CUBA IN TRANSITION

Papers and Proceedings

of the

First Annual Meeting

of the

Association for the Study of the Cuban Economy (ASCE)

Florida International University

Miami, Florida

August 15-17, 1991

Publication of these proceedings in bound form was made possible by the contributions of Development Technologies, Inc., and Florida International University. George P. Montalván and Joaquín P. Pujol undertook the task of putting together the camera-ready version of the proceedings. The cover was designed by Gustavo Araoz.

ISBN 1-879862-03-4

In Memoriam

Carlos F. Díaz Alejandro

Carlos Federico Díaz Alejandro was born in Havana, Cuba on July 18, 1937. After obtaining his Ph.D. in Economics from the Massachusetts Institute of Technology in 1961, he became Assistant Professor of Economics at Yale University (1961-65) and then at the University of Minnesota (1965- 69) where he was promoted to Associate Professor. In 1969 he returned to Yale as full Professor, and in 1984 he was appointed Professor of Economics at Columbia University, a position he held until his untimely death on July 17, 1985. As part of his distinguished career, Carlos Díaz Alejandro was also consultant to many organizations and projects and served as member of a wide variety of committees. To cite only a few examples, Carlos was a Consultant to the Commission on United States-Latin American Relations (the "Linowitz Commission"), a member of the National Bipartisan Commission on Central America (the "Kissinger Commission") and a member of the Brookings Panel on Economic Activity.

In his brief career, Carlos published more than 70 articles and four books, including Foreign Trade Regimes and Economic Development: Colombia, and his now-classical Essays on the Economic History of the Argentine Republic. He was co-editor of Política Económica en Centro y Periferie which, significantly, is subtitled "Essays in Honor of Felipe Pazos." Four years after his death a number of distinguished economists honored Carlos Díaz Alejandro by dedicating to his memory a major collection of essays on "Debt, Stabilization and Developments."

Carlos Díaz Alejandro was my teacher, my thesis director at Yale, and my friend. His kindness, his intelligence, his exceptional ability to combine theory with historical knowledge, his respect for the opinions of others and his love for Cuba will remain an unparalleled source of inspiration to me and to many of the founding members of the Association for the Study of the Cuban Economy.

Ernesto Hernández-Catá

CONTENTS

Florida International University

PREFACE

The cause of freedom and peace was enhanced immeasurably in 1989 when the Berlin Wall finally came tumbling down. (I shall never forget the exhilarating experience of personally hammering away a few pieces of that ominous symbol.) As the winds of democracy swept countries that had previously been under the yoke of communism, Cuban exiles everywhere renewed their long-frustrated hopes for the freedom and liberty of their island. Cuban scholars and intellectuals focused their energies and attention on the prospects for their fatherland. The economic, social, and moral changes of a post-Castro Cuba became the subject of speculation and debate.

For Cuban economists, this interest crystallized with the formation of the Association for the Study of the Cuban Economy (ASCE). When one of its founding members, Ernesto Hernández Catá, met with me in the summer of 1990 to explain the mission and objectives of ASCE, it seemed only natural that Florida International University (FIU), given its commitment to Cuban studies, should host the organization's first academic conference.

The papers published in this volume are the proceedings of that first meeting held August 15-17, 1991, at FIU, sponsored by ASCE together with our Cuban Research Institute and Latin American and Caribbean Center. The presentations cover a wide range of subjects, from overviews of the general economic problems of a transition in Cuba to the study of specific economic sectors such as tourism, energy, agriculture, and the sugar industry. Comments by both discussants and participants add a wider scope and further insight to each topic.

As the euphoria of 1989 gives way to the realization that advancing democracy and freedom is a painful, slow process, the value of ASCE's scholarly contributions becomes more evident. While it would be imprudent to predict upcoming events in Cuba, one can anticipate that the members of ASCE are making invaluable contributions as we prepare for the transition to a post-Castro period.

Florida International University is proud to have hosted the Association for the Study of the Cuban Economy's first conference and will continue to cooperate with the organization in the dissemination of scholarly research on the critical economic issues that inform contemporary Cuban affairs.

Modesto A. Maidique
President

Association for the Study of the Cuban Economy

First Annual Meeting

August 15-17, 1991
Florida International University
Miami, Florida

CONFERENCE PROGRAM

The Current Situation in Cuba: Panel Discussion

Moderator: Armando M. Lago (Ecosometrics Inc.)

Panelists: Ernesto F. Betancourt (Former Director, Radio Martí)
Jorge V. Domínguez (Harvard)
Jorge F. Pérez-López (Department of Labor)

Overview Approaches

Chair: Francisco Proenza (FAO)

The New Institutional Economics and the Study of the Cuban Economy
Roger R. Betancourt (University of Maryland at College Park)

Towards a Market Economy in Cuba? Social and Political Considerations
Marifeli Pérez-Stable (New School for Social Research)

Discussant: Lorenzo Pérez (IMF)

General Economic Problems of a Transition in Cuba

Chair: Alfredo Gutiérrez (J.P. Morgan)

Long-Term Objectives and Transitional Policies -- A Reflection on
Pazos's Economic Problems of Cuba
Ernesto Hernández-Catá (IMF)

El Desarrollo de una Economía de Mercado: El Caso de Cuba
Jorge Sanguinetty (Development Technologies)

Membership Requirements in the IMF: Possible Implications for Cuba
Joaquín P. Pujol (IMF)

Discussant: Elías R. Asón (Consultant)

Lessons from Other Experiences

Chair: Roger Betancourt (University of Maryland)

Lessons from Privatization in Eastern Europe and Latin America
Luis R. Luis (Scudder Group)

Discussant: José Ramón de la Torre (UCLA)

Some Lessons of Soviet Economic Reform
Kent Osband (IMF)

The Performance of Cubans and Hispanics

Cuban Economic Outcomes in the United States, 1960-1990
Jorge Salazar-Carrillo (FIU and the Brookings Institution)

The Effect of Learning English on the Earnings of Hispanic Men
Luis Locay (University of Miami)

The Industry Composition of Production and the Distribution of Income by Race and Ethnicity in Miami
Robert D. Cruz (FIU)

Specific Sectors: Sugar and Agriculture

Chair: Gonzalo de la Pezuela (Consultant)

The Cuban Sugar Industry in a Changing World
Nicolás Rivero (Rivero International) and José Alonso (Radio Martí)

Commodity-Linked Transactions and Recapitalization Needs for Privatizing
the Economy in a Democratic Cuba: The Case of Sugar
Fernando Alvarez (Fairleigh Dickinson University) and José Alvarez (University of Florida)

Notas sobre una estrategia agropecuaria para Cuba
Raúl Fernández (Retired, IDB)

Discussant: Antonio Gayoso (AID)

Specific Issues: Tourism and Energy

Chair: Carlos Seiglie (Rutgers University)

International Tourism in Cuba: An Economic Development Strategy?
María Dolores Espino (FIU)

Cuba's Transition to Market-Based Energy Prices
Jorge F. Pérez-López (Department of Labor)

Discussant: Juan J. Buttari (AID)

The Current Economic Situation in Cuba

Panel Discussion

Summary of the Presentations

Mr. Ernesto Betancourt:

The collapse of the U. S. S. R. is an important factor in changing the internal situation in Cuba. It has an ideological impact, which is certainly disorienting to those inside the island who believed in Communism. It also has a severe economic impact. Finally, it has an strategic impact which deprives Castro of the Soviet protection he counted on to promote his war against the United States. The impact of the status of Castro as a world leader and the sense of self-importance he gave to Cubans as a nation able to play an international role, way in excess of its magnitude, are key factors in explaining Castro's hold over Cuba.

• The U. S. S. R. is still interested in supporting Cuba to a certain extent. The military are not likely to want to lose the Lourdes electronic monitoring facility south of Havana. At the same time, the Soviets do not want to antagonize the United States. Therefore, their support of Castro's international adventures will cease. There will be no more overt military interventions like in Angola. However, Castro has the means to continue covert military support for revolutions as he did in the early sixties.

• The economic impact has been severe. It has been reported in the Cuban press that oil was the only item delivered to Cuba by the Soviets in the first five months of the current year. This has caused a critical economic situation. The Cuban Government had already enacted an austerity policy called "Special Situation in Peacetime", with the possibility of people having to go to the countryside a la Cambodia. Now they are talking of the "Zero Option", which means to adjust consumption to a level of zero Soviet supplies.

• Castro foresaw the present situation in the Soviet Union. In his speech on July 26, 1989, Castro predicted that, as a result of the trends there, the Soviet Union could eventually disintegrate. In a perverse way, the present chaos in the Soviet Union reinforces the image of Castro's wisdom among his hardline followers. From their perspective, events have shown him to be right in refusing to follow Gorbachev's Glasnost and Perestroika.

• The U. S. S. R. seems to wish to negotiate an orderly transition in Cuba by conditioning their withdrawal to normalization of relations with the United States and the lifting of the embargo. They want to spare themselves the humiliation to their military image as a world power of the collapse of their Caribbean advanced post. But Castro is not willing to be negotiated. Utab We must remember that Cuba joined the Soviet Bloc of its own volition. The Soviet Army did not conquer Cuba as it did conquer Eastern Europe. Therefore, the analogy being advanced that the collapse of Communism there is a predictor of what may happen in Cuba is spurious. Nationalism is not working against Communism in Cuba, quite to the contrary nationalism works in Castro's favor.

•   Cuban withdrawal from Africa is a consequence of Gorbachev's new foreign policy. Cuba lacks the logistical capability to deploy and maintain regular military forces overseas. Once the Soviets decided to cut their imperial ambitions, Cuba had to withdraw. The collapse of Ethiopia and the moves towards the West in Angola have been reported to cause dismay among Cubans. Castro sent 500,000 soldiers to Angola over the years precisely to defeat Savimbi and keep Angola Communist. His policy in Africa has been an abysmal failure for the average Cuban who served there or lost a relative. Nevertheless, Cuba has acquired the gratitude of the Africans for its role in putting an end to the South African presence in Namibia and in ending Apartheid.

•   As things stand, however, at the present time there is no likelihood of a popular uprising in Cuba. It must be taken into account that Cuba is a totalitarian state, Stalinist style. Castro has the repressive capacity and the ruthless will to use it that is required to prevent a revolt. There is no space in Cuban society to articulate and disseminate an opposition ideology and much less for a leadership to emerge to lead a revolt. Dissidents are kept under a very tight control.

•   As long as the repressive situation is what it is today, it is unlikely for the Eastern European experience to be replicated in Cuba. Contrary to the general impression that a revolution took place there, it is more precise to describe those events as the abdication of Soviet power. When Gorbachev made it clear that the Red Army was not going to be used to maintain those countries within Soviet control, he unleashed nationalist forces. The record shows that the KGB discouraged their local counterparts to repress the initial protests by the most daring opponents of Soviet rule. Demonstrations gained momentum only when people realized that the repressive forces were not going to intervene. No such thing has happened in Cuba and Castro has shown himself to be very aware of the dangers to his power to pursue such a course of action.

•   It can be expected that the repressive apparatus will be able to prevent demonstrations in Cuba. Castro is afraid of neglected small protests getting out of hand and has taken measures to control them. Witness the creation of rapid response brigades of thugs to nip in the bud any protests during the Pan American Games. The only solution in Cuba comes from the armed forces. But then we must consider what happened to General Arnaldo Ochoa. Nobody who knows anything about Cuba believes Ochoa was involved in the drug traffic. It is much more likely that he was the leader of an anti-Castro effort within the armed forces. Castro destroyed Ochoa physically as well as morally. Then, under the guise of punishing those who had been negligent--actually those who carried out his orders to help the drug barons--he also put army officers loyal to Raul in control of the MININT, which was the entity within the Cuban Government where the Soviets had the most influence. A Soviet sponsored coup a la Rumania is less likely as a result.

•   Another factor favoring Castro's survival is that U. S. foreign policy towards Cuba today is heavily influenced by the views of the Cuban American National Foundation (CANF). This influence is detrimental to the possibility of an internal solution to the Cuban problem. The Foundation is dominated by the extreme right wing of the Cuban exile community. The information coming out of Cuba indicates that the image conveyed by the Foundation of being the Administration's "chosen ones" to rule post-Castro Cuba is a factor that discourages potential disaffected people within the regime. The perception being reported is that if those inside move against Castro, they will be paving the way for the return of people who would evict them from their homes, fire them from their jobs and even subject them to Nuremberg type trials. Why should anybody plot against Castro to endure such a situation?

• Castro's propaganda takes advantage of this perception to bring cohesion to the regime. The message is very simple: no matter how bad the situation is, a return of the Miami exiles supported by a U. S. intervention looms as a worse alternative. Since those with access to the levers of repressive capacity are the only ones who can really bring some movement to the internal situation, the result is the present impasse. Ironically, Miami exiles political ambitions prolong Castro's stay in power.

• However, the Bush Administration has given some indications of broadening its approach. Assistant Secretary of State for Latin America, Bernard Aronson, hinted at this change of position in his speech to the Foundation on May 20, 1991. The new policy he announced of respect for the wishes of the Cuban people in a post- Castro period, provided a hint of a move away from the Foundation. Unfortunately, the use of the Foundation forum itself for such an announcement reflects the Administration's lack of sensitivity to what people inside Cuba think and how to reassure them. Nor has there been an unequivocal rejection of the intervention option.

• In summary, the solution of the Cuban problem has to come from inside Cuba. The basic principle that should govern any solution to the current political impasse, or U.S. policy towards Cuba, is that the more than ten million people who live there must be the ones deciding their country's destiny. For that to be possible, it is necessary first to reassure and encourage the armed forces to make their move.

Dr. Jorge Domínguez:

The current regime has managed to stay on for 30 years in power because it is not stupid. It is now attempting to reconsolidate through a series of small changes in policies. It is trying to reconstitute the political basis of the government, to open the country to political participation, and to make the leadership more viable in order to strengthen the regime. Example is the work allowed to be conducted by social scientists in the recent past. As of the end of the 1980s they had been given the opportunity to publish work abroad and to continue doing fine research work.

A recent survey was conducted by Cuban scientists. Its results were not positive toward the government, e.g., 9 out of 10 people would not vote for PCC party members. In a public opinion poll by PCC taken at the end of 1990, the results show that over 58 percent of those polled indicated that they did not have confidence in the PCC and the leadership.

On the opening of the system, human rights organizations, dissidents and opposition groups have been allowed certain latitude. Previously, these groups would have not been tolerated. There is an important debate going on in the country to allow for official political space. However, since the collapse of the Eastern European regimes and the Soviet Union, that space has narrowed.

A decision was made to allow foreign investments in the tourist sector, and by 1991 approximately 70 new foreign investments had been made. The leadership has to reconcile the activities of two very different types of economic organizations: joint ventures and government enterprises. The army is being brought in to manage enterprises because it is more efficient.

The role of the Soviet officials in Cuba was to encourage the opening up of the regime, e.g., the Havana archdiocesis received "Novedades de Moscú" as a courtesy of the U.S.S.R. Embassy. There is now a severe crisis in Soviet-Cuban relations. The Soviet Union is not able to continue supporting Cuba.
Changes in U.S.S.R. and Eastern Europe are viewed as a negative model for Cuba by the government. They will make more difficult the opening up of the regime.

Despite Assistant Secretary of State Aronson's forthright assurances about "no intervention" in Cuba's affairs, his views may not reflect the U.S. Government position.

Dr. Jorge Pérez-López:

Cuba is mired in a severe economic depression. Its severity is not known with precision, but there are indicia that it may be the worst crisis for the economy since 1959.

Cuba's economic slowdown began in the second half of the 1980s. This economic slowdown is evident from official Cuban data. The global social product, which was planned to grow at a real rate of 2-3 percent per annum, instead performed as follows:

1986	1.6 percent
1987	-3.9 percent
1988	2.5 percent
1989	1.0 percent

This works out to a cumulative growth performance of 0.7 percent over the period 1986-89, or 0.2 percent per annum growth rate. In per capita terms, the economy contracted during 1986-89: global social product declined by about 3 percent or at a rate of 1 percent (i.e., decline of 1 percent) per annum.

Reasons for the Economic Decline

Economic woes are, to a large extent, the result of inefficiencies associated with central planning. External sector problems also contributed to the economic crisis. Sugar price subsidies from the Soviet Union peaked in 1984 and declined annually since then. Hard currency debt problems intensified, and with Cuba's decision in 1986 to declare a moratorium on hard currency debt servicing, hard currency loans dried up.
The Soviet Union capped oil deliveries to Cuba. The combination of the cap on supplies and the fall in the world market price of oil reduced Cuba's ability to generate hard currency through reexports of oil.
Finally, reforms in Eastern Europe and the Soviet Union-- which began in 1989, but intensified in 1990--significantly altered Cuba's trade patterns. Cuba's ability to import a wide range of products--food, raw materials, machinery, energy--has been affected.

Thus, the economy is in a deep depression. Analysts have estimated that the global social product fell by 5 percent in 1990; this is consistent with reports of closed factories because of the lack of raw materials.
Most likely, situation in 1991 not any better and perhaps worse, since the oil supply reductions (about 25 percent) that the Soviet Union imposed in mid-1990. The 1991 zafra was disappointing, well short, by about 500,000 tons, of the 8.1 million tons produced in 1990.

Economic Strategy

Cuba's current economic strategy, in the context of the período especial en tiempo de paz, has several strands:

--   sharp reductions in energy consumption;

--   national food production plan;

--   intensification of efforts to diversify export basket and customers; and

--   promotion of international tourism. In this latter context, there have been strong efforts to attract foreign investment.

In my estimation, the most successful strand has been food production. This is not surprising since agriculture -- particularly production of staple products -- does not require high levels of imported products, including energy. Cuba has relocated workers from factories that have been shut down (called interruptos) and bureaucrats into agriculture. It should be kept in mind, however, that the increase in agricultural output has been at the expense of other sectors of the economy.

Tourism also seems to be having some success, and the goals set by the government for this sector are quite ambitious. However, the number of international tourists has been flat since 1989 at about 300,000 per annum. International tourism is creating a difficult domestic political situation, as Cuban citizens are not given access to hotels, restaurants, and other recreational facilities reserved for foreign travelers.
Cuba's attempts to broaden its export basket have not been successful. The economy continues to be heavily sugar- oriented, despite efforts by the government to reduce the dependence on the sugar industry. The Cuban leadership's assertions that biotechnology is the linchpin of export growth is preposterous. Cuba's biotechnology industry is essentially copying processes and products developed elsewhere, has quality control problems, and no distribution system.

Efforts to increase trade with Latin American countries are not likely to succeed. Cuba's export structure is very similar to the rest of the continent and there are few opportunities for Cuba to sell its commodities and semi-manufactured goods. However, Brazil and Argentina could provide a wide range of machinery and equipment to Cuba if the latter had the hard currency to pay for them.

Energy conservation is, of course, a defensive action; the current energy conservation program is essentially an effort to make do with the reduced energy supplies that are available. In this context, opción cero (the possibility that in the near future there will not be any energy imports and the economy will return to pre-industrialization) is increasingly being discussed. Although it may well be posturing by the government, the probability that opción cero would have to be implemented is non-zero, i.e., it needs to be considered. The changes that are occurring in the Soviet Union, including the tug-of-war between the central government and the republics over the ownership of oil resources and the necessity to sell oil for dollars, have to be a matter of serious concern to Cuba.

The current economic strategy is not sustainable in the medium or in the long term.

The New Institutional Economics and the Study of the Cuban Economy

Roger R. Betancourt

Introduction

A central feature of the Cuban economy throughout its history is that it has been a "developing" country, to use the politically correct euphemism adopted by our profession for describing economic systems that are unable to enjoy sustained economic growth. This condition has characterized the economy before the Revolution and during the Revolution. One critical question at the current historical juncture is whether or not this condition will continue to characterize the economy after the inevitable structural changes that it presently faces. What makes these structural changes inevitable is the dramatic shift in fundamental relative prices recently experienced, in particular for oil and sugar, as a result of the demise of the centrally planned systems in Eastern Europe and the Soviet Union. What is not inevitable are the specific forms that these structural changes will take and, consequently, whether or not they will shift the system onto a path that generates sustained economic growth over the long term.

Understanding of this process requires the application of the tools of our profession, especially certain advances that have become increasingly important over the last twenty years. These advances I will lump together under the rubric of the "New Institutional Economics." The aims of this essay are: first, to bring attention to the nature of this diverse literature; second, to emphasize its legitimacy as a natural extension of standard tools; and, finally, to illustrate its relevance for the present context. There are, perhaps, two sources of novelty in what follows. First, the obvious one which derives from bringing together a diverse literature in a manner germane for a particular topic. Second, a more subtle one which derives from asking a question that I found useful in the analysis of distribution systems: What is the economic function of an institution? For instance, in considering this question in the context of distribution systems certain aspects of the role of technology came to the surface which were not evident otherwise.

The paper is structured in the following manner. Section I provides the conceptual background through definitions, a sketch of various components of the literature, their connection within themselves and to various subdisciplines, as well as brief comments of a methodological nature. Section II discusses an important historical application of these ideas to the analysis of growth and development, a well known institution in Cuban and Latin American history, and a lesser known institution in Cuban history which is proposed for further analysis. Section III discusses applications of these tools to nonmarket settings and some implications especially relevant for the analyses of early stages of a transition from socialism. Section IV discusses an application of these ideas to market settings in advanced countries and important considerations which arise in extensions to the Cuban setting. Section V discusses the application of these ideas to the analysis of institutional change, in particular constitutions and certain types of redistributive laws. Finally, a brief conclusion highlights the nature of the questions raised in this essay.

I. Conceptual Background

Three strands of what has by now become mainstream literature constitute the core of the new institutional economics: the transaction costs literature, especially that emphasizing information costs; the property rights literature and the literature on collective action, especially that contained in the new subfield of economics referred to as public choice.[1] In this literature one can find contributions that are viewed as part of modern mainstream economics and those that are not, although most contributions would be viewed as mainstream. Nevertheless, it is useful to point out the criteria for distinguishing among them and their methodological origins.

Simply put, a contribution is viewed as within the mainstream paradigm if it develops from its postulates or even if it changes some of them, as long as they are contained in the protective belt and not in the hard core of the paradigm. I am applying Lakatos' (1970) distinction following in the spirit of Eggertsson (1990). What this means is that as long as a contribution assumes optimizing agents subject to constraints and analyzes interactions between agents in terms of displacement from one well defined equilibrium to another, it is a welcome contribution to enhancing the fruitfulness of the basic paradigm. For practical purposes, the controversial issues are exclusion of models based on nonoptimizing behavior such as Nelson and Winter's (1982) evolutionary models or models that appeal to unstable preferences or that include variables capturing notions of fairness or altruistic behavior in the objective function. Most importantly, contributions within the paradigm include models that specify costs of transaction as part of the environment and that allow for uncertainty or lack of full information about the environment. For instance, this group represents most if not all of the new industrial organization as contained, for example, in Tirole (1988).

One factor in enhancing the relevance and professional legitimacy of the new institutional economics for modern microeconomics is that some of the most distinguished members of our profession have been fundamental contributors to this literature, for example see Joe Stiglitz's discussion in the recent symposium on Organizations in Economics (1991). Another factor has been the incorporation of modern theoretical tools into the explicit analysis of institutions as such, for example the use of a game theoretic framework by Milgrom, North and Weingast (1990) in their analysis of Champagne Fairs. Finally, a third factor is that contributors to the various strands of literature represent a very diverse cross-section in terms of political or ideological orientation.

It is not surprising that a well known economic historian (North) and a well known development economist (Nugent) are at the forefront of this new field of analysis. In these two subfields of economics it is much more difficult to escape the obvious conclusion that institutions differ and seem to matter in determining outcomes. Of course, it is a long distance from such a trivial recognition of a fact to the integration of three different strands

---

[1] This general distinction of three strands of literature is taken from Nabli and Nugent (1989) but my further characterization is not necessarily in agreement with their views.

of modern literature in an attempt to develop a systematic explanation of this phenomenon. Indeed, the task is so difficult that both writers in the end feel compelled to go beyond the mainstream paradigm and challenge assumptions at the hard core to explain some aspects of the phenomena that interests them. I shall refrain from doing so while acknowledging the need to do so in some settings. A useful operating procedure is to explain as much as one can within the context of the mainstream paradigm; an important advantage is that it makes it easier for others to build upon any results obtained. One can argue that appeals to reject the hard core of the paradigm can frequently be the result of insufficient efforts at modifying its protective belt.

What is an institution? Nabli and Nugent (1989, ch. 1) answer this question in the following manner. An institution is a set of constraints which governs the behavioral relations among individuals or groups. While there are alternative definitions, this one is attractive because of its ability to encompass a wide range of issues. This characteristic seems especially relevant in the present context. These constraints can take the form of either rules or behavioral norms. Both formal and informal organizations fall within the definition as well as implicit and explicit contracts and rules of conduct.

Transaction costs are clearly relevant for the analysis of institutions. First, the constraints that evolve in the operation of economic systems can be viewed as institutions designed to accommodate one or more of these costs. Indeed, a classic contribution to this field, Coase (1937), argues that the existence of firms as organizations or economic institutions is due to their function as a mechanism for lowering some transaction costs incurred by participating in market exchange. While uncertainty plays a role in generating these costs, Coase stresses the coordinating function exercised by the firm. Moreover, he argues that the boundary between firms and markets is determined by the minimization of transaction costs. A vast literature has emerged in recent years that analyzes various aspects of this issue. The introduction of uncertainty and information costs into economic analysis, in particular, has stimulated many of these contributions. Since these factors create an agency problem between the principal, or owner of the firm, and the agents, or managers and workers, it underlies the various contributions to the principal agent literature. This agency problem exists in many organizational contexts, for example public and regulated enterprises as well as representative bodies of government and bureaucracies. Moreover, it raises new questions on why different organizational forms exist. The latter issue has been one of the main themes in O. Williamson's (1985) analyses of governance structures and opportunistic behavior.

Issues of this nature focusing on complex organizational forms such as firms have their counterpart at a lower level of aggregation. Indeed, many of the analyses in the industrial organization literature surveyed in the Handbook of Industrial Organization (1989) fall within this category, as can be seen from Porter's (1991) insightful essay on these two volumes. In particular the explanations of many business practices and market interactions among firms are developed in terms of arrangements to accommodate specific transaction costs. It lies beyond our scope to summarize all these contributions. Instead,

I will provide a brief illustration on a topic familiar from my own research, Betancourt (1991).

In observing interactions between retailers and suppliers, several practices are common. For instance, manufacturers employ the assignment of exclusive territories to the retailers of their products. A standard view of this practice is as a limit to competition among retailers. Nevertheless, Matthewson and Winter (1986), for example, point out that one can also explain this practice as a means for the manufacturer to provide an incentive to retailers not to under provide selling effort or to internalize an externality. Rey and Tirole (1986) show that in the presence of uncertainty this practice or institution has the beneficial effect of using decentralized information more efficiently than other alternatives, although competition is preferable from the point of view of consumer welfare. Rey and Tirole, however, do not allow for the under provision of selling effort emphasized by Matthewson and Winter. The transaction costs associated with the provision of selling effort at the end of the channel are, thus, crucial to an evaluation of the effects of this institution on consumer welfare. Hence, an economic evaluation of legal restrictions on this practice must recognize the role of this transaction cost.

According to Barzel (1989), who is one of the leading contributors to the property rights literature, the existence of transaction costs is the starting point of the property rights literature. Property rights are the right to consume, obtain income from and alienate (sell) an asset. These rights are difficult to delineate because transactions are costly. The transaction costs he identifies are those associated with the transfer, capture and protection of property rights. What underlies the costliness of transactions is that commodities have many attributes that vary from one item to another. This allows wealth to spill over into the public domain in every exchange and provides individuals with an incentive to spend resources in capturing this spillover. As a result, divided ownership of commodities yields increased gains from exchange by allowing transfers of subsets of attributes. Restrictions that enhance the separation of individual rights enhance the gains from exchange by allowing the existence of divided ownership. The latter in turn diminishes the attributes that remain in the public domain and thus economizes on resources that would be spent on wealth capture. An underlying principle in Barzel's analysis is that individuals attempt to maximize their wealth.

Barzel discusses briefly the existence of other approaches that stress the role of transaction costs and offers some criticisms that help identify what is unique about the property rights approach. The latter stresses reciprocity and gains from exchange, observability and capability of empirical implementation, and the prediction of the development of new rights and institutions. The first characteristic is especially important in the present context. To illustrate its importance let us consider a familiar example. The existence of transaction costs provides an incentive to own rather than rent assets, since the flow of income generated by some assets can be substantially affected by how it is operated or maintained. Thus, factory owners often own rather than rent capital equipment.

In the early nineteenth century, the work day of capital was not separated from the work day of labor and it generated onerous working conditions as well as Marx's view of surplus value, Morishima (1973). As I have noted elsewhere, Betancourt (1987), Marshall became a strong advocate of the institution of shift-work because it allowed the reconciliation of labor's needs for shorter working days with capital's need for profits from operating long periods of the day. Shift-work as an economic institution lead to improved gains from exchange in the labor contract for both capital and labor by separating the right of a worker to operate a machine during a day from the right of another worker to operate the same machine during another part of the day. On the same topic, one can note that modern technological developments in telecommunications and computers allow the use of services from computer equipment without requiring ownership. Hence, it becomes feasible in some sectors to lease computer services rather than own the computer equipment. These technological developments make possible other institutions, leasing contracts for computer services, that enhance gains from exchange by allowing the separation of the right to use equipment at a particular time from the right to own the equipment at that time.

The third strand of literature relevant for our topic is associated mainly with a specific new subdiscipline, public choice, which already has gone beyond the first edition of a leading textbook, D. Mueller (1979), and has made it to the JEL classification of books and articles. Here, I will merely note two important aspects: its relation to transaction costs and its position at the intersection of economics and politics. Early contributions emphasized the role of externalities as an impediment to collective action, Olson (1965). Externalities lead to market failure when there are transaction costs. Indeed, North (1990) in discussing Coase's (1960) famous essay stresses the interpretation that if there are no transaction costs "the competitive structure of efficient markets leads parties to arrive costlessly at the solution that maximizes aggregate income regardless of the initial institutional arrangements." His ultimate point is, of course, that there are transaction costs and that institutions do matter.

An important theme underlying this literature is that governments are actors in the economic scene with their own preferences. Once again if there are no transaction costs, especially information costs, political institutions would merely reflect the preferences of the underlying constituents and, in that sense, would not matter. The presence of uncertainty introduces a principal agent problem in this context. More generally, transaction costs create a rich array of possibilities in terms of economic institutions, political institutions and institutions that arise to bridge the two spheres of activity.

What brings these three diverse strands of literature together to constitute an incipient new field of study is the stress on transactions costs of one form or another. Because of the range of issues thus involved, it is useful to present here a view of this new field put forth by Eggertsson (1990). He suggests that there are three levels of analysis in this new field, all of which may be useful at a particular time for our present context. At the first level of analysis the structure of property rights and organizational forms are explicitly modelled but treated as <u>exogenous</u>. The emphasis is on their impact on economic outcomes. At the second level, the <u>organization of exchange is endogenized</u>, but the fundamental structure of property rights remains exogenous... At the third level, attempts are made to endogenize both social and political rules and the structure of political institutions by introducing the concept of transaction costs. He organizes his work along these lines. I may add that it is at this third level where it is most difficult to stay within the mainstream paradigm when the hard core is defined to exclude notions of fairness or altruistic behavior in the objective function.

II. Historical Applications

A fundamental building block in both development economics and growth theory has been the predominant, essentially monopolistic role assigned to technology as a determinant of self-sustained growth. In the development literature Kuznets (1966) identifies modern economic growth as starting with the Industrial Revolution and the systematic application of science and technology to production processes. On the growth theory side, Solow's (1957) famous paper attributed most of the growth in output to a residual called technology; the Solow-Swan model showed the rate of technological change as one of the few factors that can affect the equilibrium growth rate of output. Consequently, the paramount role of technology framed economists thinking about self-sustaining growth until the last decade.

An early challenge to this view came from North and Thomas (1973) who pointed out that a variety of factors changing relative prices influenced the development of Western institutions long before the Industrial Revolution. Moreover, these changes led to changes in property rights structures which affected incentives for the generation of innovations. This work had a limited impact on the analysis of development and growth at the time, although interest in the analysis of historical institutions from a property rights perspective continued to develop on its own. For instance, of interest in our context is an insightful paper by Batchelder and Sanchez (1988) which analyzes the 'encomienda' system as an institution from this perspective. One of the main themes of the paper is to show that property rights restrictions embodied in the 'encomienda' can be viewed as a mechanism which served to increase the wealth of the Spanish Crown. Moreover, they argue that it did so precisely because it allowed the transformation of wealth in the form of the human capital of the Indian population into nonhuman capital wealth that could be transported to Spain, where it could be more easily protected.

Recent developments have led to conditions far more hospitable for integrating the analysis of institutions with the analysis of growth and development. In the development literature there is now considerable evidence of notorious successes as well as continuing failures and there are substantial differences in the institutions that characterize the two sets of countries.[2] An influential analysis of the historical experience of many countries by Reynolds (1983) leads him to conclude that a significant political event was associated with

---

[2] See the discussion of the evidence in Hernandez-Catá (1991) and of some of the institutions in Betancourt and Kiguel (1989).

the turning point into intensive growth, which roughly corresponds to the initial stage of what I have called self-sustaining growth, in 30 of the 34 countries identified as having reached this point. On the growth side there is considerable controversy on whether or not rates of growth converge as implied by the standard model. Indeed, Benhabib and Jovanovic (1991) aim at reconciling the evidence with the standard model, but end up concluding that our understanding of growth needs the engine of growth to be endogenized and that this engine is fueled primarily by something other than physical capital.[3] On the theoretical side models of endogenous growth may become a growth industry themselves, for example Grossman and Helpman (1990), Lucas (1990) and Roemer (1990). An important feature of these models lies in allowing for the possibility that economic policy has an effect on growth rates.

More generally, other scientific developments are facilitating the analysis of settings where institutions can affect outcomes. Analysis of nonlinear dynamical systems in physics, biology and chemistry have generated advances in the understanding of complex, self-organizing systems. Thus, they have enhanced the legitimacy of adopting similar concepts in economics and even in the humanities, e.g., a specially appropriate reference in the literary world is Benitez Rojo "La Isla que se Repite." For instance, over twenty years ago Georgescu-Roegen (1971) argued that economic and social processes were characterized by hysteresis, also called path dependence in recent literature. Nevertheless, his arguments had little impact on the growth and development literature of the time. In the last decade, however, hysteresis became a household word for macroeconomists analyzing unemployment and path dependence plays a critical role in recent work on technology by W. Brian Arthur (1989). Once an analysis allows for transaction costs to exist, institutions affect outcomes and if there is path dependence these effects will persist through time.

To conclude this section, let me note one interesting area for application of these ideas in the context of the Cuban economy. Upon reading parts of a recent book on Cuban rural society in the 19th century, Bergad (1990), I came across an institution which must have had a substantial effect on the rate of growth of the Cuban economy up to the 19th century and which, I believe, has not been analyzed from a modern perspective. This institution is the so-called "privilegio de los ingenios" which goes back to 1529 and was abolished in 1860. Ingenio land, slaves, animals and fixed property could not be mortgaged or embargoed. Creditors could attach liens to harvests, however, and these became the common guarantee for credit. The incidence of risk bearing is dramatically changed by this restriction on the use of assets and raises the question of why it lasted as an arrangement for so many years and what was its effect on welfare and growth on the island. Incidentally, no analysis of this issue would be complete without accounting for the different insurance aspects of liens on the harvests and mortgages on land. Recent developments in the public finance literature have shown that in the presence of uncertainty taxes on output may be preferable to taxes on land, despite their distortionary effects, precisely because of their

---

[3] While they continue to emphasize the role of technology, they begin to allow a role for institutions by arguing for persistent heterogeneity in ex-post realizations of technological shocks due to this factor.

insurance properties, Hoff (1991).

III. Nonmarket Applications

Ironically, it is in the writings of economists that are avid advocates of free markets where one may find the most useful tools for the analyses of nonmarket settings. Barzel (1989, ch. 8) makes this argument himself and proceeds to illustrate by applying the tools of property rights analysis to three types of nonmarket allocation: allocation by voting, allocation of blood by donation or by market exchange and allocation by government.

In adapting his insights to the present context, it is useful to start by examining two points he makes in this chapter. The first point is that it is a myth that private property has been abolished in communist states. If one defines property rights as he does and as we have replicated in Section I, this claim is logically unassailable. The right to consume commodities in the form of physical goods or intangible services can be restricted but it cannot be eliminated from any society. Parenthetically, even in capitalist societies the right to consume some commodities, for example drugs and prostitution, is restricted. Similarly, the right to obtain income from an asset can be restricted but not eliminated, especially when informal means of exchange are taken into consideration; this right, of course, is also restricted in capitalist societies, for example restrictions on the use of home premises for business purposes in residential areas. Finally, the right to sell an asset is perhaps the one most easily restricted, especially for highly visible items, but once again as informal sectors everywhere demonstrate it is difficult to eliminate this right in its entirety.

A second point he makes which is useful to stress in the present context is that "exchanges constitute a reassignment of property rights." In particular exchanges within <u>any</u> organization involve such reassignments, including the rights to allocate resources. In all such exchanges, it is impossible to delineate all the attributes of what is being exchanged and opportunities for wealth capture are provided. Wealth maximizing agents will exploit these opportunities within the constraints allowed by the system. It is these constraints which vary most dramatically between market and nonmarket settings as well as among different nonmarket settings. Furthermore, they determine differences in outcome. One conclusion he derives from this view is that "The details of such operations cannot be guessed from one's armchair, ..." This conclusion juxtaposed to the importance of path dependence indicated in the previous section has important implications for analyzing the evolution of the Cuban economy at this time.

Predictions as to the form of this evolution are fraught with difficulty; at best one can identify a range of structural changes, starting from limited liberalizations, as reported for example in J. Domínguez' (1991) recent testimony to the U.S. Congress, to the more substantial changes experienced in various degrees in Eastern Europe, the Soviet Union and Nicaragua. In understanding any of these outcomes, however, it is imperative that one begin with informed knowledge about the current situation. Thus, those who have devoted their energies to following the detailed operations of the system play a critical role in this process.

In addition, the constraints that determine the outcomes of wealth maximization under a centrally planned system lie to a much greater extent outside the realm of the usual economic variables than in a market setting. Hence, in understanding this process we have to integrate expertise from other areas into our analyses in order to identify the relevant constraints and margins of optimization.

A second implication that follows from these considerations stems from the transaction and informational advantages that derive from being a participant in the existing type of exchanges. In market settings these advantages also exist and the literature abounds with terms that capture aspects of these advantages, asymmetric information, insider-outsider analyses, first mover advantage, power of incumbency, etc. What changes in the nonmarket setting is the structure of the rules as well as the relevant margins over which optimization by agents takes place. In this connection, it is also worth noting that under some rule changes those with experience in participation in market exchanges or organizational forms not currently in existence in the nonmarket setting enjoy transaction and informational advantages, although of a different nature. That these issues are important can be easily deduced from the complaints of the early reform period in Eastern Europe with respect to members of the nomenclature being among the main beneficiaries of the changes. Similarly, in recent testimony on the Nicaraguan situation, Penn Kemble of Freedom House states the following about the Sandinista Army: "Its finances raise eyebrows: it is widely believed to be the major conduit for cash payments to the FSLN political leadership." Identification of existing constraints and the relevant margins for optimization is a necessary task in the design and analysis of any particular institutional changes.

To conclude, let me note some implications for an important issue in any process of structural change: the supply and distribution of basic food products to consumers. This area is an attractive one for privatization, regardless of the system, because farmers everywhere, including Cuba, have demonstrated their capacity to increase output when offered economic incentives to do so. Since independent distribution networks do not exist in Cuba, however, it would be difficult to dismantle the state's wholesale distribution system instantaneously while assuring a minimum supply to urban centers through the existing retail outlets. Moreover, the dismantling of a rationing system may also be impossible to accomplish instantaneously. This suggests the need for coexistence of very different forms of organization with very different incentives for operating, leading to opportunities for wealth capture that undermine the feasibility of any process of structural change. A partial solution for this problem in the early stages of any such process is to grant secure property rights for a limited period of time on the use of assets (land and retail stores) to generate income by the current users of the assets, namely farmers and the operators of the retail outlets. This would provide incentives to increase and assure the distribution of food to consumers as well as information that would help monitor the performance of the wholesale operation. Monitoring would be essential because the wholesale operation is difficult to privatize immediately and would thus have considerable incentives to withhold food from retailing outlets and sell it on the side under any rationing scheme.

The time limit on the use of the assets would need to be long enough to lower incentives to consume or destroy the value of the asset, especially in the presence of uncertainty about the possibility of acquiring full ownership rights. Moreover, actual application of any such scheme must be modified to accommodate the existing situation at the time of its introduction, including the distribution of retail outlets among state run enterprises, cooperatives and other forms as well as their degree of specialization on food distribution. Some form of reasonable compensation should be collected for these rights and the rights could be made negotiable. Instituting a full system of property rights instantaneously has proved impossible in all the cases we know. Hence, it may be worthwhile to use the insights of the property rights literature to evaluate schemes in which these rights are introduced gradually. This gradual approach seems eminently sensible in a setting where the transportation system has major problems. Many famines take place because goods cannot be transported where they are needed in the required time frame and/or for lack of entitlements to the goods, Sen (1981).

IV. Market Applications

In this section, the ideas previously discussed will be applied to a more familiar market setting. A principal objective in doing so is to illustrate that these tools are in the process of development and constitute a continually evolving method for looking at problems rather than turn-key projects that can be pulled from a shelf of knowledge. Another objective is to bring out explicitly the connection between developments in the literature on transaction costs and in the analysis of property rights.

Recently my research activities have centered on understanding the operation of retail markets. An important finding of this research is the characterization of retail markets as institutions in which producers (retailers) furnish consumers with a set of distribution services together with the explicit goods or services that consumers purchase. These services are costly to produce and higher levels of these distribution services reduce the distribution (transaction) costs that consumers experience. This characterization defines the economic function of retail markets as an institution. In doing so, it provides a framework for analyzing and evaluating the performance of this function as well as for understanding why different organizational forms (types of firms) of both a formal and informal nature emerge to perform this function. Designing research projects around the question of what is the economic function of an institution is becoming popular, especially in the area of services where the intangible nature of the output obscures the nature of the answer. For example, Hornstein and Prescott (1990) ask this question about the insurance industry (1990), Bresnahan, Milgrom and Paul (1990) ask this question about stock markets and Hanak (1991) does the same for banking.

Six broad types of distribution costs can be identified in any interaction between consumers and a retail system: direct time costs and transportation costs, adjustment costs as a result of unavailability of products or services at the desired time of consumption or purchase, information costs, storage costs, and psychic costs of unappealing characteristics of the retail environment. A retail system, on the other hand, determines the level of distribution costs experienced by consumers through the level of distribution services it provides. These services can be classified into five broad categories: accessibility of location, product assortment, assurance of product delivery in the desired form, information and ambiance.[4] There is joint production of some dimensions of these services and they may affect more than one distribution cost experienced by consumers. Some retail institutions specialize in offering very high levels of some of these services, but all of them provide some level of each of these broad categories. Examples of these services, how they may be shifted between consumers and retailers, and how they affect consumers distribution costs are available in Betancourt and Gautschi (1988) and (1986).

From an economic perspective, a critical assumption in this analysis is that the levels of distribution services provided by retail institutions play the role of fixed inputs in the consumption and/or purchase activities of consumers. Thus, increases in the levels of these services by retail institutions lower the costs to consumers of obtaining a given level of satisfaction by reducing their distribution costs. The implications of this view for demand analysis have been examined in two papers (1990a, 1991a). Three aspects of this analysis are worth emphasizing. There is a strong tendency toward complementarity between all the items in any given assortment of a retail institution; distribution services tend to be complementary with all items in an assortment; distribution services that are common to all items in an assortment have stronger complementary effects than those that are specific to a single item. Common distribution services act as public inputs in the production functions of consumers. The role of distribution services is shown to be fundamental in understanding the nature of competition in retail markets and the creation of retail agglomerations.

On the cost side distribution services act as outputs of retail institutions. An important implication of this view is that higher levels of these services entail higher costs for the institutions that provide them. Putting together both sides of the market in the framework of monopolistic competition leads to several insights. In the short-run, the distribution services provided by retail institutions generate economic incentives for expansions of assortments and into market dimensions segmented by spatial or other characteristics. In the long run, these distribution services provide a rationale for equilibria characterized by the coexistence of different institutional forms specializing in the provision of different distribution services as well as for price dispersion in the same market (1988). Explicit modelling of these distribution services brings out the complex relationship between pricing policies and the provision of various levels of distribution services. Furthermore, this explicit modelling also brings out the conditions under which competition in retail markets enhances consumer welfare, Betancourt and Gautschi (1990b).

An important aspect in demonstrating the usefulness of the above conceptualization is its use in the empirical explanation of economic phenomena. In the analysis of retail

---

[4] In a recent paper Oi (1990) asks the question what is the output of a retail firm and comes up with a list that is easily reconciled with these five categories.

firms, a great deal of emphasis has been placed on retail margins. This approach provides a sound conceptual framework for the economic explanation of retail margins. Furthermore, it suggests how to devise empirical constructs that correspond to these distribution services. Finally, and perhaps more importantly, it has been implemented with aggregate data for the U.S. and France. The results show that distribution services are critical determinants of retail margins in both cases, Betancourt and Gautschi (1991b, 1991c). Another important aspect in demonstrating the usefulness of any conceptualization is its applicability in policy analysis. Leunis and Vandamme (1991) use this approach fruitfully to evaluate the effects of the Business Premises Act in Belgium.[5]

A current area of research in this context is the explicit identification of the links between this literature and the analysis of property rights. The literature just described has identified a subset of the valued attributes that are exchanged in any retail market as well as two characteristics of the operation of these markets important for the analysis of property rights. First, the implicit allocation of distribution costs between retailers and consumers as a result of providing any particular levels of distribution services. Secondly, the fact that these outputs (distribution services) are not explicitly priced.

The first characteristic provides a framework for identifying the gains or losses from exchanges associated with the emergence of particular retail institutions. The second one points to the need for the development of institutions that allow cooperation between retailers in order to internalize the costs of jointly providing these services. A particular example of institutions where these issues are important are retail agglomerations, either shopping malls or the informal markets that prevail in developing countries. The set of transaction costs emphasized in the property rights literature are important in determining the operation of these institutions, the actual forms that emerge and the nature of the gains from exchange. To my knowledge no analyses exist of these institutions that integrate both perspectives. There are, however, analyses which may provide a useful starting point. Barzel himself notes the gains from exchange generated by contracts which partially transfer ownership rights to security and maintenance firms in buildings. The divided ownership made possible by these contracts allows these firms to take advantage of economies of scale in the provision of these services and, thus, generates gains from exchange. Similarly, in their analyses of the development of equilibrium contracts for factors of production in rural markets, Nabli and Nugent (1989) suggest the possibility of extending these analyses to product markets.

Another area of research relevant for the present context is the extent to which the above analyses of transaction costs and property rights must be modified for application to developing country settings or, more generally, to settings where informal arrangements are more prevalent. Part of the answer was provided in the previous section, but it is useful to indicate here other considerations not discussed earlier. There are three important

---

[5] This is an act limiting the size of retail space in different areas.

underlying forces generating the emergence of various retail forms in advanced countries: the high opportunity cost of time; the increase in the number of households due to the decreased role of extended family structures; the increase in the number of households with multiple earners. Of these three factors the last two are also relevant for the Cuban economy. Just as in other centrally planned systems, the housing sector has been singularly unable to satisfy the needs of the population. This creates a considerably pent up demand for new structures that allow the trend toward more nuclear family systems to materialize with a consequent demand for the services of the retail sector. Similarly, multiple earner households are quite prevalent in Cuba and create a powerful demand for flexibility in the timing of purchases. Analyses of the implied changes, however, is critically dependent on whether or not the satisfaction of consumer wants becomes an important consideration in the functioning of the economic system.

V. The Analysis of Institutional Change

This topic is undoubtedly the most difficult one to address, especially when it concerns changes in the basic structure of rules of a system or the third level of analysis in Eggertsson's classification. It is useful to begin with some general comments before proceeding to discuss two specific issues that are quite relevant in the present context. Eggertsson (1990) makes the case that our traditional notions of allocative efficiency (Pareto efficiency) are impossible to apply when we allow for transactions costs. North (1990) proposes the notion of adaptive efficiency for evaluating the performance of economies through time, while admitting the difficulties of implementation. Without getting bogged down in methodological discussions at this point, it is useful to note two considerations that need to be included in evaluating institutional change. Institutions can have growth retarding as well as growth promoting effects. The role of existing institutions in generating growth retarding effects has been the subject of considerable attention, e.g. Olson (1982) and Krueger (1974). Much less attention, however, has been paid to the growth promoting effects of institutions, partly because of the difficulties in doing so. In this regard, I merely note that the identification of the gains from exchange associated with the analyses of institutions in the property rights literature provides a starting point in the evaluation of such effects.

Despite the difficulties enough progress has been made to provide useful perspectives on important issues. To illustrate let us consider the analysis of constitutions. Much has been made in the popular press about the writing of a constitution for Cuba by a consultant on behalf of a particular group in the exiled community. What light can the new institutional economics throw on this activity? A standard view of a constitution in the public choice literature is as a formal social contract. According to Mueller (1991), for example, such a contract emerges to accommodate uncertainties with respect to possible opportunistic behavior by members of the polity or to spread common exogenous risks and uncertainties faced by the community. He goes on to argue that the need for a formal rather than an informal contract stems from the need to minimize transaction costs when the number of agents is large.[6] If one adopts the contractual view, it immediately follows that constitutions are of limited value unless they emerge out of a process whereby those supposed to abide by it have ample opportunity to voice their views before agreeing to their provisions!

As North (1990) points out, most of the Latin American republics got their start with constitutions not too different from the United States and about the same time but political and economic outcomes have been decidedly different. One set of factors noted by North is that the informal constraints in the operation of economic and political systems were different in the two cases. Moving on to examples closer to the present issue, the first Constitution designed in Cuba by a constitutional assembly, which was to underlie its birth as an independent nation, was never put in place. It ran afoul of the not so informal constraint that U.S. occupation troops would not leave the island because it did not contain the Platt amendment. Moving closer to the present, one can note a recent article by Manuel Ramon de Zayas (1991) in which it is pointed out that one of the most conspicuous ideas of a political group outside the island is to get the present Cuban government to abide by its own constitution. A contractual view of constitutions suggests why these violations are likely to continue. Insofar as individual agents are unable to participate freely in the process of writing and adopting the constitution, they are unlikely to feel bound by its provisions. In a totalitarian state this condition applies to government officials at the lower levels of the bureaucratic ladder and in many cases to those occupying high rungs on the ladder.

Turning to the last and most difficult subject to be considered, what can economics, including the new institutional economics, say about restitution or the return or nonreturn of nationalized or expropriated property to its original owners? Uncertainty and its reduction play a key role in bringing this issue to the fore in any type of transition from a centrally planned system to a market economy. To illustrate this role it is convenient to consider how it arises in two different versions of this process. The first version is represented by the situation that arose in the Soviet Union until very recently, where the communist party retained considerable power and the repressive apparatus of the state had not been dismantled despite progress toward democratization and market reform and considerable lip service to both issues. Public and private investments by advanced countries in this process were limited and awaited substantial evidence of credible commitments in this direction. For instance, one aspect of the Japanese insistence on the return of the islands taken by force is a demand for evidence of a public renunciation by the state of arbitrarily taking over property. Acceptance of this principle with respect to other holders of property will play a significant role in determining the level of investments by these types

---

[6] There are other aspects of the design of a constitution very relevant for the present context but I will leave it to the reader to consult Mueller's paper and the literature cited therein.

of property holders and the growth possibilities of the system.[7]

A second version of this process is taking place in Eastern European countries where substantial progress has been made in terms of both democratization and market reform, in particular East Germany, Hungary, Czechoslovakia and Poland. The issue of returning property has arisen in each one of these countries. Removal of uncertainty with respect to the direction of the process has played a role but in addition the participation of former property holders in the political process has forced these states to explicitly recognize the legitimacy of a restitution policy. Recognition of this principle removes or diminishes one source of uncertainty but introduces another, namely the issue of competing claims which must be adjudicated in some manner by the legal system. Once again until the process is clarified, the result is a paralysis of many investment possibilities due to the potential costs of legal disputes.

In this second setting an important issue becomes how the legal system is structured to adjudicate disputes on these issues. A recent paper, Scott Thomas (1991), describes the alternatives chosen or being contemplated in Poland, Hungary and Czechoslovakia with respect to this and other issues, for example including the privatization of large and medium size enterprises. For our purposes, it is useful to consider two alternative forms of compensation considered in these experiences. One is the proposed return of actual property as in Czechoslovakia; the other is the compensation with financial claims for assets, except land, proposed by the Hungarian parliament and thrown in limbo by a court decision for lack of a judicial basis to distinguish between land and other assets. The return of actual property increases uncertainty and transaction costs whenever there are alternative claims to the same assets. The legal system must evaluate these competing claims and such a process takes time. Meanwhile, private investors contemplating the purchase of such assets as part of an economic activity will be tempted to look elsewhere. The importance of this growth reducing effect stems from its greater incidence on the most dynamic sector of the system, potential and newly created enterprises. The advantage of this compensation mechanism is that in principle it eliminates the difficult task of ascertaining the value of assets although in practice this may not be the case.[8] It is also worth noting that this mechanism, by itself, is inequitable with respect to those former owners whose assets have been physically destroyed or suffered substantial deterioration. Finally, this approach requires facing the issue of determining the rights of current users or title holders who are

---

[7] Announcement of a restitution policy is a powerful signal in this context but it is not the only one. Other signals, however, are less convincing and have different incentive and growth effects, for example exemptions from the country's labor or environmental legislation.

[8] For instance in the Czechoslovak case former owners and their heirs are not supposed to receive the benefits of improvements made over the last 30-40 years and the implementation of this rule generates another source of uncertainty and the need to ascertain the value of these improvements.

dispossessed in this process.[9]

A compensation scheme based on the issuing of financial claims can remove the incidence of uncertainty on investments in potential or new enterprises. It does so by allowing current users or title holders to exchange tenancy rights or the assets free of legal disputes; it does so, however, at the cost of an obligation incurred by the government to resolve legal disputes by financial compensation of valid claims to the asset. The key issue in this approach is, of course, to establish the value of the asset. Symbolic compensation or compensation based on the value of the asset in the centrally planned economy is unlikely to be successful and will be challenged through whatever legal system is developed. The economic value of an asset is the discounted value of the stream of earnings it can generate in the future. The lack of full ownership rights for several decades in these societies and their operation as nonmarket systems would have considerably reduced the income generating abilities of these assets. Schemes based on current value would substantially undercompensate in most cases. Schemes based on the value of the asset at the time of confiscation, on the other hand, would be infeasible. The income generating capacity of the asset in a market economy did not exist for several decades. Moreover, any estimates based on compounding would lead to fiscal burdens that could not be met. Thus, compensation schemes would have to be related to the income generating capacity of assets under the new proposed market system. Devising such a scheme paying due attention to efficiency, growth and equity considerations is a difficult but worthwhile research task.[10] A small part of our profession, the so-called quants, specializes in the design of new financial instruments and on their pricing. While the present problem is more complex, the insights from this literature may be valuable.

Concluding Remarks

In this essay I have endeavored to provide a constructive perspective on many different issues relying on the new institutional economics. Important macroeconomic and international trade issues relevant for the Cuban economy have been ignored, for example see the issues discussed in Pazos' lecture (1990). In those issues I did address the emphasis has been either on those factors affecting the growth promoting features of alternative institutional arrangements or in bringing out characteristics of these arrangements which become evident when one asks the question -- what is the economic function of a particular institution? By doing so, one can enhance the usefulness of contributions to policy discussions as economists. As with most research efforts, these ideas are offered as part of an exchange involving reciprocity and mutual gains. Extensions and corrections are

---

[9] There are numerous squatter settlements in the market economies of developing countries where the capitalist state has implicitly decided not to incur the transactions costs of enforcing the property rights of formal title holders. The uncertainty of these property rights makes this alternative at most a second best policy.

[10] For instance, under most conceivable schemes a significant part of the additional taxes necessary to undertake the financial compensation would have to be borne by future generations.

therefore welcome. Finally, although I have emphasized aspects especially relevant to the Cuban economy, most of these ideas are of general applicability.

References

Arthur, W. Brian, "Competing Technologies, Increasing Returns, and Lock = in by Historical Events," Economic Journal 99, March 1989, 116-131.

Barzel, Y., The Economic Analysis of Property Rights, Cambridge University Press, 1989.

Batchelder, R. and Sánchez, N., "The Encomienda and the Optimizing Imperialists: An Interpretation of Spanish Imperialism in the Americas," mimeo, Texas A&M, 1988.

Benhabib, Jess and Jovanovic, Boyan, "Externalities and Growth Accounting," American Economic Review 81, March 1991, 82-113.

Benítez Rojo, Antonio, La isla que se repite, Editoriales del Norte, 1989.

Bergad, Laird W., Cuban Rural Society in the Nineteenth Century: The Social and Economic History of Monoculture in Matanzas, Princeton University Press, 1990.

Betancourt, R.R., "Capital Utilization," in J. Eatwell, M. Milate and P. Newman (eds.), The New Palgrave: A Dictionary of Economics, the Stockton Press, New York, 1987.

Betancourt, Roger, "The Economics of Retailing," Keynote Speech to the VI World Conference on Research in the Distributive Trades, The Hague, July 1991.

Betancourt, Roger and Gautschi, David, "The Evolution of Retailing: A Suggested Economic Interpretation," International Journal of Research and Marketing 3, April 1986, 217-232.

Betancourt, Roger and D. Gautschi, "The Economics of Retail Firms," Managerial and Decision Economics 9, June 1988, pp. 133-144.

Betancourt, Roger and Gautschi, David, "Demand Complementarities, Household Production and Retail Assortments," Marketing Science, Spring 1990, 146-161.

Betancourt, Roger and Gautschi, David, "Two Essential Characteristics of Retail Markets and Their Economic Consequences," mimeo, September 1990.

Betancourt, Roger and Gautschi, David, "The Demand for Retail Products and the Household Production Model: New Views on Substitutability and Complementarity," Journal of Economic Behavior and Organization, 1991.

Betancourt, Roger and Gautschi, David, "The Outputs of Retail Activities: Concepts, Measurement and Evidence," revised version, June 1991.

Betancourt, Roger and Gautschi, David, "The Outputs of Retail Activities: French Evidence," University of Maryland Working Paper No. 91-5, February 1991.

Betancourt, Roger and Kiguel, Miguel, "Neoconservative Economic Experimentation in the Southern Core," Latin American Research Review, Fall 1989.

Bresnahan, T., Milgrom, P. and Paul, J., "The Real Output of the Stock Exchange," paper presented to the NBER Conference on Output Measurement in the Services Sector, Charleston, South Carolina, May 1990.

Clague, Christopher (ed.), Journey Toward Market Reform, forthcoming, 1992.

Coase, Ronald, "The Nature of the Firm," Economica 4, 1937, 386-405.

Coase, Ronald H., "The Problem of Social Cost," Journal of Law and Economics, 3, October 1960, 1-44.

de Zayas, Manuel Ramón, "Who's on First: The Cuban Political Ballgame," Post Modern Notes, Spring 1991.

Domínguez, Jorge, "Cuba's Present; Cuba's Future," Testimony before U.S. House of Representatives Subcommittee on Western Hemisphere Affairs, April 30, 1991.

Eggertsson, Thrainn, Economic Behavior and Institutions, Cambridge University Press, 1990.

Georgescu-Roegen, Nicholas, The Entropy Law and the Economic Process, Harvard University Press, 1971.

Grossman, Gene and Helpman, Elhanan, "Trade Innovation and Growth," American Economic Review, 80, May 1990, 86-91.

Hanak, E., "A Service-Based Theory of Retail Banking," in Betancourt, R. and Gautschi, D. (eds.), The Analysis of Retail Activities: Implicit Markets for Distribution Services, Special Issue of Managerial and Decision Economics, forthcoming 1991.

Hernandez-Catá, Ernesto, "Long-Term Objectives and Transitional Policies--A Reflection on Pazos' Economic Problems of Cuba," paper presented to the First Annual Meeting of the Association for the Study of the Cuban Economy, August 1991.

Hoff, Karla, "Land Taxes, Output Taxes, and Sharecropping: Was Henry George Right?" World Bank Economic Review, 5, January 1991, 85-91.

Hornstein, A. and Prescott, E., "Measures of the Insurance Sector Output," paper presented to the NBER Conference on Output Measurement in the Services Sector, Charleston, South Carolina, May 1990.

Krueger, Anne O. "The Political Economy of the Rent-Seeking Society," <u>American Economic Review</u>, June 1974, 64, pp. 291-303.

Kuznets, Simon, <u>Modern Economic Growth: Rate, Structure and Spread</u>, Yale University Press, New Haven, 1970.

Lakatos, Imre, "Falsification and the Methodology of Scientific Research Programs," in Lakatos and Musgrave (eds.) <u>Criticism and the "Growth of Knowledge</u>, Cambridge University Press, 1970.

Leunis, Joseph and Vandamme, Rik, "Welfare Implications of the Belgium Business Premises Act, paper presented at the VI World Conference on Research in the Distributive Trades, the Hague, July 1991.

Lucas, Robert, "Why Doesn't Capital Flow From Rich to Poor Countries," <u>American Economic Review</u> 80, May 1980, 26-91.

Mathewson, G. and Winter, R., "The Economics of Vertical Restraints in Distribution," in Stiglitz, J. and Mathewson, G. (eds.), <u>New Developments in the Analysis of Market Structure</u>, Cambridge, Mass.: The MIT Press, 1986.

Milgrom, Paul, North, Douglas and Weingast, Barry, "The Role of Institutions in the Revival of Trade: The Law Merchant, Private Judges and the Champagne Fairs," <u>Economics and Politics</u> 2, 1990, 1-23.

Morishima, Michio, <u>Marx's Economics</u>, Cambridge University Press, 1973.

Mueller, Dennis C. <u>Public Choice</u>, Cambridge: Cambridge University Press, 1979.

Mueller, Dennis C., "Choosing a Constitution in East Europe: Lessons From Public Choice," mimeo, University of Maryland, 1991.

Nabli, M. and Nugent, J., <u>The New Institutional Economics and Development</u>, North-Holland Publishing Co., 1989.

Nelson, R. and S. Winter, <u>An Evolutionary Theory of Economic Change</u>, Cambridge, Mass.: Harvard University Press, 1982

North, D., <u>Institutions, Institutional Change and Economic Performance</u>, Cambridge University Press, 1990.

North, Douglas and Thomas, Robert, <u>The Rise of the Western World: A New Economic History</u>, Cambridge University Press, 1973.

Oi, Walter, "Productivity in the Distributive Trades: The Shopper and the Economics of Massed Reserves," paper presented to the NBER Conference on Output Measurement in the Services Sector, Charleston, South Carolina, May 1990.

Olson, Mancur Jr. <u>The Logic of Collective Action</u>, Cambridge: Harvard University Press, 1965.

Olson, Mancur Jr. <u>The Rise and Decline of Nations: Economic Growth, Stagflation, and Social Rigidities</u>, New Haven: Yale University Press, 1982.

Pazos, Felipe, "Problemas económicos de Cuba en el período de transición," first C.F. Díaz-Alejandro Lecture, Washington, D.C., December 1990.

Porter, Robert, "A Review Essay on Handbook of Industrial Organization," <u>Journal of Economic Literature</u> 29, June 1991, 553-572.

Rey, P. and Tirole, J., "The Logic of Vertical Restraints," <u>American Economic Review</u>, December 1986, 76, 921-939.

Reynolds, Lloyd, "The Spread of Economic Growth to the Third World," <u>Journal of Economic Literature</u> 21, September 1983.

Roemer, Paul, "Are Nonconvexities Important for Understanding Growth," <u>American Economic Review</u> 80, May 1990, 97-103.

Sen, Amartya, <u>Poverty and Famines: An Essay on Entitlement and Deprivation</u>, Oxford University Press, 1981.

Solow, Robert, "Technical Change and the Aggregate Production Function," <u>Review of Economics and Statistics</u> 39, August 1957, 312-320.

Stiglitz, Joseph, "Symposium on Organizations and Economics," <u>Journal of Economic Perspectives</u> 5, Spring 1991, 15-24.

Thomas, Scott, "Political Economy of Privatization: Poland, Hungary and Czechoslovakia," in C. Clague (ed.), <u>Journey Toward Market Reform</u>, forthcoming 1992.

Tirole, Jean, <u>The Theory of Industrial Organization</u>, MIT Press, 1988.

Williamson, Oliver, <u>The Economic Institutions of Capitalism</u>, New York: The Free Press, 1985.

Towards a Market Economy in Cuba?
Social and Political Considerations

Marifeli Pérez-Stable

Cuban socialism as it has existed for the past three decades is increasingly unviable. Crisis in the Soviet Union has undermined the bulwark of the development model which, especially since the 1970s, had sustained the Cuban economy. Preferential sugar prices, below market petroleum prices, low-interest loans, and soft currency trade were essential for Cuba. Since the early 1960s, the United States has severely limited Cuban development within the international economy. The Soviet Union and, to a lesser extent, Eastern Europe had provided the island with an alternate, if not always satisfactory, framework to develop. That alternative is gone. And it is gone under the worst possible circumstances for Cuba.

Politically, the past two years have demolished state socialism -- what Rudolf Bahro once upon a time called "actually existing socialism" -- which, in one form or another, served as a model for Cuban socialism. Whatever the variations during the 1960s, the period of institutionalization, and the post-1986 rectification, vanguard party politics and central planning complemented well the realities of U.S. besiegement and charismatic authority. Today, the "world which actually exists" seems to be rather intolerant of the one-party political system and command economy which the Cuban leadership insists is imperative for the survival of the nation and the revolutionary heritage.

In Cuba, moreover, the fact that the original leadership is still in power and that a transition has to occur sooner rather than later compounds the crisis of the model. Had that transition happened -- say in 1978 or 1982 -- the Cuban Communist Party might have carried it through and survived its immediate consequences relatively well. Now, the transition is very much in question not only because the model has been considerably weakened, but also because the effectiveness of Fidel's leadership is in doubt and he is still very much alive. The transition was inevitable and, whatever the circumstances, it probably would have meant a crisis of one sort or another. But, Cuba is approaching that moment today under the worst possible setting.

Contemporary Cuban society likewise challenges the status quo of the past three decades. Most Cubans alive today became adults or were born after the social revolution of 1959. They are the best educated, healthiest, and most urban generations of Cubans ever. Their profile -- especially their relative equality -- is a product of the revolution. Many of them -- perhaps the most significant segment because of their technical and professional skills -- have middle class status in all but consumption. The command economy, particularly under present circumstances, is probably incapable of meeting their aspirations for better standards of living. The one-party system is likewise unlikely to satisfy their expectations for more meaningful political participation. One of the more lasting achievements of the social revolution has, indeed, been the consolidation of a significant middle class in Cuban society. The big unknown is how committed these younger generations of Cubans are to the ideals of nationalism and social justice which inspired the revolution of 1959.

International and domestic circumstances, thus, have led many analysts to conclude that the restoration of a market economy and the constitution of representative democracy are inevitable in Cuba. These analysts may well be right. Nonetheless, I would like to offer some observations in pondering the prospects Cuba faces as we near the twenty-first century. I too believe Cuban socialism as it has existed is increasingly unviable. I am not convinced, however, that the only alternative is an unmitigated market economy. I know those are the current winds, but I believe we need to develop a fuller appreciation of past and present as Cuba advances towards a still quite uncertain future. I am convinced, notwithstanding, that some form of competitive politics -- of meaningful political contestation -- is practically unavoidable and, indeed, desirable.

Where was Cuba going during the 1950s?

The revolution did not preempt Cuba from the path of becoming the only Latin American country to enter the ranks of development. Neither did the revolution save Cuba from the depths of poverty and underdevelopment. Cuba before 1959 was a complex society -- perhaps somewhat "schizophrenic" -- in which modernity and backwardness coexisted in unique ways. The social revolution did derail the directions which Cuban development seemed to be taking during the 1950s and steered it down another course which bore quite different consequences, costs, and benefits. In either case -- what did happen and what might have happened -- Cuba constituted and might have constituted a singular development path in Latin America. The revolution brought socialism. The Cuba that might have been might have brought what I call a "tropical model" of what Peter Evans termed dependent development in post-1964 Brazil.

The nature of Cuban dependent capitalism is a question which, off and on over the decades, has elicited enormous controversy with, however, surprisingly little research. Albeit we can never prove one or another outcome that never was, where Cuba was going during the 1950s is, nonetheless, important in examining the possible restoration of a market economy in Cuba. What kind of capitalism did Cuba have before 1959? One answer, of course, is rather simple: one which allowed the making of a social revolution. But, that is somewhat facetious and not the response I am presently striving for. Nonetheless, the link between what was and what could be is the revolution and just as Cuban history before 1959 created the conditions which permitted the socialist option, so have the past thirty-two years established the framework from which to carry out the possible transition to a market economy. I am arguing for a sense of historically grounded realism in understanding what the revolution preempted and the options which are currently possible.

Quickly and generally, what were the main characteristics of Cuban capitalism during the 1950s? The first and foremost was the relative stagnation of the sugar sector. After spectacular growth during the first two decades of the twentieth century, crisis overcame the sugar industry. World demand was slackening, Cuba was losing ground in the U.S. market, prices were falling, especially relative to import costs. Only wars brought temporary respite from what was evidently an industry bearing few prospects for long-term development. Output, moreover, was not keeping up with population growth. The one-ton per capita average of the 1920s had fallen drastically during the 1930s and recovered partially during the 1940s and 1950s. In 1955, nonetheless, the National Bank made starkly clear that sugar-centered growth meant declining standards of living. In order to maintain -- let alone increase -- 1947 living standards, unrealistically large sugar harvests were needed. And there were no markets for the output of an expanded sugar industry in Cuba.

Diversification -- as the reformers in the Asociación Nacional de Industriales de Cuba (ANIC), the communists and others in the Central de Trabajadores de Cuba (CTC), Gustavo Gutiérrez and other economists who formulated various official plans during the 1940s and 1950s, and the 1951 World Bank report all aptly noted and advocated -- was the only solution. Diversification did not, however, mean abandoning sugar. On the contrary, modernization of the sugar industry and by-products development might have partially served as the basis for economic transformation. Two especially pernicious consequences of sugar-dependent development need to be emphasized. The first is the problem of employment. Between the early 1940s and the late 1950s, the proportion of unemployed and underemployed in the labor force remained basically unchanged. The second is the debt problem--from the vantage point of the 1950s -- which dependence on sugar export earnings was beginning to create. During the 1940s, Cuba had accumulated some 280 pesos per capita in trade surpluses. By the late 1950s, those surpluses had plummeted to 61 pesos.

Notwithstanding, the second important characteristic of Cuban capitalism during the 1950s was the modest progress that was being made towards diversifying the economy. Non-sugar industry was growing at an annual rate of nearly 7 percent. Since the 1930s, consumer goods had declined to about one third of total imports. A new tariff to update the Customs-Tariff Law of 1927 was being worked out. In 1950, the National Bank had started operations. Credit to the non-sugar sector was increasing, sugar credit declining. Public and private support for research and development, particularly for sugar industry derivatives, was slowly rising. At the same time, foreign investors were being encouraged. Tax exemptions and more liberal terms for profit remittances were enacted. Between 1956 and 1960, U.S. capital had projected the first significant expansion since the 1930s -- $205 million in new, non-sugar investments, that is, about a 20 percent increase of total U.S. investments in Cuba.

Progress was, nonetheless, uneven. Domestic investments were still not decisively abetting economic transformation. While investment rates had risen through the 1950s, their structure had not changed significantly since the 1940s. Wages were falling as a proportion of national income and Cuban capitalists were thus enjoying a more favorable climate. But, they continued to prefer real estate, U.S. bank deposits, U.S. stock and securities, and idle bank balances in Cuba over investment in national industry and agriculture. Agriculture was especially neglected as modernization was not progressing rapidly. Industry -- sugar and non-sugar -- absorbed most capital goods imports.

Development trends, moreover, were increasing regional disparities. Between 1952 and 1958, Havana's wage bill grew 22 percent; that of the other five provinces contracted 22 percent. More than half of all wage earners whose monthly wages totaled 75 pesos or more lived in Havana.

The relative strength of the working class was a third outstanding characteristic of Cuban society during the 1950s. Unemployment levels notwithstanding, Cuba had one of the highest unionization rates in the world. Often violently repressed through the 1930s, organized labor became a central component of the compromise which followed the near-revolution of 1933. Maintaining social peace required significant state intervention on behalf of the working class. Labor laws were very progressive and the union movement strong enough to secure their minimal enforcement. Cuban capitalists insistently argued the nation would not advance until labor demands became more "realistic." That the Communist Party (PSP) controlled the CTC until 1947 rendered their arguments even more strident and urgent. Labor's strength, however, was not dependent on the PSP, but rather on the "economistic consciousness" of the working class and the often-enough responsiveness of the state to its demands. While the 1950s witnessed a moderation of labor demands and a willingness by the official labor movement to contemplate a more "realistic" accommodation with capital, a new labor pact had not yet been worked out and the working class still constituted a brake of sorts on Cuban capitalism.

The final characteristic of Cuban capitalism during the 1950s which I want to emphasize is its political weakness. Most obviously, the Batista dictatorship cast a pall over the political system which hindered the emergence of a national coalition to promote and implement reform. More profoundly, however, the political weakness of Cuban capitalism dated back to the origins and the development of the republic. Cuba had attained independence with a seriously dislocated upper class and under the Platt Amendment. The logic of twentieth century Cuban politics was clearly spelled out from the beginning: Cuba was sugar and Cuban sugar needed the U.S. market. I do not mean to reduce republican politics to sugar and the United States, but both were crucial components in governing Cuba and projecting development. Notwithstanding, after the 1930s, the state proved to be quite ingenious at implementing reform supportive of the status quo. The just-mentioned pact with labor and the 1937 Sugar Coordination Law are two outstanding examples of reform for the sake of social peace. The state, political parties, and the different sectors of Cuban society proved to be a lot less resourceful in diversifying the economy, forging a new social pact with labor, renegoting relations with the United States, and institutionalizing representative democracy. Had the politics of Cuban capitalism been more efficacious, a Cuba different from that of the revolution might well have happened.

I am suggesting the trends evident during the 1950s were transforming Cuba in the direction of some form of tropical dependent development. Cuba had a highly capitalized economy, quite extensive wage labor, an expanding non-sugar industry, a growing middle class, and a socio-economic profile, in many ways, comparable to those of Argentina, Uruguay, Chile, and Venezuela. The elements of dependent development -- the state, domestic capital, and foreign capital -- were certainly in place, if not yet coordinated. Without the revolution, a friendlier international ambience might have more easily allowed for diversification and growth. Tourism, mass media and entertainment industries, a modernized cattle industry, and winter crops exports were emergent economic prospects. So were underworld operations of gambling and drug trade as well as a banking sector not unlike that which later developed in Panama. Tropical dependent development might have also brought increased migration to the United States. Compared to the early 1950s, nearly four times as many Cubans left their country between 1955 and 1958. Growing class and regional inequalities might likewise have been aggravated. What kind of political system might have brokered these transformations is more difficult to speculate. Like most other countries in Latin America, I suspect Cuba without the revolution would have oscillated between civilian and military governments.

Where is Cuba headed during the 1990s?

I started out by saying that, as it has existed until now, Cuban socialism is increasingly unviable. My observations about where Cuban capitalism was and what might have happened without the social revolution were made to emphasize that the past thirty-two years did not preempt the transition to development. The revolution charted a different path than the one in the making during the 1950s. Today, when that path is all but concluded, I suggest we especially need to understand the past. The old saying, "Cuba país rico, pueblo pobre," needs to be modified. Cuba was not, would not have been, is not, and will not be a wealthy country. From whatever perspective we approach the future of Cuba--as scholars, as Cubans, as Cuban-Americans, as Americans, in Havana, Miami, or Washington, D.C.--we need to be realistic about the prospects for development. During the 1950s, Cubans and foreigners alike had inordinate expectations about the economic potential of Cuba. The early revolutionary years -- putting aside the euphoria which usually accompanies the birth of revolutions -- bred much optimism, in part, because the hopes were already in the air. Whatever the transition from the present situation in Cuba, I suggest we should refrain from falling into the same trap. Whatever forms markets take in the Cuban economy, the point of departure is the outcome of a social revolution and more than three decades of socialism.

The history of working class struggles and the confrontations between capitalists and workers in 1959 were significant factors in making the social revolution possible. As repository of the legitimacy of socialism, workers have borne a special place in Cuban society during the past three decades. The relationship between the state and the working class, however, has not been easy. Trade unions have undergone many changes -- their controversial reorganization to complement the goals of the planned economy during the early 1960s, their demise as mass organizations during the late 1960s, their reconstitution as "transmission belts" during the 1970s, and their uncertain present under the "periodo especial en tiempos de paz." Workers as citizens, especially in the early years, proved to be crucial for the consolidation of the revolution. Workers as workers have never quite shed their economistic conciencia. In theory, workers might be the owners of the nation's wealth. However, Cuban socialism, like the other experiences of twentieth century socialism, has failed to forge the conciencia of owners among workers. Immediate, material interests are the primary motivation for Cuban workers. Indeed, one of the reasons I contend Cuban socialism is increasingly unviable is because alternate incentives to produce efficiently have not been created and the establishment of more effective work compensation requires resorting to some form of the market.

Nonetheless, the transition from the present will have to contend with the legacy of militant unionism which, however constrained by vanguard party politics, persists to this day. Over three decades, the Cuban state has confronted the dilemma of labor discipline without the recourse of widespread unemployment and has instituted a variety of ways to deal with it. In 1980, a decree was passed to strengthen administrative control over workers. By 1985, however, unions had proven rather effective in defending workers against management. About one percent of the labor force appealed discipline sanctions, but municipal courts confirmed only 38 percent of the administrative decisions. Unions came better prepared to argue the workers'cases than management did to defend their sanctions and, consequently, the courts ruled for the workers in three out of five cases. After 1986, the Cuban leadership has chastised the unions for pursuing "particular" interests over those of the nation. Indeed, the rectificacion has often invoked a discourse on labor discipline, wages, and benefits such as vacation days which is not totally unreminiscent of the appeals by Cuban capitalists during the 1940s and 1950s. An important setting for assessing the possible transition to a market economy is the growing, albeit modest, role of foreign investments in Cuba. So far, the largest presence is in tourism and foreign management exercises almost total control over their Cuban employees. How will workers and unions react to the possible presence of foreign capital in productive enterprises which will necessarily change, at least in part, the rules of the game?

More generally, what does it mean for that possible transition to a market economy that Cuba had a social revolution? I do not think we can gauge the consequences of that fact by the experiences of the Soviet Union and Eastern Europe. The historical leadership and millions of Cubans whose lives have been committed to the revolution and socialism are still alive. The Soviet Army did not bring revolution and socialism to Cuba. So far, there is also an enduring legitimacy about the social revolution. What is currently being questioned in Cuba -- again, so far -- is the present and the future--not the past. Any transition from the status quo is likely to confront what is one of the most important outcomes of the past three decades: the widespread sentiment in favor of social justice, that is, relative equality. Indeed, the crisis of legitimacy which the Cuban government presently faces is, in part, due to the contravention of the popular expectation of equity. Corruption and privilege among high-ranking public officials have been long-standing sources of popular discontent which current circumstances have seriously aggravated. The "us-them" dichotomy permeating the social awareness of many Cubans is particularly damning for a government whose origins are rooted in a social revolution.

I believe the popular sentiment in favor of social justice is likely to survive the status quo and would probably find new avenues for expression. Many would probably see the right to some forms of private enterprise and the ability to profit honestly from their entrepreneurship as a realization of their just expectations. Many would consider justice being paid according to their job performance and having the ability to purchase goods and services commensurate with their wages and salaries. Many would, perhaps, not be too affronted by tolerable levels of unemployment, especially if accompanied by economic growth and improving living standards. I do not know whether the same can be said about privatizing the public health and educational systems, large-scale unemployment, significant undermining of the safety net, widespread foreign and Cuban-American investments, or claims to recover confiscated properties. How the sense of social justice, how the nationalism so central to the past thirty-plus years would be manifested in the event of a transition to a market economy is, right now, imponderable. In thinking about that transition, there is, nonetheless, a need to process the fact of the widespread sentido de derecho in the Cuban population.

The other central outcome of the past thirty-two years which likewise needs to be computed in the possible reconstitution of a market economy in Cuba is the sense of national identity independent from the United States which the revolution consolidated. Had the Soviet Union not become Cuba's ally, the revolutionary government would probably not have survived for very long. Collapse, defeat, or compromise with the United States would likely have been its prospects. Now that the Soviet Union can no longer provide Cuba with the same kind of support, the ways in which the Cuban government has defined and maintained national sovereignty over three decades are growing increasingly unviable. Strictly speaking, Cuba today is more independent than ever before. The question is for how long.

Before 1959, the United States seriously compromised national sovereignty and Cuban society proved to be incapable of negotiating a more acceptable dependence. After 1959, the revolution highlighted the radical elements of Cuban nationalism as the sole purveyors of national sovereignty. Today, those elements are losing the international and domestic sustenance which nurtured them since 1959. Nonetheless, nationalism is a potent force in Cuba. In contrast to Cuban-American public opinion, most Cubans in the island do not favor a U.S. invasion of Cuba. Whatever their allegiance to the government, most Cubans have a rooted national identity--albeit not necessarily in the terms the Cuban leadership espouses--and that fact should also be considered in the possible transition to a market economy.

My point is politics will play a crucial role in the transition from the status quo in Cuba. How that transition happens will have lasting consequences. If the current leadership is able or willing to engineer meaningful reforms, the outcome will be more likely to incorporate, one way or another, many of the social achievements of the past three decades. Continued inability or unwillingness to institute meaningful reforms will undoubtedly reinforce the weight of those inside and outside Cuba who favor the total uprooting of the revolutionary legacy. It is no small irony that current resistance to reform might lead to the restoration of capitalism in Cuba given that a similar inability or unwillingness before 1959 contributed to its collapse and the making of the social revolution.

An important factor in thinking about the transition is the nature of the Cuban leadership. Fidel Castro and many other high-ranking leaders believe they have a right to govern Cuba. Their rule is not likely to collapse as easily and peacefully as that of most communist governments in Eastern Europe. A complementary factor is the fact that the Cuban government so far retains sufficient support -- not a majority, but not an insubstantial minority either -- which would allow it to put up a fight -- a very bloody one probably -- in the event of U.S. intervention or a similar threat to reverse absolutely the heritage of the revolution. In other words, as of now, the proposition of total rupture with the past three decades espoused by the most powerful voices of the Cuban-American community and the Bush administration carries with it an unfortunate potential for widespread violence and U.S. intervention.

It is fruitful and necessary to think about the possible transition to a market economy in Cuba. I do not know how, when, in what forms, or if it will happen. As it has existed, Cuban socialism is, however, increasingly unviable. More realistic approaches will almost inevitably introduce considerable market mechanisms in the economy. Politically, I am suggesting that possible transition requires a discourse which takes into account the social revolution and the aspirations for social justice and national sovereignty, at present, widely diffused in Cuba. There is certainly a need to rethink Cuban nationalism and the question of equality. The platform of the past three decades will clearly not serve the next three. But, these issues should not be disregarded and they should be addressed. To disregard them or fail to address them might well undermine the future prospects for democracy in Cuba.

Cuba, indeed, is faced with momentous challenges: reorganizing the economy to secure growth, expand the satisfaction of basic needs, and motivate skilled and professional labor to work productively; establishing meaningful political contestation; and finding new ways for expressing national sovereignty which, sooner or later, will include an accommodation with the United States. Whether or how Cuba meets these challenges will, in important ways, depend on the politics of the transition. The dominant leaderships in Havana and Miami are not presently committed to meaningful reform programs. The U.S. government, moreover, insists on a Cuba policy which encourages the intransigence of both leaderships. However we approach the future of Cuba -- as scholars, Cubans, Cuban-Americans, Americans, in Havana, Miami, or Washington, D.C. -- we should not forget that, indeed, men and women do make their own history, albeit not as they please or in circumstances they have chosen. I hope the political alternatives to both leaderships and those in the U.S. government who might have longer vision avoid falling into new forms of determinisms and contribute to charting the future of Cuba from present circumstances with realism and imagination.

Comments by Lorenzo Pérez

Dr. Pérez-Stable's paper argues that Cuban socialism is increasingly unviable because of the reduction of the Soviet Union subsidies, the continuation of the United States blockade, and the increasing demands for political changes by the middle class. She notes that this has led many observers to believe that the restoration of a market economy and democracy are inevitable in Cuba. However, the author does not believe that the only alternative for change is the "unmitigated" (my italics) market economy, and she argues that to analyze possible future changes in Cuba one should keep in mind the nature of the Cuban development in the 1950s and where is Cuba heading in the 1990s.

Dr. Pérez-Stable identifies as the main characteristics of Cuban capitalism during the 1950s a relative stagnant sugar sector, relative lack of diversification of the economic structure, a highly unionized labor force, and a weak political system. She notes that notwithstanding these factors, it was reasonable to expect that Cuba would have still developed in the decades after the 1950s and that with a friendlier international ambiance the economy would have diversified. Although Dr. Pérez-Stable identifies important economic and political characteristics of the Cuba of the 1950s, I feel that her analysis does not include important factors which might explain the Cuban pattern of development prior to the revolution. For example, to what extent were there relative price distortions? How protected was the manufacturing sector? How open was Cuba to foreign investment?

Dr. Pérez-Stable believes that the transition in Cuba in the future would have to contend with a legacy of militant unionism and the widespread sentiment in favor of social justice. The author believes that the Cuban population is likely to accept some tolerable level of unemployment associated with the introduction of a market economy, if accompanied by improved living standards but that efforts to privatize public health and educational systems and a significant undermining of the social safety net, as well as efforts to recover confiscated properties would be resisted. She also feels that how the political transition takes place has important implications for the transition to the market economy.

I believe that Dr. Pérez-Stable has identified some possible important factors of recent years that need to be taken into account when developing a strategy toward a market economy. Indeed, a sound political strategy might call for a policy of gradual change, but I would warn against going too slow in making necessary changes. It would be important "to set the prices right" and to establish a clear system of property rights. I also believe that the Cuban population might react more favorable to these type of changes than the Dr. Pérez-Stable feels because of the opportunities for improving the standards of living.

On the negative side, I find some of the author's assertions rather subjective or without any clear justification. For example, assertions such as that the Cuban population today is the best educated, healthiest, and most urbanized needs to be documented. Other assertions such as that the Cuba has never been more independent or that the Cuban population has a strong "sentido de derecho" appear to be highly questionable.

Long-Term Objectives and Transitional Policies--
A Reflection on Pazos' "Economic Problems of Cuba"

Ernesto Hernández-Catá 1/

In the first Carlos F. Díaz Alejandro lecture presented before a recent meeting of the ASCE, Felipe Pazos provided a lucid and comprehensive presentation of the key economic problems that are likely to face Cuba in the event of a decision to re-orientate the economy away from central planning and toward a market-based system. 2/ In concluding his lecture, Pazos expressed the hope that his thoughts would provide a framework in which the economic problems that Cuba was likely to face in the period of transition could be further discussed and analyzed. In this paper I attempt to respond to Felipe Pazos' challenge and take the discussion of some of the important issues that he raised one small step further. In doing so, I certainly do not aim to be comprehensive. Indeed, I will deliberately leave aside some of the fundamental questions raised by Pazos (for example in the all-important areas of privatization and property rights) and concentrate on a limited number of specific policy issues, including trade policy, the exchange rate system, monetary policy and price reform.

In examining these issues, I will stress the importance of arriving at a clear understanding of the link between long-term policy objectives and the policies adopted during the transitional period. In his lecture, Pazos suggested that "we must distinguish between the basic policies that we should apply once we have overcome the problems of the transition, and those temporary measures that we will have to implement initially." I will argue that there are some risks in applying too rigidly this principle of separation between transitional measures and long-term economic goals. Specifically, I will argue that long-term strategic objectives will need to be clearly defined and carefully explained at an early stage, and that transitional policies will need to be framed in such a way as to avoid the risk of permanent deviations from those long-term goals.

Before turning to an examination of these issues, I would like to make two related observations. First, the policies that will be implemented during and after the transitional period will be largely the outcome of a political process of decision making--hopefully one in which the entire Cuban population will be allowed to express its views freely and fully. Therefore, where this paper adopts a normative tone, the intention is to be persuasive rather than prescriptive. Second, since the paper moves into uncharted territory, its conclusions should be regarded as tentative, and its recommendations are intended to encourage, rather than to preclude, further discussion.

1/ I am grateful to Armando Linde and Kent Osband for helpful comments on an earlier draft. The views expressed in this paper are those of the author and in no way represent the official views of the International Monetary Fund.

2/ Felipe Pazos, "Problemas económicos de Cuba en el período de transición," Cátedra Carlos F. Díaz Alejandro, Washington, D.C. (December 1990).

I. Long-Term Objectives: The Experience of Other Developing Countries

Much of the recent discussion concerning the future of the Cuban economy has focussed on how best to achieve the transition from a highly centralized form of economic planning to a market-oriented economy on the assumption that the political conditions for such a transformation would somehow emerge. This section addresses a different, albeit related, question: what is the form of economic organization and the economic policy framework that Cuba should adopt over the long term.

Reforming the Cuban economy without a clear view of the ultimate economic goals that are being pursued would involve serious risks: without a long-term strategy that serves as a guide for action in the near term economic policies could drift aimlessly, and serious mistakes could be made which may prove very difficult to correct subsequently. The basic objectives underlying the new economic policy must therefore be clearly stated by the authorities at an early stage, and these objectives must be well understood by the population. Otherwise, irrealistic expectations of a quick improvement in living standards will outrun the possibilities faced by policymakers, who initially will face severe constraints, giving rise to demands for unsustainable policies, excessive wage increases, and possibly to labor unrest. In that situation, the competitive position of the economy will be eroded, instability will hinder tourism and discourage investment by local as well as foreign residents, and the exodus of human capital--now presumably unfettered by domestic legal restrictions--will be difficult to contain.

The search for the basic principles that should govern the country's economic strategy cannot be disassociated from the political goals pursued by society. I will assume that these goals will involve the building of a democratic and pluralistic society based on the rule of law. I will also assume that the process of economic transformation will aim at establishing an economic system capable of achieving growth <u>on a sustainable basis</u>, and therefore a <u>durable</u> improvement in the standard of living of the population. The achievement of both objectives would seem to require an evolution of the Cuban economy towards a decentralized system where private enterprise and the free operation of markets would play a significant role. But market-based economic systems can differ significantly in terms of the extent and the nature of government intervention in the economy. They also differ considerably in terms of economic performance. It is therefore important to specify in some detail the policy framework within which market forces are most likely to bring about strong and sustained growth.

Developing countries: contrasts in performance

The search for a policy framework that will achieve Cuba's long-term economic goals must be grounded in experience. Indeed, only the lessons of experience will provide reasonable assurance that the mistakes made by other countries in the past will not be repeated, and that the actions of the successful countries will be emulated. Cuba is a developing country, and therefore it is the experience of developing countries that is most relevant. To be sure, the recent experience of the U.S.S.R. and of the countries of

Eastern Europe is invaluable, but this experience relates more closely to the tactical considerations associated with transition than to the strategic considerations relating to the definition and the pursuit of long-term economic goals. Those considerations require an examination of the growth performance of developing countries.

Over the past two decades, **there have been dramatic differences in the growth performance of various groups of developing countries.** As illustrated in Chart 1, the developing countries of Asia have experienced strong and sustained growth of per capita GDP during the period 1970-90, while the performance of other regions has been, to say the least, disappointing. 1/ It is not easy to generalize about the precise reasons for these differences, as experience has differed considerably among countries, even within a particular region. However, the sharp contrast between the successful Asian countries and the other developing countries raises a fundamental question about the relation between public policies and the observed differences in economic growth. While many aspects of this question remain unanswered, a growing body of empirical evidence suggests that there is indeed a strong link between economic policies and growth performance. Specifically, the more successful countries generally have pursued outward-oriented trade policies and maintained relatively unrestricted foreign trade systems; they have followed prudent fiscal and monetary policies and avoided very high rates of inflation; and they have generally limited government intervention in markets.

Saving and investment

Most importantly, **the successful countries have attained high rates of investment and saving.** The evidence in this area is quite strong. For example, the average contribution of capital formation to the growth of output in the 1980s has been more than twice as large in Asia as in the Western Hemisphere and the Middle East and four times larger than in Africa. It is also interesting to note that while the growth of multifactor productivity in the Asian countries in that period averaged roughly 2 3/4 percent a year, it was only 1 percent in the Middle East and it was negative in Africa and the Western Hemisphere. The importance of saving and investment for growth has been underscored by a recent study dealing with a sample of 71 developing countries. 2/ The results of that study, which are summarized in Table 1 below, indicate that countries with high rates of national saving and domestic investment have had considerable higher rates of growth

---

1/ Growth in the Asian region has been particularly impressive in a group of countries including Hong Kong, Indonesia, Korea, Malaysia, Singapore, Taiwan, Province of China, and Thailand, but it has also been above-average in the other countries of Asia taken as a group.

2/ See World Economic Outlook, May 1991 (International Monetary Fund, Washington, D.C.), Chapter IV.

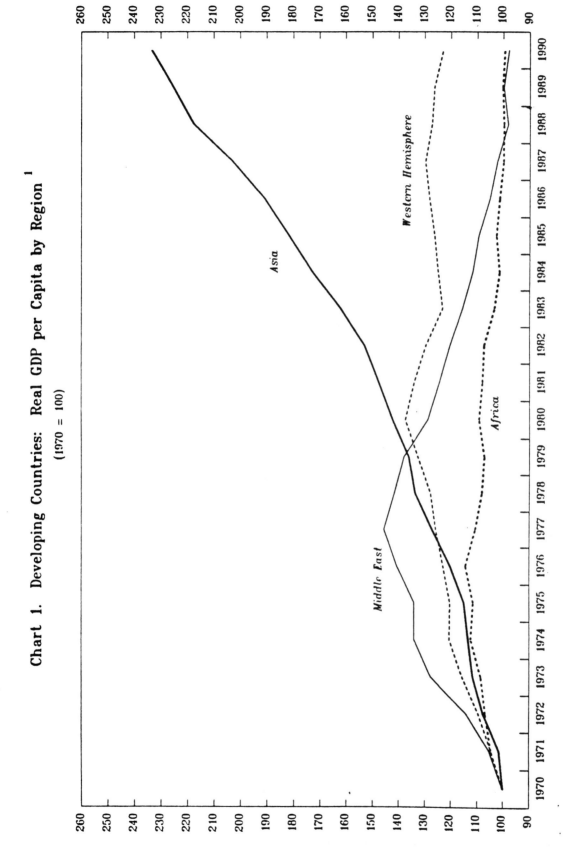

Chart 1. Developing Countries: Real GDP per Capita by Region [1]

(1970 = 100)

1 Composites are averages for individual countries weighted by the average U.S. dollar value of their respective GDPs over the preceding three years.

in per capita income than the countries with low savings and investment rates. 1/ Also, the high savers generally have experienced lower inflation, significantly lower debt/export ratios and a considerably lower incidence of debt servicing difficulties during the debt crisis in the 1990s.

Table 1. Net Debtor Developing Countries: Saving and Economic Performance, 1983-90

(In percent of GDP, unless otherwise noted)

	National Saving	Domestic Investment	Growth of Per Capita Income 2/	Inflation Rate 2/	Debt-Export Ratio 3/	Proportion with Debt-Servicing Difficulties in 1980s 3/
High savers	25.8	26.6	2.2	20.2	151	33
Moderate savers	16.2	20.0	-0.2	53.1	295	67
Low savers	6.9	14.1	-1.1	93.4	464	91

1/ Based on sample of 71 net debtor developing countries. Countries are divided into three groups according to the ratio of national saving to GDP. All figures are unweighted averages.

2/ Percent per annum.

3/ In percent.

1/ Against this background, it may seem surprising that saving rates in the formerly centrally-planned economies of Europe have been high by international standards. In large measure however, these high saving rates reflected forced saving in an environment of disequilibrium prices and shortages, and they often were used to finance inefficient investments, with adverse effects on the growth of total factor productivity and potential output. Indeed, a recent study suggests that the proportion of wasteful investment in Czechoslovakia, Hungary and Poland in the period 1965-85 may have been in the range of 50 to 75 percent. See Eduardo Borensztein, "Saving, Investment, and Growth in Eastern Europe," IMF Working Paper, May 1991. Furthermore, it cannot be taken for granted that saving rates in these countries will remain high after the implementation of price liberalization and other market-oriented reforms, unless economic policies are deliberately aimed at this objective.

The saving-investment-growth connection has strong implications for economic policies. First, macroeconomic policies must aim at achieving a general climate of stability and confidence conducive to appropriate levels of private saving and capital formation. In a situation of high inflation, volatile real interest rates and exchange rates, and large fiscal deficits, investment plans will be adversely affected because of uncertainty about the prospects for the economy and the authorities' likely policy response. A recent study of private investment behavior in 23 developing countries found that high rates of inflation-- taken as a measure of macroeconomic instability and uncertainty--had a significant negative impact on private investment. 1/ Second, policies that discourage private saving, such as financial controls that keep interest rates below market levels, should be avoided. Third, and but perhaps most important, fiscal policy should be conducted so as to avoid the absorption of national saving by the public sector, except to finance government investments in areas such as infrastructure, provided that these investments are clearly justified by a sufficiently high social rate of return. The evidence from cross-section data suggests that in the period 1983-89 developing countries with relatively high rates of national saving rates had higher government saving rates and lower fiscal deficits than other countries.

Inflation

The empirical evidence strongly suggests that the successful countries have generally avoided very high rates of inflation. Inflation involves serious costs, many of which apply with particular force to the high-inflation developing countries. High inflation is typically associated with high inflation variability, which creates uncertainty and undermines the confidence of domestic investors and foreign lenders. At very high levels of inflation, the economic horizon is shortened and financial instability disrupts economic decisions. High inflation is usually a symptom of fundamental problems in macroeconomic management: while it persists, private investors expect that the government eventually will be forced to take corrective monetary and fiscal measures. The longer these measures are delayed, the more disruptive the effect on the economy. It is therefore not surprising that countries with low inflation tend to have sharply higher investment ratios and growth rates of output and exports than the high inflation countries. 2/ This finding, of course, has important implications for the appropriate stance of monetary policy, which are discussed in some detail in Section IV.

Market distortions

Finally, there is considerable evidence that the successful developing countries generally have avoided the distortions associated with heavy-handed government interference with markets. For example, these countries have avoided financial repression

---

1/ Joshua Greene and Delano Villanueva, "Private Investment in Developing Countries: An Empirical Analysis," Staff Papers. (International Monetary Fund, Washington, D.C., Vol. 38 (March 1991) pp. 33-58.

2/ See World Economic Outlook, May 1990, pp. 57-61. The annual rate of growth of per capita GDP in the low inflation countries (i.e. countries with annual rates of increase in consumer prices of less than 6 percent) averaged 4.3 percent in 1983-89, but it was approximately zero in the high-inflation countries taken as a group.

Table 2. Trade Orientation and Growth

(In percent a year)

	Growth of Potential GDP	Contribution of		
		Capital	Labor	Total Factor Productivity
Strongly outward-oriented countries				
1975-82	8.4	4.6	1.1	2.7
1983-89	7.7	3.3	0.7	3.7
Moderately outward-oriented countries				
1975-82	4.6	2.8	1.3	0.5
1983-89	4.1	1.7	1.2	1.2
Moderately inward-oriented countries				
1975-82	4.0	2.6	1.5	-0.1
1983-89	2.7	1.4	1.5	-0.2
Strongly inward-oriented countries				
1975-82	2.3	1.6	1.6	-0.9
1983-89	2.2	0.7	1.6	-0.1

Note: All figures are unweighted averages. The classification of countries by trade orientation is based on World Bank, World Development Report 1987.

(as reflected in the fact that they have consistently maintained positive real interest rates), and they have pursued outward-looking trade policies. The importance of this last factor is illustrated in Table 2, which breaks down a sample of about 40 developing countries according to their trade orientation. Clearly, the more outward oriented countries have experienced much higher growth rates of potential output in the 1980s and, significantly, considerably higher growth of total factor productivity.

A policy framework for the long-term

This quick review of the economic performance of the developing countries suggests that Cuba's long-run economic strategy should be based on the following principles:

- a competitive and dynamic economy where the allocation of resources is based on the free play of market forces, except in those cases where market failure demonstrably justifies government intervention, for example in the case of environmental protection;

- a predominant role for the private sector in the production and distribution of goods and services, except as regards the supply of public goods and services such as infrastructure and social safety nets;

- an outward-looking economy, open to the free flow of international trade and capital;

- a strong fiscal policy that helps to achieve national saving and domestic investment rates sufficiently high to sustain strong growth of output over the long term;

- a tax system that is administratively simple and transparent, that avoids distorting decisions about saving and investment by emphasizing consumption taxes (rather than direct taxes on income or foreign trade), and that preserves reasonable incentives to work and to invest;

- and, last but not least, a climate of confidence and economic stability, which requires a monetary policy aimed primarily at keeping inflation under control, with adequate support from fiscal and exchange rate policies.

These, in my view, are the basic objectives that should be kept in mind in designing policies for the transitional period.

II. Price Liberalization, Subsidies and Macroeconomic Stabilization

I fully agree with Felipe Pazos that an essential element of the transition toward a market-based economy will be the liberalization of Cuba's price structure. He rightly stresses that price liberalization will need to occur at a very early stage: "as soon as production units are privatized, or even earlier." Of course, price decontrol will need to take place at both the consumer and producer levels. To free retail prices while maintaining restrictions on producer prices would involve a squeeze on enterprise profits--at a time when demand may be weak for various reasons--with the risk of potentially serious adverse effects on output.

Price reform will need to go hand in hand with measures to ensure the autonomy of firms from centralized control and to provide firm managers with the right to hire and fire workers and determine the desired levels of inputs and production on the basis of considerations of profitability. At the same time it will be necessary to break up existing state monopolies, to eliminate the present practice of "soft budget constraints", and to allow unprofitable firms to experience losses or even to go bankrupt. In this connection, the introduction at a very early stage of comprehensive antitrust and bankruptcy legislation will be of the utmost importance. A thorough examination of the legal and economic principles underlying such legislations should be viewed as a top priority item on which preparatory work should begin without delay.

The dismantlement of Cuba's distorted price structure will need to involve the elimination of a wide range of existing subsidies. This will be required not only as an integral part of the process of bringing prices in line with market conditions, but also in order to relieve pressure on a fiscal position which is already difficult and may well become even more serious in the period ahead. As indicated by Pazos, the present system of subsidies and price controls, as is generally the case in centrally planned economies, tends to artificially reduce the price of wage goods. Therefore, price reform and the elimination of subsidies will initially result in a fall in the real incomes of the majority of the population . As noted by Pazos, this would occur at a time when real incomes--which already have been reduced as a result of the cut in Soviet subsidies to Cuba and the disruption of Cuba's trade with the members of the now extinct CMEA--might be further reduced by the economic dislocations that could take place in the wake of a change in Cuba's political and economic system. Therefore, an important question is how to cushion the decline in real income resulting from price reform and subsidy cuts without derailing the reform process.

1.   Alternative approaches to price liberalization

The experience of the Eastern European countries and the current debate in the U.S.S.R. suggest three possible solutions to this problem. These solutions are not mutually exclusive and a variety of intermediate solutions would, in principle, be possible. **First,** the full abolition of subsidies could be accompanied by a system of temporary price ceilings for specific "essential" commodities, including selected food items. Of course this would lead to excess demand for those commodities subject to price ceilings, which would necessitate the maintenance of a complementary system of rationing--a system which would last as long as the price controls are maintained. **Second,** the termination of all price controls might be coupled with the temporary subsidization of a limited range of "essential" consumer goods, although not necessarily at pre-transition levels. **Third,** both price controls and subsidies might be eliminated for all goods, and the effects on the poorest sectors of the population might be cushioned by the introduction of welfare payments and a system of unemployment compensation. Unfortunately, all three methods present significant problems. The third one, however, is likely to be preferable, as it is most compatible with the principles of the long-term economic strategy. 1/

The price ceiling cum rationing solution would introduce a significant exception to the principle of free-market pricing, an exception that may prove hard to reverse and therefore may involve a lasting disincentive to the supply of a number of goods, including in particular some key agricultural commodities. It would also deprive the government of the political benefits of what might be one of the most popular results of price reform: the elimination of shortages and "lines" in food stores. Moreover, as argued in the following section, the retention of price controls would introduce a serious risk of rapid inflation combined with growing shortages if macroeconomic policies failed to keep the growth of aggregate demand under strict control.

The second option--combining full price liberalization with temporary subsidies for a specified list of products--would have the advantage of avoiding shortages and rationing. But it would involve a budgetary cost and would introduce distortions which, judging by the experience of those developing countries that have relied heavily on subsidies, could be politically very difficult to remove. The third option--full price decontrol and elimination of all price subsidies coupled with "safety net" payments--would also involve budgetary costs. It would, however, be most compatible with the concept of a free-market economy where poverty issues are tackled through a system of direct government transfers rather than through subsidies and price-distorting measures.

The specific solution that will be adopted will inevitably be influenced by political considerations. Nevertheless, budgetary constraints and efficiency considerations would need to be given the importance they deserve. Thus, if price controls and/or subsidies are to be retained for some time, the list of "essential" commodities will need to be kept to a minimum, and the government should firmly and publicly commit itself to a specific schedule to phase out the transitional measures over a brief period.

If a safety net is used to cushion the temporary effects on real incomes of price decontrol and subsidy cuts, budgetary considerations strongly suggest that unemployment compensation and other welfare payments must be kept at realistic levels. In this connection, the social and economic incidence of the fall in workers' real incomes and the rise in unemployment that will inevitably occur during the transition should not be exaggerated. As noted by Lipton and Sachs, the implications for the well-being of workers of the decline in real income resulting from price reform would be offset, at least in part, by the welfare gains stemming from the elimination of shortages and queues. 2/ It should also be noted that the consequences for production of the rise in joblessness would be

---

1/ A method that will not work at all is the indexation of nominal wages. Since gains in productivity are likely to be modest in the early stages of transition, nominal wage indexation will fail to support real wages and will only succeed in translating the one-shot price increase associated with decontrol into an inflationary spiral.

2/ David Lipton and Jeffrey Sachs, "Creating a Market Economy in Eastern Europe: The Case of Poland," Brookings Papers in Economic Activity, 1990:1, (The Brookings Institution, Washington, D.C.).

limited, because this rise would represent in part a shift from disguised to open unemployment. Of course, those who become openly unemployed would lose their salaries, which provides the rationale for unemployment compensation.

Finally, the fiscal burden of financing social safety net systems need not fall entirely on the budget. In several Eastern European countries, unemployment benefits schemes are now partly financed by employer's contributions (e.g. in Poland and Bulgaria) or by employer/employee contributions (Hungary).

2. Price liberalization, shortages, and stabilization

There is no dispute that full price liberalization is ultimately essential to eliminate shortages and queues and to promote efficiency in the use of resources. Still, it might be argued that price liberalization should be introduced gradually so as to avoid unleashing inflationary pressures that otherwise would need to be contained through highly restrictive financial policies. In this vein, it might be argued that there is a trade off between the objectives of controlling inflation and reducing shortages in the sense that a gradual process of price decontrol will diminish the degree of stringency required on the part of financial policies. I will argue that this is a dangerous fallacy, and that a strategy of **gradual price liberalization combined with loose demand policies will lead to both rapidly rising prices and to growing shortages.** This kind of situation, which actually developed in Poland in 1989, has been described as "shortageflation". 1/

To illustrate this proposition, consider Figure 1, where the price of goods (p) is plotted on the vertical axis and the excess aggregate demand for goods (e) on the horizontal axis. (For simplicity it is assumed that the aggregate supply of goods is fixed and that all prices are controlled.) The distance between the vertical axis and the downward sloping curve ED_1 represents the excess demand for goods if the price is regulated at any level below p_1^*. For example, if the regulated price is $\bar{p}_1$, the shortage of goods will be indicated by s_1.

If aggregate demand remains unchanged, full deregulation will bring the price level from $\bar{p}_1$ to p_1^*, thus eliminating the shortage. This rise in the price level could be substantial given the severity of the price distortions currently affecting the Cuban economy. Table 3 shows that in 1987 the gaps between regulated and parallel market prices for a number of important commodities were extremely large. More recent data is unavailable, but there are indications that shortages have increased for many commodities, and that the number of commodities subject to rationing has risen. 2/ But the sharp increase in prices resulting from deregulation will, if monetary and fiscal policies are appropriately restrained

---

1/ See Grzegorz W. Kolodko, "Transition from Socialism and Stabilization Policies: The Polish Experience," Seminar Paper, June 11, 1991.

2/ Jorge Pérez-López and Carmelo Mesa Lago report that the Cuban government recently has re-introduced rationing of 28 food products and 180 consumer goods, including clothing, footwear and household appliances. See "Cuba: Counter Reform Accelerates Crisis," Transition, Volume 1, No. 8, (The World Bank, Washington, D.C.: November 1990).

Fig. 1. EXCESS DEMAND AND PRICES

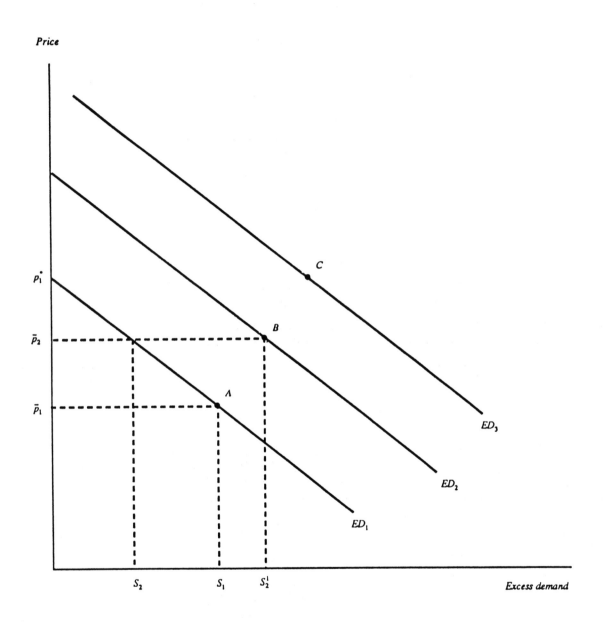

(i.e., if the schedule ED in Figure 1 does not shift upward), involve a one-step adjustment. The measured rate of inflation will show a rise for some time, but there would be no lasting effect on the rate of inflation.

Table 3. Cuba: Retail Prices for Selected Food Items, 1988
(In pesos per Kilogram, unless otherwise noted)

	Controlled Market	Parallel Market	Percentage Difference
Pasteurized milk 1/	0.25	1.00	300
Rice	0.52	3.26	526
Refined sugar	0.30	1.74	480
Raw sugar	0.17	0.87	412
Onions	0.54	2.60	381
Vegetable oil	0.87	10.53	1,110
Beans	0.46	5.28	1,048
Bananas, green	0.24	0.74	208
Bananas	0.22	0.40	82

Source: "Estudio Económico de América Latina y el Caribe, 1988, Cuba," Comisión Económica para América Latina y el Caribe, Naciones Unidas (Agosto 1989).

1/ Pesos per 946 gram jar.

Returning to Figure 1, a policy of partial liberalization would bring the price level from $\bar{p}_1$ to, say, $\bar{p}_2$, reducing the shortage to s_2. This would appear to indicate a trade off between the size of the price increases and the magnitude of the shortage. But this trade off exists only as long as the excess demand curve remains at ED_1. If the curve shifts up to ED_2, for example, the shortage will increase to s_2'. Thus, a policy of partial price liberalization coupled with loose control of aggregate demand (for example along the path A-B-C) would be associated with growing shortages and rising prices.

These considerations strengthen the case for rapid and full price liberalization. The experience of Eastern Europe demonstrates that such liberalization is possible. In Poland, for example, the share of sales at market-determined prices in the total value of sales increased from 50 percent in 1989 to 90 percent in early 1990. In the Czech and Slovak Republic, price liberalization in early 1991 brought the share of sales at free market prices to 85 percent of total sales. More recently, Bulgaria and Rumania have introduced comprehensive programs of price liberalization. In all four countries, however, governments have retained the power of intervention to limit "excessive" price increases resulting from monopolistic price setting.

The experience of Czechoslovakia is particularly illustrative in discussing the case of a country like Cuba where price distortions are pervasive. 1/ It is also particularly encouraging as it indicates that a comprehensive price reform need not evolve into a lasting inflationary process. The reform program launched in January 1991, which involved large-scale liberalization of both prices and foreign trade as well as a switch to world prices and convertible currencies in trade with members of the CMEA, did result in a sharp increase in prices: consumer and producer prices surged by 41 percent and 48 percent, respectively, in the first quarter of 1991. 2/ However, this was followed by a quick and pronounced deceleration of prices: by April-June 1991 the monthly rate of increase was down to an average of about 2 percent for consumer prices and less than 1 1/2 percent for producer prices. In recent months, prices in Czechoslovakia have been essentially stable.

The success in avoiding an inflationary spiral following price liberalization in Czechoslovakia was due to the pursuit of restrictive monetary and fiscal policies, including a swing from deficit to surplus in the government's overall budget balance. It was also supported by measures to avoid excessive wage increases. In January 1991, agreement was reached to place a cap of 10 percent on wage increases during the year ended December 1991, with increases above this norm being penalized by prohibitive taxes on enterprises.

3.   Price liberalization and the monetary overhang

By reducing the real value of the money supply, the one-shot increase in the price level associated with liberalization also would help to deal with any monetary overhang that may have built up over three decades of price controls and rationing. The monetary overhang, which is reported to be sizable in a number of Eastern European countries and particularly in the U.S.S.R., reflects the involuntary accumulation of financial saving associated with a prolonged excess demand for goods resulting from disequilibrium prices. A rise in the price level reduces the monetary overhang by acting as a tax on the real value of financial wealth.

An alternative way to reduce the overhang would be to cut the nominal value of the broad money supply through a monetary reform involving the write down or conversion of the financial balances held by the public. 3/ This method, which appears to have worked

---

1/ In contrast with the experience of Poland and Hungary, where some progress in liberalizing prices had been made in recent years, the price structure in the Czech and Slovak Republic had not been corrected over 40 years of central planning.

2/ As noted above, prices of goods representing 85 percent of sales were freed on January 1, 1991. About half of the items that remained subject to temporary price regulation freed in June 1991. In addition, consumer subsidies on virtually all goods were eliminated over the period July 1990-May 1991.

3/ See R. Dornbusch and H. Wolf, "Monetary Overhang and the Reforms of the 1940s," Seminar paper, Massachusetts Institute of Technology, October 1990.

well in several European countries in the period following World War II, does require difficult estimates of the size of the monetary overhang. Moreover, a monetary reform could raise political difficulties for a new government that is striving to gain the confidence of the population and establish its credibility. 1/

No estimate of the monetary overhang is currently available in the case of Cuba. However, on the basis of data provided by the Economic Commission for Latin America, the monetary savings of the Cuban population increased by more than 240 percent from 1980 to 1988, compared to a rise of roughly 50 percent in the nominal value of Social Global Product. While these data are subject to a very wide margin of uncertainty--particularly as regards the Social Global Product--the implied magnitude of the fall in velocity suggests that the size of the cumulative excess demand for money could be quite large.

III. Trade Policy and the Balance of Payments

Felipe Pazos correctly emphasizes the issue of how and where to sell Cuba's sugar production as one of the key problems of the transitional period. He may well be right in warning that, for an extended period, Cuba will have to continue selling an appreciable part of its crop to the U.S.S.R.--hopefully at world prices and in hard currency. Unfortunately, Soviet demand for imported sugar is unlikely to be sustained as domestic sugar production is rising. Therefore a critical item in Cuba's foreign economic agenda will be the urgent need for negotiations aimed at the reestablishment of a sugar quota for Cuba in the U.S. market--unless, of course, the protectionist barriers and distortions that presently characterize the sugar sector in most industrial countries, notably in the European Community and the United States, were to be dismantled as a result of multilateral trade negotiations.

As important as it is, sugar will be only a part of Cuba's foreign trade. Cuba's external sector will cover a wide range of exportable and importable goods and services some of which, like tourism, are likely to grow much more rapidly than sugar exports during the transition. Thus, there is a general issue of what trade system would be most appropriate for Cuba. In this regard, Pazos observes that "after normal conditions are re-established, we should adopt a tariff regime with very low duty rates." I fully agree, and I would add that tariff reduction should be accompanied--or even preceded--by the elimination of quantitative barriers on trade. However, Pazos goes on to caution that "the establishment of such a regime prior to the re-equipment of our industry and the re-establishment of our population's will to work would result in a flood of imports and a serious disequilibrium in our balance of payments."

1/ Another option that could have a role in the Cuban case as a complement to price liberalization would be to mop-up part of the excess liquidity by open market sales of government assets in the context of a program of privatization.

Pazos is undoubtedly right that Cuba's balance of payments is likely to come under pressure following the liberalization of its trade system. However, a number of forces will be set in motion that will tend to restore equilibrium in the external accounts. First, as Pazos notes, low levels of real incomes are likely to prevail at the start of the transition period, and this would tend to limit the demand for imports. Second, an incipient balance of payments' deficit would result in a fall in the value of the peso--spontaneously under a floating exchange rate regime or through a discrete devaluation under a fixed but adjustable rate system--which would help to further reduce import demand and to stimulate exports and tourism (the implications of such a depreciation are examined in more detail in Section IV). Third, the adjustment process could be smoothed by obtaining temporary external financing, for example under an adjustment program with the I.M.F.; such a program would make particular sense in the context of a domestic plan to dismantle restrictions on foreign trade.

Balance of payments adjustment along the lines described above would appear to be far preferable to the maintenance of a system of import restrictions aimed at protecting the balance of payments. First, if free-trade is the ultimate objective--a point on which Pazos and I fully agree--a restrictive trade system would not avoid, but would only postpone, the need for balance of payments adjustment. Second, import protection, even if it is meant to be temporary, would run the risk of encouraging the organization of pressure groups with a vested interest in making protection permanent, and such groups may be difficult to reign in once they have been given the opportunity to flourish. This is a serious risk. Cuba should not replace the inefficiencies resulting from bureaucratic control of central planners with the inefficiencies resulting from an uncompetitive private sector operating under the protection of trade barriers.

It should be noted that rapid, large-scale trade liberalization is not merely an ideal. It has increasingly become a reality in many developing countries, including notably in Mexico, and in the majority of the formerly centrally planned economies. All the Eastern European countries have now abolished the state monopoly of foreign trade. And whereas various degrees of tariff protection remain in place, considerable progress has been made in reducing or eliminating quantitative restrictions. Up to 90 percent of all non-tariff import restrictions have been removed in Hungary and in the Czech and Slovak Republic and the proportion is even larger in Poland. Even in the Soviet Union, there has been a significant, albeit incomplete, reduction of government involvement in foreign trade.

IV. Exchange Rate Policy

Few decisions will be more important than the determination of Cuba's exchange rate system. That decision will not only have a major influence on the evolution of Cuba's balance of payments, it will also determine to a large extent the context in which the country's monetary policy will operate. I will suggest that this is an area in which Pazos' "separation principle" between what is appropriate for the transition and what is appropriate in the longer-run may have some relevance. Specifically, I will argue that while the best solution for the long term will be to establish a fixed parity between the Cuban peso and the U.S. dollar, the appropriate solution for the initial phase of the transition may need to involve a degree of exchange rate flexibility.

1. Long-term objective: fixed nominal exchange rate with the U.S. dollar

For the long term, the potential importance of the United States in the geographic structure of Cuba's trade in goods and services, as well as in capital movements, suggests that a fixed nominal exchange rate with the U.S. dollar is likely to be the best solution. A fixed parity between the peso and the U.S. dollar would introduce an element of predictability for the bulk of Cuba's external transactions. In particular, it would greatly facilitate transactions by U.S. tourists by allowing the U.S. dollar to circulate freely in Cuban territory. This kind of system worked well in Cuba prior to 1959 and it has worked very well in tourist-oriented economies such as the Bahamas and the member countries of the Eastern Caribbean Central Bank. 1/

More importantly, a fixed exchange rate would provide an anchor for price stability as it would, in effect, tie the monetary policy of the Cuban central bank to that of the U.S. Federal Reserve. So long as the Federal Reserve continues to pursue a monetary policy aimed at resisting inflation in the short run, and at achieving a reasonable degree of price stability in the long run, a fixed exchange rate policy will ensure that Cuba's price performance is also favorable. Cuba would thus avoid the episodes of high inflation (and the subsequent episodes of sharp monetary tightening that high inflation inevitably requires at some point) that have inflicted so much damage on the economies of many Latin American countries.

Another argument in favor of the fixed exchange rate system is that it would make it easier to protect the independence of Cuba's central bank from eventual pressures from the government and its spending agencies. Of course, the exchange system will not guarantee independence as governments will always have the option of modifying the exchange rate rule and breaking the parity with the dollar. The avoidance of inflation will therefore require legislative guarantees including strict limitations on the provision of domestic credit. 2/ Most importantly, it will require a sound fiscal policy that avoids the need--and therefore the temptation--to resort to the inflation tax. Of course, this will require firm control of public expenditures and a strong system of revenue collection. It may also require legal restrictions on the size and on the rate of expansion of the public debt.

It could be argued that a fixed exchange rate system would imply a loss of independence of domestic monetary policy and thus would deprive the Cuban authorities

---

1/ Panama's fixed exchange rate system goes one step further by adopting the U.S. dollar as the sole domestic currency and thus avoiding the need for a central bank.

2/ One possibility that deserves full consideration would be to prohibit the central bank from expanding domestic credit, so that changes in foreign exchange reserves would constitute the full counterpart to changes in high powered money.

from a powerful tool of demand management. For several reasons, I find this argument to be unconvincing.

First, the ability of monetary policy to influence the real economy should not be exaggerated. In the long run, monetary policy cannot influence either the real interest rate or the real exchange rate. Accordingly, monetary policy cannot, beyond the short run, influence real economic magnitudes such as output and employment. As emphasized in Section I, these variables will be determined by the factors that account for the long-run growth of productive capacity: capital formation and saving; the intensity and the quality of the labor force; and total factor productivity--which means technological progress and the whole spectrum of managerial, administrative and structural factors that influence the overall level of economic efficiency.

There is, however, one way in which monetary policy can influence investment and productivity in the long run. It can do so by helping to establish a framework of macroeconomic stability and confidence in which the private sector, both domestic and foreign, can operate at its best. First and foremost, monetary policy can ensure that inflation remains at levels sufficiently low that they will not hinder investment and economic activity by distorting resource allocation and investment decisions, by creating uncertainty about future prices, wages and interest rates, and by encouraging activities whose sole purpose is to hedge against inflation. Therefore, if the "loss of independence" of monetary policy means the maintenance of price stability, this loss will be a blessing in disguise.

Second, it is not realistic to count on monetary policy to isolate a small economy like Cuba from cyclical fluctuations in its major trading partners. For example, in the event of a recession in the United States, Cuba's economy unavoidably would be affected through a reduced demand for Cuban goods and services by U.S. importers and tourists. However, the intensity of these adverse effects would be cushioned by the operation of automatic stabilizers, both in the United States and in Cuba. For example, a fall in economic activity in the United States would exert downward pressure on U.S. interest rates and on the value of the U.S. dollar. Under a fixed exchange rate system, Cuban interest rates also would be allowed to fall, thus boosting the interest-sensitive components of domestic demand, and the Peso would depreciate against other major currencies, thus stimulating Cuban exports to countries other than the United States. Exports to the United States also would rise, as the competitive position of Cuban producers in the U.S. market would improve owing to the Peso's depreciation vis-à-vis third currencies.

Automatic stabilizers also would operate in response to fluctuations in domestic output. For example, a cyclical decline in **domestic** economic activity would temporarily reduce tax revenue and thus cushion the decline in disposable income; unemployment compensation payments also would provide a stabilizing influence. It is true, however, that under a fixed exchange rate system the country would forego the additional stabilizing effect that could result from a depreciation of the Peso against the U.S. dollar and from a cyclical decline in domestic interest rates.

The need for an instrument of domestic demand management may arise in particular in the event of a major but temporary change in the terms of trade, for example as a result of a large drop in the world price of sugar. 1/ In that situation, there is a question whether the stabilizing role of fiscal policy should be limited to the working of automatic mechanisms or whether within limits, there may be a role for an active fiscal policy as a tool of stabilization. The limits are likely to be narrow. Longer-term objectives require that expenditure be kept under firm control, and the basic structure of the tax system clearly cannot be altered frequently without introducing serious costs in terms of uncertainty. Moreover, the free mobility of goods, capital, skilled labor and entrepreneurship will mean that tax arbitrage will set a limit to the extent to which taxes in Cuba can differ from those in the United States. Nevertheless, there could be scope for using temporary tax cuts and the front-loading of certain expenditure projects to provide temporary support for aggregate demand and economic activity in exceptional circumstances. The challenge will be to introduce the appropriate rules and mechanisms to ensure that these temporary fiscal measures do not give rise to lasting departures from the long-term budgetary goals.

2. Exchange rate policy in the transition

So much for the long term. The next question is which exchange rate system is feasible and desirable for the transitional period. I will consider two possibilities: (i) a fixed nominal exchange rate vis-à-vis the U.S. dollar and (ii) a temporary floating exchange rate system. I will discard a third possibility: exchange controls, as it would involve serious distortions and would be inconsistent with other elements of the transitional strategy, including in particular full and rapid trade liberalization.

a. Fixed nominal exchange rate

The first possibility would be to fix the value of the peso at an early stage, probably following a large, once-and-for-all devaluation. It could be argued that the early establishment of a fixed nominal exchange rate vis-à-vis the U.S. dollar would have all the advantages mentioned in the previous section's discussion of exchange rate policy in the longer term. In particular, it would provide an "anchor" to a noninflationary monetary policy and help to bring about a rapid convergence of domestic and U.S. inflation. If monetary policy were, for some time, more expansionary than that compatible with the maintenance of the fixed exchange rate, the central bank would lose international reserves, and it would be forced to reduce the growth of money and credit. If the authorities' commitment to the fixed rate system is credible, the convergence of inflation would take place without significant costs in terms of output and employment.

1/ If the deterioration in the terms of trade were to be permanent--for example if it reflected a permanent decline in the world demand for sugar--the situation could require a more drastic adjustment process including a permanent depreciation of the Peso. This, of course, would be possible under the "Bahamian" solution, but not under the "Panamean" solution where adjustment would need to involve changes in domestic demand and prices.

Several objections could be raised, however. 1/   First and foremost is the issue of credibility. If the authorities' commitment to the fixed exchange rate is not credible, central bank reserves, which initially are likely to be quite small, could come under speculative attack, ultimately forcing the abandonment of the system and the adoption of a floating rate system and/or exchange controls. Even if the central bank can hold the line for some time serious problems could arise. If monetary policy is sufficiently tight but inflationary expectations fail to adjust--because the public expects that monetary restraint will not be maintained--domestic inflation will continue to outpace external inflation and the **real** exchange rate will appreciate. This would have adverse effects on exports, output and employment; the current account position will deteriorate, thus further eroding confidence in the authorities' ability to maintain the exchange rate. Perseverance with a tight monetary policy eventually will convince markets that the exchange rate will be maintained, and the real exchange rate will gradually depreciate. But the process of stabilization without credibility could involve serious output losses.

Second, there may be serious difficulties in establishing the exchange value of the peso in the initial stage of the transition. If the initial exchange rate is seriously overvalued, there could be an immediate speculative attack on the central bank. If reserves are inadequate, this could force the abandonment of the currency peg, perhaps under disorderly conditions, with possibly lasting adverse consequences for the credibility of a nominal exchange rate anchor. The early establishment of a fixed exchange rate will be complicated by the fact that price liberalization most likely would result in a radical change in the structure of relative prices and costs. Because the present structure of relative prices and costs is so distorted, it is virtually impossible to establish a priori the level of the exchange rate that would ensure, in the short term, an appropriate level of competitiveness and satisfactory balance in the country's external transactions.

b.   Floating exchange rate

In view of the fundamental uncertainty as to how the cost structure will evolve, it could be argued that a transitional system of floating exchange rate would have considerable advantages. In particular, it would allow the exchange rate to "find its value" in the foreign exchange market as trade flows adapt to the country's cost/price structure while avoiding the risk of speculative crisis that would be inherent in a process of occasional, discrete adjustments in temporarily fixed exchange rates.

Two important questions arise about the implications of this initial period of floating exchange rate. The first question relates to the strong possibility that the introduction of external convertibility and the creation of a free foreign exchange market would result in a sharp fall in the value of the peso. In this regard, Pazos notes that "if the disequilibria of the transition were to result in a strong depreciation of the peso, and consequently in a fall

---

1/ Similar objections could be raised with respect to a preannounced "crawling peg" system such as the "tablita" system used in Argentina in 1979-80 and at various times in several other South American countries.

in the foreign currency value of all Cuban assets, the free entry of foreign capital would be tantamount to giving away Cuba's wealth to the new investors." 1/

It is not clear, how such a depreciation could be avoided. One possible interpretation of Pazo's concern is that a system of temporary controls on capital inflows would be appropriate. However, such a system would deprive Cuba of a source of external capital at a time when such capital would be most urgently needed and most reluctant to flow in. Furthermore, capital controls would deprive the country from an automatic mechanism of balance of payments adjustment. By lowering the foreign currency price of domestic assets, a devaluation of the peso would increase the expected (risk-adjusted) rate of return on such assets from a level which, initially, is likely to be very low. The resulting inflow of foreign capital would, for some time, finance a higher current account deficit than would otherwise be possible, thus allowing a higher level of capital goods' imports and giving time for the country's export capacity to develop.

The second question relates to the conduct of monetary policy. Without the nominal anchor provided by a fixed exchange rate, monetary policy would have to target on some monetary or credit aggregate. But monetary targeting, often a technically difficult matter, is likely to be particularly complicated in the wake of price liberalization, when monetary velocity is likely to experience large changes. In those circumstances, the objectives of monetary policy will be difficult to explain and its results hard to evaluate. Without the yardstick provided by the nominal exchange rate, monetary policy would be unable to establish credibility and would therefore fail to keep inflation under control. This is a serious risk. But it is a risk that argues against a floating rate system as a permanent or even a lasting solution, and does **not** rule out that such a system might play a useful role for a relatively brief transitional period, particularly if care is taken to avoid the (formal or informal) indexation of nominal wages.

c.   A possible solution

The observations made above suggest that exchange rate policy might go through three distinct phases. In the **first phase**, a program of price liberalization and subsidy reduction will be designed and formally announced, and the exchange rate will be allowed to float. Most probably, as suggested by the analysis of Calvo and Frenkel, the Peso will then depreciate in anticipation of price reform. 2/ A number of other important things would be done during this phase. First, legislation guaranteeing the independence of the central bank and imposing strict limitations on the expansion of domestic assets would be enacted. Second, a stabilization fund could be negotiated with the United States and other industrial countries and, if possible, with support from international financial institutions. Third, trade and price liberalization will be implemented which, most probably, would result in a further depreciation of the peso. This would be accompanied by restrictive monetary

---

1/ Presumably, this concern would also apply to a large, discrete devaluation under a fixed-rate system.

2/ Guillermo A. Calvo and Jacob A. Frenkel, "From Centrally Planned to Market Economy." IMF Staff Papers, Vol. 38, No. 2, June 1991.

and fiscal policies with a view to bringing down the rate of price increase to low levels over a relatively short period, following the recent example of Czechoslovakia. In the **second phase,** a crawling peg would be introduced, with a pre-announced schedule of progressively smaller devaluations that would continue until convergence between Cuban and U.S. inflation is achieved. The **third phase** would then begin with the establishment of a fixed nominal exchange rate against the dollar.

El Desarrollo de una Economía de Mercado:
El Caso de Cuba[1]

Jorge A. Sanguinetty

I. INTRODUCCION

Los astrónomos aprovechan los eclipses de sol para estudiar fenómenos que sólo ocurren o que son mejor observados en esas circunstancias. El eclipse de las economías socialistas--en este caso, un eclipse permanente--ofrece oportunidades especiales para mejorar nuestra comprensión de las economías de mercado. Como se observa en los países de Europa del Este, el establecimiento de una economía de mercado partiendo de un sistema de propiedad estatal con planificación centralizada presenta dificultades que van más allá del dominio de la política económica, pues exige la identificación de factores institucionales y de otra índole que normalmente tomamos por dados. El caso de Cuba, donde es razonable esperar que en un futuro cercano se pueda instaurar una economía de mercado, presenta condiciones extremas en cuanto al grado de centralización alcanzado actualmente y, por ende, a la profundidad y complejidad de las reformas que se harían necesarias para lograr tal transición.

El objetivo general de este ensayo es ayudar a identificar los factores que deben tenerse en cuenta para que tal transición se lleve a cabo de la mejor manera posible y con base en el interés público cubano. Además, este trabajo persigue varios fines específicos en el corto plazo. Uno es contribuir al estudio de problemas económicos para los cuales no existen soluciones "enlatadas" de fácil aplicación y éxito garantizado. En este sentido, los economistas constituyen una de las audiencias principales del ensayo.

Otro objetivo de corto plazo es el de identificar aquellos factores no económicos que deben ser tomados en cuenta en cualquier transformación profunda de una sociedad. Por ejemplo, el establecimiento de una economía de mercado requiere cambios trascendentales del sistema legal, cubriendo una amplia gama de aspectos como son los derechos de propiedad, la normación de las diversas formas de relaciones contractuales, la regulación de actividades monopolísticas, la definición de las autoridades fiscales y los procedimientos para la venta y adquisición de bienes y servicios por el Estado. Es, además, prácticamente imposible concebir una transformación profunda de la economía cubana sin cambios constitucionales. Todo esto significa que la "ingeniería" de la transición requiere no sólo economistas si no también juristas, lo que los hace parte de la audiencia intentada de este ensayo.

---

[1] El autor desea dejar testimonio de su deuda intelectual con Felipe Pazos, quien al comienzo de la década de los ochenta escribió un trabajo pionero sobre este tema. Posteriormente, el 28 de diciembre de 1990, dictó la Cátedra Carlos F. Díaz Alejandro en Washington, D.C. bajo el título "Problemas Económicos de Cuba en el Período de la Transición" donde plasma y desarrolla sus ideas iniciales.

Generalmente se ha supuesto que la transición hacia una economía de mercado en Cuba deberá llevarse a cabo en el contexto de una transición hacia una sociedad democrática. De hecho, muchos suponen razonablemente que el advenimiento de un Estado que reconozca una mayor libertad individual, que al mismo tiempo evite los abusos que se derivan de cualquier concentración desmesurada de poder (tanto económico como político) es el objetivo principal de cualquier transformación profunda del Estado cubano. Por lo tanto, la transición hacia una economía de mercado no se percibe tanto como un objetivo en sí mismo, sino que es más bien una de las partes, o acaso un medio, en la instauración de una democracia.

Con este supuesto en mente, el tercer objetivo inmediato de este trabajo es contribuir a elevar el nivel de comprensión económica del ciudadano cubano medio. O sea, en la medida que una transformación del sistema económico nacional precisa de cambios de naturaleza legal, desde el nivel constitucional hasta el de las leyes y regulaciones más específicas, y suponiendo que tales cambios han de ser sometidos a consultas democráticas directas e indirectas, es preciso que el ciudadano común, como votante o como representante de otros ciudadanos, tenga un mínimo de comprensión sobre los aspectos económicos de aquello sobre lo cual se manifiesta y oportunamente vota.

Esto define la tercera y no menos importante audiencia de este ensayo. No basta que los economistas nos pongamos de acuerdo sobre cómo resolver ciertos problemas críticos de una transición hacia una economía de mercado si la mayoría ciudadana no acepta lo que los técnicos determinan. Esto es especialmente válido si se tiene en cuenta que los primeros años de la transición no sólo no han de producir milagros sino que van a requerir ajustes macro y microeconómicos que generarán incertidumbre y que incluso pueden llegar a afectar negativamente a algunos segmentos de la población.

Puede postularse que la solidez de una nueva República de Cuba dependerá del grado de conocimiento de la ciudadanía sobre lo que es posible y lo que no es posible en materia de política pública. En este sentido, insto a mis colegas economistas y a todos aquellos profesionales y técnicos que puedan contribuir a resolver los problemas de la transición a que dediquen parte de su esfuerzo no sólo a las soluciones respectivas si no también a mejorar el nivel de comprensión del ciudadano medio.

Además de esta sección introductoria, la sección II presenta una discusión de las condiciones políticas y económicas que pueden existir al comenzar una transición y que pueden ejercer un peso determinante sobre la misma. La sección III se concentra en los acciones más perentorias que deberán ser consideradas en los primeros momentos de la transición, mientras que la sección IV pasa a detallar los elementos más importantes que debieran considerarse en la formulación de un plan para la transición. La sección V se dedica a un pensamiento breve a manera de conclusión del ensayo.

I. LAS CONDICIONES INICIALES

A. La Situación Política al Comienzo de la Transición

No tiene sentido tratar de pronosticar las condiciones en que ocurriría un cambio de poderes en Cuba y si tal cambio propiciaría una transición democrática y una economía de mercado. Es de esperar que una transición pacífica del poder político facilite la transición hacia una economía de mercado, mientras que un cambio político violento entorpecería dicha transición, al menos durante los primeros tiempos. Cada forma de traspaso del poder político corresponde a un conjunto de opciones de transición económica. Es posible que un nuevo gobierno en Cuba adopte medidas que marquen una transformación radical de la economía al punto de reducir a un mínimo el grado de intervención estatal en la economía. Sin embargo, no es prudente descartar la posibilidad de que un nuevo equipo gobernante adopte políticas más cercanas a las de China que a las de Checoslovaquia, Polonia o Hungría. Por otro lado, es necesario tener en cuenta que una transición política como la que sucedió en Rumanía, la que parece estar ocurriendo en Albania mientras se escribe este trabajo o incluso la de la propia Unión Soviética dificultaría enormemente cualquier transición económica, pero especialmente aquéllas que dependan intensamente del funcionamiento eficiente de los mercados.

Como no sería práctico escribir un ensayo para cada uno de los escenarios más verosímiles, este trabajo se basa en unas condiciones iniciales hipotéticas relativamente simples para estudiar los problemas de la transición. La razón de usar supuestos simplificadores es de tipo expositivo o didáctico: la transición hacia una economía de mercado es un proceso complejo en si mismo. Si conducimos el análisis bajo supuestos de una transición escabrosa, con violencia y profundas divisiones entre diversos segmentos de la población perderíamos el foco de nuestro tema principal: los problemas económicos por sí solos. Por lo tanto, es conveniente adoptar unos supuestos simplificadores en cuanto a las condiciones iniciales para poder comprender mejor la complejidad de la transición económica sin las complicaciones que introduciría la transición de poderes.

Supondremos para los efectos de este análisis, que el proceso de traspaso del poder político será muy corto, de naturaleza pacífica y que la implantación de una economía de mercado contará con el apoyo de la mayoría de la población. Al suponer estas condiciones iniciales, el gobierno a cargo de la transición podrá concentrarse en la reconstrucción económica sin que tenga que distraer demasiada atención ni recursos excesivos a problemas de seguridad interna o de orden público. Es obvio que la reconstrucción económica se haría más difícil en tales condiciones, pues la base de recursos disponibles sería menor y no se lograría el ambiente de tranquilidad interna que se requiere para atraer la actividad inversionista que ayudaría en la transición. El lector queda a cargo de hacer su propio análisis en la medida que crea que las condiciones iniciales, ya bien difíciles como vamos a ver, serán menos favorables.

B.   La Situación Económica al Comienzo de la Transición

Los cambios ocurridos en la Unión Soviética y en los otros países de Europa Oriental están forzando al gobierno cubano a adoptar medidas de ajuste macroeconómico que restablezcan el equilibrio entre ingresos y gastos del país, en presencia de una reducción gradual y presumiblemente significativa de los subsidios y préstamos recibidos hasta ahora. A grandes rasgos, las medidas de ajuste son similares a las que un gobierno de transición tendría que adoptar para enfrentarse a una economía ineficiente, distorsionada y endeudada en extremo: principalmente equilibrar el balance de pagos por medio de reducciones drásticas de las importaciones al mismo tiempo que se adoptan medidas para aumentar los ingresos por exportaciones.

Tales medidas de ajuste presentan algunas características interesantes e irónicas que merecen ser destacadas. Una es que el ajuste ha sido impuesto por el propio gobierno y no por un organismo financiero multilateral como el Fondo Monetario Internacional o el Banco Mundial como condición para establecer programas de financiamiento. Esto implica que el impacto del ajuste sobre la población puede ser más severo en el corto plazo pues, habiendo Cuba renunciado a ser miembro de dichas instituciones desde el comienzo de la década de los sesenta, no tiene la posibilidad de acceder a financiamientos que de alguna manera aliviarían los dolores inevitables del ajuste.

Al aplicar las medidas de ajuste, el gobierno cubano actual, obviamente sin quererlo, está facilitando una transición futura hacia una economía de mercado, pues el establecimiento de la misma requiere un saneamiento mínimo de las finanzas públicas. Si, por el contrario, fuese un gobierno de transición el que se viera forzado a aplicar las medidas mencionadas, la transición hacia una economía de mercado se vería seriamente obstaculizada pues la población sólo vería al comienzo las dolorosas consecuencias de un ajuste que son inevitables bajo cualquier régimen económico que busca su propio sostenimiento.

Los esfuerzos para aumentar las exportaciones conducen a la que acaso sea la más flagrante de las ironías o contradicciones de la política económica cubana: el reclutamiento activo de capitalistas internacionales para invertir en el desarrollo turístico del país. Aunque el gobierno cubano ha rechazado reformas que lo conduzcan al establecimiento de economías de mercado, no le ha quedado otra alternativa que recurrir a actividades de mercado (circunscritas al sector externo para mantener la asepcia ideológica interna) para incrementar sus ingresos por exportaciones y evitar lo que percibe como una crisis económica que puede tener repercusiones políticas impredecibles.

El origen de la crisis, sin embargo, no radica en los acontecimientos recientes en los países del difunto bloque socialista. Tales acontecimientos no han hecho otra cosa que revelar la crisis crónica de la economía cubana durante las últimas tres décadas; una crisis que consiste en la incapacidad nacional de producir para su propio sustento sin necesidad de inyecciones masivas de recursos externos que han convertido al país en una economía esencialmente parasitaria.

En este sentido, el fracaso económico del gobierno actual es doble. En primer lugar, por haber seleccionado un modelo de desarrollo intrínsecamente ineficiente y tribal y en segundo lugar porque, aún dentro de los cánones socialistas, Cuba logró ser la más ineficiente de todas las economías planificadas como lo demuestra su dependencia secular de los subsidios y el volumen de los mismos. Ellos parecen ser de tal magnitud que debemos plantearnos una gran interrogante: **¿es capaz Cuba de alimentarse a sí misma si los subsidios desparecieran abruptamente?** Si la respuesta es negativa, la transición se tendría que llevar a cabo en condiciones difíciles de describir, mientras que la ayuda internacional para evitar una hambruna puede ser indispensable.

En tal contexto y aunque sea aventurado decirlo, es importante señalar que el éxito que el gobierno actual tenga en independizar la economía cubana de los subsidios facilitaría la labor de un gobierno de transición. Si por otra parte, las medidas de ajuste llegan a exasperar a la población hasta el punto de provocar la desestabilización y ulterior caída del régimen, el gobierno de transición tendría igualmente que continuar tales medidas, a menos que se obtengan cantidades masivas de ayuda externa, lo cual no es realista ni prudente esperar. Esto, por supuesto, resolvería el problema de corto plazo en cuanto al sostenimiento de actividades mínimas de consumo para la población, pero no resolvería el problema de largo plazo de restaurar la capacidad productiva nacional hasta el punto en que alcance nuevamente su autosuficiencia.

La misma paradoja puede aplicarse al tan debatido tema de la inversión de capitales extranjeros en el desarrollo turístico como un medio de alcanzar un equilibrio externo. Muchos parecen estar de acuerdo con la premisa del gobierno cubano actual que el desarrollo turístico puede salvar el socialismo en Cuba. ¿Por qué no se razona en otra dirección? ¿Por qué se piensa que un gobierno que durante tres décadas se ha distinguido por su ineptitud económica ha de tener éxito esta vez? ¿Por qué, por otro lado, no se considera la posibilidad de que un cierto grado de éxito en el desarrollo turístico representaría un gran fracaso para el gobierno pues él mismo estaría demostrando que la economía cubana no es sostenible sin capitalistas, empresarios y actividades de mercado? ¿Haría esto más fácil la remoción del equipo dirigente del gobierno que persiste en mantener a Cuba dentro del régimen actual?

Durante las últimas tres décadas, el país ha venido sufriendo serias dificultades económicas que, aunque interrumpidas por breves períodos de ilusoria y marginal prosperidad, parecen haber conducido sistemáticamente a un deterioro generalizado de los niveles y calidad de la vida de la población. Sin embargo, las dificultades económicas nunca han parecido estar cerca de provocar un cataclisma de tipo político. Tampoco fueron las condiciones económicas por sí solas las causantes directas de las transformaciones ocurridas en los países de Europa Oriental.

Independientemente del grado de éxito que el gobierno cubano alcance en los frentes del ajuste y del desarrollo turístico, es de esperar que en el mediano plazo la economía cubana mantenga las características actuales, que en favor de la unidad de este trabajo repasamos en los puntos siguientes:

- Predominio de la propiedad estatal en las actividades productivas,

- Rigidez de precios de bienes y factores,

- Distorsiones de precios con desviaciones de magnitud desconocida con relación a lo que serían precios de equilibrio competitivo, o sea, aquéllos que reflejen relaciones de libre oferta y demanda,

- Racionamiento de casi todos los bienes de consumo,

- Volumen desconocido de actividades de mercado negro pero presumiblemente marginal,

- Administración centralizada de las empresas productivas de manera que las mismas no tienen control sobre sus inversiones, los precios de lo que producen, sus ingresos y sus gastos,

- Sistema financiero nacional que asemeja a una caja común,

- Inexistencia de la intermediación financiera, el crédito y el ahorro,

- Producción de alimentos a niveles precarios basada en el sistema estalinista de acopio de productos agropecuarios que se distribuyen por el Estado hasta llegar al consumidor,

- Bajos niveles de productividad del trabajo y del capital,

- Poca diversificación de la producción exportable nacional,

- Capacidad industrial exigua como resultado del deterioro de la planta física y la baja eficiencia productiva,

- Infraestructura física (incluyendo vivienda) en estado de deterior progresivo,

- Tecnología generalmente atrasada aunque puede haber excepciones,

- Un alto nivel de endeudamiento externo con diversos países e instituciones de crédito,

• Niveles desconocidos de competencia en la fuerza de trabajo,

• Niveles desconocidos de desempleo abierto y disfrazado,

• Educación gratuita con racionamiento de acceso a ciertos planteles y a niveles superiores,

• Servicios gratuitos de salud,

• Monto de las pensiones en curso de pago y de próximo vencimiento de magnitudes desconocidas.

En resumen, la transición a una economía de mercado en Cuba probablemente tenga que comenzar con un país profundamente endeudado, de economía ineficiente e incapaz de crecer rápidamente en los primeros años.[2] En estas condiciones, más o menos aliviadas (o empeoradas) por el éxito (o el fracaso) de las actuales políticas del gobierno y más o menos complicadas por las condiciones en que ocurra el traspaso del poder político, el gobierno de transición se enfrentará a enormes desafíos, entre ellos, la gigantesca tarea de formular una estrategia y poner en práctica el plan de acción correspondiente para construir una economía de mercado.

Para mejor identificar los factores más importantes a ser tomados en cuenta en semejante empresa, los conceptos que siguen se han ordenado en forma de la agenda que pudiera tener el gobierno de transición de manera de identificar las prioridades pertinentes y separar, en cada fase de la transición, lo que debe hacerse en esa fase y lo que debe dejarse para una siguiente. O sea, el éxito en la instauración de una economía de mercado en Cuba dependerá, entre otras cosas, del sentido de propósito y la capacidad organizativa y ejecutiva del nuevo equipo de gobierno. El éxito depende de mucho más que de una formulación inteligente de política económica.

II. LAS PRIORIDADES Y DECISIONES INICIALES

Antes de entrar en la materia de esta sección, es preciso visualizar el problema de tipo logístico que enfrentará un gobierno de transición desde el primer momento en que aborde sus nuevas responsabilidades. Es útil enfatizar que dicho equipo de gobierno heredará un sistema que desde el comienzo se postula como arcaico y que deberá ser radicalmente modificado.

Sin embargo, las modificaciones deberán respetar ciertos principios para no crear nuevos problemas y complicar innecesariamente el proceso de la transición. El gobierno

---

2 No es posible predecir si para entonces los subsidios soviéticos habrán sido reducidos ni en qué magnitud.

de la transición deberá actuar de manera análoga a la de una tripulación que debe abordar una nave en mal estado, abandonada en alta mar y cuya carga debe ser salvada. Lo primero que la nueva tripulación deberá hacer es aprender a conducir esa nave, por obsoleta que sea, es ella la que en ese momento lleva la carga que debe ser salvada. Una vez en control de la nave, entonces se podrá proceder a designios más ambiciosos como el de trasbordar la carga y llegar a destinos más lejanos.

La analogía sirve para dramatizar la necesidad de que el gobierno de una nueva República de Cuba formule sus agendas con una concepción clara de lo que se puede y no se puede hacer en cada momento. El cumplimiento de esta condición es de importancia crítica para el éxito de la transición y debe contemplarse en cada fase de la formulación de la política económica y del plan de acción correpondiente.

De aquí en adelante, las decisiones de política económica que se discuten se plantean en los términos individuales de los funcionarios a cargo de las mismas. Se ha adoptado este método para llevar al lector una visión más clara de la finitud de la capacidad decisoria y administrativa para construir un nuevo sistema económico, visión que de otro modo se perdería si se siguiera la costumbre de emplear la abstracción impersonal de que son los organismos del Estado los que manejan la política pública.

A. Los Primeros Días de la Transición

1. En el Despacho del Ministro de Economía[3]

La prioridad más alta de cualquier ministro de economía en un gobierno de transición deberá ser evitar que se deteriore el precario sistema de producción y distribución de alimentos a la población.[4] El alto grado de centralización del sistema productivo cubano actual y que seguramente heredará el gobierno de transición implica que no hay redundancias de capacidad que permitan a una parte del sistema compensar las ineficiencias o incumplimientos de alguna otra parte. Los productos agropecuarios forman una parte crítica del sistema alimentario cubano y los mismos llegan a la población mediante el llamado sistema de "acopio", donde las granjas le "venden" al Estado parte de su producción para ser distribuida en los distintos centros de consumo. Este sistema, de naturaleza netamente estalinista, generalmente incumple con los planes de producción, lo cual causa oscilaciones de gran amplitud entre períodos de escasez--los más frecuentes--y períodos de abundancia excesiva--los menos comunes. Este sistema está estrechamente ligado al sistema de racionamiento con precios fijos dictados por el gobierno, lo cual es parte intrínseca del sistema estalinista. El sistema de racionamiento está sujeto igualmente a oscilaciones en el cumplimiento de las cuotas estipuladas. Dichas oscilaciones no sólo

---

[3] Es de esperar que este cargo sea simultáneamente el de Director de la Junta Central de Planificación.

[4] El uso del género masculino en la descripción de cargos se hace por simplificar el lenguaje y no denota preferencias de ningún tipo.

tienen su origen en contingencias en la fase productiva misma, sino también en las que afectan independientemente los sistemas de transporte y de administración de la distribución.

Antes de que semejante anacronismo pueda modificarse, es imperativo comprender que el mismo es el único sustento alimentario de la población, aparte de las exiguas importaciones de alimentos y de lo aparentemente poco que logra distribuirse mediante el mercado negro. Esto conduce a la paradójica conclusión de que el ministro de economía a cargo de la transición hacia un sistema de mercado tendrá que aprender primero a manejar un sistema estalinista para no causar una crisis alimentaria de proporciones incalculables. La experiencia actual de la Unión Soviética y de Albania corroboran esta preocupación.

Es necesario tener en cuenta que el sistema vigente que administra la producción y la distribución de alimentos está basado en un régimen de disciplina en el cual los factores políticos y el propio partido comunista representan de facto la verdadera autoridad empresarial. Aunque este aparato sea muy ineficiente y sólo logre niveles mediocres de productividad, los volúmenes que sí logra producir son de los cuales depende el país para su alimentación. En una transición política que de entrada destruya la autoridad del partido y en ausencia de un sistema autoregulado y descentralizado de propiedad privada, es razonable pensar que habrá una desarticulación generalizada y posiblemente acelerada del sistema productivo y distributivo, que a su vez provocará una reducción severa de las disponibilidades de alimentos al consumidor.

En estas circunstancias, el reto que enfrentará el nuevo ministro de economía (y con él todo el gobierno) es el de transformar el sistema productivo de alimentos sin afectar el delicado equilibrio que hoy lo mantiene apenas a flote, teniendo en cuenta que ni el ministro ni el gobierno se espera que gozen de los poderes totalitarios de sus antecesores. Aceptando que el nuevo ministro de economía logrará evitar una catástrofe alimentaria, ¿cómo deberá proceder en su tarea de construir una economía de mercado? ¿Cuáles deberán ser los primeros pasos que se tomen? ¿Dentro de qué marco legal podrá actuar? ¿Dónde están los límites de su autoridad para introducir cambios en el sistema y quién determina esos límites?

2.   En los Otros Organismos Públicos

Aunque no es posible, por razones de espacio y tiempo, abordar con el mismo nivel de detalle las agendas y los problemas de todos aquellos altos funcionarios públicos que estén responsabilizados con la transición, es necesario bosquejar muy brevemente algunas de sus responsabilidades para establecer la interdependencia entre los diversos aspectos y variables del proceso. En este punto es crítico resaltar la necesidad imperiosa de que el equipo de la transición no sólo alcance una coordinación precisa entre las políticas y acciones a tomar en cada ramo, sino que también coordinen la puesta en práctica de las definiciones de política y las agendas individuales de cada organismo y funcionario involucrado en la transición.

No es posible exagerar el costo para Cuba de que los miembros del equipo de gobierno actúen independientemente sin una fuerte coordinación entre ellos. Por ejemplo, la decisión de asegurar el flujo de alimentos a la población requiere que el ministro de economía autorice las transferencias de recursos necesarios, mientras que los titulares a cargo de la administración de las empresas agrícolas, de transporte, etc. administren esos recursos en concordancia con esa política. Lo mismo es válido para quien dirija el Banco Nacional.[5]

La falta de coordinación será un peligro permanente, especialmente si el gobierno de transición tiene que hacerse cargo súbitamente de la administración de un país que por tres décadas ha estado habituado a funcionar siguiendo instrucciones del centro. Además del riesgo de la improvisación inicial y de lo enormemente difícil que será mantener una coordinación precisa de planes y acciones, es de esperar que surjan contingencias de todo tipo que conspirarán a diario con la unidad de acción de cualquier plan de gobierno.

Una de estas contingencias puede aparecer como desequilibrios financieros no previstos que tendrán que ser corregidos adecuadamente. Por ejemplo, el Banco Nacional de Cuba puede determinar que los niveles de precios fijados para los alimentos no son suficientes para cubrir los costos de producción y distribución correspondientes. Las alternativas que se presentan son: a) subsidiar los alimentos con ingresos de otras fuentes, b) emitir moneda si el punto anterior no es factible, c) aumentar los precios de los alimentos o dejarlos flotar y/o d) reducir los costos de producción y distribución mediante reducciones de salarios o despidos.[6]

¿Quiénes deberán tomar las decisiones al respecto? ¿Qué fuerza legal tendrán las decisiones que se adopten? El gobierno de transición tendrá que operar en un vacío legal durante los primeros tiempos, posiblemente hasta dos años, mientras no exista un nuevo sistema legal y un nuevo marco constitucional. Pero la decisión sobre las alternativas señaladas en los cuatro incisos de arriba no puede esperar tanto tiempo. Los problemas económicos requieren respuestas rápidas y congruentes con la intención supuesta de establecer una economía de mercado. Para que este tipo de economía realmente contribuya

---

[5] En la práctica, la planificación socialista consiste en un proceso dual de asignación de recursos físicos y financieros, dada la casi nula autonomía de las empresas. Como este es el sistema que heredará el gobierno de transición y que tiene que saber manejar mientras lo transforma, se corre el riesgo que las decisiones entre las asignaciones físicas y las financieras no sean congruentes, lo cual empeoraría la eficiencia de las empresas estatales recibidas.

[6] En este tipo de disyuntiva es donde se hará notar de manera más dramática el efecto pernicioso de los subsidios y de las distorsiones de precios con que está contaminada la economía cubana. Es de notar también que este tipo de situación no ocurrirá durante la transición si el gobierno actual tiene éxito en ajustar la economía para reducir la dependencia de los subsidios soviéticos. Nótese igualmente que en la medida que perdure un cierto nivel de subsidio externo, perdurarán las distorsiones a un nivel congruente con el nivel de los subsidios. En tal caso, el gobierno de transición evitaría un trauma interno si obtiene de los soviéticos que los subsidios se mantengan y/o se reduzcan gradualmente para darle tiempo a la economía cubana de adaptarse a un nuevo equilibrio.

al desarrollo económico general de una manera equitativa tiene que evitar caer en los caminos fáciles que representan los puntos a) y b) y adoptar las medidas responsables aunque dolorosas del tipo c) o d).[7],[8] Los problemas endémicos de las economías latinoamericanas y los todavía más graves de la economía cubana actual se derivan del manejo arbitrario de precios y salarios mediante la intervención del Estado. Si el gobierno de transición es serio con respecto a la creación de una economía de mercado, deberá adoptar medidas en torno a los dos últimos puntos (c y d), aunque no debe descartarse que en una situación excepcional se justifique algún subsidio (interno) temporal.[9]

B.   Después de los Primeros Días

1.   Hacia la Formulación de un Plan de Gobierno

La sección anterior plantea la necesidad de contemplar un principio de simultaneidad en las definiciones de política y en las acciones que se adopten en la transición.[10] Es obvio que el ministro de economía no puede ni debe actuar por su cuenta, aun cuando ejerza una posición de liderazgo. Sin embargo, la necesidad de actuar simultáneamente en varios frentes va más allá de las etapas iniciales de manejo apropiado del sistema heredado y que se desea modificar.

El establecimiento de una economía de mercado partiendo de una de planificación centralizada es una tarea infinitamente más ardua que el proceso inverso y exigirá la participación de un elevado número de profesionales. Aunque el establecimiento de una economía socialista requirió la creación de nuevas instituciones, el proceso fue eminentemente uno de desmantelamiento de estructuras de alta complejidad que no tenían símiles en el mundo de la planificación socialista.[11] Actividades enteras desaparecieron

---

[7]   Tales medidas obviamente tienen que ser puestas en práctica con gran consideración por el costo social y humano que las mismas conllevan. Esto es parte de la política económica y debe ser un punto importante en la agenda de la transición. Un manejo torpe o insensible de estos problemas pueden crear, en el corto plazo, reacciones políticas que interfieran con la creación de una economía de mercado y en el largo plazo pueden contribuir a un sistema económico despojado de toda valoración humanística. El gran desafío para cualquier sociedad (no simplemente su gobierno) es cómo crear o desarrollar un sistema económico que sea eficiente y humano sin ser paternalista.

[8]   Liberar los precios antes de que se logre una cierta privatización en condiciones competitivas de las actividades productivas puede no ser posible en todos los casos pues, en las primeras etapas de la transición habrá un gran número de empresas monopolísticas que harían subir los precios significativamente mientras restringen una oferta presumiblemente inadecuada para satisfacer a la población.

[9]   Aunque este tópico siempre es debatible, no debe descartarse. Por ejemplo, mientras la economía cubana no pueda alcanzar una cierta normalidad y persistan grandes desajustes en los ingresos de los consumidores y en los precios de los artículos de consumo, puede ser aconsejable subsidiar el precio de la leche que consumen los niños como una medida preventiva de salud pública que males mayores.

[10]   Aquí no damos por sentado que la definición de política es equivalente a su implantación. La experiencia de otros países enseña que existen grandes diferencias entre ambas.

[11]   Curiosamente, el proceso fue uno de aumento de la entropía del sistema económico en su conjunto, lo cual resulta paradójico viniendo de un gobierno que prometía un estado superior de organización social en beneficio del ser humano.

especialmente en el sector de los servicios, por ejemplo, todo el espectro de la intermediación financiera, las agencias de publicidad, las empresas de seguros y los servicios legales de todo tipo.

En la mayoría de las empresas de la llamada "esfera de la producción material" (agricultura y ganadería, pesca, industria, construcción, transporte y comunicaciones) el proceso de socialización fue uno de concentración de plantas y fusión de sistemas administrativos, proceso que dió lugar a la creación de los monopolios estatales.[12] Mientras tanto, el sector comercial sufrió severas reducciones pues el mismo era considerado parasitario (no creador de riqueza; otra aberración del pensamiento marxista) dentro de los preceptos oficiales. En resumen, la economía socialista posee una estructura institucional más simple, de menos complejidad y diversidad que una de mercado.

El esfuerzo de instalar una economía de mercado en Cuba será, por lo tanto, uno de recreación de instituciones y actividades necesarias para la operación del nuevo sistema. Es importante aclarar en este punto, sin embargo, que en la recreación de instituciones y actividades el papel del Estado será el de facilitador y no el de empresario. Si lo que efectivamente se desea es establecer una economía de mercado, tales actividades e instituciones deberán ser gestadas por el sector privado. El proceso también incluirá una diversificación productiva y empresarial, que consistirá primordialmente en la división de los monopolios estatales. Esto, por otra parte, deberá llevarse a cabo con la ayuda de un proceso paralelo de privatización el cual deberá tomar algún tiempo y del que trataremos más adelante.

2. El Uso Eficiente del Tiempo del Gobierno de Transición

Muchas serán las fuerzas que obstaculicen la formulación y ejecución eficiente de un programa económico en Cuba durante la transición. Cabe destacar aquí dos de las más importantes. Primeramente, el establecimiento y organización de un equipo de gobierno para la transición no será un proceso fácil. Todo dependerá, en gran medida, de las características del traspaso de poderes. En cualquier caso, no es de esperar que el gobierno de la transición (que puede llegar a ser un gobierno provisional con mandato de un par de años) tenga tiempo de articular su equipo y programa de gobierno antes de tomar posesión. Esto significa que tendrá que comenzar la administración del Estado cubano con muchos poderes y pocas ideas concretas de lo que va a hacer. En estas condiciones, su tarea más perentoria será la de lograr un mínimo de integración del conjunto de hombres y mujeres que formen el equipo de gobierno.

---

[12] En la cosmovisión de la planificación socialista, la competencia se percibe como un desperdicio de recursos pues aparenta padecer de un cierto nivel de redundancia en la asignación de los mismos entre diversas empresas, mientras la concentración se ve como un proceso de racionalización. Se ignoraban dos cosas: la posible existencia de costos medios crecientes de largo plazo y la necesidad de contar con un mecanismo que incentivara la eficiencia de cada empresa.

El segundo gran obstáculo hacia una administración eficiente es que aún cuando el gobierno comience su gestión con un programa bien estructurado, recibirá presiones de todo tipo de fuentes para atender otros problemas y modificar consecuentemente la agenda oficial. Es obvio que tales presiones serían más eficacez en la medida que el gobierno comience su gestión sin una agenda definida. Algunos ejemplos de las presiones, peticiones o demandas que el gobierno recibirá se listan a continuación:

- Reclamaciones de compensación por acciones del gobierno anterior, por ejemplo, devoluciones de propiedades expropiadas y reestablecimiento de pensiones y jubilaciones suspendidas;

- Solicitudes de acreedores externos (gobiernos y organismos privados) para que el nuevo gobierno defina un programa de pago de la deuda;

- Demandas provenientes de diversas comunidades y segmentos de la población para atender problemas que se fueron acumulando durante la administración anterior como pueden ser, reparaciones de infraestructura, mejoramiento de los abastecimientos, mejoramiento de otros servicios públicos, rectificación de injusticias del gobierno previo, etc.;

- Demandas provenientes de los diversos partidos o facciones políticas para que el gobierno acelere el proceso de institucionalización y llame a unas elecciones tempranas, acaso precedidas de la formación de una asamblea constituyente;

- Peticiones de mediación en conflictos internos de todo tipo, desde laborales hasta políticos, tanto a nivel de empresa como de comunidad;

- Solicitudes de individuos, gobiernos y empresas extranjeras para que funcionarios del gobierno atiendan propuestas de todo tipo supuestamente dirigidas a mejorar la gestión del gobierno y las condiciones económicas del país, por ejemplo, proyectos de inversión privados, ofrecimientos de asistencia técnica y otras formas de ayuda, peticiones de concesiones especiales para poder iniciar ciertos negocios o inversiones, etc.

Siempre que se instala un nuevo gobierno, el desfile de este tipo de solicitudes es interminable y coloca una gran presión sobre el tiempo disponible de los funcionarios públicos a los más altos niveles. Encima de estas solicitudes, todo funcionario de alguna prominencia recibirá una serie interminable de invitaciones y solicitudes de representación en actos de todo tipo, inauguraciones, conmemoraciones, sepelios y recepciones en el territorio nacional, más la consabida cuota de invitaciones a eventos en el extranjero.

En conjunto, esta demanda del tiempo de los funcionarios públicos puede llenarles sus respectivas agendas sin necesidad que formulen un plan de trabajo con otros propósitos, mucho menos dedicarle tiempo a ejecutarlo y darle seguimiento. El punto se trae a colación porque plantea la necesidad de resolver un serio conflicto desde los primeros momentos de la transición.

Muchas de las peticiones tienen que ser atendidas más tarde o más temprano y, de hecho, representan cuestiones que pertenecen al ámbito de la política pública que el gobierno tiene que atender. Sin embargo, el tiempo y los recursos del gobierno de transición son sumamente escasos y muchas de las peticiones tendrán que ordenarse en una línea de espera mientras que otras deberán ser pospuestas para un cierto período futuro o indefinidamente. ¿Mediante qué criterios el gobierno podrá establecer prioridades para atender los problemas que les plantean desde afuera, mientras separa suficiente tiempo para la tarea misma de la transformación institucional del país? La respuesta está obviamente en un plan deliberado en que el gobierno asigna tiempo y recursos para atender tareas que de antemano sabe que tiene que abordar, mientras que al mismo tiempo deja espacio para atender algunas de las presiones más urgentes.

El tamaño de esta tarea administrativa es incalculable. Puede decirse que, en la práctica, la primera prioridad económica del nuevo gobierno es organizarse eficientemente, definir metas específicas y optimizar el uso de los recursos disponibles para alcanzarlas en el menor tiempo posible. Si por el contrario, el gobierno no desea o no es capaz de formular y ejecutar una agenda factible, el sufrimiento de la población cubana no acabará con la desaparición del equipo actual de gobierno.

III.   EL PLAN PARA ESTABLECER UNA ECONOMIA DE MERCADO

El principio cardinal que debe regir el diseño de un programa económico factible consiste en separar en diversos plazos las tareas que deban y puedan ejecutarse con los recursos disponibles. El plan, por supuesto, estará sujeto a contingencias, pero parte de la responsabilidad del nuevo gobierno consistirá en prepararse para enfrentar contingencias de una manera inteligente y eficaz. Con esto en mente, definiremos tres períodos para la ejecución de un programa económico (que incluye muchos aspectos no económicos). El plan se define al principio y cubre los tres plazos, aunque tenga que ser modificado a medida que sea ejecutado y de que surjan nuevos elementos de juicio. Los plazos los llamaremos simplemente corto (uno a dos primeros años), mediano (hasta cinco años) y largo (después de cinco años). El mayor detalle se le asigna a las medidas de corto plazo, dándosele un tratamiento muy breve a los otros dos.

Adicionalmente, el plan deberá contemplar acciones simultáneas y/o interdependientes en tres frentes generales de actividades que denominamos: a) político-administrativo, cubriendo aquellas acciones que pueden llevarse a cabo con el sistema económico existente en cada momento; b) el institucional, que incluye acciones dirigidas a transformar el sistema económico en uno de mercado y c) el humano, donde se incorporan actividades encaminadas a mejorar la comprensión pública de los problemas económicos y a estimular los valores y las formas de comportamiento congruentes con una economía que depende de la iniciativa individual y no de un Estado omnipotente y paternalista. Diversas metas y acciones en estos tres frentes pueden corresponder a cualquiera de los tres plazos. En lo que sigue el mayor énfasis se pone en las medidas político-administrativas e institucionales.

A.   El Plan en el Corto Plazo

El objetivo general de las actividades en el corto plazo es mantener y mejorar los niveles generales de producción de las empresas mientras se comienza la transición hacia una economía de mercado. Todo lo demás debe quedar supeditado a este objetivo. En este contexto, es importante separar las actividades que deben acometerse en el corto plazo de una manera realista y aquéllas que deben ser abordadas más adelante. Las secciones siguientes recogen las que, en opinión del autor de este ensayo, deben y pueden ser acometidas en el corto plazo. Cada uno de los temas abordados posee sus propias complejidades conceptuales y metodólogicas y requiere un tratamiento más amplio del que aquí podemos darle por limitaciones de espacio y por las propias limitaciones del autor. Este tratamiento, sin embargo, sirve para dar una visión de conjunto de los diversos temas y su interdependencia, al mismo tiempo que se ofrece un "catálogo" con algunas características individuales.

1.   El Mejoramiento de la Eficiencia de las Empresas

Virtualmente toda la actividad productiva en Cuba está en manos de empresas estatales que oportunamente dejarán de estar bajo la tutela del sector público. La privatización de las empresas será un proceso prolongado que debe ser planeado cuidadosamente con base en el interés público. Mientras tanto, el país seguirá dependiendo de la producción de estas empresas para el uso directo de lo que producen o para la exportación. En consonancia con el objetivo de evitar un deterioro de los niveles de producción, especialmente en materia alimentaria, los procesos productivos de dichas empresas deben ser apoyados siempre y cuando las mismas puedan producir de una manera eficiente.

El criterio cardinal de eficiencia productiva es que sus costos sean iguales o menores que sus ingresos. No hay información suficiente para saber cuántas empresas operan eficientemente en Cuba en la actualidad. Sin embargo, la magnitud de los subsidios es muy elevada y es muy probable que muchas empresas operen a costos demasiado altos en relación a sus ingresos. Eso significa que el déficit se cubre en la caja única del gobierno central y que los subsidios soviéticos acaban financiando. De hecho los subsidios ayudan a ocultar estas ineficiencias.[13] Como esta situación es intolerable, las empresas deberán comenzar a operar cuanto antes en condiciones de equilibrio financiero, lo cual requerirá, como ya fue señalado, que suban los precios de lo que venden y/o bajen sus costos.

---

[13]   Uno pudiera especular que si todos los subsidios son en forma de ayuda militar, la ineficiencia de la economía cubana no sería tan elevada, sin embargo tal extremo no parece ser probable.

Es muy posible que muchas empresas no sean viables y que deban ser cerradas. Muchas veces es más eficiente mandar para su casa a los trabajadores con sus salarios pagados que mantener la ficción de una empresa que opera en condiciones de ineficiencia permanente. También es importante tener en cuenta que una empresa puede ser hoy eficiente y mañana no, como resultado de las condiciones cambiantes de la economía nacional o de factores externos.

En cualquier caso, el objetivo es ir creando las condiciones y los incentivos para aumentar la eficiencia, la productividad y los niveles de producción, mientras se eliminan aquellas actividades que representan una carga para el Estado y la población. Esto requerirá que las empresas tengan cada vez mayor libertad para administrarse mientras ellas y no el Estado se encarguen de subsistir y desarrollarse o fenecer.

En la situación actual, las empresas están unidas al resto del aparato estatal no por uno sino por varios cordones umbilicales que deben ser seccionados. Uno de ellos es el de la tutela por medio de las llamadas empresas consolidadas que agrupan, a modo de consorcio, todas las empresas de un mismo giro, y que pertenecen a la esfera superior de algún ministerio o super ministerio. Otro de los cordones umbilicales es con el sistema fiscal ya que los pagos no son hechos por las empresass a sus proveedores ni las empresas disponen de sus ingresos. Un tercer cordón umbilical--generalmente entrelazado con los otros--es el del Partido Comunista que supuestamente rige, vigila o supervisa que las empresas se mantengan dentro de las líneas trazadas por el gobierno actual. Es de suponer que, a menos que la transición en Cuba siga un camino parecido al de China o al de la Unión Soviética, este cordón desaparecerá rápidamente en los primeros momentos de la transición, como sucedió en Polonia, Checoslovaquia, Alemania y Hungría.

El primer problema que una mayor autonomía de las empresas plantearía es el de quiénes serían los administradores de esas empresas. ¿Puede confiársele a sus trabajadores la selección de los administradores? ¿Pueden mantenerse algunos de los administradores actuales en sus posiciones? ¿Quién debe tomar estas decisiones?

El enorme número de empresas diseminadas por las ciudades y los campos de Cuba hace impracticable que estas decisiones sean tomadas centralmente. Por otra parte, los ministerios y empresas consolidadas correspondientes son eminentemente grandes burocracias que deberán ser eliminadas oportunamente, pero en el menor período de tiempo posible. El criterio para el nombramiento de administradores tampoco puede ser político, pues se estaría repitiendo el estilo socialista y se atrasaría el proceso de ganancia de eficiencia y el de instalación de una economía de mercado.

Si los trabajadores de estas empresas serán los primeros beneficiados o perjudicados por un proceso de autonomía en busca de eficiencia, es lógico que sean ellos los que decidan quiénes serán sus administradores. ¿Pero bajo qué autoridad pueden los trabajadores decidir sobre sus propios jefes? Sólo si se les otorga una autoridad que los vincule de una manera más estrecha a sus lugares de trabajo que como simples empleados.

Una alternativa es mediante el otorgamiento de acciones o derechos parciales de propiedad sobre sus empresas. Aunque deben considerarse otras alternativas en la medida en que se vayan planteando, ésta puede tener la virtud de que serán los propios trabajadores los que tengan que decidir el destino final de la empresa, tanto en el esfuerzo que hay que desplegar para alcanzar su solvencia, como en el caso de que la misma sea intrínsecamente insolvente. Es muy posible que una gran cantidad de empresas tengan que adoptar medidas drásticas de ajuste interno, incluso despidos y reducciones salariales, simplemente porque no hay recursos para mantenerlas, ni porque, aunque los hubiera, deben penalizarse las actividades más eficientes de una economía obligándolas a transferir recursos para sostener a las menos eficientes. De hecho, lo que se estaría manteniendo no son las empresas mismas sino el empleo artificial de sus trabajadores. Esta situación se hará más probable en la medida en que vayan desapareciendo los subsidios soviéticos a Cuba. Es obvio que el nuevo gobierno no puede acoger este problema como si fuera suyo, imagen que erróneamente crearía si mantuviera un vínculo "propietario" con tales entidades.

Como puede notarse, este tema, mientras más se explora, más abre nuevas interrogantes y dilemas. Para poder pasar a otro tópico, sólo listamos otros de los muchos temas que dentro de la autonomía de las empresas deberán ser tratados con más profundidad:

- En la medida en que las empresas ganen en autonomía, ¿dentro de qué límites podrán aumentar los precios de los bienes y servicios que venden aquellas empresas que tengan una posición monopolística en su sector respectivo, por ejemplo, la generación de electricidad o los servicios telefónicos?

- ¿Cómo podrán adquirir bienes intermedios y de capital que no son producidos en el país? ¿Deben utilizar las otras empresas estatales para tales fines o deben ellas alcanzar también su autonomía?

- ¿Dentro de qué normativa jurídica y sistema de administración de justicia operarían estas empresas para realizar contratos con otras entidades nacionales y extranjeras?

- ¿Será posible promover rápidamente un sistema, al menos rudimentario, de crédito para financiar las operaciones de las empresas en su búsqueda autónoma de eficiencia? Muchas empresas pueden ser eficientes pero pueden tener problemas momentáneos de caja que las harían cerrar. ¿Pueden los propios trabajadores (o los de otras empresas) financiar el capital de trabajo mediante la postergación del pago parcial de sus salarios?

2. El Equilibrio Macrofiscal

Uno de los objetivos de la autonomía de las empresas es liberar al Estado de la carga de apoyarlas financieramente y comenzar la instauración de un sistema fiscal en concordancia con las necesidades de una economía de mercado. Una vez que el gobierno de transición tenga una visión clara de la situación financiera del país, tanto en lo interno como en lo externo, podrá decidir sobre las cuestiones más urgentes en materia de gasto público e ingresos fiscales. Por el lado del gasto, hay dos grandes decisiones que tomar. Una es cuánto se va destinar para servir la deuda externa, lo cual va a ser una función parcial de los acuerdos a que llegue el país durante las negociaciones correspondientes. Habrá voces que demanden el no reconocer la deuda, pero es de esperar que la cordura impere y que el país, independientemente de quién lo gobernó cumpla con sus obligaciones financieras externas, de lo contrario se convertiría en un delincuente internacional con consecuencias devastadoras para su recuperación económica. La experiencia reciente del Perú durante el gobierno anterior es de particular pertinencia al caso cubano.

La otra gran decisión con relación al gasto público es cuánto debe gastarse en servicios del Estado. Este también será un tema de gran potencial polémico, ya que el gobierno actual se distinguió en promover programas en educación y salud que en gran medida se financian con los subsidios soviéticos. Sin subsidios y con una economía posiblemente en bancarrota ¿cuánto se podrá financiar del gasto en educación y en salud? Otros renglones importantes de gastos públicos a definir son los siguientes: a) administración de justicia, b) seguridad interna, c) defensa, d) infraestructura y e) regímenes de retiro (invalidez, vejez y muerte).

Las asignaciones presupuestarias de años anteriores no servirán de mucho en la definición de los nuevos montos ya que la situación financiera del país está sufriendo cambios casi traumáticos como resultado de la reducción y posible eliminación de los subsidios. Por otra parte, las razones hasta ahora predominantes para determinar el monto y la estructura del gasto público han de ser modificadas en la medida que se desee y se marche hacia un nuevo régimen económico. Por ejemplo, una economía pujante de mercado requiere de una buena dotación de capital humano, tanto en términos educativos como de salud, además que ambos tipos de gastos son deseables en sí mismos por su contribución al bienestar del ser humano. Por lo tanto, es deseable que se inviertan cantidades significativas de recursos en la educación de la población y en su salud. Sin embargo, puede justificarse una re-estructuración del gasto educativo de manera de mejorar la calidad y el acceso de la educación pública durante los primeros nueve años de escolaridad, y comenzar a aplicar planes de recuperación de costos de ahí en adelante. Hay muchas razones para eliminar la gratuidad de la enseñanza universitaria y otras muchas, por otro lado, para desarrollar mecanismos de préstamos educativos que permitan acceder a tal nivel a aquellos ciudadanos de talento que no pueden costear estudios caros, como son los de medicina.

En lo que se refiere al gasto en salud pública puede debatirse que el Estado sólo debe hacerse cargo de financiar y hasta administrar los bienes y servicios públicos involucrados con la prevención de la salud pero no necesariamente con los servicios asistenciales o curativos que son más de naturaleza privada. Actualmente se escuchan informaciones de que el Estado cubano ha conseguido brindar servicios asistenciales a toda la población prácticamente sin límites. Aunque no sabemos cuánto hay de mito y cuánto hay de realidad hasta que no se tenga un diagnóstico libremente conducido en el país, observadores independientes informan de manera fragmentaria que efectivamente hay una gran cobertura y profundidad de tales servicios. Si esto es cierto, los mismos no pueden ser eliminados hasta que no se instaure un sistema sustituto con características similares. Pero, ¿podrá el Estado cubano costear el nivel de los servicios actuales después que desaparezcan los subsidios soviéticos?[14]

Muchas consideraciones similares habrá que hacer en torno a los otros sectores del Estado. ¿Qué clase de administración de justicia se desea y cuánto cuesta? ¿Qué se puede costear hoy y qué se tendrá que hacer más adelante? ¿Cuáles son las preferencias del público y cuáles las del gobierno? ¿En qué nivel y estructura del gasto en este sector se aproxima al óptimo en función del interés común? Interrogantes similares pueden aplicarse a los sectores de seguridad interna y defensa. Es de esperar que en una sociedad más abierta y sin la paranoia de una invasión de los EE.UU. ambos renglones de gastos se vean disminuídos significativamente. Pero en algún nivel hay que parar las reducciones. Incluso los que propongan la eliminación total de las fuerzas armadas seguramente aceptarán la necesidad de un servicio de guardacostas o guardafronteras, especialmente para enfrentar el tráfico de drogas y otras formas de contrabando o hasta movimientos subversivos.[15]

Otra gran incógnita es el estado de mantenimiento y de operaciones de la red vial del país, sus puentes, puertos, y otras construcciones necesarias para el transporte. Dicho estado será el principal determinante de la demanda por fondos públicos. Aquí sin embargo se abre una posibilidad de privatización por medio de la cual inversionistas de distinto origen--sin descartar al propio Estado cubano--financien algunas facilidades a cambio del pago de peajes.

Concluyendo las consideraciones sobre el gasto público, el gobierno de transición deberá determinar el monto de las obligaciones contraídas anteriormente en materia de regímenes de pensiones (invalidez, vejez y muerte) y establecer la viabilidad financiera de las mismas con base en proyecciones actuariales. Las variables a ser examinadas son las edades de retiro, el monto de las contribuciones, el monto de los beneficios y la estructura etaria de los derechohabientes para pronosticar la trayectoria futura de las erogaciones. Una de las grandes interrogantes será cuál es el monto de los beneficios a ser pagados por el Estado y si el mismo podrá ser cubierto dentro del panorama fiscal que se vislumbra, o requerirá un ajuste drástico del régimen en términos de, por ejemplo, aumento de la edad de retiro, disminución de los beneficios o aumento de las cuotas contributivas.

---

14   Esta interrogante es tan válida para el gobierno actual como para el que le siga. Es en este tipo de situación en que se puede afirmar que al gobierno de transición le conviene que el gobierno actual logre el ajuste total de su economía, de lo contrario ese gobierno tendrá que aplicar el ajuste, como ya se discutió, y no le sería fácil a la población identificar la verdadera causa del corte en el gasto en salud. Por eso es necesario que se dedique una gran parte del esfuerzo de la transición a exponer al público cubano los diversos problemas económicos que aquejan la nación.

15   Este es otro punto cuya definición final dependerá significativamente de la naturaleza del traspaso de poderes políticos.

La experiencia latinoamericana enseña que este tema presenta situaciones explosivas como resultado de la frecuencia con que los gobiernos han hecho promesas de largo plazo que no podían ser cumplidas. El gobierno cubano actual tendría menos problemas que un gobierno democrático en incumplir sus obligaciones por su capacidad represiva y porque puede manipular otras variables sin afectar los valores nominales de las variables que caracterizan estos regímenes, por ejemplo, las cuotas de racionamiento y ciertos precios. Otra variable es propiciar la salida del país de las personas que estén recibiendo pensiones para aliviar la carga financiera del estado socialista. Es obvio que un gobierno que se rija por una economía de mercado no podría recurrir a tal alternativa, pues tendría que pagar las pensiones aún cuando las personas abandonen el país.

Pasando ahora del gasto a los ingresos fiscales es importante recordar que, en el sistema actual, los ingresos del Estado teóricamente son los de las empresas, excepto que bajo las condiciones predominantes de ineficiencia crónica de las mismas, una parte sustancial de los ingresos provienen de los subsidios. Eliminados éstos y con la autonomía financiera, los ingresos de un nuevo Estado tendrán que provenir de un sistema tributario que tendrá que ser construído a partir de cero.

El primer punto a definir es el nivel deseado de ingresos en función del nivel deseado de gastos. ¿Podrá la economía cubana al comienzo de la transición sostener un nivel tal de actividad compatible con el nivel de gasto público que se desea? Los ingresos fiscales tendrán que generarse por impuestos de diversos tipos, entre ellos a la población y a las empresas. Independientemente de la estructura tributaria que se adopte, la cuestión del monto de la recaudación va a ser una gran incógnita y un gran dolor de cabeza para el nuevo gobierno, pues sin los subsidios es dudoso que la recaudación fiscal pueda cubrir el gasto deseado. Aunque parte de los subsidios están destinados a financiar gastos militares, hay razones para sospechar que una parte sustancial apoyan gastos civiles.

Otro tema que deberá salir a colación oportunamente es el del uso de los impuestos para fines de política económica, o sea para fines distintos a los del financiamiento del gasto público. Es importante que el gobierno de la transición comprenda el peligro de establecer una estructura tributaria que puede introducir distorsiones, privilegios e inequidades de todo tipo en la economía. El principal objetivo de la imposición tributaria es financiar los gastos del Estado de una manera neutral, o sea, de manera que unos no sientan la carga tributaria más que otros y que las actividades económicas no se sientan unas más favorecidas por ciertos impuestos y otras perjudicadas.

De los varios peligros que existen en este aspecto, seleccionamos uno que es de particular importancia y gravedad. El éxito del gobierno de transición va a depender en gran medida de su capacidad para elevar el nivel de actividad de la economía cubana, lo cual a su vez depende de la actividad inversionista que tenga lugar. Puede darse por sentado que el gobierno recibirá, de múltiples fuentes, numerosas propuestas de inversión a cambio de incentivos fiscales y de protección arancelaria. Tales propuestas serán de gran atractivo al gobierno de turno pues ofrecen ventajas en el corto plazo que pueden ser mostradas a la población como prueba de decisiones inteligentes y beneficiosas, mientras que sus posibles resultados negativos para la economía no sólo no se mostrarían de inmediato sino que siempre estarían ocultos en las distorsiones que así se crean. Por otra parte, el gobierno puede verse tentado a aceptar las otras falacias de un régimen proteccionista como el argumento sobre la industria insipiente, etc.[16] La capacidad que el nuevo gobierno tenga para rechazar tales propuestas será una medida significativa de su competencia y/o de su integridad.

3.   La Oferta Monetaria, la Tasa de Cambio y el Crédito

La principal responsabilidad del presidente del Banco Nacional de Cuba hacia la instauración de una economía de mercado es mantener la oferta monetaria de manera que no haya inflación. Sin embargo, como resultado de las distorsiones de precios que resultan, entre otros factores, del régimen de control de precios instituído por la planificación socialista, los precios existentes deberán sufrir ajustes de gran magnitud para lograr el equilibrio financiero de muchas empresas.

A menos que dicho ajuste se obtenga por medio de reducciones de costos (mayormente salarios, lo que puede no ser sicológica y políticamente aconsejable) las subidas de precios forzarán a un aumento de la oferta monetaria, a menos que los ajustes de precios puedan ser absorbidos por algún exceso de circulante en manos de la población y de las empresas.[17]

El segundo problema que de inmediato ocupará la atención del presidente del Banco Nacional es el determinar una tasa de cambio para el peso cubano que sea compatible con la situación económica del país. Las transacciones privadas en monedas extranjeras en Cuba están tan perseguidas y severamente castigadas que no parece haber un mercado paralelo de suficiente extensión para dar un indicio del vecindario de una tasa de cambio realista. Por otra parte, las necesidades más perentorias de convertibilidad provendrían de las empresas para sus compras de materias primas, piezas de repuesto y equipos, necesidades que hasta ahora han estado manejadas por el aparato de planificación a tasas arbitrarias y es imposible predecir cuál sería la demanda por importaciones de estas empresas cuando las mismas tengan que actuar autónomamente.

Las dos fuentes más importantes de ingresos por exportaciones de Cuba son generalmente volátiles, o sea, el azúcar y el turismo. Dependiendo de la coyuntura de ambas en el momento en que comience la transición se sabrá la tasa que prevalecerá, aunque es de esperar que la misma fluctúe ampliamente durante mucho tiempo. Esto por

---

[16]   Para un estudio sobre las falacias y los costos del proteccionismo que es altamente ilustrativo y fácil de seguir léase a Jagdish Bhagwati, Protectionism, The MIT Press, Cambridge, Massachusetts, 1988.

[17]   La oferta monetaria en la economía cubana es eminentemente M1. Es de suponer que el volumen de las cuentas de ahorro es muy bajo y que los otros componentes sean de magnitudes despreciables, si existen. En ocasiones, el gobierno actual ha informado de "excesos" de circulante que en la práctica implican ahorros o atesoramientos ("hoarding") involuntarios.

supuesto generará una cantidad de incertidumbre que pondrá presión hacia el establecimiento de un control de cambio, lo cual no es compatible con una economía de mercado. El control de cambio, de todos modos, no resolvería el problema de la incertidumbre en el largo plazo. Si existen fuerzas subyacentes en la economía que causan una gran inestabilidad en la tasa de cambio, las mismas deben encontrar salida en los mecanismos de mercado. Además, el control de cambio siempre implica una gran cantidad de burocracia en términos de manejo de cuotas, permisos de importación, etc. El tema es complejo y será objeto de debate por mucho tiempo dentro de los círculos de decisión económica del gobierno de la transición.

Finalmente, las autoridades monetarias tendrán que definir un plan para propiciar la creación de instituciones de crédito. Este posiblemente sea el ejemplo donde más urgentemente se necesita crear una de las instituciones desmanteladas por el régimen socialista. Donde más se necesitará el crédito será, como se indicó anteriormente, en las empresas que en su nueva autonomía tendrán que procurar los medios para subsistir, entre ellos, las formas de financiamiento de corto y largo plazo. En el contexto de la creación de una economía de mercado, las instituciones de crédito que aparezcan deberán ser privadas. Sin embargo, es de esperar que las necesidades de crédito surjan primero que las instituciones privadas de crédito. En estas circunstancias, ¿deberá el Estado cubano suplir esta necesidad temporalmente? Es posible, pero el tema, como muchos otros, tiene que ser examinado por especialistas para encontrar las mejores alternativas para el país.

4. Restauración de los Derechos de Propiedad

Al comienzo de la transición, la propiedad privada de los bienes o riqueza existente en Cuba tendrá una mínima expresión. Las formas de propiedad privada de bienes de producción más importantes serán posiblemente algunas pequeñas fincas y las nuevas inversiones que el gobierno actual está tratando de llevar a Cuba, especialmente en el sector turístico. Una vez se libere la prohibición de poseer privadamente bienes de producción, es razonable esperar que surja una demanda creciente por los mismos y posiblemente de fondos para su financiamiento. Es igualmente razonable esperar que surjan iniciativas para abrir pequeñas empresas de todo tipo, iniciativas que deberá facilitar el nuevo gobierno por varias razones, a saber: a) promover el espíritu empresarial que se necesita en una economía de mercado, b) propiciar la generación de empleos que sirva para absorber el empleo desplazado en las empresas que así lo necesiten para sobrevivir y c) facilitar la producción de bienes y servicios que necesita la población.

Simultáneamente, la búsqueda de un sistema que dé autonomía a las empresas del Estado puede incluir alguna forma de propiedad para sus trabajadores, como se discutió más arriba. Cuba se beneficiará enormemente de la experiencia que van acumulando en este aspecto los países de Europa del Este. Además, puede haber iniciativas de capitalistas extranjeros que deseen invertir en Cuba en condiciones competitivas atractivas para el país.

Todas estas oportunidades plantean la necesidad perentoria de establecer una normativa jurídica y su concomitante administrativa sobre los derechos de propiedad que se adquieran y necesiten ser registrados, así como la normación y registro de las transacciones sobre la compra y venta de activos y demás actividades complementarias. Este es un punto donde se requiere un trabajo intenso de equipos multidisciplinarios, especialmente economistas, juristas, expertos en administración de justicia y especialistas en registros de propiedad y disciplinas afines. Aún cuando sea necesario adoptar una normativa temporal, la misma tendrá que dar garantías lo suficientemente sólidas para no desestimular las iniciativas inversionistas del tipo que acabamos de señalar.

Aquí se presenta uno de los problemas que pudiera convertirse en una gran distracción del esfuerzo de reconstrucción nacional si no se maneja con sumo cuidado por el nuevo gobierno. Nos referimos a las posibles demandas de devolución o compensación de activos expropiados por el régimen socialista. Aunque puede haber muchos otros tipos de reclamaciones al Estado cubano (pensiones cuyos pagos se interrumpieron por abandono del país, por ejemplo), aquí sólo discutiremos los primeros con la esperanza de que sirva para ilustrar la complejidad de este tipo de problema.

Los bienes expropiados durante las distintas fases de consolidación del Estado socialista tuvieron una amplia gama de destinos, dependiendo de sus características, del momento de la expropiación y hasta de quiénes participaron en la misma. El hecho es que la mayoría de dichas propiedades, en diversas medidas, sufrieron grandes cambios desde el acto de la expropiación. Por ejemplo, algunas fábricas y talleres fueron unidas a otras instalaciones mientras otras fueron desmanteladas, canibalizadas (para utilizar las piezas de repuesto en otros lugares) o abandonadas. Otras propiedades simplemente desaparecieron como edificios que fueron demolidos, inventarios (físicos y de ganado) que fueron liquidados, plantaciones permanentes cuyas cepas fueron removidas y activos líquidos que fueron absorbidos por el gobierno sin dejar huellas. Incluso la tierra de fincas donde se encontraban o aún se encuentran edificaciones puede haber sido modificada por la adición de otras construcciones, movimientos de tierra y contaminación ambiental.[18] En otros casos, las antiguas propiedades pueden haber sufrido mejoras sustanciales durante las últimas tres décadas, mientras que también existen nuevos activos que fueron enteramente creados, todo como parte de los programas de inversión de la planificación socialista.

De modo análogo a los profundos cambios sufridos por las propiedades estatizadas, los propietarios mismos han cambiado simultáneamente. Muchos han muerto y no hay información sobre cuántos dejaron testamentos identificando a sus herederos, mientras otros se separaron de sus familias durante la emigración (o sin ella) y crearon nuevas familias. Algunos pocos llegaron incluso a donar sus propiedades al Estado.

---

[18] Como se ha venido descubriendo en los países de Europa Oriental, la destrucción del medio ambiente ha alcanzado proporciones devastadoras, además de causar daños que no son reversibles fácilmente.

Este autor no está calificado para discutir las doctrinas y tecnicismos legales que pudieran servir para orientar la política que un nuevo gobierno deba seguir en relación a los posibles reclamos. Una cosa es cierta; dicho gobierno debe estar preparado adecuadamente para enfrentar los mismos con planes bien definidos y explicados. Las consideraciones que siguen reflejan las de un economista y no pretenden sentar la pauta que se deba seguir para solventar este problema. Sólo tienen como objetivo contribuir algunos elementos de juicio pertinentes y que puedan ayudar a encontrar aquella solución que más convenga al interés nacional cubano.

En la medida que un nuevo gobierno y la población cubana deseen seriamente instaurar una economía de mercado, donde la propiedad privada, pequeña o grande, familiar o en sociedad, representa uno de los pilares institucionales del sistema, lograr alguna forma de reconocimiento o compensación de las propiedades perdidas es necesario, precisamente en reconocimiento del valor social de este régimen. Dicho valor no se limita a los propietarios, sino que se extiende hasta los que no lo son pero que se benefician de una mayor eficiencia económica, cuando la propiedad productiva se usa de modo competitivo y no monopolístico.

Por otra parte, es necesario visualizar la madeja de problemas logísticos y legales que habría que enfrentar si, en una decisión extrema, un gobierno decidiera "devolver" los activos expropiados. Una devolución propiamente dicha no es factible, por lo problemas apuntados más arriba. Aquéllos que fueron propietarios de bienes que no existen pudieran reclamar sobre las propiedades que en ese momento pueden ser identificadas. Simultáneamente, los que tenían propiedades que fueron sustancialmente mejoradas por las inversiones hechas durante el socialismo podrían recibir mucho más de lo que perdieron. Adicionalmente, estaría el problema de desalojar a los habitantes de casas cuyos propietarios las reclaman. Todas estas consideraciones y muchas otras sirven para ilustrar que una simple "devolución" pudiera crear más problemas de los que resolvería, efectivamente si lo que se desea de la desaparición del socialismo en Cuba es la reconstrución del país de la manera más justa para todos y expedita.[19]

Queda abierta la posibilidad de reconocer alguna forma de compensación para los que sufrieron pérdidas. Cuba iniciaría su reconstrucción económica con un profundo endeudamiento que no parece haber resultado en un aumento de su capacidad productiva. A esta deuda habría que añadir la deuda en que llegue a valorarse el monto de las compensaciones. ¿Es justo pedirle a la mayoría del pueblo no propietario y que no tuvo la oportunidad de emigrar que trabaje para compensar a los que tuvieron la fortuna de poder salir del país?

---

[19]   Las formas de propiedad son muchas y no es posible inventariarlas aquí. Algunas se prestan más fácilmente que otras para devoluciones o compensaciones. Por ejemplo, los derechos de la propiedad intelectual (derechos de autor, marcas registradas, etc.) son más fácilmente reconocibles porque no había activos físicos que podían ser alterados.

Los argumentos en pro y en contra de alguna forma de compensación o las alternativas al respecto deben ser discutidas y evaluadas en Cuba para que exista un consenso nacional en cuanto a la decisión final que se tome. Trabajos como éste pueden contribuir ideas al debate pero la solución definitiva tendrá que partir de la voluntad, democráticamente expresada, de la población.

5. La Liberación Gradual de los Precios y la Eliminación del Racionamiento

La flexibilidad de precios es una condición sine qua non de una economía de mercado. Los precios deben ser determinados por relaciones de oferta y demanda que, por el lado de los compradores, representan la libertad de selección (nadie los obliga a comprar o a no comprar, como en el sistema planificado), mientras que por el lado de los vendedores debe ser una expresión de libertad de opciones y de la competencia entre ellos, de manera que se logren los precios más bajos, pero que sean suficientes para cubris los costos.

Dejar que los precios fluctúen es algo que genera incertidumbre en las mentes de los que tienen mayor aversión al riesgo, pero es necesario para que los productores y los consumidores ajusten sus decisiones respectivas a lo que ellos estimen sea más eficiente. Sin un sistema de precios que sea flexible, la economía pierde de vista dónde se encuentran las actividades más eficientes socialmente (para invertir en ellas) y dónde están las menos atractivas para la sociedad (para no desperdiciar recursos en las mismas). Este mecanismo es precisamente el que la planificación socialista eliminó con las consecuencias que ya conocemos de estancamiento económico crónico.[20]

Sin embargo, a pesar de lo dicho arriba, no es fácil moverse abruptamente de un sistema de precios rígidos por mucho tiempo a uno de flexibilidad total, pues los diversos miembros de la sociedad, en función de sus distintas actividades, han ajustado las mismas a los precios existentes, estén o no distorsionados. Si el reajuste de los precios del sistema rígido al flexible fuese pequeño o afectará a sólo unos pocos bienes o servicios, el cambio hacia la flexibilidad sería más fácil.

Pero es muy probable que la diferencia entre los precios actuales y los que resultarían después de la instauración de un régimen flexible sea sustancial y haya muchos productos básicos que no puedan ser adquiridos por la población sin que existan ajustes salariales. Esto, a su vez puede no ser posible sin desatar un proceso inflacionario de un potencial devastador, pues los salarios son partes de los costos de producción y los mismos

---

[20] Uno pudiera preguntarse: si era tan obvio, ¿por qué se insistió en mantenerlo tanto tiempo? La respuesta no es necesariamente fácil y pudiera radicar en una combinación de ignorancia y de oportunismo. La flexibilidad de precios es un instrumento de la libertad de selección para todos los miembros de una sociedad, sean consumidores, ahorristas, inversionistas, empresarios o trabajadores. Los oligarcas del socialismo, como cualquier otro oligarca, detestan la libertades individuales. Libertad es poder político y económico.

deben estar por debajo de los ingresos de las empresas, los cuales dependen a su vez de los precios.[21]

Esta causación circular entre precios y salarios es una buena noticia en una economía de elevada eficiencia, pues los salarios (que son parte del costo) pueden ser cubiertos por los precios y satisfacer las necesidades mínimas de la población e incluso ir más allá. Sin embargo, si la economía es de una baja eficiencia, la combinación de precios altos con salarios bajos puede resultar en que muchos, acaso la mayoría, no pueda comprar los bienes mínimos que necesita para el sustento propio y el de los que dependen de él.

Independientemente de cuán ancha sea la brecha entre los precios rígidos y los niveles que alcancen en sus posiciones de equilibrio cuando se liberen, la liberación es indispensable para la normalización de la actividad económica nacional, especialmente para que las empresas comiencen a operar bajo condiciones de autosuficiencia financiera. No existe, por otro lado, un método analítico que permita determinar ex ante la magnitud de la brecha en cada caso. Por lo tanto, será necesario conducir la liberación empírica pero gradualmente para evitar situaciones traumáticas de efectos secundarios indeseables. El proceso deberá ser vigilado de cerca, para observar sus efectos y tomar las acciones correctivas o aceleradoras que sean aconsejables.

La transición hacia una flexibilidad de precios se facilitará en la medida que surjan mercados fuera de la esfera de las empresas estatales o incluso como iniciativas de las mismas.[22] El mercado negro en productos agrícolas pudiera ser un precursor de las organizaciones de mercado, pero no hay evidencia sólida de su extensión, ni se sabe cuánto ha dependido de la venta de productos que tenían vendedores legítimos o de individuos que robaban a las empresas del Estado. En la medida que este último aspecto haya sido de una importancia más que marginal, se constituirá también en un problema para la nueva economía, pues conspirará contra el establecimiento de un nuevo orden legal, de la eficiencia de las empresas víctimas de tales prácticas y del desarrollo de una economía de mercado.[23]

---

[21] El argumento se ha simplificado un poco para enfocar la noción de interdependencia entre precios y salarios, pero las relaciones son algo más complejas pues hay que tener en cuenta que no todo el ingreso de los consumidores proviene de salarios, ni todos los precios se refieren a bienes de consumo, como es obvio.

[22] En este punto hay que vigilar que no se formen arreglos monopolistas especialmente en la intermediación de los productos agrícolas, uno de los grandes males de la época pre-revolucionaria en Cuba y que contribuyó a darle un mal nombre al papel de la iniciativa privada en una economía.

[23] El gobierno de la transición deberá estar alerta frente a anomalías que conspiren contra sus planes. Trabajadores poco escrupulosos de empresas estatales, aún cuando se hagan propietarios parciales de las mismas en un nuevo sistema, pueden encontrar ventajas en violar las nuevas reglas si perciben que el beneficio que obtienen por esos medios es superior. Esta condición puede ser especialmente peligrosa en el caso de la venta de activos de las empresas como equipos, partes de maquinaria y ganado.

Es posible que el racionamiento pueda ser eliminado muy rápidamente en aquellos artículos de los que no dependa la población para su subsistencia diaria. De hecho es aconsejable que se pueda eliminar el racionamiento lo más pronto posible para que los nuevos precios indiquen dónde están las prioridades de la sociedad en materia productiva y de consumo y de ese modo guiar la actividad inversionista desde su comienzo.

No existen razones para que una vez se decida liberar algún producto del racionamiento se adopten posiciones intermedias entre el control de precios y la completa liberación de precios. La única excepción tendrá que hacerse en aquellos bienes y servicios que se producen por monopolios y cuyos precios deberán ser regulados por una autoridad oficial competente y especialmente dedicada a estos menesteres. El control de precios de monopolio, por otra parte, no tiene como fin subsidiar al consumidor o minimizar el precio para favorecer a éste, si no evitar que se abuse la posición monopolítica en contra del bienestar común. Es muy posible que los precios actuales de tales productos estén por debajo de lo que sería socialmente eficiente y, por lo tanto, puede que tengan que sufrir aumentos sustanciales. Esto puede ser el caso de los servicios telefónicos, eléctricos y la venta de combustibles. Otros muchos artículos pueden sumarse a la lista dependiendo del grado de concentración de los sectores respectivos.

Los procesos de liberación de precios y de reducción del racionamiento en Cuba generarán mucha incertidumbre, confusión y conflictos. No debe esperarse que los precios pasen de su situación al inicio de la transición hacia una posición de equilibrio y se estabilicen en esa posición por un tiempo, pues esas posiciones de equilibrio no se conocen de antemano ni se sabe cuáles serán las posiciones respectivas de las relaciones de oferta y demanda en el mediano y largo plazo. Por ejemplo, muchos precios dependerán de productos importados y los mismos costarán internamente según la posición que alcance la tasa de cambio, la cual a su vez fluctuará de acuerdo a otras variables económicas. Todo esto significa que la flexibilidad de los precios no se mostrará a través de un solo cambio sino por medio de oscilaciones alrededor de una o varias posiciones de equilibrio.

La población debe estar sicológicamente preparada para enfrentar estas contingencias y aprender a actuar frente a ellas. De hecho, ellas constituyen un reto a la necesidad del ajuste individual del comportamiento a un sistema en que en lugar de ser el Estado el que absorba todo el riesgo a cambio de las libertades individuales, el ciudadano puede enfrentarse a la incertidumbre a cambio de la libertad que le dá el derecho de seleccionar lo que él decida dentro una gama mayor de oportunidades. El valor político de la flexibilidad de precios radica en que facilita la democracia en el aspecto económico de las sociedades.

6.   La Liberación de los Mercados de Trabajo

En casi toda su extensión, la sección anterior puede aplicarse a los mercados de trabajo, pues durante la planificación socialista no ha existido la libertad de contratación por parte de las empresas, ni la libertad de los trabajadores de ofrecer sus servicios a diversas empresas, ni la posibilidad de mejorar salarios en función de la eficiencia. Los mercados de trabajo han sufrido de una rigidez similar a la que prevalece en otros mercados y la misma tiene que ser reemplazada por un sistema flexible que permita que los trabajadores de toda clase puedan seleccionar sus lugares de trabajo y cuenten con suficiente libertad para negociar sus salarios en función de sus productividades.

El sistema, cuando no está afectado por distorsiones monopolísticas y está integrado en un ambiente con amplias oportunidades de inversión, estimula la productividad del trabajo pues premia al trabajador capaz y ambicioso, mientras castiga al rezagado.[24] La eficiencia de las empresas precisa que las mismas tengan la libertad de contratar a los trabajadores más eficientes y deshacerse de los menos eficientes para poder operar a los costos que les permitirán cargar precios ace-quibles a los consumidores. Las empresas no pueden ser instrumentos de caridad pública donde por una combinación de piedad y paternalismo a veces se mantienen empleados individuos que no producen lo suficiente. Los instrumentos caritativos deben estar fuera de la empresa.[25]

Se plantea entonces la cuestión de la normativa jurídica que debe regir los mercados y contratos laborales. La experiencia de los países latinoamericanos de las últimas dos o tres décadas es de especial pertinencia para Cuba. Dicha experiencia indica que la legislación laboral puede llegar a tales extremos que cree condiciones que desestimulen la generación del mismo y la inversión tanto doméstica como extranjera.

Otras limitaciones de los códigos del trabajo que abundan en la región son los salarios mínimos y otros beneficios excesivamente elevados, lo que causa que los empleadores empleen menos mano de obra, de lo que lo harían si el precio de la misma no fuera artificialmente alto. Lo paradójico de esta situación es que la misma hace coexistir una población trabajadora y sindicalizada relativamente pequeña con una masa de trabajadores desempleados que estarían dispuestos a trabajar por menos que el salario mínimo legal si hubiera plena libertad de contratación. Este sistema sólo beneficia a una minoría de trabajadores en detrimento de la mayoría.[26]

Una vez más, el tema es vasto y requiere un tratamiento mucho mayor del que aquí podemos darle. Lo importante es mantener en mente que la legislación laboral debe garantizar la libertad de contratación tanto en beneficio del trabajador como el de las

---

[24] Obviamente, el sistema también crea un problema social serio cuando ignora aquellos individuos que son intrínsecamente incapaces.

[25] Ninguno de estos razonamientos debe tomarse como una afirmación tácita de que la empresa debe operar de una manera inhumana. La cuestión es comprender la responsabilidad social de producir eficientemente, lo cual puede hacerse sin perjuicio de los más altos valores éticos y humanistas en cada entidad.

[26] Tal inequidad no está sola pues los trabajadores así privilegiados son los que suelen trabajar en empresas protegidas con privilegios otorgados por los gobiernos y las respectivas legislaturas. Los casos más típicos de estos privilegios son la protección arancelaria contra la importación de productos competitivos del exterior que son más baratos, la imposición de restricciones cuantitativas con el mismo fin y la exención de impuestos sobre ingresos o sobre importaciones de capital y materias primas.

empresas. El requisito económico es que la norma jurídica establezca el marco que facilite la formación y dilusión de contratos laborales de todo tipo en beneficio de ambas partes. Lo que no puede hacer la legislación es determinar el monto de esos beneficios ni los términos de cada contrato en favor de una parte u otra sin perjudicar a toda la sociedad. Después de todo, la felicidad no puede legislarse.

7. La Liberación Gradual de las Importaciones

En el instante en que Cuba dé las primeras señales de una apertura hacia una economía de mercado, el país se verá invadido de vendedores de todas partes del mundo ansiosos de mostrar sus productos y ofreciendo todo tipo de facilidades para su importación en el país. La mala noticia será que no habrá suficientes divisas para comprar todo lo que se ofrece, pero este será el primer paso hacia la restitución del un comercio internacional libre. Antes del socialismo, la actividad importadora era libre y cualquiera podía ejercerla. La misma estaba además facilitada por un régimen de cambio libre. Con el advenimiento del socialismo, el sistema de planificación centralizada estipulaba que lo más eficiente desde un punto social era la creación de un monopolio de importación al cual debían dirigirse todas las solicitudes y planes de importación. De este modo se eliminaron todas las actividades de importación y la infraestructura comercial que se había creado durante muchos años desapareció rápidamente. La institución del Ministerio de Comercio Exterior conllevó a una verdadera "tupición" en el flujo de información y decisiones necesario para lograr las importaciones que las empresas, ya de por si ineficientes, requerían.

El gobierno de la transición deberá propiciar la rápida creación de empresas importadoras privadas, posiblemente a partir de la desmantelación de los organismos respectivos, lo cual tendría la ventaja de utilizar la experiencia existente. Sin embargo, la principal restricción será la disponibilidad de las divisas. Es posible que la obtención de créditos comerciales de corto plazo para las empresas de mayor solvencia en Cuba pueda servir para iniciar el movimiento de recuperación productiva del país, de ahí la importancia de estimular y crear las condiciones para que las empresas operen eficientemente.

8. La Promoción de las Exportaciones

El bajo nivel de los ingresos por exportaciones será uno de los grandes cuellos de botella de la economía cubana. Una gran parte de esos ingresos proviene de la producción de azúcar, como es sabido, y esta dependencia no es de esperar que se modifique en el corto plazo.[27] Tampoco es de esperar que Cuba pueda recuperar una parte sustancial del mercado azucarero de los Estados Unidos con sus precios preferenciales, lo cual ya ha sido

---

[27] La incapacidad de liberar a Cuba de la dependencia de casi un solo producto es la prueba más concluyente de la ineptitud del régimen actual. Esta continua dependencia no debe tomarse como una indicación de que la diversificación de las exportaciones no es posible.

señalado por Pazos.[28]

¿Qué debe hacer un nuevo gobierno para aumentar en un plazo breve los ingresos por exportaciones de Cuba? Lo mismo que el gobierno actual: promover el turismo internacional agresivamente. Bajo las condiciones actuales el turismo parece tener un cierto potencial de crecimiento y podrá desarrollarse aún más en el marco de una reforma económica profunda que pueda llevarse a cabo en condiciones de paz.

Aunque el horizonte aparece sombrío en este aspecto, ya que no es posible identificar actividades con suficiente potencial exportador, la propia depauperación económica de Cuba puede determinar una tasa de cambio tan baja que la producción exportable aparecerá con una alta competitividad exterior. El lado negativo consiste en que esa misma tasa hace que los activos cubanos tengan un precio internacional muy bajo lo que crea el peligro, como también Pazos[29] señaló, de que Cuba acabe regalando sus activos y su riqueza a inversionistas extranjeros si no se pospone este proceso hasta que existan mejores condiciones para el país o se puedan canalizar los capitales extranjeros de una manera más beneficiosa.[30]

En este punto es donde se puede presentar un fuerte argumento en favor de la ayuda exterior, lo cual este autor no favorece, ya que perpetuaría el carácter de sociedad parasitaria que el régimen actual ayudó a establecer en el país. Los que prefieran que Cuba salga adelante con base en su propio esfuerzo, favorecerán otras soluciones.

La solución principal parece radicar en una recuperación rápida de la eficiencia de las empresas del modo señalado anteriormente. Las mismas actuarían en dos frentes primordiales: el de la producción de alimentos y el de la producción de exportables, incluyendo el turismo. Esto pone nuevo énfasis en la necesidad de que el gobierno a cargo de la transición lleve a cabo una acción concertada para lograr estos objetivos.

9. Otros Aspectos de la Transición

El gobierno de la transición se enfrentará a una importante encrucijada en cuanto a las políticas para atraer inversión extranjera. Aunque las mismas sean muy aconsejables, al comienzo de la transición es donde el valor de los activos en monedas extranjeras puede ser sumamente bajo, como ya se mencionó; la inversión extranjera debiera ser controlada para evitar que una proporción inaceptable de la riqueza nacional pase a manos foráneas. La cuestión es decidir cuánta inversión es estrictamente necesaria aún cuando implique

---

[28]   Op. cit., pags. 8 y 9.

[29]   Ibid. pag. 3.

[30]   Este es un caso donde la intervención estatal puede ser inevitable para evitar una consecuencia catastrófica de una falla del mercado. La situación puede ser más grave aún si el efecto combinado de la desaparición de los subsidios y el bajo nivel de los ingresos por exportaciones obliga a Cuba a vender activos en el exterior para evitar una crisis alimentaria.

venta de activos a precios excesivamente bajos para reactivar la economía cubana cuanto antes.

Simultáneamente, deberá contemplarse la formación de mercados de capital de modo que las transacciones de propiedades otorgadas por el Estado a trabajadores de empresas estatales puedan llevarse a cabo. La creación de los mercados de capital proveería también un medio facilitador del proceso de privatización y de estímulo al ahorro y la inversión nacionales.

El gobierno tendrá una agenda llena con otros temas que aquí sólo podemos listar. Una lista parcial es la siguiente:

• La necesidad de definir una política para la distribución de los derechos de transmisión por radio y televisión;

• La regulación de las empresas aseguradoras con especial énfasis en los seguros de negocios que reduzcan el riesgo individual de la actividad inversionista;

• La evaluación de las condiciones en que Cuba debiera unirse al tratado de libre comercio con los Estados Unidos;

• La necesidad de dedicar suficientes recursos para explicar a la población en general y con suficiente detalle los problemas económicos del país, las diversas alternativas y las soluciones que parecen más aconsejables.

B.   El Mediano Plazo

El objetivo de esta fase es la consolidación legal de la economía de mercado, hecho que estará estrechamente vinculado a las otras necesidades jurídicas de la nueva República y que incluirán un nuevo marco constitucional. El mediano plazo también se podrá caracterizar por un proceso de consolidación de una economía abierta donde será necesario lograr la diversificación de las exportaciones y la definición de aquellas actividades económicas que sean compatibles con el desarrollo económico del país. Tales actividades, por supuesto, serán identificadas principalmente por empresas privadas, pero es necesario estudiar si el Estado puede jugar un papel coordinador en este esfuerzo.

Otro aspecto característico del mediano plazo es la remodelación de la estructura institucional del Estado cubano, en consonancia con el nuevo marco constitucional y la instauración de una economía de mercado. Para entonces, una gran parte del aparato burocrático del socialismo habrá sido demolido y reemplazado por un aparato estatal más ligero y eficaz.

Finalmente, el mediano plazo será el marco en que se pueda definir una estrategia de largo plazo en el frente educativo. Si Cuba desea perseguir metas ambiciosas de desarrollo económico y social, deberá invertir fuertes sumas en el desarrollo de su capital humano. Este proceso debe comenzar desde el principio mismo del traspaso de poderes políticos. Es posible que el proceso pueda aprovechar los avances supuestamente logrados en materia educativa durante el socialismo, pero evaluaciones independientes de tales logros siempre impidieron conocer a ciencia cierta la naturaleza de los mismos.

C.   El Largo Plazo

Acaso sea prematuro hablar de lo que pueda o deba hacerse en materia de política pública en Cuba más allá de cinco años desde el comienzo de la transición hacia una economía de mercado. En verdad luce algo aventurado si se piensa en los innumerables problemas que el gobierno y la población deberán enfrentar, como hemos visto, en los dos primeros años. No obstante, el largo plazo puede empezar hoy mismo con las tareas que requieran años de concepción y de puesta en marcha, y entonces no resulta tan ocioso indagar en horizontes lejanos.

¿Cuáles son las metas que Cuba debe perseguir como nación? ¿Que clase de estructura productiva debe el país estimular para lograr esas metas? Es obvio que el país necesita aprender a vivir de actividades diferentes a la producción azucarera. Pero ¿cómo se logra reestructurar toda la base productiva de un país? La experiencia enseña que la respuesta está en la versatilidad de la dotación humana de una nación. Tal riqueza no consiste sólo de destrezas de tipo cognocitivo, sino que también cubre todo el espectro de atributos afectivos o no-cognocitivos que forman parte de los objetivos educativos más elevados. Esto tiene que ver con lo que algunos llaman de manera muy general la formación del carácter pero que más específicamente se identifican por medio de un alto número de variables, por ejemplo, el sentido de responsabilidad, la capacidad de trabajar en equipo, la capacidad de construir y mantener organizaciones sociales complejas, la integridad, la propensión a cumplir con contratos sociales, etc. La lista de atributos es interminable y sólo se da aquí para ilustrar este ámbito de acción para la futura orientación de la política pública.

La educación de una nación puede ser un acto deliberado, parte de un contrato social. Los males que han aquejado a Cuba durante tantos años, no sólo durante los últimos treinta, pueden ser atribuídos en gran medida a deficiencias de tipo educativo. Sin querer proponer una nueva panacea, es necesario, en opinión de este autor, que la construcción de una nueva República de Cuba cuente con un esfuerzo de gran envergadura en este frente y que dicho esfuerzo sea una parte clave de la política pública por un largo período de tiempo.

IV.   CONCLUSIONES

La complejidad de las tareas que tienen que llevarse a cabo para construir una economía de mercado es evidente. Muchos reaccionan negativamente ante este tipo de planteamiento, pues lo consideran pesimista al sentir que los problemas se tratan sin eufemismos y generalmente las soluciones que se proponen no son fáciles. Tal estilo de presentación, también se argumenta, no genera el optimismo necesario para promover los cambios que Cuba necesita.

El economista, como cualquier otro profesional, puede ceñirse o no a algún código de conducta. Como se espera de un médico al examinar un cuerpo enfermo, el economista, al buscar soluciones para una sociedad con problemas, debe producir un diagnóstico preciso. Tal diagnóstico, tanto en el médico como en el economista, es necesario para hallar la cura o la solución adecuada. Si el diagnóstico falla por limitación del conocimiento o por falta de cuidado, las consecuencias pueden ser catastróficas.

No hay justificación ética que conduzca a dibujar un cuadro rosado de la economía cubana actual, como tampoco la hay en proyectar un camino fácil hacia el futuro. Sería una gran irresponsabilidad no mencionar las barreras que yacen en el camino hacia una economía más eficiente y más justa. El economista, como el médico, se enfrenta a dos tipos de "pacientes": el que quiere la verdad y el que sólo quiere oir buenas noticias. Si efectivamente queremos contribuir a mejorar la situación cubana no hay otra alternativa que la verdad. Si hay una lección que aprender sobre el origen de los males económicos y de toda clase que hoy aquejan al país y que lo seguirán aquejando por un cierto tiempo aún después de la transición, es que Cuba debe llegar a tener suficientes mentes claras y voces honestas para impedir que otro demagogo, prometiendo lo que no puede cumplir, se apodere nuevamente del país entero por tantos años.

Membership Requirements in the IMF:
Possible Implications for Cuba

Joaquín P. Pujol 1/

This paper gives an overview about the requirements and procedures that a country must follow in order to become a member of the International Monetary Fund (IMF). The first section explains the main purposes and characteristics of the IMF as an international organization. A second section explains the role of the member's quotas in the Fund and the procedures for their determination. A third section presents a historical remembrance of Cuba's past relationship with the IMF. A fourth section discusses recent developments in the membership of the Fund. A fifth section provides some information on the Fund's financial activities. A sixth, and final section draws some possible implications for Cuba of membership in the IMF.

What is the International Monetary Fund (IMF)?

The IMF is a cooperative intergovernmental monetary and financial institution. Its name assigns it to the dry, remote domain of monetary matters, balance of payments and the international monetary system, with its seemingly archane problems. But the reality is that these activities are very close to every day life, and that no country can ignore them. The job of the Fund is to cope with international monetary problems and to seek a cooperative approach among nations in resolving these problems. The policies and activities of the Fund are guided by its charter, known as the Articles of Agreement. Article I establishes as one of the main purposes of the Fund: "To facilitate the expansion and balanced growth of international trade, and to contribute thereby to the promotion and maintenance of high levels of employment and real income and to the development of the productive resources of all members as primary objectives of economic policy."

When the founders of the IMF specified its mandate in this way, they sought to ensure that the world would not repeat the mistakes of the inter-war years, especially the proliferation of restrictions on trade and payments, which had greatly aggravated the impact of the Great Depression and ultimately contributed to the social and political problems that led to World War II. In the 45 years since then, the world has successfully avoided such disasters, although--of course--many other problems have emerged. The successes achieved so far are due in part to the development of a more open system of international trade, but they are also due to the fact that the major participants in the world economy--governments, business, and workers--have more generally accepted the key principles of responsibility, mutual support, and cooperation. Today everyone knows that, in an interdependent world, each partner has an essential role to play, and none can play it alone. Every country, no matter how small, carries a responsibility for the overall success of the world economy, and its own successes will only be partial or precarious without the support and cooperation of the others.

1/ The views expressed in this paper are those of the author and in no way represent the official views of the International Monetary Fund.

The Fund is unique among intergovernmental organizations in its combination of regulatory, consultative, and financial functions. These functions derive from the various tasks that the IMF was assigned to carry out by its founders:

--to facilitate the balanced growth of international trade;

--to promote exchange rate stability; and

--to assist in the establishment of a multilateral system of payments in respect to current international transactions between members and in the elimination of foreign exchange restrictions that hamper the growth of world trade.

To help achieve these goals the Fund has available and can provide to its members financial resources to enable them to correct balance of payments disequilibria without resorting to trade and payments restrictions, and it provides a forum for consultation and collaboration among its members toward the solution of international monetary problems.

The Fund is thus concerned with the economic and financial problems of individual countries, as well as with the working of the international monetary system. Its activities are focused on promoting policies and strategies through which its members can achieve balance of payments viability on an individual basis and work together to ensure a stable international financial system and sustainable economic growth of the world economy.

Aside from its responsibilities associated with overseeing the international monetary system to ensure its effective operation, the Fund exercises specific surveillance over the exchange rate policies of its members. It is the guardian of an agreed international code of conduct with respect to these policies. The procedures for surveillance adopted by the Fund are designed to identify and encourage the correction of inappropriate exchange rate policies, and each member upon joining the institution must accept the obligation to provide the information necessary for such surveillance.

The Fund maintains a large pool of financial resources from which to help finance temporary disequilibrium imbalances in the balance of payments of its members. These resources are primarily derived from the currencies subscribed by its members through their quotas and they can become available to those members having a balance of payments need on a temporary basis while the member adopts the adjustment policies required to correct its balance of payments problems. In addition, the Fund may supplement these resources by borrowing. To use Fund resources a member must represent that it has need of them, because of the evolution of its balance of payments, or because its reserve position is weak, or is being affected by factors beyond its control, and that it is taking appropriate policy actions to improve its balance of payments situation.

Use of the Fund's resources is based on an equivalent and nondiscriminatory treatment of members, with due regard to their domestic, social and political objectives. Fund policies try to encourage members to have recourse to the Fund's financial facilities at an early stage of their balance of payments problems. The financial assistance provided by the Fund is designed to allow members to correct their payments disequilibrium without having to resort to trade and payments restrictions that affect the well being of other members. The Fund also acts as an important catalyst of financial resources for its members, insofar as policy adjustments implemented by members undertaking Fund-supported programs help to generate additional financial assistance from other sources, such as private and official creditors. Moreover, the granting of the stamp of approval of the Fund to a country's economic adjustment program is often sufficient to expedite access to significant credits from other sources of financing.

The catalytic role of the Fund has been enhanced significantly since the development of the international debt crisis. Since 1985, there has been a sharp reduction in voluntary flows of financing from commercial banks and other sources to developing countries in general, and to highly-indebted countries in particular, and the Fund has played an important role in mobilizing financial resources for those members that have adopted adjustment programs.

The Fund maintains close contacts with other international organizations, particularly its sister Bretton Woods institution, the International Bank for Reconstruction and Development (also known as the World Bank). Although relations with the Bank are mainly of a nonfinancial character--since each institution has separate funding, purposes, functions, and operations--there is also a structural link of a legal character in that the Bank's Articles of Agreement (Article II, Section 1) restrict the membership of the Bank to countries that have become members of the Fund; however, a country is not required to join the Bank once it joins the IMF. Based on the Articles of the two institutions, guidelines have been established for collaboration between the two organizations, with the Fund's activities centering on the provision of temporary balance of payments assistance and focusing on the macroeconomic aspects of the member's economies, whereas the Bank is more concerned with longer term projects and financing of economic development.

In terms of policy areas, the Fund has primary responsibility for working with members on the aggregate aspects of macroeconomic policies, including policies on public sector spending and revenue, wages and prices, money and credit, interest rates, and exchange rates. The Bank, on the other hand, has primary responsibility for policies on development strategies, sector and project investments, structural adjustment programs, and the efficient resource allocation in both public and private sectors. The two organizations also collaborate closely in efforts to mobilize resources from official and commercial sources in support of strong programs of macroeconomic adjustment and structural reform undertaken by members and endorsed by the Fund and the Bank.

There is also close collaboration between the Fund and the General Agreement on Tariffs and Trade (GATT). Article XV of the GATT provides that: "The CONTRACTING PARTIES shall seek cooperation with the International Monetary Fund to the end that the CONTRACTING PARTIES and the Fund may pursue a coordinated policy with regards to exchange questions within the jurisdiction of the Fund and questions of quantitative restrictions and other trade measures within the jurisdiction of the CONTRACTING PARTIES."

As part of its normal activities in support of member countries, the Fund also provides technical assistance to its members. Such assistance normally consists of providing highly qualified and experienced economic experts to work with a country on particular problem areas. In this context, since 1989 the Fund became an Executing Agency for the United Nations Development Program (UNDP); this cooperative arrangement has enabled the Fund to expand the amount of technical assistance it provides, as well as to help UNDP achieve its development aims. Under this arrangement, the UNDP finances some of the project cost while the Fund provides technical management and direction.

The Fund's Articles do not permit it to engage its general resources in guarantee or reinsurance schemes, including those for commercial bank lending or suppliers' credits; nor does the Fund participate as a party in negotiations between debtor countries and banks. There are, however, various links that have emerged between Fund financial arrangements with member countries and the loan agreements between private banks and these members. For example, such loan agreements may stipulate that the borrowing country should be "a member in good standing of the Fund" and be "eligible to use the Fund's resources." Also, the Fund--at the request of the member--may provide information to the banks about the eligibility of the member to make purchases under Fund arrangements, or help explain the nature of the economic program being undertaken by the member. From the onset of the debt crisis, commercial banks generally have been more willing to extend loans to debtor countries if the Fund has approved an arrangement for that country, because the approval of such arrangement is seen as a sign that the adjustment program is adequate to the circumstances of the country.

Other multilateral organizations and governments also have indicated a preference to provide financing for adjustment programs if such programs are supported by the Fund. The Paris Club, 1/ in particular, has made the existence of a Fund arrangement almost a **sine qua non** for proceeding with their debt rescheduling operations. Such mechanisms exemplify the role of the Fund as a catalyst in generating additional international credit and capital in support of its members.

Fund quotas

The subject of Fund quotas is of great interest to any country considering membership in the Fund. Each Fund member is assigned a quota which determines its financial and organizational relations with the institution. Quotas determine the member's subscription

---

1/ The Paris Club is the forum where representatives of the main creditor countries get together to consider rescheduling proposals for official bilateral debt of debtor countries.

to the Fund, its relative voting power, its maximum access to financing from the Fund, and its share in any SDR allocations. 1/

The amount of a member's quota is expressed in terms of SDRs and it is equal to the subscription the member must pay to the Fund. Up to 25 percent of the subscription has to be paid in international reserve assets specified by the Fund (these are usually SDRs or convertible currencies which are easily usable in international transactions), and the remainder can be paid in the member's own currency. This latter part usually is deposited in an account in the name of the Fund in the member's central bank, or equivalent monetary institution.

Each member has 250 basic votes plus one additional vote for each SDR 100,000 of quota. A member's voting power is important for two reasons. First, many of the principal policy and operational decisions of the Fund require a certain majority of votes. (For example, an increase in member's quotas needs an 85 percent majority, while the determination of charges on use of Fund credit requires a 70 percent majority.) Second, the voting power of a member has a bearing on the member's representation in the Executive Board. Each of the five members with the largest quota, as well as each of the two members with the largest net creditor positions in the Fund over the two years preceding the regular biennial elections, are entitled to appoint an Executive Director. The remaining Directors are elected by groups or constituencies of members.

Access to Fund resources under the various Fund lending windows (i.e., facilities) are usually specified in terms of member's quotas. For example, the limits on access to Fund resources under stand-by or extended arrangements are currently 110 percent of quota on an annual basis, or 440 percent of quota on a cumulative basis (the latter defined net of outstanding obligations).

The Articles of Agreement do not specify how a member's quota should be determined. However, from the start of the Fund, quotas have been related to--although not strictly determined by--economic factors. Under the Articles, the Board of Governors is required to conduct a general review of quotas at intervals not longer than five years and to propose any adjustments that it may deem appropriate. 2/ Such reviews provide an opportunity to consider the adequacy of the Fund's resources to fulfill its systemic responsibilities and to respond to the temporary balance of payments needs of its members, while maintaining the revolving character of its resources. In connection with the latest review of quotas (the Ninth Review), five quota formulas were agreed to serve as broad measures of the member's relative position in the world economy. These formulas use economic data relating to the member's gross domestic product (GDP), current account transactions in the balance of payments, the variability of current receipts from international

---

1/ SDRs are international reserve assets that were created in 1969 to enable the Fund to meet long-term needs to supplement global liquidity by adding to international reserves of members. The SDRs are valued in relation to a basket of major members' currencies. The quotas of the Fund and members' transactions with the Fund are denominated in SDRs; currently, one SDR is worth about US$1.30.

2/ Currently Fund quotas amount to SDR 91.1 billion, but a 50 percent increase has been proposed under the Ninth Review of Quotas.

transactions, and the level of official international reserves. The Board of Governors is also the one who holds the power to admit new members. However, it delegates the power of running the Fund on a daily basis to the Executive Board.

When a country applies for membership, relevant macroeconomic data on its economy are collected, and a quota range is calculated. Data are then compared with those of existing members of comparable economic size and characteristics, and an initial quota or quota range is proposed by the Fund staff. This quota can be expected to be within the same range as the quotas of members the Fund considers to be in a comparable situation. The other terms of membership, such as the proportion of subscription to be paid in reserve assets, are to be set so as not to discriminate in other respects between applicants and existing members in similar circumstances.

A member is not eligible to use the Fund's resources until it has paid its subscription in full. Likewise, a member's quota cannot be increased until it has consented to the increase and paid the subscription in full. These requirements ensure that the Fund's paid-up capital equals its authorized capital, and there is therefore no component of "capital on call" as is the case of some domestic financial institutions or even some international development banks.

Cuba's past relations with the IMF

Cuba was one of the founding members of the International Monetary Fund (IMF). It should be of particular interest to this group that a Cuban delegation attended the Bretton Woods Conference that gave birth to the IMF and the World Bank. It was composed of men who are well known in Cuban and international economic circles:

Eduardo I. Montoulieu	J.M. Menocal
Oscar Garcia Montes	Miguel A. Pirez
Ramiro Guerra	Eduardo Durruthy
Luis Machado	Felipe Pazos

In fact, Mr. Montoulieu became the chairman of the Credentials Committee at Bretton Woods, and the Cuban delegation took a very active part in the deliberations of the conference, helping to shape the foundations of the IMF. Luis Machado became an Executive Director at the World Bank and Felipe Pazos joined the staff of the Fund in its early years, before returning to Cuba to help establish the Cuban National Bank.

Cuba officially joined the Fund on March 14, 1946. At that time, it was assigned a quota of US$50 million. Other countries being assigned a similar quota at the time were New Zealand, Norway, and Chile; meanwhile, Greece's quota was set at US$40 million,

Egypt's at US$45 million, and Yugoslavia's at US$60 million. 1/ Cuba accepted the obligations of full convertibility of its currency under Article VIII of the Articles of Agreement in December 1953.

Cuba withdrew from membership in the Fund on April 2, 1964. This withdrawal was the culmination of a period of difficulties in Cuba's balance of payments starting in 1959. Cuba had drawn US$25 million from the Fund in September 1958, undertaking to repurchase this sum within six months. However, it repeatedly asked permission to defer repurchasing, and the Executive Board of the Fund agreed in March and April 1959, in March 1960, and in December 1961, to set new dates for the repurchase obligations to fall due. During the three years 1959-61, however, the process of converting the island into a communist state disrupted both its internal organization and its economic relations with the Western world, resulting in a sharp deterioration of its economy in general, and of its balance of payments position in particular.

The agreement reached in December 1961 provided that Cuba would make three purchases of US$5 million each at half-yearly intervals beginning in September 1962, and to agree with the Fund before the latter date on arrangements for the repurchase of the final US$10 million within the five-year period that ended in September 1963. However, in August 1962 the Cuban authorities asked the Fund for a further deferment, undertaking to make a first repurchase in March 1964. In doing so, it drew attention to paragraph 2 (d) of the Executive Board's Decision No. 102-(52/11, of February 13, 1952) which read as follows:

"When unforeseen circumstances beyond the member's control would make unreasonable the application of the principles set forth .... [that repurchases should be made within an outside range of three to five years], the Fund will consider extensions of time."

In a subsequent letter, Cuba supported its plea for deferment by pointing out that since December 1961, when it entered into its undertaking to repurchase from the Fund, the United States had placed a total embargo on all interchanges of goods and services with Cuba, resulting in so marked a decline in Cuba's international assets as to prevent it from fulfilling its commitment. It was hoped, however, that a prospective increase in its exports in 1963, especially sugar, together with a decline in its needs for imports, would enable Cuba to start repurchases in 1964.

In replying to these communications, the Managing Director of the Fund stressed that five years was regarded as the maximum period for repurchases. The Cuban authorities failed to respond and in September 1963 the Managing Director sent a notification to the Executive Board to report that Cuba was not fulfilling its obligations under the Fund Agreement. He informed the Board that five years had elapsed since Cuba's drawing from

---

1/ The quotas of these countries have been adjusted over time in line with the general revisions of the Fund's quotas and their own individual economic performance. Currently the quotas of these countries are: New Zealand (SDR 462 million); Norway (SDR 699 million); Chile (SDR 440 million); Greece (SDR 400 million); Egypt (SDR 463 million); and Yugoslavia (SDR 613 million).

the Fund, but that no part of the drawing had been repurchased, although all the charges had been paid. Further, since July 1961 Cuba had stopped supplying the monetary, banking, and balance of payments data required under Article VIII, Section 5 (a), of the Articles of Agreement and no data on monetary reserves had been supplied since the Fund's 1959/60 financial year. Finally, since June 1960, Cuba had furnished no information about its foreign exchange practices, nor had it removed the exchange restrictions imposed since late 1959, which it had been formally enjoined to discontinue by the Fund because it was in contravention of the obligations under Article VIII. The Executive Board agreed that the Managing Director should inquire into Cuba's intentions regarding these defaults, and he did so by letter on October 11, 1963 and again on December 3, 1963.

No reply was provided by the Cuban authorities to these enquiries, and on April 2, 1964, the Cuban authorities announced that they were withdrawing from the Fund. At that time, they proposed to settle the sum due to the Fund by handing over title to Cuba's gold subscription (equivalent to US$12.5 million) and repaying the remainder in five annual installments of US$2.5 million, with interest at 2 percent per annum, beginning on July 1, 1964. The Managing Director recommended that this proposal be accepted, even though 2 percent was a low rate of interest, in order to secure a quick settlement. This was accepted by the Executive Board and Cuba completed payments under this settlement in January 1969.

Evolution of membership in the Fund

At the time of its founding the Fund had 40 members. The membership has risen over the years and has now reached 155 members. Of the 159 nations belonging to the United Nations (UN), 152 are Fund members. Moreover, three countries (Kiribati, the Republic of Korea, and Tonga) are members of the Fund even though they are not members of the UN. A membership resolution for another country, Switzerland, which is not a member of the UN has been approved.

To apply for membership to the Fund, the applicant must be a country in control of its own foreign affairs, and both willing and able to meet the obligations of membership contained in the Articles of Agreement. Under those obligations, a member must conduct its exchange rate policy and related economic and financial policies in accordance with the Articles, and provide requested economic and financial information to the Fund. A member must also pay a subscription--its quota. Although member countries do not have to adopt a market-type economic system to qualify for membership, nor do they need to adhere to a particular exchange rate regime, they are expected to pay regard in their foreign exchange policies to the purposes of the IMF and to take steps toward lifting any existing exchange restrictions, as soon as possible. Moreover, the Executive Board's decision to consider an application and subsequently submit it to the Board of Governors depends on whether it is considered that the country can meet the obligations of membership; thus, an applicant must have sufficient political support from the membership at large. Therefore, potential applicants tend to explore carefully the likely response of various important member countries and groups of countries before formally submitting an application. The actual timing of the acceptance of the application may hinge on domestic political and economic events.

Once an application has been received, the IMF sends a fact-finding mission to the country to collect the necessary data for quota calculations and to prepare documentation on the economic and financial system of the country, its history and current policies. At the same time, the mission informs the country about the IMF's rules and policies, as well as about the financial, legal, and procedural steps of membership. The World Bank may also participate in such a mission, and it will use the quota arrived at by the IMF to determine the prospective member's capital subscription for the Bank.

The information gathered by the Fund's mission is used to prepare a "quota paper" for consideration by a committee of members of the Fund's Executive Board. Based on the data supplied to the mission on national accounts, gold and foreign exchange reserves, and current payments and receipts of the balance of payments, five different formulas are used to estimate a calculated quota. Actual quotas, however, are on average smaller than calculated quotas, and the initial quota of a new member has to be fitted into the structure of the existing quotas of members of comparable economic size. Comparisons are made also with other subgroups of countries that have similar characteristics. This normally results in a recommended quota range. The staff's recommendations as regards the quota and the proportion of the subscription to be paid in international reserve assets are then considered by a committee of the Executive Board. The committee of Executive Directors is the body that has the power to recommend a quota.

Once the applicant agrees to the quota recommended by the committee, the quota and other terms of membership are considered by the Executive Board as a whole, which submits a resolution to the Board of Governors for a vote. To be adopted the resolution requires a simple majority of the votes cast, but two-thirds of the membership must vote. After approval of the resolution, the country must enact any legislation necessary to enable it to sign the Articles of Agreement, after which it becomes a member. When a country that previously was a member re-applies, it is treated in the same manner as a new applicant.

In recent years the Fund has received a flurry of membership applications, particularly as a result of the economic and political changes in the eastern bloc. New applicants have included:

Angola: applied to the Fund in October 1987 and became a member in September 1989 with a quota of SDR 145 million.

Albania: applied to the Fund in January 1991; its application is being processed.

Bulgaria: applied to the Fund in February 1990 and was admitted in September 1990 with a quota of SDR 310 million.

Czechoslovakia: originally joined the Fund in December 1945 but had ceased to be a member in December 1954; submitted applications for membership in the Fund and the World Bank in January 1990 and was readmitted to the Fund in September 1990 with a quota of SDR 590 million.

Marshall Islands: applied to the Fund in May 1991, but its international status is currently being reviewed by the Fund.

Mongolia: applied to the Fund in July 1990 and was admitted in February 1991 with a quota of SDR 25 million.

Namibia: became a sovereign nation in 1990; it applied to the Fund in June 1990 and was admitted in September 1990 with a quota of SDR 70 million.

Switzerland: which, although an important center of international finance, is neither a member of the Fund nor of the United Nations, applied for membership of the Fund and the World Bank in May 1990. The Board of Governors has adopted the membership Resolution and Switzerland's membership will become effective when the legislative steps necessary for it to sign the Articles of Agreement have been completed.

The only other UN members which are not members of the Fund are: Brunei, the Byelorussian Soviet Socialist Republic, Cuba, Liechtenstein, North Korea, the Ukranian Soviet Socialist Republic, and the Union of Soviet Socialist Republics. The latter has recently indicated its interest in joining the Fund, and procedures are being discussed; its formal application for membership was received on July 22, 1991. (The Soviet Union was one of the principal negotiators at the Bretton Woods Conference in 1944 which adopted the original Articles of Agreement by the Fund, but it did not accept and sign the treaty as an original member.)

Fund financial activity

There are currently 78 member countries with outstanding credits from the Fund for a total of SDR 25.6 billion. Of these, 45 countries have ongoing adjustment programs being supported by the Fund. Over the last year, particularly, there has been an upswing in Fund financial activity in connection with new financial arrangements between the Fund and East European member countries in support of major economic restructuring programs. Fund arrangements are now in place with Bulgaria, Czechoslovakia, Hungary, Poland, Romania and Yugoslavia. In the first half of 1991 the Fund entered into new commitments for a total of SDR 7.6 billion, of which SDR 4.7 billion was to East European countries.

Possible implications of membership in the Fund for Cuba

Membership in the IMF can help bring a country into the mainstream of the international economic and financial activities. It gives it access to valuable information about the economy and economic policies of other countries and about the general economic developments in the world economy. It involves potential access to substantial resources, both human--in terms of technical assistance and economic advice--and financial. Such resources are not limited to the Fund alone, since membership in the Fund opens the doors to membership in the World Bank and the potential for easier access to other international financial institutions (such as the Inter-American Development Bank) and to the world financial community as a whole. Access to such types of assistance would be particularly important if the country was engaged in a major transformation of its economy as has been the case for the East European countries.

At the same time, membership requires a willingness on the part of the prospective member to adopt a cooperative approach to its international internationalfinancial relations, open its economy to international transactions, free its economic system of restrictions, share with other members information about its economy, and be prepared more generally to engage in a frank discussion of the appropriateness of its economic policies.

Bibliography

Admission to Membership in the International Monetary Fund, Manual of Procedures, (Washington, D.C. 1990).

Articles of Agreement, International Monetary Fund (Washington, D.C.).

Financial Organization and Operations of the IMF, by the Treasurer's Department of the International Monetary Fund, (Washington, D.C. 1990), Pamphlet Series No. 45.

"How does a Country Join the IMF?" Questions & Answers by Marina Primorac, Finance and Development, (Washington, D.C., June 1991).

Proceedings and Documents of United Nations Monetary and Financial Conference, (Bretton Woods, New Hampshire, July 1-22, 1944), U.S. Department of State, Volumes I and II.

Selected Decisions of the International Monetary Fund, 14th Issue, (Washington, D.C., April 30, 1989).

The International Monetary Fund: Its Evolution, Organization and Activities, Fourth Edition (1984), Pamphlet Series No. 378.

<u>The International Monetary Fund, Twenty Years of International Monetary Cooperation</u>, by J. Keith Horsefield, Vols. I-III, (Washington, D.C., 1969).

Comments by Elías R. Asón

Felipe Pazos has expressed the view that in the transition from a centrally planned to a market economy, a policy of gradualism seems to be optimum. Hernandez-Catá differs from Pazos on this issue, proposing a more frontal and radical approach. I would argue that it will not be easy to sell such an approach to the politicians, unless we identify and confront the possible negative impacts of such a recommendation.

Hernandez-Catá is concerned with what is the optimum economic policy to be followed in various areas and as a background for his prescriptions he compares the economic development experience of the developing countries in Asia against those in other parts of the world. On the basis of his analysis he concludes that the policy framework for the long term must include: (a) a competitive market economy; (b) privatization; (c) free flow of goods, services and factors of production in and out of the country; (d) a strong fiscal policy that fosters savings and investments; and (e) a monetary policy that aims primarily at keeping inflation under control, with adequate support from fiscal and exchange rate policy.

A competitive market economy is the cornerstone of the policy package. He asks for price decontrols at all levels and concludes that the social welfare of the population will not change significantly because everyone will benefit from the elimination of "lines" in stores. But we should realize that the proposed policy may result not only in a decline of real income but in a significant redistribution, and that when real income is redistributed no social welfare conclusions can be derived.

To cushion the impact on the poorest section of the population, Hernandez-Catá allows for some transfer payments. He proposes that unemployment benefits be financed, at least partially, by the firms to avoid the budgetary costs and the inflationary repercussions. But given that real incomes are already low and falling we should not underestimate the potential budgetary costs of any alternative chosen. Moreover, such an approach will increase the costs of the firms and push them to try to increase their prices (lowering their competitiveness). There is no free lunch.

We should realize that price liberalization is also a rationing devise; the shortages are real for those who do not have the economic means to acquire essential goods. While price mechanisms may be economically efficient, the welfare costs may be very high and the optimal path from a political point of view may not be evident.

I disagree with Hernandez-Catá's assessment that during the transition Cuba's external sector will encompass a wide range of exportable goods. I think that the balance of payments will provide meager resources to pay for imports, because the exporting producing industries will suffer as a result of the changes in the economic and political structures. But I agree with his prescription that a flexible exchange rate regime should prove far superior to a fixed exchange rate system with exchange controls as an instrument to help reduce the balance of payments situation.

Perhaps the most important point made in the paper is that we should always keep a clear view of our ultimate objectives in framing the policies of the transition period, so that we can ensure that they guide us in the appropriate direction. However, if we do not identify and offer some kind of solutions to the short run problems, we are doomed as political economists and we may end up losing the war, because politicians will look for someone else in search of "better" solutions.

Lessons from Privatization in Eastern Europe and Latin America

Luis R. Luis

This paper draws some conclusions from the experience with on-going privatization programs in the emerging market economies of Central and Eastern Europe. The experience of these former members of CMEA, the disintegrating communist economic block, is the most relevant for Cuba, also a member of CMEA, with an economy modeled on the central planning and state ownership once dominant in Eastern Europe. Although privatization is only now beginning to gather steam in Central and Eastern Europe, much can be learned from this initial experience. Insights can be obtained on the obstacles in the way to privatization and regarding alternative approaches to the sale or transfer of assets. However, because of the short duration of their efforts with privatization and the incipient development of a market economy, the CMEA experience has important limitations. Drawing some lessons from the longer experience of many Latin American countries with privatization enriches the analysis. Furthermore, the mixed economic systems in Latin America provide a varied framework for an assessment of the approaches to privatization.

Privatization involves the transfer of economic activity from the public to the private sector. In its more widely practised form, it involves the sale of state enterprises and other public assets to individuals or private firms. In CMEA countries privatization is also understood to encompass the entry of **new firms** into sectors of activity previously reserved to the state, an important phenomenon in low-capitalization firms that operate in the light manufacturing and service sectors. In Latin America, privatization has largely involved the sale of state companies in the industrial and public utility sectors to private domestic or foreign interests, and, to a lesser extent, the granting of leases and other concessions from the public sector to private firms. However, there has been only limited entry of new firms into activities controlled by state firms because the state in Latin America largely has concentrated its involvement in capital-intensive sectors such as mining, steel and telecommunications.

I. Objectives of Privatization Programs

Privatization programs aim to accomplish a number of major economic objectives. Foremost among these objectives is the increase in economic efficiency at the firm level derived from improved and more flexible management. Because profits and other efficiency criteria have been largely absent from the management of state-run firms in CMEA countries and as a result of the large distortions in an arbitrary price system, state companies generally operate at cost conditions well above international levels or produce goods and services of inferior quality. For many, if not most firms, redressing this uncompetitive structure may not be feasible in the short run. Plants may not have access to raw materials at a competitive cost, or the cost of replacing and refurbishing the capital equipment may be higher than the cost of a greenfield plant. Hence in many cases, the best course of action may be to liquidate the companies, which is a form of privatization. In the absence of liquidation, restructuring of the firm should be undertaken. Although restructuring would start under state ownership and management, privatization will become a central part of the restructuring process. Important questions arise as to the most appropriate mechanism to carry out the restructuring before and after privatization.

A second related reason for privatizations in socialist economies, is that private firms, whether privatised or newly established, bolster an emerging market economy. Firms with independent managers are more likely to react flexibly to market signals than are state-owned companies, which more likely have to satisfy objectives other than profit maximization and cost efficiency.

The need to strengthen the fiscal position of the government has provided a major rationale for privatizations in Latin America and also in Eastern Europe. The transition to a stable macroeconomic framework in a liberalizing economy requires progress towards fiscal balance. Privatizations can boost the public finances in two major ways. First, the sale of firms and other state assets has a direct revenue-generating impact, whether classified as capital gains or other extraordinary revenues. In addition, privatization will generally be accompanied by the elimination or reduction of operating and investment subsidies. Among operating subsidies that are eliminated are direct transfers to the firm from the central government, its agencies or state banks. Indirect subsidies to be eliminated include those provided to the state enterprise by other state firms in the form of inputs priced below their economic cost. Obviously, if firm valuation is low, as apparently is the case with many state enterprises in East Germany (GDR), the fiscal benefit from privatization can be negative. That is, subsidies are likely to exceed income derived from the privatization process.

A fourth objective of privatization programs is to facilitate relief on the country's external debt. The conversion of foreign debt instruments at a discount into equity of state enterprises can be used to reduce the country's external debt to banks and other institutions. This mechanism has been utilized in Latin America, most notably in Argentina, but substantially also in Brazil, Chile, Mexico and Venezuela. In Eastern Europe, privatizations have not been utilized yet in a major way as a mechanism to obtain relief on the external debt.

The development of domestic capital markets is an important complementary objective of privatization. Capital markets in Central and Eastern Europe and in Latin America are either practically non-existent in the former, or illiquid and largely short-term in the latter. New share issues can help boost the liquidity of stock markets. Stocks of privatized companies are the most widely traded in the Mexico City and Santiago de Chile stock exchanges.

A well designed privatization program can also help foster foreign investment through direct sales to foreign investors and by providing core facilities that attract complementary foreign capital. Concessions to foreign firms for the development of natural resources controlled by the state can also play an important part in bringing foreign capital, skills and technology. The granting of management contracts to qualified foreign firms can also pave the way for future inflows of direct and portfolio investment. Attracting foreign investment in a socialized economy will require the sale of some state assets to foreign investors, in addition to the establishment of joint ventures, management contracts and marketing arrangements.

Privatization can also aim to widen equity ownership among the population, thus cementing support for the difficult and very costly process of restructuring the economy. Chile in 1982-87 was very successful in placing a majority of the equity of large state companies in the retail market through qualified institutional fund managers. The recent Mexican experience with the privatization of commercial banks is also relevant in this regard.

Privatization programs often have generally not been well focused. In many of the programs in Latin America, for example in the earlier Mexican experience during 1984-87, the importance given to fiscal objectives meant that privatizations not always were carried out with careful consideration of the proper restructuring of the company's assets. This delayed the gains in efficiency that can be derived from the process. The rush to privatize either because of fiscal, foreign debt or other reasons has often not been consistent with the development of an adequate institutional framework to support the operation of private companies. Private utilities, for instance, require a regulatory framework which will assure stable and balanced contracts between producers and consumers or among suppliers.

The presence of multiple objectives does not mean that they are mutually exclusive. Many of the objectives of privatization programs listed above can be attained simultaneously. For example, fostering foreign investment is consistent with the goals of boosting the public finances and increasing company efficiency, and, at the same time, through well coordinated offerings of shares in domestic and foreign markets, privatization could help with the development of a domestic capital market.

II. The Mechanics of Privatization

The placement or distribution of equity in existing state enterprises in Central and Eastern Europe and in Latin America has been carried out under a variety of mechanisms. Most of them involve the sale of shares to residents or non-residents under established rules. Some Central European countries, notably Poland and Czechoslovakia, are beginning to experiment with schemes for the free distribution of shares among wide groups of the population.

The main mechanisms used in the placement of shares are the following: a) direct sales to an investing group by the government; b) auctions or other competitive bidding; c) spontaneous privatization by state companies; d) free distribution of shares to the public; e) profit and equity sharing with employees of the firm; f) retail sales to the public; and g) selling blocks of shares in foreign stock markets.

Direct Sales to an Investing Group

Direct sales to an investing group through a two way deal under a clear set of rules is one of the fastest routes to privatization. If done properly it can also bring complementary capital, technology and management skills from the acquiring group. In CMEA countries, direct sales have been of two types. In one widely practised form in Poland and Hungary, direct sales to a management group have taken place. This management buyout has the advantage of familiarity with the firm and the market, but are unlikely to attract substantial investment capital or bring much new technical knowhow to the firm. Direct sales to multinational companies have also been employed widely. These have involved some of the best known examples of privatization in Eastern Europe and in Latin America. The acquisition or joint ventures with foreign companies of Skoda in Czechoslovakia, Tungsten in Hungary and the GDR's banking system are among the best examples in the CMEA area.

Direct sales of assets or associated joint ventures, are used by critics of privatization as examples of hasty action. Much of this criticism extends to the valuation process. Hero Brahms, deputy president of the East German privatisation agency (Treuhandanstalt) acknowledged recently that his agency did not initially have the experience to value companies properly. Mr. Brahms added that the Treuhandanstalt still has problems "with reliable valuation information. Profit and loss accounts, are, for example, often unreliable".

The argument is also made that speedy sales prevent proper restructuring of companies that would enhance their value. This assumes that the agency in charge of privatization has the managerial and technical ability to proceed with a restructuring, which even in Germany has proven to be difficult to acquire.

Auctions and Other Competitive Bidding

This is the most widely used mechanism for privatization. It has been employed in all privatizing countries in Eastern Europe and Latin America. In the latter, it has been associated with domestic and foreign offering of shares to competing groups sometimes accompanied by the underwriting or placement of shares in major stock markets. The 1990-91 privatization of TELMEX, the Mexican phone company, is probably the best example of a balanced bidding process involving both block sales to competing groups of investors and retail placements of stock in the domestic and foreign markets. In Eastern Europe, auctions are being employed in Germany and Hungary under the close coordination of privatization agencies.

Spontaneous Privatization

This mode of privatization can involve either direct sales or auctions, except that instead of being closely guided by a central privatization agency such as the Treuhandanstalt, the State Property Agency (SPA) in Hungary or Corporación de Fomento de la Producción (CORFO) in Chile, it is done in a decentralized fashion by state companies themselves.

Spontaneous privatizations are initiated by private managers, subject to the approval of the privatization agency. The arrangements with investment banks, the valuation process, debt-restructuring and other preliminary steps needed prior to privatization are arranged largely by the company managers. This process can be swift. It was employed with some success by the Hungarians in 1990 as the modus operandi for their first privatization package. Hungary is currently trying a mix of both Spontaneous Privatization and SPA-directed efforts. The aim has been to execute the divestment of 5 to 8 percent of state property per year. The goal of Hungary's privatization program is to reduce state property from 90 percent in early 1991 to 40 percent by 1996.

Free Distribution of Shares to the Public

In such schemes shares in state enterprises are distributed among the adult population of the country free of charge or at nominal distribution cost. The most notable and sophisticated example of this is the proposal by the Polish government announced at the end of June 1991.

The Polish scheme would cover the privatization of 400 state-owned factories, representing 25 percent of the country's industrial sales and 12 percent of total employment. This would be a key element in the goal to sell companies representing 50 percent of GDP within three years. In the scheme, prepared by S.G. Warburg of London, 60 percent of the equity in the 400 companies would be transfered to up to 20 investment groups to be known as National Wealth Management Funds (NWMF). Management of these funds would be carried out by foreign fund managers under contract to the shareholders. The government will keep a 30 percent shareholding in the groups while employees will retain 10 percent of the equity.

Other schemes for free transferral of shares have been proposed in Czechoslovakia and Hungary. These "voucher schemes" have yet to be implemented on any significant scale in these two countries.

Profit and Equity Sharing with Employees of the Firm

This is a complement to other forms of privatization. It usually involves the sale or transfer of a minority shareholding to company employees. It can be done gradually through profit sharing, or it can be a component of a larger privatization package. The privatization of Mexican banks and utilities and the prospective privatizations in Venezuela have components of this form of privatization. Employee or management buyouts have also taken place in Poland and Hungary, although the earliest experience with this modality of divestment of state property in Central Europe took place in Yugoslavia in the 1970s.

Profit and equity sharing has limited value as a capitalization mechanism. It is also unlikely to contribute substantially to the improvement of management conditions, although often it can contribute to the betterment of morale among employees. Management buyouts have been the exception in recent privatization experience, but there is scope for such schemes particularly in skill and technology intensive industries, for example tool and dye making, pharmaceutical and biological companies.

Retail Sales to the Public

Efficient retail sales to the public require some prior development of the domestic capital market, but direct distribution to shareholders may prove initially successful. In the absence of a functioning stock market, however, shares will have poor liquidity, limiting their desirability and thus lowering their value. One of the ways of tackling this problem has been through the privatization of social security and pension funds, as illustrated by the experience of Chile beginning in the mid 1970s. In Chile, private pension funds provide considerable depth to the capital markets and have raised inmensely the returns received by participants in the plans. CMEA countries are not yet ready to operate with the same institutional arrangements as Chile. However, in a privatization horizon of 3 to 7 years, there would be sufficient time to create a domestic capital market capable of handling the widening of share ownership.

Selling Blocks of Shares in Foreign Stock Markets

This can only be done by sizable companies with an established operating record, and only after extensive restructuring and preparation by management, the government and investment bankers. It has been used in Latin America by a handful of large companies, among them telephone companies in Chile and Mexico (CTC and TELMEX), the leading Mexican cement company (CEMEX) and a few other large enterprises. In CMEA countries, major changes in operating procedures, financial and legal structure and accounting are necessary before this form of privatization and access to new capital can be employed. However, for companies with high international competitive potential, early restructuring could prepare the road for access to foreign stock markets within a few years. The establishment of a joint venture with foreign partners could be a way to accelerate this process.

III. Lessons from Privatization

After considering the objectives of privatization and the alternative mechanisms that have been employed in the light of the recent experience in Eastern Europe and Latin America, conclusions are derived that should help to structure the privatization process in state controlled economies.

The main conclusions that can be derived are the following:

1. From an efficiency point of view, the entry of new firms is the best mechanism for privatization.

Existing firms in CMEA countries have such deep structural problems that in many or most cases the organization of productive resources may have to start from scratch. The key question is how to foster and best support the entry of entrepreneurs into areas of activity heretofore reserved to state enterprises. A change in regime and the initiation of reform by itself can do much. By one estimate over 500,000 new firms were created in Poland in the first year after the installation of a democratic government in the country. But the absence of adequate financial markets, will mostly relegate new domestic companies to labor-intensive activities in the service sector. Companies with foreign capital should be allowed to operate at the outset, but not much will happen until property and legal rights are well established.

Encouraging new firms is highly desirable, but this still leaves the problem of the restructuring of the existing firms and the massive challenge of retraining and reemploying workers from the old state sector. For a number of years, the rate of job creation of new firms is likely to be well below the rate of employment contraction in the state sector. Hence, the focus would have to remain on launching privatized firms that can operate profitably within a reasonable time span.

2. Institutional reorganization of the economy must begin at once.

A major roadblock to privatization either through the establishment of new firms or through sales or transfers of existing state assets is the lack of clear contractual rights and relationships. Time can not be wasted in restablishing land and other property rights. Legal mechanisms that assure the validity of contractual relationships must be established.

A scheme to provide insurance for contractual relationships involving privatized firms or newly established companies could be helpful in attracting domestic and foreign investors. The insurance could cover titles and breach of contract under certain conditions. Fees would be assessed on the investors on a case-by-case basis. Insurance contracts could cover the title to the land of a privatized company, a guarantee from the government against expropriation or rights of access to natural resources. Insurance covering foreign investments possibly can be reinsured in international markets or could be covered by agencies such as the Overseas Private Insurance Corporation of the United States (OPIC) or similar agencies in other OECD countries.

3. Rules for privatization have to be clearly established.

This applies to all forms of sales and transfers, direct sales to investor groups, auctions, transfers and spontaneous privatizations. One of the reasons for the widespread criticism of spontaneous privatization in Hungary has been the inconsistency of procedures relating to valuation, awarding of contracts, technical transfers and other arrangements. The main object of the rules is to guarantee a fair, transparent and speedy process for all parties involved in the privatization process. Obscure procedures will also lead to investor delays as they seek to protect their investment. The repeated delays in the privatization of Aerolíneas Argentinas, which took close to two years to complete, more than double the projected timetable, is an example of the problems that can arise when procedures relating to the investment (as well as contractual relationships) are not clear to participants.

4. Sales of equity are preferable to voucher or other transfer schemes.

Although there is as of yet only a small amount of evidence regarding the workings of voucher schemes, the controversy surrounding the implementation of such programs in Czechoslovakia and Poland provide some warning about their practicality. The appeal of transfer schemes appears to be largely political rather than economic or managerial. While profit and equity sharing with workers could well work in the case of some enterprises, it appears that the generalized distribution schemes under consideration in CMEA countries will not help achieve most of the major objectives of privatization described in the first section of this paper. The main exception is that it would help to widen equity ownership among the population.

The advantages of sales over transfers of equity are clear in regards to other major objectives of privatization, in particular the likelihood of having access to improved management and technical expertise, enhancing competition among prospective investors and generating positive effects on the fiscal accounts or the external debt.

This does not mean that some form of discount sale of shares may not prove to be effective. For instance, it may be worthwhile to study the possible sale of shares in farm enterprises at some discount to workers and residents of agricultural communities. Still, practical considerations would probably make this approach difficult.

5. Privatizations are highly effective in attracting foreign investment.

There has been great success in this regard in Latin America as shown by the cases of Argentina, Chile and Mexico. Mexico has carried out some of the more sophisticated and well structured transactions involving the sale of common equity to foreign shareholders and to direct investors as well. It has been able, for instance, to sell important stakes in key companies such as Mexicana de Aviación and Telmex to foreign companies which will have a substantial say in management and operations. Mexico has also been able to attract large inflows of portfolio investment into shares of formerly state companies, even under still restrictive regulations that limit foreign holdings of voting shares.

In CMEA countries, foreign investment in state companies will have to be largely of the direct form since capital markets are still in an embryonic stage. But other mechanisms would have to be assessed. One mechanism which is very likely to be appropriate is the direct placement of securities with investor groups abroad. This has taken place already in Poland and Hungary among emigré groups, but it could well be taylored to other specific investor groups. A good example could be the placement of shares in tourism enterprises among companies in the same activity abroad. Ordinarily, direct placements tend to be most effective when the investors already understand well the business.

6. Fiscal objectives must not drive the privatization process.

Fiscal balance is highly important and the privatization process must contribute to it. But centering the privatization process on the need to achieve specific revenue goals is likely to distort the process or to exert pressure to carry out transactions without proper preparation. One way to approach this problem is to budget conservatively the revenues derived from privatization, assigning the bulk of the revenues to a special fund earmarked for discretionary spending, preferably capital expenditures.

The reduction in net subsidies arising from privatization is a better criterion to guide the privatization process than are revenue goals. Realistic pricing must be restored to the economy. Privatization could become a key instrument in butressing the functioning of a proper price system.

IV. Comments About Privatization in Cuba

Cuba has probably the most rigid and distorted economy of any socialist country. Unlike some of the Eastern European countries, the process of reform and decentralization has not been started in any significant way. Management, technology, marketing knowhow and the productivity of Cuban firms are well below international standards. Because of this and the lack of a proper institutional framework, privatization of some firms through sales of assets in general may not be feasible. Manufacturing companies linked to Eastern European suppliers are not likely to be profitable. Liquidation of many of these firms will have to be accomplished in an orderly fashion.

However, a number of large firms with a dominant market position will be good candidates for early privatization. Typically this may involve cement, beverages, mining, petroleum, utilities, some chemical industries as well as others. Sugar mills and other agroindustrial plants are also early candidates for privatization since their cost structure could be aligned with international prices in the short-term. Opportunities for foreign direct investment will also be strong in the case of the larger firms and in the tourism sector.

Substantial entry of new firms can be expected in the service sectors. Retail activities are likely to be at the forefront of this process as would be firms offering personal services. The lack of capital will restrain firm formation largely to labor intensive activities.

Cuba's exile community offers major assets in the restructuring of state firms as well as in the formation of new businesses. The community's professional and managerial skills, capital and linkages to international markets and companies will be important boosters in the implementation of successful privatizations. But the great problems with privatization in East Germany illustrate the difficulties of the process under even stronger conditions of support from fellow citizens and the government of the Federal Republic of Germany. Cuba's relative advantage would be to learn from the trials of the privatization processes in Eastern Europe and Latin America and to be able to improve upon the design and implementation of such programs.

Comments by José Ramón de la Torre

I concur with Luis on the basic premise that privatization is an essential ingredient of a broad-based package of liberalization measures. Although costly and potentially disrupting in the short term, it must be done relatively fast and in parallel with the development of measures that provide the necessary infrastructure for the efficient function of a modern market economy. Where Luis fails is in distinguishing between the often contradictory goals of equity and efficiency in the choice of privatization tools and programs. What is just and fair is not necessarily what is best.

The example of Eastern European countries' handling of the return of confiscated properties is an excellent case of the dangers involved in such programs. Insuffient attention to the uncertainly introduced by complex restitution policies into such consideration as the permanency of property rights can bring serious difficulties to the best intentioned program. Also, different types of assets (real property vs. businesses, large vs. small, agricultural land vs. regulated utilities, etc.) require significantly differentiated treatment, a point Luis does not develop.

Finally, related issues such as the valuation of foreign exchange, the role of foreign investment, and the desire for establishing a broad distribution of property rights must be considered within the same equity/efficiency paradox. In closing, Luis has provided us with a first attempt, and a valuable one, to discern the lessons from a variety of experiences under highly diverse circumstances. But much remains to be done in terms of a generalized model of privatization that must be rooted in economic analysis and enriched by the ample empirical evidence. Being last in this process is a definite advantage.

Some Lessons of Soviet Economic Reform

Kent Osband 1/

The progress, or lack of it, in Soviet economic reform is by now broadly familiar to every student of socialist and formerly socialist economies. In addition to the nearly daily discussions in the press, two comprehensive surveys, including assessments of alternative reform strategies, have been published within the last nine months--one by the EC 2/ and one jointly by the IMF, IBRD, OECD, and EBRD. 3/ In search of a comparative advantage, I shall in this paper neither review Soviet economic development systematically nor forecast future developments, but will instead try to extract some lessons for market-oriented reform.

The basic problem with Soviet economic reform is very simple: there has not been enough of it. There are noble visions, debates galore, swarms of Western well-wishers flying in and out of Moscow, and reform legislation by the bucket, but not much in the way of implementation. What makes this especially tragic, albeit darkly ironic, is that a more successful path was and is so near. Its cornerstone is less a determination to do than a willingness to let happen. Let people trade, let them produce, let them move, let them own property and let them sell it. Let them hire and fire and be hired and be fired. In short, let the Soviet economy rise or fall with the initiatives of a couple of hundred million individuals. This path will succeed as no other path will.

In saying this, I am not suggesting that reform is easy, that concerted action by the state is unnecessary, or that ideals of social justice must be abandoned. On the contrary, a thorough transformation in the Soviet Union, even under the most radical variant, will take decades. The material infrastructure must be thoroughly overhauled and modernized. More importantly, a new legal, commercial, financial, and social security infrastructure must not simply be built--in some respects from scratch--but also must become sufficiently routine and traditional that people can and will rationally plan on its continuation. In this process of construction and reconstruction, there is a chance to create societies that more fundamentally equal, more harmonious, and more protective of the environment than any that exist today. But if they are to endure--much less to respect other human values--these societies must work with the market and not against it. They must safeguard property rights, and through the very design of their institutions assure that commitments made today, whether to their own citizens or to foreigners, will not lightly be breached tomorrow.

1/ International Monetary Fund, Washington, D.C. 20431. The views expressed are those of the author and do not necessarily represent those of the Fund. This paper was written before the recently-foiled coup.

2/ "Stabilization, Liberalization, and Devolution", European Economy, No. 45, December 1990.

3/ International Monetary Fund, The World Bank, Organization for Economic Cooperation and Development, European Bank for Reconstruction and Development, A Study of the Soviet Economy (3 Volumes), Paris: OECD, February 1991. The main findings are summarized in The Economy of the USSR: Summary and Recommendations, Washington, D.C.: The World Bank, December 1990.

The Primacy of Reform

Having sketched the ethereal grand picture, I shall now draw specific lessons from Soviet experience. The first concerns the primacy of reform. When Gorbachev came to power, he and his colleagues were less concerned about reform than about modernization, which they saw as essential both to civilian economic development and to long-term political and military strength. To this end they planned, under the banner of "acceleration", for large investments in engineering and machine-building, strict quality control, and better labor discipline. Reform was secondary. 1/

On virtually all important counts, the modernization program was a failure. Quality control caused bottlenecks, and foundered on the lack of market assessments of quality. Investment targets in machine-building in effect assumed the productivity improvements they were supposed to foster. They could not be met, and thereby added to unfinished construction and other structural imbalances in the economy. Surprisingly, the labor discipline campaigns, which were thought to be harmless, caused perhaps the most damage. Clampdowns on speculation and other "non-labor" income chilled legitimate private production. Worse still, the prohibitionist campaign against alcohol cost the budget 1-2 percent of GDP, exacerbated shortages of other goods through diversion of consumer expenditures, and encouraged massive bootlegging and corruption, without delivering more than a transitory shock to alcohol consumption. Failure was sealed by the slide in world market prices for Soviet oil, the nuclear disaster at Chernobyl, and, especially, the destabilization ensuant on **glasnost** and political liberalization.

The Market as Organizing Principle

Open discussions and setbacks in modernization quickly brought market reform to the fore. However, the market was still seen primarily as an adjunct to state planning, as a tool for improving plan design and implementation, rather than as the basic organizing principle of the economy. This was a second mistake.

The intended centerpiece of reform, the Law on State Enterprises, was adopted in June 1987 for implementation in January 1988. Enterprise managers were given wide-ranging autonomy, and mandatory output targets were abolished. Direct government needs would be met through procurement contracts ("state orders"), while central planners and the ministries would concentrate on long-term strategy.

In practice, state orders extended far beyond direct government needs, embracing over 80 percent of output in 1988. On the one hand, planners and ministries sought through state orders to ensure the production of unprofitable items; on the other hand, enterprises

---

1/ It has been argued that reform was always high on some leaders' agenda but had to be promoted slyly and in piecemeal fashion against conservative resistance. See, for example, Anders Aslund, Gorbachev's Struggle for Economic Reform, Ithaca, New York: Cornell University Press, 1989. The present analysis is less concerned with an individual leader's psychology than with the policy choices made, for whatever reasons, by the leadership as a whole.

clamored for state orders to improve their chances of receiving centrally-allocated supplies. The Law on State Enterprises also failed to clarify enterprise rights vis-a-vis the ministries or to set up procedures for enforcement. It did, however, loosen controls over input and output mixes and leave a greater share of profits with enterprises to use as they wished. Uncertain about future policy, enterprises sought to convert their monetary windfall into immediately tangible benefits. Average wages and salaries, which traditionally increased about 2-3 percent per year, rose by over 8 percent annually in 1988 and 1989. The number of new construction projects rose by 40 percent in 1988 alone.

With prices controlled and budget constraints soft, greater autonomy did not yield the hoped-for improvements in productivity. On the contrary, bottlenecks spread in production, while consumer goods shortages disheartened workers. In 1989, the rise in "above-norm" unfinished construction absorbed close to the entire officially-recorded increase in national income. 1/

Price Reform

Shortages could have been eased by freeing prices or--if liberalization was too frightening--by raising prices administratively. Retail prices for food staples, which had been frozen since 1962, had fallen far below their opportunity costs, as had the wholesale prices for fuel and raw materials. By 1988, direct subsidies of meat and dairy products amounted to 5 percent of GDP, and indirect subsidies for perhaps another 3 percent. Domestic oil prices were less than one third of world market prices, even at the overvalued official rate.

The authorities repeatedly balked at price reform. This was a third mistake, although at the time it may have seemed politically wise. Unquestionably, price reform was and is unpopular. Low fixed prices had over the years acquired a moral symbolism, allegedly reflecting both victory over market volatility and social commitment to the poor. Perhaps more important, various groups had privileged access to deficit goods, and were as reluctant to relinquish their **de facto** property right as any other property owner would be. For example, subsidized meat is distributed exclusively in the cities, especially the main cities, and much of it is channeled to the elite through closed distribution systems. 2/ With fuels and raw materials, first claim has traditionally gone to heavy industry. As late as spring 1990, as then-Prime Minister Ryzhkov discovered, to advocate price reform was to court political suicide. Nevertheless, price reform could not be postponed indefinitely: wholesale prices were raised in late 1990, and retail prices in April 1991. As a result of the delay, the economy is weaker; the transition, still incomplete, must be harsher; and public confidence in the government is even lower.

1/ Soviet investment trends under **perestroika** are analyzed in Boris Rumer, "Investment Performance in the 12th Five-Year Plan", Soviet Studies, Vol. 43, No. 3, 1991, pp. 451-472.

2/ According to the government newspaper Izvestia of November 19, 1987, meat, on average, was almost 50 percent more expensive for relatively poor families (per capita earnings of less than 50 rubles per month) than relatively rich ones (per capita earnings of more than 150 rubles per month). When differences in amounts purchased were taken into account, relatively rich families received three times more meat subsidies than relatively poor ones.

Unleashing the Private Sector

The growing imbalances in state production and pricing had their bright side. They offered fantastic opportunities to private entrepreneurs. With or without a crisis, unleashing the so-called "Second Economy" would have been a sure economic winner, as the experiences of every single centrally-planned economy attest. Indeed, the non-state sector has grown markedly under Gorbachev. However, it could have grown much more--and in more aboveground, tax-bearing channels -- if the authorities had let it. This was a fourth mistake.

The legal high point was the Law on Cooperatives of May 1988. It accorded cooperatives, defined broadly enough to embrace both giant collective farms and three-person families, equal status with state enterprises. Coops could lease property, subcontract to other coops or individuals, hire outside labor, and raise capital from banks and outside shareholders. At reformers' insistence, clauses were inserted to simplify registration, prevent arbitrary closure, and limit state regulation of production and sales. By October 1990, over 200 hundred thousand cooperatives had been registered, employing 5 million people, or 3.5 percent of the labor force. Yet the Law fell far short of its promise, in part through its own loopholes, in part through unpunished violations, and in part through subsequent amendments.

Private business continues to face a public resentful of high markups, state enterprises hostile to competitors, planners anxious about erosion of price controls and tax revenues, and corrupt officials, not to mention outright gangsters, eager for spoils. Not surprisingly, many private businesses do evade taxes, pay off criminals, link up with monopolies, and charge high markups. However, the main policy response should be more liberalization, not less. Reducing entry barriers and providing private entrepreneurs better legal protection would stimulate competition, limit criminal opportunities, and lead to lower markups. While policies have generally improved over the last year, the overall regulatory environment recalls the pre-reform Peru described in The Other Path 1/ more than it does any OECD country.

Unbundling Property Rights

The impact of small-scale private enterprise would be greatest in trade and services. Without "marketizing" the state sector, however, improvements in agriculture and manufacturing will be slow. Unfortunately, in complete contrast to the liberalization of the private sector, reform of the state sector in socialist or formerly socialist economies has nowhere yet been a major success. The core problem is the failure to unbundle property rights. A typical socialist enterprise is not simply a business under state ownership, but also an administrative department, a jobs scheme, an apartment builder, a landlord, a provider

---

1/ Hernando de Soto, The Other Path, New York: Harper & Row, 1989. The regulatory environment varies greatly by republic and sometimes even by region within republics. The Baltic republics are approaching the standards of, say, Poland or Hungary in the 1980s. The least restructuring has occurred in Central Asia, but there the "Second Economy" has long thrived with official complicity.

of day care, an operator of recreation centers and vacation resorts, and a sponsor of public works. To provide the right incentives--both internally and to potential competitors--the enterprise must become, at the very least, an independent public corporation, with clearly-specified assets and liabilities, clearly-defined public responsibilities, and clearly-limited claims on or from the budget. 1/ This is a fifth lesson of reform.

While the Soviets are moving in this direction, they are not moving nearly rapidly enough. Shortcomings of the Law on State Enterprises were mentioned above. In addition to state orders and overbearing production ministries, enterprises face a bewildering and ever-changing array of taxes, rents, and other levies. Tax reform is hampered by the instability of authorities and jurisdictional struggles between them, as is the enforcement of commercial contracts. Western-style balance sheets often cannot be calculated, for lack of knowledgeable accountants or because state agencies cannot agree on who owns what. Responsibilities for employee benefits or public works are left hanging.

Except in the Baltic republics, there is not a strong constituency for restoring expropriated property to its former owners or their heirs, and hence, little need to separate old value from new value. Unfortunately, this blessing is more than offset by competing national and regional claims on assets. For the Soviet Union as a whole, the crucial contest involves some partly-frozen real estate in northwest Siberia, under which happens to lie some of the world's largest deposits of oil--at least half a trillion dollars' worth, at current prices--and about 30 percent of the world's confirmed natural gas reserves. Currently, ownership is being ceded to the Russian republic, but the Union government claims the oil wells, the pipelines, and hefty royalties. Local authorities have staked claims too, partly on behalf of minority native peoples but mostly on behalf of the two-million-plus European migrants. The latter tend to be highly paid by Soviet standards but poorly housed and starved for modern amenities.

Ownership rights are difficult to clarify even at a local level. Privatization of housing in Moscow, for example, has been mired in disputes over rights of disposal, not only between the city government and higher authorities, but also between the city government and neighborhood councils.   However property rights are allocated, it is important to give the new owners the right to sell or lease long-term to others, independently of their other activities. 2/ Paradoxically, the right to sell property encourages owners to invest in it. Also, a market in property encourages more efficient owners to buy out less efficient ones. Many of the vaunted union and republican proposals for turning over land to the peasants suffer from exactly this defect: the peasant who stops cultivating the land must surrender it to the collective farm or local authorities.

1/ Some would argue that enterprise property rights cannot be effectively unbundled short of a mass transfer to private ownership. Soviet experience as yet neither confirms nor refutes this. It does show--although less vividly than does, say, Polish experience--that debates about the proper forms and scope of privatization can be used to postpone needed layoffs and other aspects of unbundling.

2/ For example, it is fine to give workers shares in their enterprises, provided workers can dispose of the shares without regard to labor status.

Political Stability

In any event, property rights are only as good as the expectations of their enforcement. For foreign businessmen, enforcement is much less certain now than it was before **perestroika**. Then, the authorities looked after whatever foreign economic ties they deigned to permit. Now, the authorities hustle foreign investment, but no one knows whether agreements will be followed through. For example, the Chevron Corporation, which thought it had negotiated a long-term share in the Tenghiz oil fields of Kazakhstan, now finds itself assailed both by old-guard foes of Western investment on any terms and by free-market democrats convinced the bidding was bungled. This brings us to a sixth lesson of Soviet economic reform, regarding the need for stability.

Disunion

Instability in the Soviet Union reflects the heritage and decay of Communist Party rule, and of the tsarist rule that preceded it. At risk now is not simply the political or economic stance of the Union but its very existence as a multinational state. The various republics and ethnic groups differ vastly in language, demographics, religion, education, economic activity, and political perceptions. 1/ **Glasnost** gave vent to long-standing resentments, and in the process inadvertently helped kindle new ones. Political decentralization is inevitable.

As the Western studies of the Soviet economy point out, political decentralization need not rule out economic integration. The latter should be encouraged. Realistically, however, the trends are not auspicious. The existing interregional division of labor, while extensive, rests on a central administrative fiat that has become increasingly difficult to sustain. The alternative is voluntary exchange, but shortage makes producers reluctant to sell at official prices, and local authorities naturally try to prevent the export of deficit goods. Labor mobility is severely constrained by housing shortage and by the **propiski,** or permits, required for residence in large cities. Voluntary capital flows across regions are discouraged by fear of seizure--indeed, foreign investment is better protected than interregional investment.

Another challenge of economic union is to delineate budgetary authority between different levels of government, lest each government be excessively tempted to spend at the others' expense. 2/ Years ago the Union officials had worked out an effective though extreme solution: the republican budgets were line items in the unified union budget approved by the center. Now that independent budgets are allowed, some other controls must be found. Also, more explicit transfer mechanisms must be devised--in particular, for subsidy of Central Asia, whose population is growing 1-3 percent faster per year than the

---

1/ For a survey of ethnic and republican issues bearing on economic reform, see A Study of the Soviet Economy, Volume I, Appendix II-4, pp. 185-234.

2/ Presently the various fiscal authorities quarrel over not simply how the tax revenues will divided, but who will collect them, because the collectors of taxes cannot be trusted to hand them over.

population of the European republics, and whose near-term economic prognosis is poor. At stake are republics' wealth and power, relative to the center and to each other, so agreement will not be easy.

In short, an economic union cannot simply be preserved, but to a considerable extent must be recreated. Given the present tensions, attempts to recreate it through central decree may be counterproductive. Local leaders will be tempted to portray the center as carting off domestic products, fostering the immigration of outsiders, and asserting claims on local property. References to past behavior could lend credence to such claims.

Also, although an economic and monetary union is often described (e.g., in the Soviet presidential guidelines of October 1990) as being compatible with considerable republican discretion over the forms and pacing of economic reform, in fact it is not. A republic raising or decontrolling the price of deficit goods would tend to draw in rubles and supplies from the other republics. Republics losing supplies would presumably respond with direct export controls, while the reforming republic would probably restrict purchases by nonresidents. Similar considerations would apply to privatization. Already there is much evidence of this. Russia's 1990 hike in procurement prices for meat prompted the Ukraine to restrict meat exports to Russia. Proofs of local residence have been imposed at various times for purchase at official stores in the Ukraine, Estonia, Leningrad and Moscow. Internal customs barriers are proliferating.

Under those conditions, separate currencies might offer better prospects for reform, with less distortion of trade and greater incentives for fiscal discipline. The key problem would be to assure the credibility of the currency, first as a means of exchange and second as a store of value. The Ukraine's introduction of the **kharvonets** (soon to be superseded by the **griven**) illustrates these issues. Technically, the **kharvonets** was not a currency but a coupon issued for use with rubles. Many purchases inside the Ukraine required equal numbers of **kharvontsy** and rubles, but the former was the binding constraint since there are fewer of them. Their introduction reportedly caused an immediate recovery in state retail trade. However, methods of distributing alternative monies, regulating their supply, and ensuring their acceptability as payment are still being ironed out.

If republics or groups of republics issued new currencies, the ruble overhang would resolve itself. What would happen next is unclear. On the one hand, a hardened Russian currency might quickly supplant the rest, with less turmoil than if rival currencies had never been tried. On the other hand, rival currencies might encourage autarky and discourage external investment. In any event, separate currencies are at best an aid to market reform, and not a substitute for it.

Indecisiveness

Soviet instability has been exacerbated by a vacillating, indecisive economic policy. The main hallmark of "Gorbonomics" seems to have been the search for a happy medium between the old system and a normal market economy. 1/ To what extent this search has been voluntary, and to what extent it has been forced by political struggle between reformers and conservatives, is difficult to judge. From a political standpoint, the search has not been completely fruitless. Early in **perestroika**, deferring economic choices may have facilitated ideological and political liberalization, because interest groups hurt by those choices might otherwise have thrown in their lot more forcefully with political conservatives. Equivocation also may have helped Gorbachev portray himself domestically as an indispensable moderator between extremes.

From a purely economic view, however, equivocation has done little good. First, as we have seen, the resulting measures do not add up to a coherent reform program. Second, the ebb and flow of schemes encourage low-level officials--who may be hostile to reform to begin with--not to enforce them, or to enforce them arbitrarily. Third, people and firms are reluctant to invest for the long term, because they do not know where policy is heading.

While such difficulties are not peculiar to the Soviet economy, they are vastly more serious than in developed market economies, in large part because of the design of Soviet government. There are relatively few legal restraints on state institutions, jurisdictional boundaries between insitutions are fuzzy, and the judicial system is unreliable. These characteristics are not oversights, but reflect a conscious decision to increase the power of the top leadership and let the Communist Party mediate disputes. While the top leadership could and did change course, the edifice as a whole suffered less from wobbliness than from rigidity, but only as long as the Party was hegemon.

Some people, both Soviets and non-Soviets, think that substituting majority decisions for Party decisions would suffice to restabilize the government. Unfortunately, it would not. Majority rule, when unrestrained by constitution or tradition, tends to be cumbersome, fickle, and predatory. Hence, a stable and growth-promoting democracy figures ways to tie its own hands. It may require super-majorities on certain issues, prohibit action on others, and delegate still other issues, such as enforcement of contracts or regulation of the money supply, to quasi-independent authorities. 2/

Creating a Constituency

Economic reform would have been more popular in the Soviet Union, and the political situation less precarious, had more people been offered a tangible opportunity to prosper from reform. In China, for example, the **de facto** redistribution of collective farm lands created an enormous constituency to stick with reform and extend it. In the Soviet Union, by contrast, there has so far been no mass privatization. New businesses still employ but a small percentage of the work force. Higher wages and social benefits, the real value of

---

1/ This aim is clearly spelled out in Abel Aganbegyan, The Economic Challenge of Perestroika, Bloomington, Indiana: Indiana University Press, 1988. Aganbegyan was Gorbachev's chief economic advisor in the early stages of **perestroika**.

2/ These issues are discussed in more depth in Dennis Mueller, "Choosing a Constitution in East Europe: Lessons from Public Choice", Journal of Comparative Economics, Vol. 15, 1991, pp. 325-348.

which have been eroded through shortage, provide few incentives to work harder or better. The need to actively create vested interests in reform, instead of simply searching for pre-existing ones, is a seventh lesson.

A quick expansion of private plots would have been very popular among both farmers and customers in private food markets. Admittedly, however, land redistribution would not have had the same impact in the Soviet Union as it did in China. Less than 20 percent of Soviets work in agriculture, and farming is more dependent than in China on state-controlled industrial inputs, storage, or processing.

For a bigger reform boost in the cities, state-owned apartments could be turned over free, or at very low cost, to their tenants. Private housing arouses little antipathy, partly because Marxism tended not to treat owner-occupied housing as capital (although it did consider resale for profit to be exploitative), and partly because the interiors are hidden from public view. Hence, housing is a convenient shelter for wealth. Relaxing the restrictions on private resale or lease would let the existing housing stock be used more efficiently and reduce constraints on labor mobility.

Privatization of housing would break the state monopoly (albeit a monopoly riven by competing republican, municipal, and enterprise jurisdictions) over the lease of commercial space. The difficulty cooperatives have in securing legal accommodation often serves as a pretext for denying licenses or forcing their subordination to state officials.

Privatization of housing would, furthermore, increase employment opportunities in the repair and refurbishing of the existing housing stock. Legal and underground employment of private craftsmen is already widespread, but the average volume of activity per housing unit is much greater for private housing (e.g., summer cottages in the countryside).

Even where businesses have nothing to do directly with housing, privatization of housing can assist their development by providing entrepreneurs with potential collateral for loans.

One objection to giving tenants title is that some people will benefit considerably more than others. However, differential benefits are common to any mass privatization. In any case, it is difficult to define a completely fair allocation, much less enforce it. Depending on the context, better-than-average housing could be a form of wage payment in kind or recompense for years in below-average housing, or it could have been purchased at high prices on the black market. Assessments of fair value, in the absence of a history of market prices for similar property, would be extremely crude.

Another objection to housing giveaways is that the state allegedly needs the revenues from sales. However, mass auctions would be impossibly unwieldy. People would grumble, with justification, that the authorities had broken yet another implicit contract (low charges for housing), while evictions would grab unfavorable media attention. Scarce managerial expertise would be diverted from the more demanding task of restructuring and/or privatizing state enterprises. Finally, current rents are so low as to fall below maintenance costs, so even turning properties over free would save the state money.

The Role of Culture

The eighth lesson concerns the role of culture. It is often alleged that Soviet citizens as a whole are too inured to the old system to respond flexibility and rapidly to market incentives, or to put it another way, that the entrepreneurial stuffing has been kicked out of them. Most of the evidence is strongly to the contrary. To begin with, one can simply observe the sharp contrast between the goods at citizens' disposal and the (lack of) goods in state stores. The contrast suggests that Soviets are very enterprising, but that the market incentives favor socially wasteful shopping over production. One should also note the explosion in cooperative membership since entry was eased.

A joint Soviet-American team recently tried to compare popular attitudes to free markets in the Soviet Union and the United States. 1/ Administering identical telephone surveys in Moscow and New York, the researchers concluded that the two groups were basically very similar in their attitudes towards fairness and income inequality and in their understanding of how markets work.

While culture does not seem to strongly influence receptivity to markets, it is crucial to economic development in another way; namely, the thirst for skills and knowledge. Here the Soviet record is mixed. The Russians, for example, have made a determined effort to absorb Western technology and arts. Russian mathematics, physics, literature, and ballet, each of which has drawn heavily on others' contributions, is justifiably world-renowned. Unfortunately, in the social sciences, the dominant Soviet ideology held for most of this century held that Soviet organization was so advanced that the rest of the world had little to offer. With hindsight, shamefully, Soviet scientists concede they may have traveled up a historical dead end. Still, they are only just emerging from their isolation, and remain sketchily informed even of experiences in other socialist countries. In this respect the past does indeed die hard.

Foreign Aid

The ninth lesson concerns appropriate foreign aid. Foreign training and technical assistance can speed up the transfer of knowledge and skills. It is relatively inexpensive, easy to administer, and, for the donor, essentially risk-free. The international financial institutions and Western statistical agencies are experienced in training officials, while Soviet students would be welcome in Western universities. A few hundred million dollars annually in Western government aid--a pittance compared to the credits already being extended to the Soviet Union and the much larger credits being discussed--would suffice to train tens of thousands of bankers, managers, accountants, economists, and corporate lawyers. In

---

1/ Robert Shiller, Maxim Boycko, and Vladimir Korobov, "Popular Attitudes Toward Free Markets: The Soviet Union and the United States Compared", American Economic Review, Vol. 81, No. 3, June 1991, pp. 385-400.

addition to the immediate benefits to the Soviet Union, the training offers diplomatic returns to the donors in terms of good will and improved communication. To facilitate training and make sure it reaches those who need it, technical assistance should be extended to republican levels as well as to the center, and at times even to municipal levels.

The wisdom of large-scale economic aid is less obvious. In the press, and even among some economists, the question is typically posed as follows: Is a guarantee of radical, whole-hearted Soviet reform worth, say, 100 billion dollars? Considering the political and military stakes, presumably the answer is yes. The question is fundamentally misleading, however. No guarantee is for sale, because short of occupying the Soviet Union militarily and/or rebuilding the political and legal institutions -- as was done in post-war Japan and Germany, with which the Soviet Union today is often, though wrongly, identified -- no guarantee could be enforced.

Criticisms along these lines prompt the aid question to be reformulated: How much is an extra x percent probability of radical, whole-hearted Soviet reform worth? However, this version is also disconcerting. The number symbolized by "x" is rarely, if ever, specified. It is not even clear that large-scale aid will raise the probability of economic reform. Indeed, what little evidence we have suggests the contrary. Why, for example, did the Soviet Union, in contrast to China, Hungary, and Poland, not embark on economic reform in the 1970s? A crucial differences seems to have been the foreign exchange cushion provided by Soviet oil reserves.

Even now, future claims on Soviet natural resources could easily be sold in international markets for hard currency, provided these claims were secure. The Soviet inability to offer this security is simply the flip side of its unstable commitment to reform. Also, large-scale economic aid could take pressure off the Soviet Union to seek out and encourage private investment.

Hence, it would appear wiser to defer consideration of large-scale economic aid, as the Group of Seven did, pending sturdier assurances of Soviet dedication to reform.

Conclusions

The main conclusions of this paper, lessons drawn from Soviet experience, are summarized below:

-- Reform takes precedence over modernization.

-- The basic organizer of the economy should be the market.

-- Price liberalization is deferred at great peril.

-- Unleash the private sector, quickly.

-- Property rights in the state sector must be unbundled.

-- Political stability should be encouraged through delegation and demarcation of authority.

-- Mass constituencies for reform should be actively fostered, by giving people tangible stakes in its continuation.

-- Cultural attitudes to markets do not matter much, but cultural attitudes to human capital do.

-- Foreign technical assistance is invaluable, but large-scale foreign economic aid is double-edged.

These lessons are very elementary, and address only the initial questions of reform. Tomorrow the Soviet Union will face more advanced questions, of the sort that much of Eastern Europe faces today. How to privatize? What should be done with the industrial behemoths, and how quickly? How can budget constraints be tightened without strangling credit? What are appropriate social safety nets and environmental safeguards? What is the best path to convertibility? Neither Soviet nor East European experience as yet offers clear answers, or more precisely, whatever answers are there we do not yet clearly see.

I continually feel that the economic policy needs in reforming socialist countries far outstrip our profession's current technical capacity. It is as if we economists were 19th century biochemists learning about microbes, or 19th century physicists learning about electricity, who are asked to advise on major surgery or light bulb production. From tomorrow's perspective, we will surely not have worked very efficiently. Let us hope we can at least be useful. Most of the lessons drawn above concern basic hygiene and safety, on the order of "wash your hands and knives before you cut" and "don't stick your fingers in the socket". Sadly, in the present context such advice still bears repeating.

Abstracts

Cuban Economic Outcomes in the United States, 1960-1990
Jorge Salazar-Carrillo

This paper examines the characteristics of the Cuban diaspora in the United States, and its propensity to achieve business success. The results are based on the <u>Survey of Minority-Owned Business Enterprises</u>, 1987 Economic Census issued by the U.S. Department of Commerce in April 1991. These statistics conclusively depict the breadth and depth of entrepreneurship displayed by the Cuban Americans. Some of the obstacles and the forces molding the outcomes observed are succinctly considered.

The Effect of Learning English on the Earnings of Hispanic Men
Luis Locay and Arthur Diamond

Previous work on Hispanic men finds that earnings rise with English proficiency. Several studies have found, in fact, that previously found non-Hispanic/Hispanic earnings differentials can be accounted for completely by differences in English proficiency. We question existing work on two grounds. First of all, the more able are more likely to be proficient at any point in time, so that English proficiency may simply be a proxy for unmeasured ability. Ignoring this role of English proficiency will understate non-Hispanic/Hispanic earnings differentials and overstate the return to learning English. Our second question of existing work causes biases in the opposite direction. At least some Hispanics who are proficient in English at any point in time acquired their proficiency after entering the U.S. labor market. Such individuals cannot be expected to have had the same wage growth as those who were proficient from the start. Ignoring the history of when proficiency was acquired will overstate differences between non-Hispanics and Hispanics, and understate the return to learning English.

We use data from the 1976 Survey of Income and Education to construct a model of the acquisition of English proficiency. Using predicted as opposed to actual levels of English proficiency, we are able to avoid some of the pitfalls of previous work. We find that Hispanic men we <u>predict</u> to have been proficient prior to entering the U.S. labor market do <u>not</u> earn less than non-Hispanics with the same measured characteristics (schooling, work experience, etc.). This confirms previous results, but apparently because the above mentioned biases approximately cancel each other out. We also confirm that there is a positive return to learning English. Individuals who enter the U.S. labor market with low predicted English proficiency, but then experience rapid improvement in their English skills, earn less than you would expect of individuals with their English skills at the time of the survey. This is consistent with our hypothesis that an individual's history of English proficiency, and not just his current level, is important in determining earnings. We also find, contrary to previous work, that Cubans in the Northeast earn considerably more than other Hispanic groups in that region. We suspect this is due to selection. That is, Cubans in the Northeast are atypical of Cubans in general, the overwelming majority of whom have chosen to locate in South Florida.

The Industry Composition of Production and the Distribution of Income by Race and Ethnicity in Miami

Robert David Cruz

Employment Growth and Income Distribution in Miami

Miami is the central city of the greater Miami metropolitan area in southeastern Florida. It encompasses only approximately 28 square miles in an MSA that is nearly 332 square miles in total developed land area. One might consider the city to represent the urban core of the metropolitan area: it remains the largest employment center; it is characterized by the highest residential densities and intensities of land uses; and contains much of the metropolitan area's lower income housing. Approximately 21 percent of the MSA's population resides within the City's boundaries. Although Miami is a relatively young city (most of its growth occurred after World War II), economic and social trends over the past two decades have been similar in many ways to those trends witnessed in older U.S. cities. Despite a slight decline in official population estimates, the number of persons who work within the city's boundaries has grown steadily. The industry composition of employment, however, has changed significantly. An increasing proportion of those who work in the city, live outside its boundaries and the city's housing stock has been steadily "filtering" down to lower income groups. Household income of city residents has declined sharply. Between 1979 and 1983, the median family income of city residents declined by 17 percent in real terms (Cruz, 1989).1 The median family income of black residents, however, declined by 43 percent in real terms during this same short period. Median family income among Hispanics declined in real terms by 15 percent.

The observed declines in income reflect changing residential patterns in the metropolitan area with poorer families moving into city neighborhoods and more affluent families migrating to higher quality housing outside the city. The out-migration of black families to destinations with typically higher income, moreover, was particularly strong in the late 1970's.2 Similar patterns have been witnessed in other U.S. metropolitan areas (Kain, 1968; Mills and Price, 1984; Kasarda, 1985). Kasarda notes: The transformation of older cities from centers of production and distribution of material goods to centers of information exchange and service consumption has profoundly altered the capacity of these cities to offer employment opportunities for disadvantaged residents. [This result has been aggravated by] ... the exodus of middle-income population and general retail and service establishments from much of the city beyond the central business districts. (Kasarda, 1985, p.43)

Kain suggested that housing segregation limited black earnings because of higher commuting costs which discouraged employment, lack of labor market information, and higher incidence of discrimination as distance from black residential areas increases. Price and Mills (1985) provide empirical estimates of the negative effect of segregated housing on earnings of blacks, as this group may find housing only in the central city where job opportunities for their skill levels are relatively scarce.

In 1980, 314,000 persons worked within the City of Miami's boundaries. Only 28 percent of those employed in the city actually lived within the city's boundaries. Yet the City represented the place of employment for most of the city's black residents. This would be expected, given that poorer families are less likely to own private automobiles and the MSA's mass transit system provides relatively poor access to non-central city employment centers. The city's Hispanic population also depended heavily on central city jobs.3

Between 1970 and 1980, the number of persons working within the city's boundaries increased by 66 percent. A large proportion (49 percent) of the growth was concentrated in executives, managers, professional, technical and sales occupations. Yet few of the city's minority population were employed in such occupations in 1980. Approximately 18 percent of blacks who held jobs and lived within the City of Miami were employed in these occupations. By contrast, 27 percent of Hispanic workers and 52 percent of "non-Hispanic white" workers were employed in such occupations.4 The growth in employment by occupation is, of course, related to the growth of employment by industrial classification. The fastest growing industries during the 1970s were transportation, communication and utilities, professional and related services, and wholesale and retail trade (Rodríguez, 1987).

By 1980, dissatisfaction among black residents with their lack of participation in the city's economic expansion was quite evident, and this alienation has been cited among the causes of civil disturbances in the 1980's (Porter and Dunn, 1984).5 Although economic deprivation is not sufficient to explain civil disturbances (Lieberson and Silverman, 1965), poverty together with a perception of being excluded from the social system has been a common element of race riots (Caplan and Paige, 1968). While Porter and Dunn assert that Hispanic immigrants had taken jobs from black residents, and undoubtedly this was a widespread perception, no objective evidence of this conclusion has been put forward. Indeed, Table 1 reveals that significant gains in the number and proportion of blacks employed in higher paying "white collar" jobs occurred between 1970 and 1980. Hence, the reasons for the lack of participation of blacks in the City's economic progress may lie more with occupational distribution rather than with a loss of jobs to immigrant groups.6 Despite the small gains in the occupational distribution of black residents, however, the distribution of income changed very little for black city residents over the 1970s. In 1969, the income accrued by blacks within the city represented 15 percent of all income, although blacks represent 23 percent of the population. By 1979, the income of black residents represented 18 percent of all city income, but blacks then represented 25 percent of the population. The economic status of blacks relative to Hispanics, however, did worsen. In 1969, Hispanics comprised 59 percent of the population and their income represented 41 percent of the city's total income. By 1979, Hispanics' share of income had increased to 50 percent, while their share of the population had declined to 56 percent (see Table 2).

Estimates of employment growth within the city's boundaries during the 1980s are difficult to ascertain, but several indicators suggest a continuation of the pattern established in the previous decade. While the pace of employment growth has mostly likely decelerated along with the growth of employment at the MSA level, white collar employment has probably grown and blue collar jobs most likely have declined. The stock of prime office space within the city's downtown increased by 40 percent between 1980 and 1987.7 Between 1979 and 1988, the City of Miami Planning Department estimates that the area of land used for commercial activity grew by nearly 200 acres (10.3 percent growth over 1979), while industrial land uses fell by 205 acres (a 30 percent decrease over 1979).8 Commercial activity refers to retailing and office uses, while industrial refers to manufacturing and warehousing uses.

The number of workers in retail and wholesale trade activity within the city's boundaries grew by 9.4 and 3.1 percent, respectively, between 1982 and 1987. Service sector employment grew by 33 percent within this same period, with very large gains witnessed in hotel and lodging (93 percent), and engineering, accounting, management, et al (70 percent).

To the extent that income distribution across racial and ethnic groups is the result of the growth and composition of economic production, as well as changing residential patterns, the income trends observed during the 1970s are likely to have continued in the 1980s. The extended input-output model presented in the next section provides some empirical evidence on the link between income distribution and production.

The Model and Its Calibration

The model developed for the City of Miami consists of 31 productive activities or industries, eight labor occupations, and three household groups. The metropolitan region is separated into the urban "core" (ie., the City of Miami) and rest of the urban area (the Miami MSA). Each industry within the "core" faces demand for its output from both firms and households located within the core and from firms and households located outside the core. In order to produce output, local firms must purchase intermediate goods from other firms and hire labor and capital services. Payments for labor services are assumed to accrue to locally available labor, while profit type income is assumed distributed to households outside the region. Some labor commutes to work from outside the urban core, and so not all labor income accrues to city residents. The labor income that does accrue to city residents generates demand for locally produced goods and services. To a much lesser degree, the labor income accruing to noncity residents also results in demand for goods and services produced within the urban core. That is, workers that are employed in the city but who live outside its boundaries may consume some goods and services within the city. All prices and wages rates are taken as exogenously given and fixed.

Production in the model is characterized by an input-output structure. There are 31 industries identified in the model. The direct input coefficients were determined by regionalizing a national table of direct coefficients that had been updated to 1985.9 The location quotient technique for regionalizing the direct coefficients was used (see Miller and Blair, 1985, pp.296-99). A special tabulation of employment within the City was prepared by the U.S. Department of Commerce from County Business Patterns (unedited subcounty data). These employment figures, although unofficial estimates, were used to determine the location quotients for each of the 31 industries.

Labor income per unit of output was disaggregated among eight occupational categories. Labor compensation per unit of output by industry was determined from the national input-output table, and an employment by occupation and industry matrix for Florida was used to distribute per unit compensation to each occupation.10 Compensation per unit of output by occupational group was computed by:

$$u_{kj} = (e_{kj}/e_j) \cdot (w_k/\bar{w}) \cdot u_j$$

where

e_{kj} ≡ the number of workers in occupational group "k" employed in industry "j";

e_j ≡ total industry "j" employment;

w_k ≡ the median weekly earnings of occupational group "k";

$\bar{w}$ ≡ the average of median earnings for all occupation groups; and

u_j ≡ total labor compensation per unit of output for industry "j".

Median weekly earnings were obtained from Current Wage Developments and refer to national wages. The ratio $w_k/\bar{w}$ is taken as a proxy for the ratio of average wages paid to a particular type of worker relative to the industry-wide average wage.

From Journey to Work data we were able to estimate the proportion of laborers in each occupation that lived within the City's boundaries. Since only a fraction of workers in each occupation lived within the City, only a fraction of labor compensation from each industry accrues to City residents. Each unit of income accruing to labor of a specific occupational group was, therefore, distributed to city households according to the proportion of MSA workers (in 1980) belonging to that occupational group that resided within the city. Labor income to noncity residents was distributed according to the proportion of MSA workers residing in the remainder of the MSA. This practice treats workers as though they are homogeneous within the same occupation and receive the same wage rate regardless of where they chose to live in the region.11

The average (and marginal) propensities to consume were determined in a two step procedure. In the first step, the national propensities (based on the updated 1977 I-O table) were regionalized using the location quotient technique with national employment data as the reference point. In the second stage another set of location quotients were calculated using MSA employment levels as the reference point. In those cases where the location quotient with the MSA as the reference point was less than unity, a second adjustment was performed to allow for consumption purchases by city residents in the remainder of the MSA rather than from city firms. Accordingly, the consumption coefficients of city households, in those cases, were determined by:

$$b_i = \left[\frac{(e_i/e)}{(e^*_i/e^*)} \right] \cdot \left[\frac{(e_i/e)}{|(E_i/E)|} \cdot B_i \right]$$

where "e_i" refers to industry employment within the city; the absence of the subscript refers to total employment; the superscript "*" refers to MSA employment; the uppercase "E" refers to national employment; and B_i is the national propensity to consume industry "i" output.

To determine the propensity of noncity residents to consume goods and services from city firms, location quotients for the remainder of the MSA were calculated using MSA employment levels as the reference point. In those cases where these location quotients were less than unity, the propensities to spend on goods and services produced in the city were determined by:

$$b_i r = \left[1 - \frac{(e_i r/e_r)}{(e^*_i/e^*)} \right] \cdot \left[\frac{|(e_i r/e_r)}{|(E_i/E)} \cdot B_i \right]$$

The mathematical structure of the model, which is provided in an appendix, is linear and can easily be solved to yield the output and payroll multipliers.

Once the payroll multipliers by occupation have been calculated, the impacts can be disaggregated among the different racial/ethnic groups according to the representation of each racial/ethnic group in each occupational category. This practice implies that all workers within an occupational category receive the same wage regardless of their race or ethnicity, and, thus, the multipliers over-estimate the impact on income for minority groups whenever wage discrimination is present.

Income Multipliers and Income Distribution

The payroll multipliers, disaggregated by race and ethnicity, for each of the 31 industries are presented in Table 3. Given the assumption that profit income accrues to nonresidents, the payroll multipliers represent the household income multipliers. The income multipliers are expressed as additional income per dollar of additional final sales in the respective industries. As one would expect, the income multipliers sum to less than unity, revealing the high degree of openness of such a small economy. The income multipliers for all household groups combined range from a low of 0.14 (for the Real Estate industry) to a high of 0.81 (for Other Financial industry).

The income multipliers also indicate considerable differences in the relative importance of various industries to the income of each social group. In a ranking of industries from highest income effect to lowest, only two industries (Textile and Apparel Manufacturing, and Other Transportation and Warehousing) appear among the top five for both blacks and Hispanics. Only one industry appears among the top five industries for both Hispanics and non-Hispanic whites, while blacks and non-Hispanic whites have no industries in common.

As a group, business and financial services and manufacturing (except for Textile and Apparel) rank relatively low in their impact on black income. Yet, it is only the growth of output in financial service industries that would lead to a decline in the relative income of blacks. In order for an increase in industry output to lead to a deterioration in the distribution of income for a given social group, the income multiplier for that group relative to the total income multiplier must be less than that social group's share of income. This difference between income (ie., payroll) multiplier share and 1970 income share is illustrated in Figure 1. The industries in Figure 1 are arranged by those with approximately the highest growth rates at the top to the slowest growing or declining industries at the bottom. All industries listed above Construction in Figure 1 grew at higher than average rates. The industries whose growth would be accompanied by a decline in the relative income of blacks are the Finance-Insurance and Real Estate group, Wholesale Trade, and Communication. Between 1970 and 1980, however, the industries that experienced the fastest growth rates were largely those whose growth adversely affected black income shares (see Table 4) or had no effect on their share of income. Indeed, within the last decade Miami has developed into a regional and international financial center.

The relative income of blacks is improved substantially by output growth in Agricultural Services, et al, Personal Services, Eating and Drinking Establishments, Hotel and Lodging, and Textile and Apparel Manufacturing. Manufacturing industries on the whole were either neutral or had a positive effect on blacks' share of income. During the 1970s, however, employment in Personal Services declined and employment in Retail Trade grew below the average rate. Manufacturing employment, moreover, expanded at a very slow pace. The remaining industries, which grew at above average rates, are approximately neutral in their effect on the relative income of blacks.

One may also note from Figure 1 that the scatter diagram of points for blacks are more clustered around the zero axis than the points for Hispanics. That is, in general, the growth of output is likely to have less of an impact on black income shares than on Hispanic income shares.12 In addition, despite the larger income multipliers for Hispanics, fewer industries are likely to have a positive impact on Hispanic income shares than are likely to increase black income shares. As in the case of blacks, those industries which grew faster than average between 1970 and 1980 were industries whose growth coincides with a decline in Hispanics' share of income. The growth in the share of income earned by Hispanics during the 1970s, therefore, could be attributed to the increase in this group's labor force participation rate (Table 1) and to increases in Hispanic representation among higher skilled occupations.

We should also emphasize that the growth and composition of production has not been the only determinant of the actual changes in income shares that have occurred within the city. Changing residential patterns (especially the out-migration of more affluent blacks), no doubt, played a critical role in this phenomenon. The results of the model indicate the potential impact on income distribution, when the residential patterns across racial groups and/or across income groups do not change, and the extent to which the composition of production influences the distribution of income. The results also show how the growth of production may be of little significance to a large proportion of the city's population. Figure 1 illustrates that the fastest growing industries during the 1970s were the ones whose income effects were disproportionately concentrated among non-Hispanic whites. Since relatively few non-Hispanic whites live in the city, most of the income effects accrue to non-residents.13 These results are, of course, consistent with an increased feeling of economic alienation on the part of black residents.

Conclusions

Demographic trends in U.S. urban centers have resulted in the decline of average income in major cities and a worsening of income distribution. The growth and composition of output within urban centers has also contributed to the increasing disparity of income among racial and ethnic groups. In the preceding sections, we have illustrated the empirical link between output and income distribution by looking at the specific example of Miami. In the case of Miami these structural changes in the urban economy have heightened social tensions to the point where confrontation between police and black residents have sometimes erupted into civil unrest. For this reason much of the focus of this paper has been on the period between 1970 and 1980, but the conditions which contributed to the decline in the relative income position of blacks in the 1970s continued into the 1980s, and so did the incidences of civil disturbances. As 1990 census data becomes available, it will be interesting to see if increases in black labor force participation rates and representation of blacks in "white collar" occupations were able to offset the negative distributional impacts of growth in financial service-type employment. It is clear that economic growth, in its present form, will not be able to improve the relative income position of black residents and upward mobility among occupations is required to narrow the income gap.

While Hispanics incomes performed relatively well during the 1970s, several factors suggest that this may not have continued into the 1980s. Factors that contributed to the increase in the relative income of Hispanics -- increases in labor force participation rates and representation in white collar jobs -- are not likely to have persisted in the 1980s. Labor force participation rates by 1980 had already reached levels near reasonable upper bounds, and the immigration of Hispanics during the 1980s, mainly from Mariel, Cuba and

Central America, included many semi-skilled and unskilled laborers.

As these demographic and economic trends continue, the economic growth experienced within the city becomes less of an important factor in the determination of economic welfare among city residents. Local economic development initiatives which target the growth of office type employment, moreover, become less significant to the objective of increasing the income of existing city residents.

Acknowledgements

I am very grateful to Robert Hessler for his valuable hours of research assistance in regionalizing the national I-O coefficients and debugging some of the software routines. Professor Maria Willumsen has provided me with her many insights into the problem of income distribution and economic development. Professor Antonio Jorge provided important comments and coordinated the research project with the City of Miami that served as the background for this study. I am also grateful for the suggestions of an anonymous referee. The author, of course, remains fully responsible for any shortcomings.

Endnotes

1. This data is from the Annual Housing Survey: 1983, Housing Characteristics for Selected Metropolitan Areas, U.S. Department of Commerce, Bureau of the Census. Median family income was computed as a weighted average of median income in renter occupied and owner occupied units. Except for black families, the decline in real income was due to inflation. The local CPI rose by 37 percent between 1979 and 1983.

2. Nearly 90 percent of blacks who migrated from the city to other areas within the MSA between 1975 and 1980 moved to areas with higher median incomes than the median income of blacks in the city. Sixty-two percent moved to areas where the median income was more than 50 percent higher than the median income at the place of origin. This may indicate that black families who could afford to move to higher income neighborhoods were leaving the city. One may also note that nearly 50 percent the MSA's black immigrants from abroad (mainly from the Caribbean) settled in the City of Miami between 1975 and 1980. A similar pattern of out-migration occurred among middle-income Hispanics as well.

3. The employment and occupational data for 1980 are from the Census of Population and Housing: 1980, U.S. Department of Commerce, Bureau of the Census. Fifty-three percent of all employed blacks living in the City of Miami had jobs located in the city. Fifty-eight percent of Hispanic workers who lived within the city had jobs within the city.

4. Figures for non-Hispanic whites are estimated as a residual by deducting blacks and Hispanics from totals. A relatively small number of other races are, therefore, included in such estimates. In 1980, less than 2 percent of the MSA's population belonged to these

other races. Similarly, the proportion of Hispanics who are also classified as black represented 1.4 percent of the population in 1980.

5. The major riot of 1980 was followed by smaller, yet significant, disturbances in 1982 and 1989.

6. Only in the occupational group "laborers" and "private household services" did city blacks lose jobs while city Hispanics gained employment. In the case of "operators and assemblers", blacks experienced absolute gains in the number jobs while Hispanics experienced absolute losses. The proportion of blacks between the ages of 16 and 64 who were employed declined between 1970 and 1980. But this decline in the labor force participation rate was due entirely to an increase in school enrollment rates. Porter and Dunn also suggest that the economic progress of blacks was thwarted by Hispanic entrepreneurs who were more successful in the competition for scarce economic development assistance funds.

7. City of Miami Planning Department estimates, based on real estate market data provided by Coldwell Banker. See Cruz (1989).

8. Since their was very little undeveloped land within the city in 1979, nearly all of the growth in "commercial" land area represents a redistribution of land uses. See Barker, Hett and Roddy, 1989, p.I-4.

9. The software package ADOTMATR produced by Resource, Economics and Management Analysis (Lincoln, Nebraska) was used to update the national 1977 I-O table to 1985, to regionalize the national table and to compute the type II multipliers.

10. The occupation by industry data is for 1980, and obtained from the 1980 U.S. Census of Population and Housing subject report series.

11. The marginal impacts we are attempting to estimate are, therefore, limited to those cases where discrimination is absent.

12. The distance between the points for Hispanics and the zero axis are greater than for blacks in Figure 1.

13. Non-Hispanic whites currently represent between 45 and 50 percent of the MSA population, but less than 25 percent of the City's population. Income multipliers for city and non-city residents were also calculated. The share of additional income accruing to city residents never exceeded 34 percent for any industry, and averaged 30 percent of the total payroll multiplier.

Appendix

The structure of the model may be represented by the following equations.

The structure of production and the supply/demand balance equations are given by:

$$x1 = a11x1 + a12x2 + \cdots + a1JxJ + b1y + b1\, ryr + v-1$$

$$\cdot$$
$$\cdot$$
$$\cdot$$

$$xJ = aJ1x1 + aJ2x2 + \cdots + aJJxJ + bJy + bJ\, ryr + v-J$$

where "x" refers to the value of output, the aijs are the regionalized direct input coefficients, the b's represent the propensities to consume, "y" is the income of city residents, yr is the income of residents in the remainder of the MSA, and v − represent exogenous demand. Note that prices are fixed and set to unity (the x's are both quantity and value of output).

Labor income accruing to each occupational group is given by:

$$w1 = u11x1 + u12x2 + \cdots + u1JxJ$$

$$\cdot$$
$$\cdot$$
$$\cdot$$

$$wK = uK1x1 + uK2x2 + \cdots + uKJxJ$$

where ukj refers to compensation for labor of type "k" per unit of output of industry "j".

The income of city residents is given by:

$$y = d1w1 + d2w2 + \cdots + dKwK + y-$$

where dk represents the proportion of workers of type "k" that live within the city and y − is household income that is independent of city production.

The income of noncity residents is given by:

$$yr = (1-d1)w1 + (1-d2)w2 + \cdots + (1-dK)wK + y-r.$$

We can express this system of equations as:

$$
\begin{bmatrix} x \\ w \\ y \end{bmatrix} = \begin{bmatrix} a & 0 & b \\ u & 0 & 0 \\ 0 & \delta & 0 \end{bmatrix} \begin{bmatrix} x \\ w \\ y \end{bmatrix} + \begin{bmatrix} v- \\ 0 \\ y- \end{bmatrix}
$$

where x, w, and y are column vectors corresponding to the xjs, wks and [y, yr]', respectively. a is the 31x31 matrix of regionalized direct input coefficients. u is the 8x31 matrix of labor compensation per unit of output and δ is the 2x8 matrix of distribution parameters dk and 1-dk. b is a 31x2 matrix of marginal propensities to consume. v − and y − are column vectors representing exogenous final demands and income, respectively. The zeros represent empty cells in the matrix. Letting the matrix equation above be written as z = Az + v, the matrix of multiplier impacts is the (expanded) Leontief inverse:

$$
\begin{bmatrix} \dfrac{dz}{dv} \end{bmatrix} = \begin{bmatrix} I - A \end{bmatrix}^{-1}
$$

References

Barker, R, Hett, M. and Roddy, A. "Land Use Analysis," Miami Comprehensive Neighborhood Plan: Data and Analysis. City of Miami Planning Department, 1989.

Caplan, N. and Paige, J.. "A Study of Ghetto Rioters," Scientific American, 219 (1968). 15-21.

Cruz, R. "Economic Profile," Miami Comprehensive Neighborhood Plan: Data and Analysis. City of Miami Planning Department, 1989.

Kain, J. "Segregation, Negro Employment and Metropolitan Decentralization," Quarterly Journal of Economics, 84 (1968). 175-97.

Kasarda, John. "Urban Change and Minority Opportunities," in Paul E. Peterson (ed), The New Urban Reality. Washington, D.C.: The Brookings Institution, 1985.

Lieberson, S. and Silverman, A. "The Precipitants and Underlying Conditions of Race Riots," American Sociological Review, 30 (1965): 887-98.

Miller, R. and Blair, P. Input-Output Analysis: Foundations and Extensions. Englewood Cliffs, N.J.: Prentice Hall, 1985.

Mills, E. and Price, R. "Metropolitan Suburbanization and Central City Problems," Journal of Urban Economics, 15 (1984). 1-17.

Norton, R. D. "The Once and Present Urban Crisis," Urban Studies, 24 (1987). 480-88.

Porter, B. and Dunn, M.. The Miami Riot of 1980. Lexington, MA: Lexington Books, 1984.

Price, R. and Mills, E. "Race and Residence in Earnings Determination," Journal of Urban Economics, 17 (1985). 1-18.

Rodríguez, E. Changes in Population Characteristics and Job Opportunities: The Case of the City of Miami. Unpublished Masters Thesis, Florida International University, Miami, FL, 1987.

U.S. Department of Commerce, Bureau of the Census. Census of Population and Housing: 1970 Census Tracts, Final Report, Miami, FL, SMSA.

_____. Census of Population and Housing: 1980 Census Tracts, Final Report, Miami, FL, SMSA.

_____. Journey to Work: 1980.

_____. Occupation by Industry: 1980.

U.S. Department of Labor, Bureau of Labor Statistics, 1986. Current Wage Developments, Vol. 38, Number 3 (March).

_____. Current Housing Reports, H-170-83-28, Annual Housing Survey: 1983, Housing Characteristics for Selected Metropolitan Areas, Miami, FL, SMSA. Willumsen, M. "The Impact of Production Structure on Income Distribution: A Multiplier Approach," Review of Regional Studies, 20 (1990) (forthcoming).

Abstract

The Cuban Sugar Industry in a Changing World

José Alonso and Nicolás Rivero

Over the past hundred years the destiny of Cuba, of its sugar industry and its primary markets changed dramatically three times from Spain, to the United States, to the U.S.S.R. Now, in 1991 the question arises: is the island on the verge of yet an other change. There is a general consensus that the communist regime's days are numbered. However, it is not certain when this will happen, nor how it will impact on the sugar sector.

The two key questions on Cuban sugar revolve around: external markets and rationalization-diversification of the sugarcane industry.

On the sugar trade policy issue: For example will the Republics of the Soviet Union continue to buy sugar from Cuba and at what price? Will the United States change its trade and sugar policy in order to buy sugar from the island and, moreover, how will an opening for Cuba affect current sugar quota countries?. Will the "Uruguay Round" of GATT liberalize sugar trade?

On the rationalization-diversification issue: What resource allocations should be assigned to the sector in order to modernize it and can the island continue to be mono-culture economy?

The Cuban sugar agro-industry

Cuba is the world's single largest exporter of sugar -- excluding the European Community -- and its economy depends almost exclusively on this one crop. The state owns and operates the sugar agro-industry. According to official data, it accounts for 20 percent of the gross national product and about 80 percent of total exports. It employs 12 percent of the work force and utilizes 27 percent of the arable land.

The Cuban sugar industry is made up of 156 mills and agro-industrial complexes. The latter include under one management not only the mill but also the sugarcane farms and plants for the manufacture of sub-products such as yeast, furfural, bagasse paper and bagasse board. There are 16 refineries, 13 distilleries and seven bulk loading terminales. Harvesting is reported to be highly mechanized -- about 73 percent -- and production in 1990/91 was 7.7 mmtrv compared to 8.0 mmtrv in the previous season.

An important factor that has to be taken into careful consideration when analyzing this broad state agro-industry is that by western standards -Australia, South Africa, Brazil (South Central), U.S. sugarcane -- Cuba is not necessarily a very efficient producer of sugar. The basic industrial complex is rather old -- 95 percent of the mills were constructed before

1950 -- and is highly dependent on Soviet and Eastern European technology and machinery. Significant problems have already began to appear with regards to the replacement of equipment and spare parts.

The up-coming 1991/92 and subsequent harvests will be seriously hampered not only because of the lack of parts but also of basic inputs such as imported fertilizer, chemicals and above all petroleum.

A market for Cuban sugar

Historically the principal characteristic of Cuban sugar export strategy has been its high degree of dependency on one market. This is a consequence of political arrangements that granted the island preferential access and fixed prices at levels substantial above those of the world market. Up through 1960 Cuba was the number one foreign supplier of the U.S. market under the expired Sugar Act with annual sales of more than 3.0 mmt. From 1961 onwards the Soviet Union takes the place of principal buyer, with 53 percent -- based on 1984-90 trade data -- with the (former) Socialist countries of Eastern Europe and China accounting for a further 22 percent.

These two special arrangements had a profound impact on Cuban sugar policy makers. First, the country became dependent on the purchasing country's sugar subsidy -- granted, security in deliveries and high price were obtained -- but the industry as a whole did not have to be competitive in the world sugar market. Second, more emphasis was given to lobbying, be it in Washington or in Moscow, than rationalizing the industry in order to make it the world's most efficient sugar producer. Third, internally the industry since the mid-1930s did not operate in a free market ambiance as a result of strong government intervention. Sugarcane planting and sugar production as well as prices, were regulated.

Now that subsidized trade with the Soviet Union is drying up, and ceased to exist with former COMECON countries in 1991 -- unless Cuba pays in convertible currency -- the question is what will happen to sugar exports.

The U.S.S.R.: In the longer term, the Soviet Union, under a market oriented economy, could renew efforts to increase domestic beet sugar production. This aspiration was stated recently by the Director of the Russian Institute for Sugar and Sugarbeets who projects that beet sugar production could reach 7.0 mmt by the year 2000. There is an apparent potential to improve the yield of sugar beets with "intensive technology" -- a system to facilitate the application of more and better quality inputs on better land with strict observance of recommended cultural practices -- but changes in the Soviet agriculture and agricultural processing tend to be very slow. Therefore it is safe to assume that an import demand for sugar will continue till the year 2000.

The United States: The U.S. trade embargo on Cuba of early 1962 ended a special relation in sugar trade that existed for over sixty years. There has been a structural change in the U.S. sugar market since that date. The sugar industry continues to operate under a price support program and imports are controlled under a quota system but the market, however, is no longer a sugar one. It is now a sweetener market, where High Fructose Corn Syrup (HFCS) accounts for about half of the requirements. Also since 1962 important domestic producers like Florida, with an annual production of 1.6 mmt, have developed. The beet sugar industry will probably be able to expand due to the impact of molasses desurgarization. Consequently, unless the U.S. Congress makes significant changes in the program -- and this is difficult task but not impossible due to the politically powerful lobby of the sweetener producers -- there appears to be very little space for Cuban sugar. Also foreign relations and GATT rules have to taken into consideration.

Cuban sugar policy in the future has to be carefully framed. With regards to the U.S. sweetener market the issue is what is politically feasible to obtain in Washington. Returning to a system were 3.0 mmt of Cuban sugar are imported is a dead question. Internal Cuban macro economic and sectoral sugar policies and external market factors have to be considered jointly. Two areas of concentration that should be actively pursued are the following:

The first is related to rationalizing the Cuban sugar agro-industry. Recent history has clearly demonstrated that state owned and operated industries tend to be inefficient and costly. Ultimately the privatization of the sugar sector could establish the basis of an efficient diversified agro-business whose dimensions and allocation of resources -- human, land and capital -- would be in line with anticipated export market demands.

Second, a workable marketing strategy would have to developed with regards to the United States. If there is a political will this approach could be structured around three critical points.

In the case that the United States -- in the absence of any meaningful GATT trade liberalization- continues with a sugar support program it could be modified to include Cuba. The operational aspects would be: i) continue with the loan program with an upward adjustment of the loan rate; ii) freeze U.S. domestic marketing shares of both sugar and corn sweeteners at current levels (cane 3.2 mmt, beet 3.6 mmt and HFCS 6.4 mmt) and imports from present quota countries at 1.2 mmt; and iii) the growth in requirements over this baseline would be allocated to Cuba from page 5.

Finally, sugar sales to the (former) U.S.S.R. should continue.

Commodity-Linked Transactions and Recapitalization Needs for Privatizing the Economy in a Democratic Cuba: The Case of Sugar

Fernando Alvarez and José Alvarez

Behold: here is sugar without tears;
to say,
I have returned, do not fear;
to say,
Long was the journey, and bitter the road.

-Nicolás Guillén, "Eulogy to Jesús Menéndez"

Introduction

In his address to this Association last year, Felipe Pazos outlined a research agenda for the transition stage in a post-Castro Cuba. According to him, Cuban economists have not given enough thought neither to the problems of transition, nor to the policies to resolve them. He also stated that while it may be possible for Cuba to obtain loans and some economic aid from Western countries during the transition stage, it will be very difficult to obtain the amounts needed to rebuild the country. Pazos's challenge motivated us to think about the problems of transition and to try to find policies to solve them. In this paper we evaluate a commodity-linked transaction (CLT) as a potential tool for privatizing parts of the Cuban economy in a post-Castro Cuba. Potentially, CLTs provide an alternative to obtain funds on more favorable terms than would be possible otherwise. Furthermore, we feel that the institutional arrangements required to put in place commodity-linked transactions can guide those involved in designing transition stage rules. The specific problem addressed in this paper relates to the capitalization needs of the Cuban sugar industry, chosen because of its importance to the Cuban economy.

Since they are important to the thrust of this paper, we begin with an overview of the Cuban sugar industry and a discussion of the world sugar market. Next, some thought is given to the capitalization needs in the transition stage, followed by a discussion of commodity-linked transactions. In the next section, we simulate a sugar-linked transaction for a Cuban sugar consortium. Another section contains public policy implications suggested from our analysis. We intend these public policy prescriptions to serve as a guide to policy makers during the beginning of the transition stage in a post-Castro Cuba. The last section summarizes the contents of the paper and its conclusions.

The Cuban Sugar Industry

The literature on the Cuban sugar industry has been very prolific in the island and abroad. The reason is obvious: sugar cane has been, and continues to be, the dominant crop in Cuba's economy, and sugar the main source of foreign exchange. Data published by the

Cuban government portray the sugar industry as the source of employment for almost 400,000 persons who, with their families, make up perhaps one-sixth of the Cuban population. It also accounts for about one-third of the total means of production used in Cuban industry. Sugar represents 80% of the value of Cuban exports and the industry as a whole contributes 10% to Cuba's Global Social Product (Feuer, 1987, p. 69, from Anuario Estadístico de Cuba).[1]

The production sector has been expanding in the last decades. In the early 1960s, area harvested fluctuated around one million hectares and maximum total production reached 50 million metric tons. Today, production of sugar cane takes place on approximately 1.35 million hectares which yield about 53 metric tons of cane for a total production of over 70 million metric tons. Although state farms account for about 83% of the area harvested, their yields are slightly lower than those of private farms.

The trend toward mechanization started in the 1960s has continued. Almost all loading has been done with machines since 1970 and mechanical harvesting has increased from 25% in 1975 to 45% in 1980 and to 67% in the 1988-89 season.

The processing sector of the sugar industry has also experienced dramatic changes during the last thirty years. When the revolution took power on January 1959, the sugar industry consisted of 161 raw sugar factories, 16 refineries, over 20 distilleries producing alcohol and some press board and paper factories using bagasse as raw material (David, 1983, p. 100).

The entire Cuban sugar industry was expropriated in 1960. Today, all sugar mills and sugar refineries are owned by the State and managed by the Ministry of the Sugar Industry (MINAZ). There are 155 raw sugar mills throughout the 14 provinces and 14 refineries in 10 provinces (Table 1 and Fig. 1).

Cane-milled-per-day has increased from around 489,000 metric tons in the 1960s (somewhat below the figures in the 1950s), to 529,000 metric tons in the 1970s, and to around 619,000 metric tons in the 1980s. The effective milling season, however, has lengthened by more than three weeks.

Statistics on raw sugar production, industrial yield (recovery rate), and polarization illustrate the industry's performance in the last four decades (Table 2).

Despite heavy capital investments made to renovate and modernize some industrial facilities, "the industry is still characterized by a significant number of small, inefficient operations. About two-thirds of the mills have a daily grinding capacity of 4,000 tons or less

---

[1]When not specified otherwise, the statistics presented in this section appear in Anuario Estadístico de Cuba as shown in Buzzanell and Alonso (1989). They are used to delineate the main characteristics of the industry in the production, processing and marketing sectors.

Table 1.   Number and location of raw sugar mills and sugar
refineries in Cuba, by province, 1990.

Province	Sugar mills	Sugar refineries
Pinar del Río	5	1
La Habana	16	2
Ciudad de la Habana	1	1
Matanzas	21	3
Cienfuegos	12	–
Villa Clara	27	2
Sancti Spiritus	9	1
Ciego de Avila	9	1
Camagüey	15	1
Las Tunas	6	–
Holguín	10	1
Granma	10	1
Santiago de Cuba	8	–
Guantánamo	6	–
Total	155	14

Source: Germinsky (1990, pp. 45, 48, 109-110).

FIGURE 1

Location of Industrial Facilities in the Cuban Sugar Industry, by province, 1983. Source: Torralbas–Gonzalez (1983. p.8)

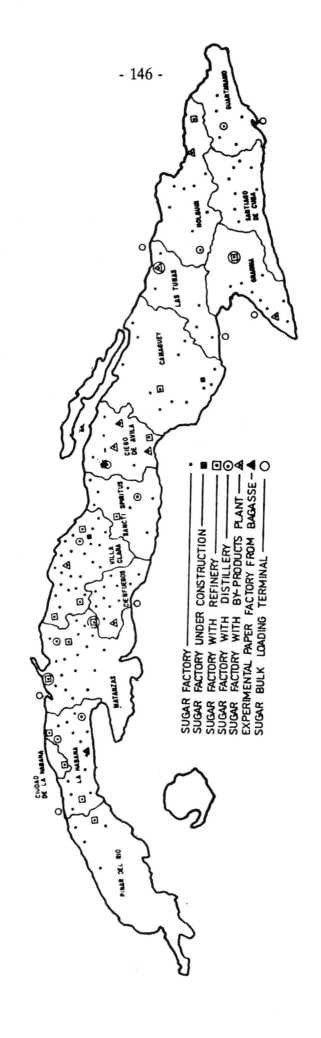

SUGAR FACTORY
SUGAR FACTORY UNDER CONSTRUCTION
SUGAR FACTORY WITH REFINERY
SUGAR FACTORY WITH DISTILLERY
SUGAR FACTORY WITH BY-PRODUCTS PLANT
EXPERIMENTAL PAPER FACTORY FROM BAGASSE
SUGAR BULK LOADING TERMINAL

and over 85 percent were built prior to 1913" (p. 22).

Table 2. Selected statistics for the Cuban sugar industry, by decade, 1950-1980.

Decade	Production (million metric tons)	Recov. rate (Percent)	Polarization (Degrees)
1950	5.59	12.89	97.19
1960	5.26	12.28	97.62
1970	6.43	11.29	97.74
1980	7.49	10.89	98.19

Sugar marketing is also under the control of the State. The domestic rationed quotas are distributed through the Ministry of Internal Trade (MINCIN), while CUBAZUCAR is the agency in charge of negotiating and marketing foreign sales.

As stated earlier in this section, sugar represents about 80% of Cuba's total exports. About 85% of the 7 million metric tons exported annually go to Eastern Europe (mainly the USSR) and China. The future of those sugar sales will be a cause of concern in a post-Castro Cuba. As stated by Pazos, sugar users in the United States will not be able to buy immediately all, or even a significant amount, of the sugar that is now being sold to the Soviet Union without reducing domestic production or foreign supplies from the Philippines and Latin America; but, since the Soviet Union will continue to need most of that sugar, Cuba could keep selling it, directly or through brokers, at world market prices (1990, p.9). Uncertainty about the future direction of trade for Cuban sugar leads to the use of world sugar prices (No. 11 Contract = SUGPRICE) in the simulations later on this paper and to a brief discussion of the world sugar market.

The World Sugar Market

The world market for sugar is not well understood. It is a market of left-overs from domestic needs and/or pre-arranged deals. In fact, there are three kinds of sugar markets (Schmitz et al., 1984). First, there is the market for sugar within sugar-producing countries. Since the bulk of the world's sugar output is consumed in the country of origin, this market is the biggest (75% of all sugar produced), and prices tend to be more stable than "world market prices". Second, there is the market resulting from various international agreements between certain importers and exporters (10%); i.e., the Bilateral Cuban Agreements with the USSR and other countries, import quotas under the US sugar program, and agreements by various countries with the European Community. Third, there is a residual "free market" in sugar (the remaining 15%), which is occasionally regulated by International Sugar Agreements.

This "free market" often becomes a dumping ground and remains relatively "thin" compared to world supply and demand. This world market can become quite volatile during periods of international tension, dramatic weather changes, and major shifts in sugar policies of major producing and/or consuming countries (Polopulus and Alvarez, 1991, pp. 30-31). For example, "since the free market for sugar is typically 15-25% of world production, a 5% change in production can represent a 25-33% change in free market sugar supply, one of the reasons for the high volatility of sugar prices" (Coffee, Sugar & Cocoa Exchange, 1990, p. 2).

Most countries seek to insulate their domestic sugar producers and consumers from the relatively volatile world market with a complex assortment of public policies and programs (Polopolus and Alvarez, 1991, p. 31). But it is protectionist sugar policies worldwide that create the volatility of the world market for sugar. Intervention begets intervention (Mises, 1979, pp. 42-46, 52), and the world sugar market is a perfect example. First, governments enter into agreements which curtail the free flow of sugar into world markets, causing the "free market" to be volatile; governments then use the volatility of this market as the reason to institute domestic policies to insulate producers and consumers from that volatility.

At present, the world sugar market seems to be entering into a new cycle (Table 3). Although total sugar production has been increasing in the last three years, consumption has been rising even more, so that ending stocks are at their lowest level since 1980-81 (Economic Research Service, USDA). The stocks/consumption ratio, an important indicator of upcoming prices, has been decreasing in the last three years indicating a future upward trend in prices from the current levels of $0.08 to $0.09/lb. We base the initial price of $0.11/lb in the simulations on this observation.

The future role of Cuba in the world sugar market can be estimated by extrapolating from current trends in exports (Table 4). During most of the 1980s, Cuban sugar exports to the world market averaged 1.66 million metric tons per year, or 24% of all sugar exports. Annual exports to Eastern Europe during the same period averaged 0.95 million metric tons, or 13.7% of all sugar exports during the 1980 decade. In 1988 Cuba also exported 1.4 million metric tons (more than twice the amount in the previous year) to China, or 20% of that year's exports. In a post-Castro Cuba, assuming no future bilateral trade agreements between Cuba and these two trading partners, Cuba could be selling up to 4 million metric tons in the world market. This represents more than 50% of total exports if domestic production and consumption[2] are maintained at the levels of the 1980s. These estimates do not include sales to the USSR (between 3.3 and 4 million metric tons in the late 1980s), which account for the remaining of Cuban sugar exports.

---

[2] The simulations described later in this paper assume total production will decline during the transition stage. It is also expected that domestic consumption will increase once rationing is abolished.

Table 3. World sugar production, supply, and distribution, 1986/87 - 1989/90.

Mkting year	Begin. stocks	Sugar product.	Imports	Tot. sup.- distr.	Exports	Domestic consumpt.	Ending stocks	Stocks/ consm.
	- - - - - - - - - - - - - - - -1,000 metric tons, raw value- - - - - - - - - - - - - - - -							
1986-87	25,969	103,371	27,247	156,587	28,124	105,055	23,408	.2228
1987-88	23,408	103,447	27,796	154,651	27,721	106,489	20,441	.1919
1988-89	20,441	105,469	29,903	155,813	28,280	107,617	19,947	.1853
1989-90	19,947	106,747	28,894	155,588	27,429	108,718	19,441	.1788

Source: Economic Research Service, USDA.

Table 4. Cuban sugar exports by trading partners, 1959-88.

Year	USSR	China	Eastern Europe	Other countries	Total	USSR	China	Eastern Europe	Other countries
	— — — Million metric tons, raw value — — —					— — — — Percent — — — —			(Share of)
1959	0.27	0.00	0.00	4.68	4.95	0.5	0.0	0.0	94.5
1960	1.58	.48	.23	3.34	5.63	28.1	8.5	4.1	59.3
1965	2.46	.40	.67	1.79	5.32	46.2	7.5	12.7	33.6
1970	3.11	.53	.96	2.31	6.91	45.0	7.7	13.9	33.4
1975	3.19	.18	.58	1.79	5.74	55.6	3.1	10.1	31.2
1976	3.04	.25	.94	1.53	5.76	52.8	4.3	16.3	26.6
1977	3.79	.23	.64	1.58	6.24	60.7	3.7	10.3	25.3
1978	3.94	.53	.61	2.15	7.23	54.5	7.3	8.4	29.8
1979	3.84	.49	.74	2.20	7.27	52.8	6.7	10.2	30.3
1980	2.73	.51	.69	2.26	6.19	44.1	8.2	11.2	36.5
1981	3.20	.57	.91	2.39	7.07	45.3	8.0	12.9	33.8
1982	4.43	.92	.80	1.58	7.73	57.3	11.9	10.4	20.4
1983	3.31	.77	1.00	1.71	6.79	48.8	11.3	14.7	25.2
1984	3.65	.71	1.17	1.49	7.02	52.0	10.1	16.7	21.2
1985	3.71	.68	1.03	1.79	7.21	51.5	9.4	14.3	24.8
1986	4.02	.31	.86	1.51	6.70	60.0	4.6	12.9	22.5
1987	3.86	.61	1.02	.99	6.48	59.6	9.4	15.7	15.3
1988	3.31	1.40	1.04	1.22	6.97	47.5	20.1	14.9	17.5

Note: Cuban exports to the United States amounted to 2.94 million tons in 1959 and to 1.95 million tons in 1960. Since July 1960 exports have been zero, reflecting the U.S. embargo on all imports from Cuba.

Sources: International Sugar Organization, various issues, and Anuario Estadístico de Cuba, 1970-1986, as they appear in Buzzanell and Alonso (1989, p. 24).

The impact of such sales on world market prices will depend on two different scenarios. If a post-Castro Cuba still faces today's world protectionist environment, world sugar prices would be expected to go down as a result of increasing supplies. On the other hand, if the Uruguay Round of trade negotiations within the General Agreement on Tariffs and Trade (GATT) are successful, Cuba will be playing on a level field and will benefit from the comparative advantage it has in sugar production. Recent research studies, summarized in Schmitz and Christian (1990), conclude that world sugar prices will rise following trade liberalization; however, sugar production would be determined by longer run price expectations, which may be lower than prices immediately following trade liberalization (Polopolus and Alvarez, 1991, p. 275).

Rather than speculate about which scenario is more likely to be in place at the time of the transition to a post-Castro Cuba, we base our simulations on data from 1979 to 1989 (Fig. 2a). We measure volatility as the six-month percentage change of spot prices (Fig. 2b).[3]

The Transition Stage and Capitalization Needs

No one has a crystal ball to provide a description of the initial conditions in a post-Castro Cuba. Nevertheless, the simulations that follow require information about (a) the organization that will be seeking financing; and (b) an estimate of the amount of money that will be needed to recapitalize the sugar industry. We conjecture that a post-Castro Cuba will be a free market economy and that the production capabilities of the sugar industry will be reduced during the transition stage.[4]

Estimates of Recapitalization Needs

There are no reliable statistics[5] on the value of assets in the Cuban sugar industry. Therefore, we believe that engaging in the development of an inventory of capital needs in a post-Castro Cuba is a worthless ex ante activity. In Appendix 1 we calculate a figure of approximately $1 billion as the value of non-land capital assets in the Cuban sugar industry.

---

[3] Volatility captures the unpredictability of future prices and, hence, commodity price risk. The month-to-month percentage change is a widely used measure of volatility (Eckl et al., 1991, pp. 2-6). The percentage change as a measure of volatility is based on static expectations. We use the six-month figure because our simulations will be based on six-month periods.

[4] No one can predict the state of the economy at that point in time since different degrees of change will bring about different outcomes. Both the type of organization seeking financing and the amount of money required will depend on the initial conditions.

[5] For example, Buzzanell and Alonso (1989) refer to official statistics of the 1981-85 Second Five-Year Plan. They state that "by the end of 1985, an estimated $3.1 billion pesos (U.S. $1.25=1 peso) had been invested in the industry..." (p. 20). That figure is overly exaggerated when one considers that the capital invested came from barter trade, perhaps at inflated prices. Since neither the Cuban peso, nor the Russian ruble, are hard currencies, it is difficult to conceive how any one can come up with a hard currency estimate for those figures. For example, in recent currency auctions, the ruble's real value has been put at about $0.02, vs. an official exchange rate of $1.70 (Business Week, July 29, 1991, p. 88).

FIGURE 2a

SUGPRICE: World Raw #11, Spot Prices (Close)

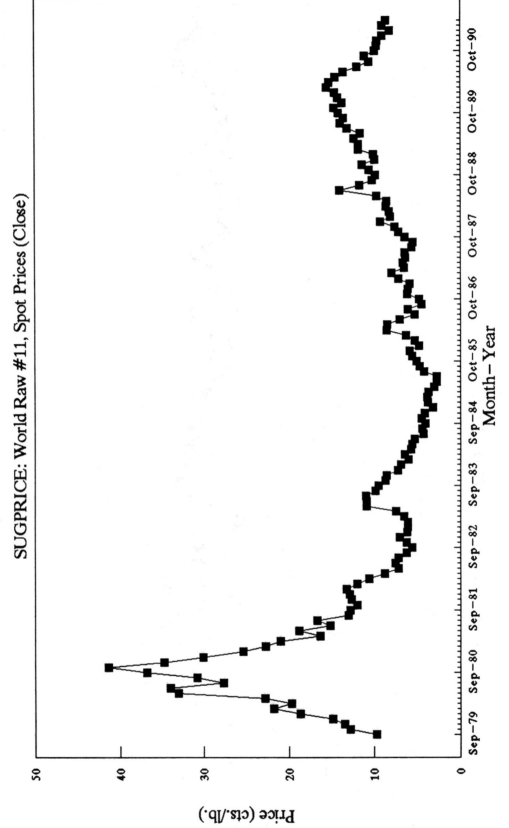

Data Source: Commodity Systems, Inc.

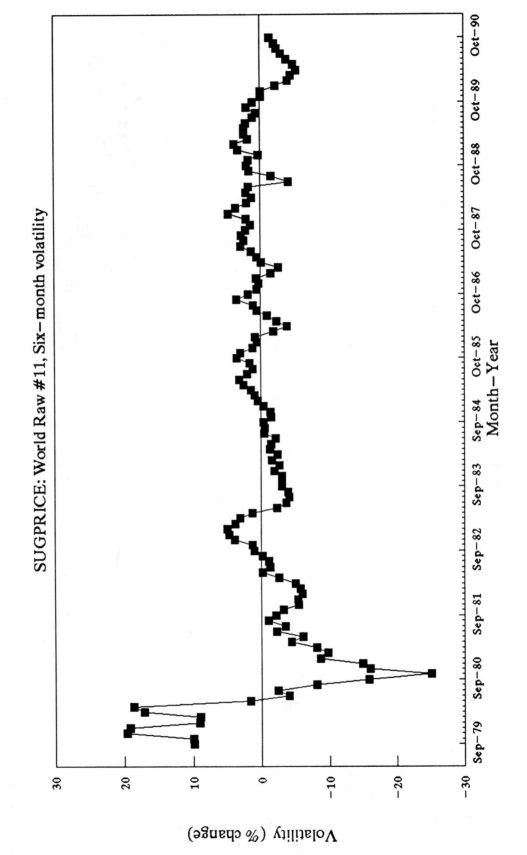

FIGURE 2b

SUGPRICE: World Raw #11, Six–month volatility

Data Source: Commodity Systems, Inc.

We base our calculations on figures of Cuban sugar production and the value of Florida's non-land capital in the sugar industry. This $1 billion figure is only meant to be an approximation and no significance should be attached to it.

A discussion on how this capital will be disbursed is irrelevant. The money may be invested in upgrading milling capacity, replacing old parts, purchasing mechanical harvesters, upgrading the infrastructure, or even in developing new markets. Again, initial conditions will determine specific needs.

Organization Seeking Financing

Who will exercise control over the sugar industry in a post-Castro Cuba is extremely hard to predict. But, regardless of who will be in power at that moment, it is fair to assume that, by a "post-Castro Cuba", we mean a democratic society with a free market economy. Who the owners will be is beyond the scope of this paper and irrelevant for our purposes once a free market economy is assumed.[6]

In the simulations that follow, a Cuban sugar consortium, Cuban Sugar Kings, Inc. (CSK), will be one of the organizations seeking financing. Total Cuban sugar production is assumed at 6 million short tons, or about 72% of the 7.5 million metric tons average production of the 1980s. The decrease reflects the reduction in production capabilities due to potential disruptions during the transition stage.

We assume CSK has control over 5% of the production; i.e., 300K per year and that CSK needs $90 million financing.[7] Since one of the stumbling blocks to recapitalization of the Cuban sugar industry in a post-Castro Cuba may be the lack of favorable financing, CSK considers the commodity-linked transaction as a viable alternative. We now digress to explain why.

Commodity-Linked Transactions[8]

Financial risk management is one of the major responsibilities of any financial

---

[6] Pazos (1990, pp. 7-8) contains general ideas on how to proceed to transform Cuba into a market economy, some of which have been challenged by O'Connel (n.d.). In addition, those interested in the problems of transition and in the privatization of state-owned assets in the former socialist countries of Eastern Europe are referred to Kaser (1991), Aslund (1991), and Fundación Sociedad Económica de Amigos del País (1991). There is a wealth of information on these topics that can be requested from Fundación Sociedad Económica de Amigos del País, P.O. Box 927, London SW1P 2ND, England.

[7] Given the gross figure of $1 billion calculated in Appendix 1, this means CSK owns about 9% of our gross estimate of the value of assets in the Cuban sugar industry. An entity that owns 9% of the industry's assets should control 9% of the industry's production. However, because of the potential disruptions in production at the beginning of the transition stage, such as sabotage, lack of qualified personnel, and many other causes, we assume that CSK controls only 5% of total production. This reflects our conservative estimate of the debt servicing capacity of CSK.

[8] The material contained in this section was taken from various issues of Euromoney.

manager. While risk can take on many definitions, the price volatility of some raw materials and final products is an important one. Commodity-linked products (CLPs) [9] have evolved into a tool for hedging that risk. Today, it is no longer acceptable for a financial manager to ignore financial risk. A decision not to hedge is a highly speculative action that can result in bankruptcy of the firm. A company can manage its operations very well and, yet, go out of business because of large fluctuations in the prices of its raw materials and/or final product. This section presents a brief overview of the literature on CLPs before discussing the specific arrangement we are proposing for the Cuban sugar industry.

Definition

A commodity swap requires two parties. A swap arranger (the facilitator) to put the deal together, and a firm desiring to hedge its risk exposure. This firm may be a user, concerned about a price increase, or a producer concerned about a price decrease (for the purposes of this definition, we will consider the deal from the viewpoint of a 'user' firm). The parties agree on the length of the agreement, payment intervals, and prices. One of the basic requirements for a successful swap is that there is a recognized benchmark, or market price for the raw materials, or product. The parties can then determine at the outset how the set price compares to the benchmark. The user agrees to pay a fixed price for the commodity to the facilitator, and the facilitator agrees to pay market price to the user. However, only the net is transferred. The user has therefore locked in a fixed price for a commodity, providing insulation from any large price increases. Locked out, however, are any advantages that a lower price would bring. The facilitator, in addition to the fees for bringing the deal together, is the beneficiary of any price decrease. As explained below, the facilitator can act as a intermediary, or as a broker.

History

Swaps first appeared in the early 1980s, with currency swaps reaching about $1 billion worth of business in 1981, and $15 billion in 1982. Interest rate swaps became popular in 1982, with about $5 billion. By the first half of 1989, interest rate and currency swaps totaled $467 billion, for an increase of 50% from the first half of the previous year. Since 1987, the market for CLTs has developed and current estimates put their value at around $10 billion, having doubled in August and September 1990 due to the scare of the Kuwait invasion. Energy products account for nearly all of the CLT business, but commodities such as aluminum, pulp paper, orange juice concentrate, ores such as copper have been the subject of many CLTs.

Risk

The primary risk in a CLT is price risk. The facilitator takes on the risk of prices

---

[9] Swaps are examples of commodity-linked products that are used to engineer commodity-linked transactions like the one we simulate for CSK in this paper.

rising above the agreed constant inflow, but can hedge this through the use of futures or mirror transactions. The user has been insulated from upside price risk, but is still exposed to extreme downside price risk. The risk here is that the price for the commodity will drop so low that the firm's competitors can drive the firm out of business. While unlikely, this risk can be covered with various hedging techniques.

Rationale

CLTs have grown explosively over the last few years. The Kuwait invasion of August 1990 made believers of many users (e.g., the airline industry), as oil volatility, which previously had run at 25-30%, hit as high as 85%. With price swings such as this, and with jet fuel representing 15% of an airline's operating expense, there is a critical need for an airline to hedge its exposure to this kind of risk. CLTs provide the means to do just that. CLTs, as opposed to other hedging instruments, do not require delivery, nor do they commit the user to a specific market. CLTs also have a substantial advantage relative to the timeframe of a contract. No other hedging mechanism available goes beyond 18 months, while CLTs really have no time limit. In addition, a CLT locks in price movements over a period of time; a forward only protects one purchase. Viewed in this light, a CLT is really a portfolio of forwards, with an agreed-to price being paid at specific intervals over the length of the contract. CLTs also look good from the viewpoint of the facilitator. With matching transactions, the risk is minimal, and with a relatively new product, the fees are well worth the effort. The fees charged by CLT facilitators are not yet public information. They are quoted on a deal-by-deal basis and, at a rate probably higher than the 4-5% charged on interest rate options, are quite expensive.

Facilitators

Currently, there is not a large group of institutions willing to act as CLT facilitators. The Commodity Futures Trading Commission (CFTC) 1989 decision to allow CLTs to be booked in the United States has brought many new players into the game, but the experience and contacts necessary to be a major player promise a long learning curve. Some commodities are dominated by as few as two facilitators, while fewer than twenty institutions will quote prices on oil swaps, with varying degrees of competitiveness. Both banks and producers are involved in facilitating CLTs, and each has reasons why the other is less suitable for the task.

The Regulatory Environment

US banks, with certain limited exceptions, have been traditionally precluded from dealing directly in commodities or commodity-indexed futures and forwards. On July 20, 1987, the Office of the Comptroller of the Currency (OCC) advised Chase Manhattan Bank that it would not object to the bank entering into matched commodity swaps. Soon after the OCC's letter, the Federal Reserve Board approved a Citicorp request to engage in CLTs through its export-trading subsidiary, which was expressly authorized to take positions in commodities and commodity contracts as long as they were not speculative. In September 1987, the New York State Banking Department also authorized CLTs for a New York state-chartered bank, assuming the bank would enter matched agreements subject to state lending limits. In November 1988, the New York State Banking Department formally approved New York State bank CLTs hedged with other available instruments. Finally, in July 1989, the CFTC established a set of criteria, referred to as a "safe harbor," for swap transactions (including CLTs) and options on CLTs. Transactions which satisfy these criteria may be transacted off-exchange, and will not be subject to the CFTC's regulatory framework.

To be eligible for the safe harbor treatment, a transaction: 1. Must be individually tailored in its material terms. 2. Must create performance obligations that are terminable, unless there is a default, only with the consent of the counter party and that are entered into with the expectation of performance. 3. Must not be supported by the credit of a clearing organization or primarily or routinely supported by a mark to market and variation settlement system designed to eliminate individualized credit risk. 4. Must be undertaken in conjunction with the parties' line of business. 5. Must not be marketed to the public.

Example

Pierce Industries, Inc. uses 1,000 barrels of oil per month. Fearing that Middle East uncertainty will bring higher prices, CEO Alan Pierce gives the go-ahead for a five-year oil swap, to be engineered by the local bank. Pierce agrees to pay \$25/barrel to the bank each quarter, while the bank will pay Pierce the benchmark price for crude. Pierce is now locked into a quarterly payment of \$75,000 (1,000 barrels x 3 months x \$25), and is totally sheltered from the volatility of the oil markets because the bank is committed to covering the market cost of the 3,000 barrels/quarter which Pierce needs. However, Pierce has bargained away any profit opportunities offered by cheaper oil, while the bank receives a substantial fee and the benefit of any fall in prices. In this example, the bank has acted as an intermediary, the CLT is carried on the bank's books, and the bank has assumed the risk of a substantial rise in oil prices, and the profit opportunity resulting from a price drop. In most cases, the bank will hedge this risk, by acting as a broker. The hedge works by entering into a second swap with a producer, who is concerned about prices falling. In that case, the deal would provide the bank with the benchmark rate, while the bank would provide a fixed price to the producer. Ideally, the deal becomes a 'mirror image' of the Pierce deal, and the bank's commodity price risk is completely hedged. But default risk still exists, and must be taken into account by the bank in pricing the CLTs.

A More Elaborate Example

Although CLTs have involved other commodities, the copper-linked transaction arranged by Banque Paribas on behalf of Mexicana de Cobre (MdC) in the summer of 1989 has attracted international attention. Paribas, leading a group of 11 banks, lent MdC US\$210 m at 11.5% (instead of the 20%-plus rate on MdC existing debt) for 38 months.

The Belgian company Sogem agreed to buy from MdC 4,000 mt/month at a price indexed to the London Metal Exchange daily prices. To reduce the risk of loan default due to drastic price falls, Paribas' payments of $2,000/ton are deposited into a New York escrow account to repay interest and principal to the banks. Payments will exceed debt servicing by about 10% insulating the banks from changes in copper prices. The residual cash built over up over time will be passed on to MdC. The actual CLT was much more complex than this brief discussion can show (Fig. 3).

The CLT of Mexicana de Cobre has important implications for the economic development of third world countries. A common goal shared by both users and producers of raw materials and other commodities is the need for long-term insurance against violent market movements. CLTs guarantee a fixed price and a steady income for those countries, making them a better loan risk. With that in mind, we now present a sugar-linked financing for CSK.

Sugar-Linked Financing for CSK

Assumptions

As discussed in the section on transition stage and capitalization needs, we base the simulations on this section on the following assumptions:

a) CSK wants to borrow $90 million for 15 years.

b) National sugar production is expected to be 6 million short tons per year.

c) CSK is a 5% player; i.e., expected annual production of 300,000 tons.

We now introduce the following assumptions:

d) CSK is currently financed with 100% equity.[10]

e) Financing available to CSK:

(i) long-term interest rate at 18% (fixed).

(ii) short-term interest rate at the 6-month London Inter Bank Offered Rate (LIBOR) + 200 basis points.

---

[10] This assumption is not unrealistic although, again, it will depend on the initial conditions. For example, if one of the policy decisions at the beginning of the transition stage gives full ownership to current cooperative members, without compensating previous owners, the resulting consortium would be 100% equity financed. The same would be true if full ownership was granted to previous owners under the same circumstances.

- 159 -

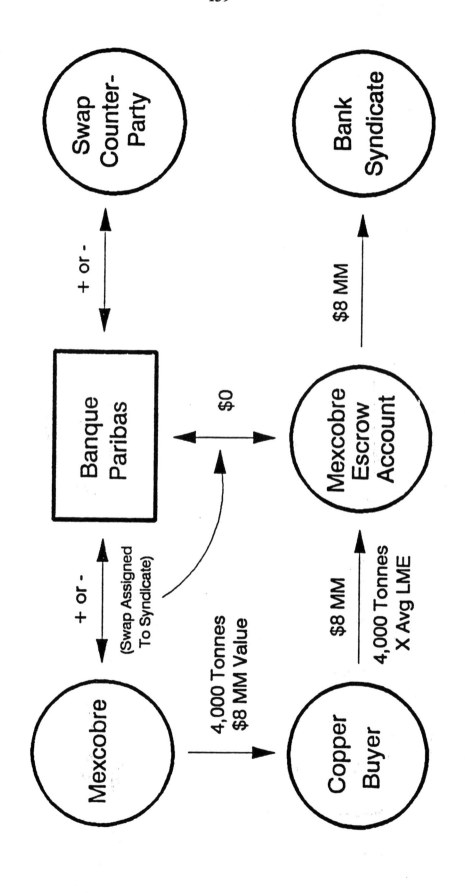

FIGURE 3

Mexicana de Cobre, S.A.: Monthly Repayment Flows

Source: Gaylen Byker

FIGURE 4
SUGAR–INDEXED FINANCING FOR CSK

Panel A: Initial Cash Flows

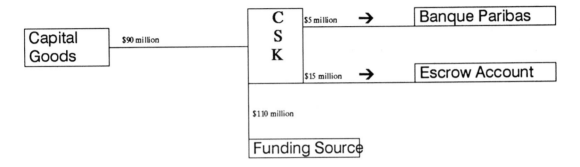

Panel B: Repayment Cash Flows

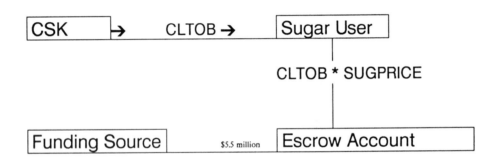

Panel C: Escrow Account Ending Balance Cash Flows

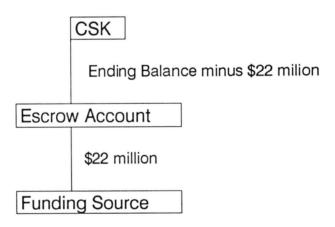

The Deal

The transaction (Fig. 4) will be three years in duration; therefore, for the life of the long-term financing, there will be five cycles. To guarantee payment, CSK will undertake two actions. First, CSK will enter into a contract to deliver a specified amount of sugar every six months to a candy manufacturer or some other credit worthy purchaser (AAA-rated). The amount of sugar to be delivered will be based on the amount needed to service 110% of the debt at the price discussed in the section on the world sugar market--$0.11/lb. Second, CSK will open an escrow account in a US bank (paying LIBOR) with an initial balance of $15 million. The initial balance of the escrow account will be borrowed and the ending balance will be used to retire the principal on the loan. The purchaser of CSK sugar will make payments directly into the escrow account. In the simulations that follow, CSK will be dealing directly with the syndicate providing the funds, the escrow account, and the sugar purchaser. Under most circumstances, an investment bank, such as Banque Paribas, would be providing those services and charging a fee.[11] We assume that this fee will be approximately 5% of the total amount of the loan; i.e., $5 million. In this way, we concentrate on the transaction from the perspective of CSK and do not take into account the swaps needed to hedge the interest rate risk and the commodity price risk. Since CSK needs $90 million usable funds, the loan will be for $110 million (110 minus 15 for initial balance in the escrow account, minus 5 for fees paid up-front to Banque Paribas).

CLTs and Risk Reduction

We conjecture that, by entering into a commodity-linked transaction, CSK will be able to borrow $110 million for 15 years at a fixed rate of 10%. Compare this 10% financing with the 18% financing available without the CLT and it is easy to see why this financing tool is so attractive. The 18% to 10% interest rate reduction is comparable to the recent interest rate reduction Mexicana de Cobre was able to obtain in US$210 million financing from Banque Paribas (from over 20% down to 11.5%). This was possible because CLTs control for commodity risk, interest rate risk, credit risk, currency exchange risk, and performance risk. Moreover, unlike many debt-for-equity swap programs of Less Developed Countries, CLTs do not involve accounting tricks and/or repudiation of principal and/or accrued interest. Now, we are specific about how this works for CSK financing.

1. Performance risk is the inability, because of bad weather, sabotage, etc., to deliver the sugar needed to cover interest expenses; we reduce this risk in three ways: by modeling CSK's crop as described below; by assuming that, during the transition stage, production will be about 72% of the average production in the 1980s; and by going from ownership of 9% of the industry's total capital assets to 5% of the industry's total production as discussed in a previous section.

---

[11] In this section, we refer to Banque Paribas, rather than "the investment bank" or "the facilitator" for editorial convenience. The fees and other responsibilities we ascribe to Banque Paribas are strictly conjectural on our part.

2. CSK does not bear interest rate risk because it borrows at a fixed 10% rate. Banque Paribas hedges interest rate risk by entering into an interest rate swap as part of the services they provide for their $5 million fee.

3. Treating the CLT as pre-export financing eliminates the risk of future tax and other retro-active legislative actions.

4. The escrow account eliminates foreign exchange risk and the risk that currency exchange controls or lack of hard currency would prevent CSK from making payments.[12]

5. The escrow account also reduces credit risk by transferring the credit rating of the sugar user to CSK. The sugar user does not require compensation from CSK because they have entered into a long-term contract for supply at the spot price of sugar. In fact, under some circumstances, the sugar user will gain from this arrangement. For example, if there were no escrow account and CSK diverted the funds from debt payments to another use, the lender may have the legal right to impound the shipment sent by CSK to the sugar user, disrupting their operations.

There is another dimension to credit risk. Credit risk entails the option of the borrower to suspend interest payments. By having the sugar user deposit directly into the escrow account the amount to cover interest payments, CSK has forfeited that option; i.e., CSK does not have the option to divert the funds from interest payments to other uses. We are assuming that CSK is an ethical entity that would not consider such action under any circumstances; therefore, the option of suspending interest payments is worthless to CSK. Nevertheless, credit risk, i.e., the suspension of interest payments, is worth something to the lender. Part of the reduction from 18% to 10% comes from CSK giving up an option, worthless to them, that is worth something to the lender.

CLTs and Debt Service

The debt service of the deal consists of $5.5 million semi-annual interest expense (10% per year on $110 million), and retirement of principal equal to $3,666,667 ($110 million divided by 30 -5 cycles with six semi-annual payments each), for a total debt expense of $9,166,667 semi-annually.

We are assuming that Banque Paribas and CSK agree that $0.11/lb is a reasonable sugar price on which to base the number of tons of sugar the value of which will be deposited into the escrow account. Recall that the initial balance of $15 million in the escrow account will act as a buffer in case there is a drastic drop in the sugar price.

---

[12] Alternatively, foreign exchange risk would not be present if, in a post-Castro Cuba, US dollars were the national currency. We will discuss this futher in the section on public policy implications.

The percentage of CSK's production dedicated to debt service is computed as follows: At \$0.11/lb and 2,000 lb/ton, CSK will need to dedicate 41,667 tons [\$9,166,667/(2,000*0.11)]. In order to fulfill the contractual obligation of 110% of debt service, CSK will have to dedicate 45,833 tons (41,667*1.1) for its CLT obligation (CLTOB).

Sources of Uncertainty

We need to model three sources of uncertainty to generate the simulations explained in the next section.[13] They are:

CSK Production (CROP)

Recall the assumption that, even though CSK owns 9% of the capital, CSK will have only 5% of total production to eliminate some of the performance risk. Performance risk will also be reduced by modeling CROP as a truncated normal distribution with mean 300K tons, standard deviation of 25K tons, a minimum of 250K tons, and a maximum of 350K tons. CROP is independently distributed from one year to the next. Again, we model CROP this way to take into account the fluctuations in production due to disturbances from man and nature.

LIBOR and SUGPRICE

Each of these variables will be modeled with their six-month continuously compounded rate of return following a log normal distribution, with period-to-period correlation, and estimated with data from 1979 to 1989 (Appendix 2). An alternative procedure would be to model LIBOR and SUGPRICE as mean reversing processes.[14] Also, we could infer forward prices for LIBOR and SUGPRICE from indications in the market place, i.e., quotations from options and futures markets, and use those prices in the simulations.

We also considered whether a relationship exists between LIBOR and SUGPRICE. Since nominal interest rates contain an expected inflation premium, the prices of most

---

[13] All of the simulations in this manuscript were performed within Lotus 1-2-3, version 2.01, with Palisade's Corporation @RISK, version 1.51.

[14] A variable follows a mean reversion process if high (low) returns are followed by lower (higher) returns; that is, returns appear to regress toward the mean (a trend, or drift, can be incorporated in the mean). First, we would test for mean reversion using the procedure outlined in Fama and French (1988). If we could not reject the hypothesis that LIBOR and/or SUGPRICE follow a mean reversing process, we would estimate the following process:

$$dP_t = k * (\mu - P_t) + \sigma \, dz,$$

where k is the speed of adjustment, μ and σ are the mean and standard deviation of the process, and z is a Weiner process with mean zero and std. deviation of one. This process would then be used to generate LIBOR and SUGPRICE in the simulations.

commodities are correlated with interest rates, albeit with a lag. But the world sugar market is driven more by its residual character than by such fundamentals. To test for any correlation between LIBOR and SUGPRICE, we ran a regression between their continuously-compounded rates of return and found no statistical relationship for any reasonable lag structure. Therefore, LIBOR and SUGPRICE were modeled as independently distributed.

CSK's Cash Flows Resulting From the Deal[15]

A major criterion for judging the success of CLTs is the possibility of CSK of meeting its financial obligation without committing a major portion of its revenues to debt service. The semi-annual cash flows (Fig. 5) are calculated to determine the proportion of income dedicated to debt service and the ending balance in the escrow account at the end of the first 3-year cycle. In this section, we first describe how the cash flows are calculated; next we discuss the results from simulating the income statements allowing SUGPRICE to float, and putting a collar on SUGPRICE.

We divided the year into two six-month periods: January/June and July/December. The deal is put in place at $t=0$ (January of the first year). The first annual crop will not be marketed until July of that year, at which time half of the crop will be sold at the prevailing price, with the remaining half being marketed during January of the next year. SUGPRICE, CROP and LIBOR are random variables generated with the processes described above.

Revenues: CROP * SUGPRICE

In July of the first year ($t=1$), six months into the transaction, we show revenues of $25,122,294 (144,381 tons times 2,000 pounds per ton times $0.0870 per pound).

Expenditures: CLTPOB * SUGPRICE

In the first period we show expenditures of $7,974,942 (45,833 tons times 2,000 pounds per ton times $0.0870 per pound). Recall that CLTOB = 45,833 tons and that, regardless of what CROP turns out to be, CSK is contractually obligated to deliver 45,833 tons to their counter party. All other expenditures are ignored. Since expenditures such as taxes, wages, maintenance, etc., are independent of the arrangement, we ignore them and concentrate on CLTOB as a percentage of revenue. We recognize that, implicit in this assumption, is the independence between financial leverage and operating leverage, but we feel this is reasonable.

---

[15] We used Lotus 1-2-3, version 2.01, to generate the figures in this section. Since Lotus uses a different rounding convention than financial calculators, the reader checking our figures may find some insignificant discrepancies.

FIGURE 5
CUBAN SUGAR KINGS: Semi-annual cash flows

Period	January 0	July 1	January 2	July 3	January 4	July 5	January 6
SUGPRICE	$0.1100	$0.0870	$0.0874	$0.1045	$0.1042	$0.1172	$0.1513
CROP		288,762		297,074		303,192	
Sugar sold		144,381	144,381	148,537	148,537	151,596	151,596
Revenues		$25,122,294	$25,237,799	$31,044,233	$30,955,111	$35,534,102	$45,872,950
CLTOB		$7,974,942	$8,011,608	$9,579,097	$9,551,597	$10,743,255	$13,869,066
CLTPER		31.74%	31.74%	30.86%	30.86%	30.23%	30.23%

ESCROW ACCOUNT

	January 0	July 1	January 2	July 3	January 4	July 5	January 6
LIBOR	8.00%	6.61%	6.48%	6.66%	5.39%	6.87%	5.35%
Beginning Balance	$15,000,000	$15,600,000	$18,672,319	$21,870,286	$26,813,498	$31,696,909	$38,209,059
Interest Payment		($5,500,000)	($5,500,000)	($5,500,000)	($5,500,000)	($5,500,000)	($5,500,000)
Deposit		$7,974,942	$8,011,608	$9,579,097	$9,551,597	$10,743,255	$13,869,066
Ending Balance	$15,000,000	$18,074,942	$21,183,927	$25,949,383	$30,865,095	$36,940,165	$46,578,125
Retirement of Principal							$22,000,000

CLT Obligation as a Percentage of Revenue (CLTPER)

We want to show that, as a result of this deal, CLTPER remains within reasonable bounds. Recall that we are assuming that, before entering into the deal, CSK was 100% equity financed (see fn. 11). Furthermore, we assume that all the production will be sold at world prices. Otherwise, CLTPER would have to be calculated as a weighted average.

For example, in period 1 we show a CLTPER of 31.74% ($7,974,942 divided by $25,122,294).

Escrow Account

The escrow account will serve as a buffer to protect Banque Paribas from low sugar prices. As a condition for the financing, CSK will borrow $15 million more than it needs and will open an escrow account that pays LIBOR. The escrow account's cash flows are as follows: withdraw $5.5 million each period for interest payments; deposit expenditures, (CLTOB times SUGPRICE); deposit interest earned during the previous period.

For example, in period 1 we show a beginning balance of $15,600,000 [15 million * (1+.08/2)], a withdrawal of $5.5 million for interest payments, and a deposit of $7,974,942 for an ending balance of $18,074,942.

Escrow Account's Ending Balance

Recall that the $110 million CSK borrowed will be retired in $22 million payments at the end of each cycle. Therefore, the ending balance in period 6 must be greater than or equal to $22 million.

For the path of CROP, LIBOR and SUGPRICE in this example, we show an ending balance in the escrow account of $46,578,125, which is well above the $22 million minimum required ending balance.

Simulation Results

Variables Simulated

We ran 2,500 iterations of CSK's cash flows resulting from the deal. The price of sugar was allowed to float from the starting price of $0.11/lb following the process described in Appendix 2 (Fig. 6a). SUGPRICE shows a range from a low of about $0.02/lb to a high of about $0.55/lb. The range in our simulations reflects the actual behavior of world sugar prices in the last 10 years (Fig. 2a).

From the perspective of CSK, prices in the low range (below $0.07/lb) instill fear while prices above $0.35/lb generate greed; the opposite is true for the sugar user. To

FIGURE 6
SUGPRICE
Range within two std. dev. from the mean

(a) SUGPRICE allowed to float

Trend in Mean,
1 Std.Dev.,
5/95 Perc.

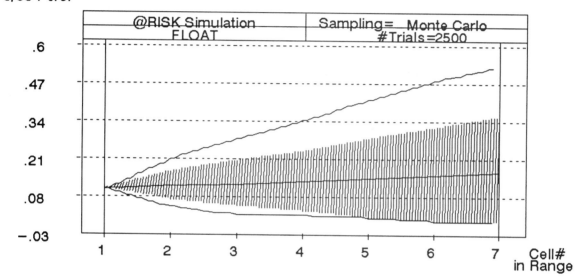

(b) SUGPRICE with a collar
Floor of $0.07 and ceiling of $0.35

Trend in Mean,
1 Std.Dev.,
5/95 Perc.

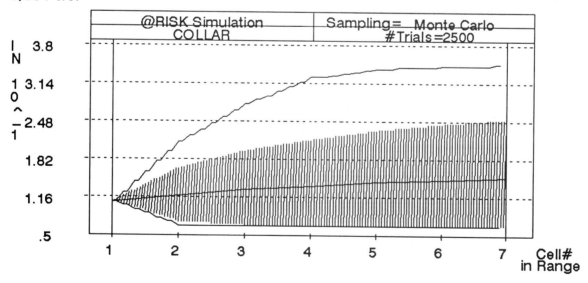

FIGURE 7
LIBOR
London Interbank Offered Rate

(a) Range within two std. dev. from the mean

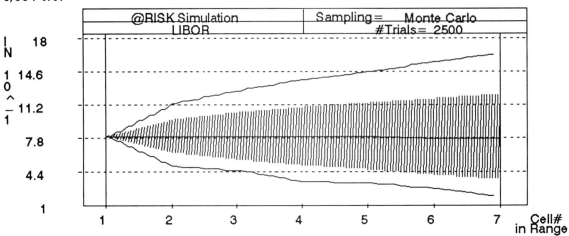

(b) Probability distribution for period 4

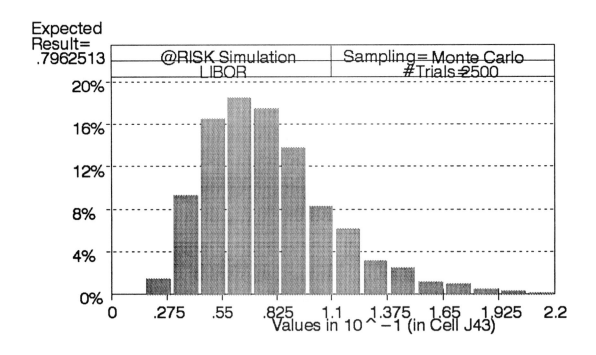

FIGURE 8
CROP

Probability distribution

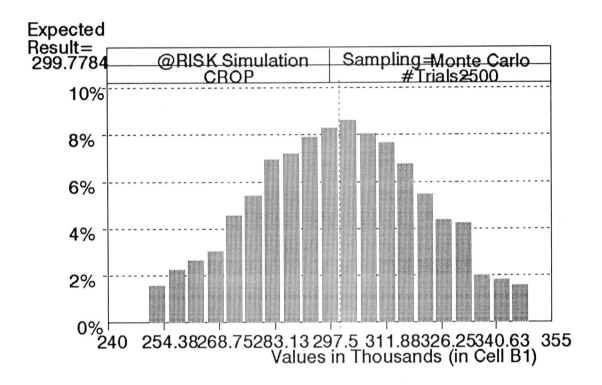

balance these extremes, Banque Paribas (as part of their $5 million fee) would set up a collar with a floor of $0.07/lb and a ceiling of $0.35/lb (Fig. 6b), thereby providing insurance for CSK against low prices at the expense of giving up the profits available to them when prices rise above $0.35/lb, with the opposite being true for the sugar user. We are assuming that this a par--i.e., a no-cash-flow transaction; in other words, CSK pays for protection from prices below $0.07/lb with foregone profits from prices above $0.35/lb, the opposite being true for the sugar user.

LIBOR goes from a low of 2% to a high of 17% per annum (Fig. 7a). The low end seems unreasonable, but recall that the major result we are seeking is the ending balance in the escrow account. The purpose of LIBOR is to generate interest income from the balance in the escrow account. Low interest rates reduce the ending balance in the escrow account, thus making our results more conservative. The expected value of LIBOR is about 8% per annum. In period 4, two years into the deal, we see that the majority of the realizations are between 5% and 10% per annum (Fig. 7b).

CROP was simulated as a truncated normal, showing the traditional bell shape with the tails chopped off (Fig. 8).

Escrow Account's Ending Balance

The escrow account's ending balance is the parameter that validates this exercise. We simulated the ending balance under two scenarios: allowing SUGPRICE to float (EBFLOAT, Fig. 9) and placing a collar (EBCOLLAR, Fig. 10) on SUGPRICE. The simulation results for each scenario are summarized below (Table 5).

Table 5a.   Simulation results for the expected value of the escrow account's ending balance and probability of obtaining $22m and $110m.

	Expected value	Probability >$22m	>$110m
EBCOLLAR	$ 66.55 million	100%	16.5%
EBFLOAT	$ 69.00 million	83%	17.0%

When we allowed SUGPRICE to float, the probabilities that the ending balance in the escrow account were higher than $22 million and $110 million were 83% and 17%, respectively. When we simulated SUGPRICE with a collar, those probabilities were 100% and 16%, respectively. The value of the collar can be discerned from the expected value

FIGURE 9
ESCROW ACCOUNT ENDING BALANCE
(SUGPRICE allowed to float)

(a) Probability distribution

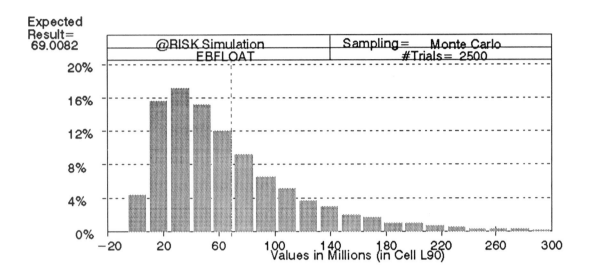

(b) Cummulative distribution

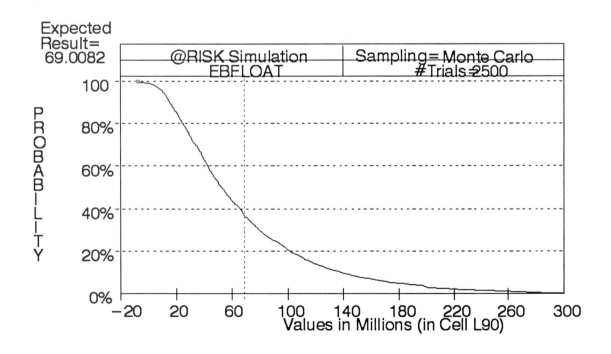

FIGURE 10
ESCROW ACCOUNT ENDING BALANCE
SUGPRICE with a Collar

(a) Probability distribution

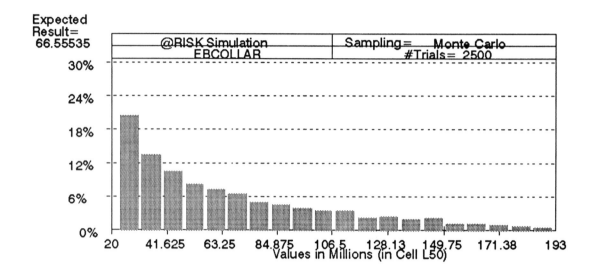

(b) Cummulative distribution

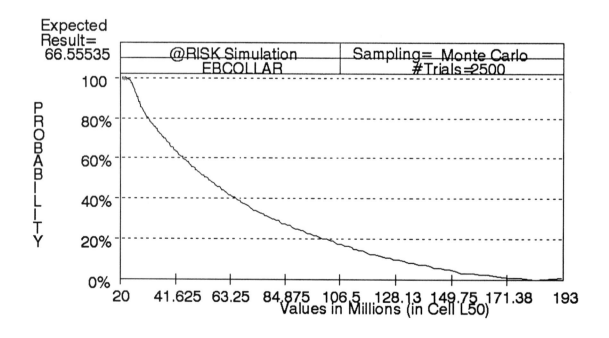

of the ending balance with and without the collar. Considering expected values only, it seems that CSK should receive compensation from the collar since the ending balance with the collar is about $2.5 million less than without the collar. However, once we allow for risk aversion, the picture is not as clear (Table 5b).

Table 5b. **Simulation results for the escrow account's ending balance obtained with 5% and 95% probabilities.**

	Probability >	
	95%	5%
EBCOLLAR	$25.2 million	$149 million
EBFLOAT	$10.0 million	$182 million

There is a 95% probability that the ending balance with the collar will be higher than $25 million, but the same 95% probability only yields an ending balance of $10 million without the collar. This reinforces the result from Table 5a that, without the collar, CSK may not end up with enough funds in the escrow account to retire the principal on the loan. Also, there is a 5% probability that the ending balance with the collar will be higher than $149 million, but the same probability yields an ending balance higher than $182 million without the collar.

These results show why we are proposing our simulations only as a negotiating tool for the chief financial officer. As investigators we have no insight into the degree of risk aversion of the owners of CSK and its bankers. Therefore, we could only speculate about what trade-offs in risk and return they would be willing to make.[16]

CLT Obligation as a Percentage of Revenue (CLTPER)

Another important result from the simulations is the percentage of revenue dedicated to debt service (Fig. 11). Panel A shows the range within two standard deviations from the mean for CLTPER. The 95% confidence interval ranges from 27% to 35% with a mean of 30%. Panel B shows the probability distribution for period 5, with results being typical for each period. Panel C shows that there is only 9% probability that CLTPER will be higher than 34%.

---

[16] In results not reported here, we found that stochastic dominance does not yield an unequivocal decision either. In a future draft, we plan to evaluate the results on the basis of "safety first" criteria (Elton and Gruber, 1991, Chapter 9).

FIGURE 11

CLT Obligation as a Percentage of Revenue

(a) Range within 2 std. dev. from the mean

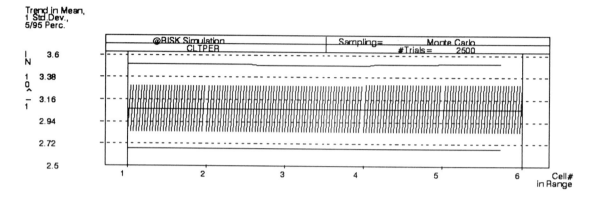

(b) Probability distribution for period 5

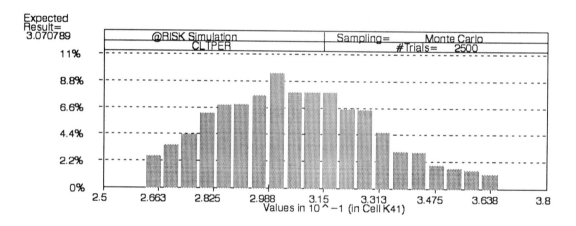

(c) Cummulative distribution for period 5

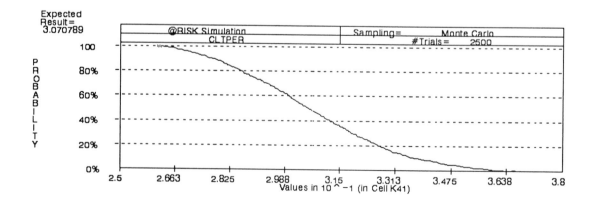

Public Policy Implications

We have demonstrated how a new financial tool, Commodity-Linked Transactions (CLTs), can improve the decision making of a sugar consortium in a post-Castro Cuba after the initial transition stage has been completed. This tool can be used by the Chief Financial Officer of the consortium to negotiate favorable terms when seeking financing. Used this way, CLTs can play an important role in the privatization of the sugar industry or any other sector of the Cuban economy. But there is more. The use of CLTs has important public policy implications for the immediate transition stage that relate to Pazos' concerns about an unregulated influx of foreign capital buying our national wealth (1990, p. 3), and to Justo Carrillo's account of Cuba's republican life (1985).

Carrillo uses the word **atimia**, meaning "loss or deterioration of status", to describe Cuba's republican existence:

An atimica Cuba -- defined by the Platt Amendment -- permitted North American capital to flood the island due to the safeguards offered by possible U.S. intervention. Thus, North American investment inadvertently became an element of corruption as politicians from every end of the political spectrum used American influence to gain power, to retain power, and/or to engage in business with the North American banking sector (p. 163).

A key feature of the CLT we propose is the escrow account in a US bank. This escrow account eliminates foreign exchange risk and interest payments risk. Other policies could accomplish the same objective. For example, using the US dollar as the national currency in a post-Castro Cuba would also eliminate foreign exchange risk. Another policy, enforcing the US commercial code in Cuba, would also reduce interest payments risk because US banks could force Cuban companies into Chapter 11 bankruptcy procedures if a Cuban firm stopped making payments.

Therefore, laws and regulations that allow Cuban companies to establish escrow accounts with foreign banks would defuse the argument that Cuba should use the US dollar as the national currency to facilitate an influx of foreign capital into Cuba. That is, a public policy that facilitates the use of escrow accounts also works in favor of establishing a national currency. In the same way, we can argue that making it easy to establish escrow accounts eliminates the argument that the US courts should have jurisdiction over Cuban companies.

There is still another important public policy implication that can be derived from our study. Our discussion portrays the world sugar market as an example of intervention begetting intervention, thus becoming the product of self-defeating policies. When a government, in order to protect the consumers and producers from the vagaries of the world market, institutes protectionist policies, these policies aggravate the conditions the government wants to alleviate. One of the major problems protectionist policies intend to alleviate is the volatility or world prices. But there is an alternative path. A post-Castro Cuban government could unilaterally move toward freer trade. Consumers and producers could use commodity-linked transactions to isolate themselves from price volatility. This is not as farfetched as it may seem to those who hear it for the first time. In fact, producers and consumers in the world oil market have used CLTs to reduce the oil price volatility that came about after 1974 (Byker, 1990b). The section on CLPs also mentions an array of CLTs that have been negotiated with raw materials and final products, describing one of them in some detail. In future research we intend to investigate the costs and benefits of using CLTs as substitutes for protectionist policies in order to provide price stability to both import and export prices in a post-Castro Cuba.

We believe that the public policy implications of our study should be seriously considered. Cuba was born atimica and remained so for the rest of its republican life, or until January 1959. According to Carrillo:

> If Cuba, during its difficult historical process, had an opportunity to be genuinely free and independent, it was during the first months of 1959 when the old political, economic, social, and military structure fell to pieces. At that moment a new and different Cuba could have been reconstructed from the roots up (p. 174).

The degree of atimia in today's Cuba has gone beyond anybody's imagination. However, it may be possible that history will allow Cuba a second chance. That thought should guide social scientists while working on the development of the institutional arrangements that should be established during the transition stage in a post-Castro Cuba. Although both authors agree with the French philosopher Bastiat (1850) that laws should minimize the ability of politicians to grant favors, they disagree on other future roles of the Cuban State. One of the authors believes with Thomas Jefferson that "government governs best that governs least," the other sees a larger role for the State. Yet, by sharing the same goals, they were able to find a solution to accommodate both preferences. We hope that this experience will be shared by Cubans engaged in the problems of transition to a free and democratic Cuba. Then, and only then, the "here is sugar without tears; to say, I have returned, do not fear" will become truly relevant.

Summary and Conclusions

The sugar industry plays an important role in Cuba's economy. It represents 80% of the value of exports, contributes 10% to its Global Social Product, covers about one-third of the total means of production, and employs 400,000 persons. In addition to infrastructure and other industrial facilities, there are 155 raw sugar mills and 14 refineries. Despite some recent capital investments, there is a significant number of small, inefficient operations. Most of the mills have a daily grinding capacity of 4,000 tons or less, and over 85% of them were built prior to 1913.

The sugar industry will have to be recapitalized in a democratic Cuba. Commodity-linked transactions (CLTs), engineered with commodity-linked products (CLPs), offer the potential for obtaining funds on more favorable terms than would be possible otherwise. Developed in the mid-1980s, the pricing and cash flows of this new financial tool are similar to those of interest rate and currency swaps, and unlike some of the schemes recently suggested to lower LCDs' external debt, CLTs do not involve accounting tricks or debt repudiation.

A commodity swap, an example of a commodity-linked product, is a financial arrangement that requires two parties. First, there is a firm desiring to hedge its risk exposure. This firm may be a user (producer) concerned about a price increase (decrease). Second, there is a facilitator who brings the deal together. The parties agree on the length of the agreement, payment intervals, and prices. One of the basic requirements for a successful CLP is the existence of a recognized benchmark or market price for the commodity. The parties can then determine at the outset how the agreed price compares to the benchmark so that only the net difference changes hands. A number of CLPs have been written on energy products, gold, copper, aluminum, nickel, pulp paper, concentrated orange juice, soybeans, coffee, and cocoa. Current estimates put their value at around $10 billion.

CLPs can be part of complex financial transactions (CLTs) that are engineered to solve a specific problem. A CLT announced in the summer of 1989 has attracted international attention. Banque Paribas, leading a group of 11 international banks, lent Mexicana de Cobre (MdC) $210 million at a fixed rate of about 11.5% (instead of the over 20% rate on MdC's debt then outstanding) for 38 months. The Belgian company Sogem agreed to buy 4,000 metric tons of copper per month from MdC, at a price indexed to the the London Metal Exchange's daily prices, over that period. To reduce the risk of drastic price falls (with the resulting inability of MdC to meet loan payments), Paribas pays MdC about $2,000 per ton for 4,000 tons of copper per month. Payments for the copper are deposited in a New York escrow account, from which interest and principal are repaid to the banks. The flow of payments will exceed debt service by about 10% to insulate the banks from changes in the price of copper. To hedge its copper price risk, Paribas entered into a swap with a copper user (not Sogem) that was the mirror image of the swap Paribas has with MdC. To hedge its interest rate risk, Paribas entered into an interest rate swap of fixed for floating rates. The residual cash in the escrow account will build over time, assuming Sogem receives shipments, and will be intermittently passed on to MdC. The interest reduction in this landmark financial transaction, which has put Mexico back in the credit map--at the time of the transaction, this was the first voluntary private lending to Mexico since 1982--was possible because CLTs control for commodity risk, interest risk, credit risk, currency exchange risk, and performance risk.

The first of five, three-year sugar based CLTs, was simulated for the Cuban sugar consortium Cuban Sugar Kings (CSK). We conjectured that the CLT would lower the borrowing rate from 18% to 10% per annum. Assumptions included (a) Cuba's annual production of 6-million short tons, with CSK owning 9% of the assets but only 5% of the production, or 300,000 tons; (b) $110 million loan for 15 years with semi-annual payments debt service payments of $9,166,167 ($5.5 million for interest expense and $3,666,667 for retirement of principal); (c) initial world sugar price (SUGPRICE) of $0.11/lb. Simulations included two cases, sugar price allowed to float, and sugar price with a collar of $0.35/lb ceiling and $0.07/lb floor; (d) initial LIBOR at 8% per annum; (e) a contract to deliver 45,833 tons semi-annually at $0.11/lb to a sugar user with a high credit rating to cover 110% of debt payments; and (f) $5 million arranger's fee and $15 million deposited in an escrow account in the US (paying LIBOR) as maintenance margin, leaving $90 million as usable funds.

Performance risk (the inability of CSK to deliver the quantity of sugar needed to cover interest expenses because of mishaps due to man or nature) is minimized by modeling CSK's production (CROP) as a truncated normal distribution; by assuming that, during the transition stage, national production will be about 72% of the average production during the 1980s; and by going form ownership of 9% of the industry's total non-land capital assets to 5% of the industry's total production. CSK does not bear interest rate risk because it borrows at a fixed 10% per annum--BANK hedges interest rate risk by entering into an interest rate swap as part of the services they provide for their $5 million fee. Treating the CLT as pre-export financing minimizes the risk of future and other retro-active legislative actions. The escrow account eliminates foreign exchange risk and the risk that currency exchange controls or lack of hard currency would prevent CSK from making payments. The escrow account also reduces credit risk by transferring the credit rating of the sugar user to CSK. Finally, the escrow account reduces the risk of suspension of payments by CSK because the sugar user deposits directly into it the amount from the semi-annual sugar sales.

The stochastic variables were: the sugar cane crop, modeled as truncated normal; the world price of sugar (SUGPRICE), and LIBOR, modeled with their six-month continuously compounded rate of change following a log-normal distribution, with period-to-period correlation, and estimated with data from 1979 to 1989. SUGPRICE was allowed to float, and was restricted by a collar between $0.07 and $0.35 per pound. The simulations were performed within Lotus 1-2-3 with the @Risk add-in. The results are based on 2500 iterations.

Results show that, when allowed to float, SUGPRICE exhibited a range from a low of about $0.02 to a high of about $0.55/lb, reflecting the actual behavior of SUGPRICE in the last ten years. To balance these extremes, BANK (as part of their $5 million fee) would set up a collar with a floor of $0.07 and a ceiling of $0.35/lb. LIBOR goes from a low of about 2% to a high of about 17% per annum. Although the low end of the range seems unreasonable, the purpose of LIBOR is to generate interest income in the escrow account, so the low rates of interest make our results more conservative. In any case, LIBOR's expected value is about 8% for each period, and most of the realizations in each period are between 5% and 11% per annum.

The ending balance in the escrow account is the parameter that validates this exercise. Results of CSK's cash flows show probabilities of 83% and 17% that the ending balance in the escrow account will be $22 million ($110 million/5) and $110 million, respectively, when the price of sugar was allowed to float; and of 100% and 16.5%, respectively, when the $0.07 to $0.35/lb collar was imposed on sugar prices. There is a 95% probability that the ending balance will be higher than $25 million with the collar and $10 million without the collar; and a 5% probability that it will be $149 million with the collar and $189 million without the collar. Results also show that the CLT obligation, as a percentage of revenue, range from 27% to 35%, with a mean of 30% for a 95% confidence interval; and that there is only a 9% probability that it will be higher than 34%.

In addition to showing how CLTs can improve the decisionmaking of a sugar consortium in a post-Castro Cuba, this paper conveyed important policy implications for the immediate transition stage. Policies that facilitate the establishment of escrow accounts in foreign banks (to eliminate foreign exchange risk and interest payment risk), would defuse the arguments that Cuba should have the US dollar as the national currency to facilitate the influx of foreign capital, and that US courts should have jurisdiction over Cuban companies. CLTs could also be used as substitutes for protectionist policies to provide price stability to both imports and exports, whenever possible, making post-Castro Cuba a leader in the movement toward freer trade.

References

Anuario Estadístico de Cuba. La Habana: Comité Estatal de Estadísticas, various issues.

Aslund, Anders "Principles of Privatization for Formerly Socialist Countries," Working Paper No. 18 (Preliminary), Stockholm Institute of Soviet and East European Economics, Stockholm, Sweden, January 1991.

Bastiat, Frederic. The Law. Irvington on the Hudson, New York: The Foundation for Economic Education, 1964. 4th printing of the 1950 translation by Dean Russell from the 1850 original in French.

Brady, Simon, "Swap your Risks Away. Commodity Swaps Market For Energy Producers" Euromoney pE35(4) June, 1990.

Business Week Editorial, "Stabilize Reform Along with the Ruble," Business Week July 29, 1991, p. 88.

Buzzanell, Peter J. and Jose F. Alonso. "Cuba's Sugar Economy: Recent Performance and Challenges for the 1990s," Sugar and Sweetener Situation and Outlook Report, SSR14N2, Economic Research Service, U.S. Department of Agriculture, Washington, DC, June 1989, pp. 17-28.

Byker, Gaylen. "Introductory Remarks." Euromoney Conference SE 957. London, England: Financing and Hedging with Commodity-Linked Products, 1990a.

Byker, Gaylen. "Structuring Financings with Commodity Hedges," Euromoney Conference SE 957. London, England: Financing and Hedging with Commodity-Linked Products, 1990b.

Carrillo, Justo, in Suchlicki et al. (Eds.) "Vision and Revision: U.S.- Cuban Relations --1902 to 1959," pp. 163-174.

CITIBASE: Citibank Economic Data Base [Machine-Readable Magnetic Data File]. 1946-, New York, Citibank N.A. 1978.

Clauson, Annette L., Ron Lord and Frederic L. Hoff. "1989 Crop Sugarbeet and Sugarcane Production and Processing Costs," Sugar and Sweetener Situation and Outlook Report, SSRV 16N1, Economic Research Service, U.S. Department of Agriculture, Washington, DC, March 1991.

Coffee, Sugar & Cocoa Exchange, Trading Sugar Futures and Options, New York, NY, 1990.

Commodity Systems, Inc. (CSI), 200 West Palmetto Park Road, Boca Raton, Fl 33432.

David, Eduardo. "Sugar Production in Cuba," Sugar y Azúcar 78:2 (1983): 100-108.

Economic Research Service. Sugar and Sweetener Situation and Outlook Report. Washington, DC: U.S. Department of Agriculture, various issues.

Eckl, S., J.N. Robinson, and D.C. Thomas Financial Engineering: A Handbook of Derivative Products, Cambridge, MA: Basil Blackwell, 1991.

Elton, Edwin J. and Martin J. Gruber, Modern Portfolio Theory and Investment Analysis, Fourth Edition, New York: John Wiley and Sons, 1991.

Fama, Eugene F. and Kenneth R. French. "Permanent and Temporary Components of Stock Prices" Journal of Political Economy 1988 vol. 96, no.
2, pp. 246-273.

Feuer, Carl Henry, in A. Zimbalist (Ed.). "The Performance of the Cuban Sugar Industry, 1981-85," pp. 69-83.

Fundación Sociedad Económica de Amigos del País. "The Compensation and Restitution of Property, Confiscated by Communist Governments, to Former Owners: The Examples of Eastern Europe," Interim Report 1, London, England, April 8, 1991.

Henderson, Schuyler K. "A Legal Eye on Hedging's Newest Club." Euromoney p95(2) May, 1990

Germinsky, Robert A. (Ed.). 1990 Sugar y Azúcar Yearbook. Englewood Cliffs, NJ: Ruspam Communications, Inc., March 1990.

Kaser, Michael. "Moving from a Centralized Command Economy to a Free Market: Problems and Solutions. How the West can Help?" Ditchley Conference Report No. D90/13, The Ditchley Foundation, Offordshire, England, 1991.

Lewis, Julian. "The Bandwagon Starts to Roll. (Banks and the Commodity Swaps Market) Euromoney p. 87 (5) May, 1990.

Mises, Ludwig von. Economic Policy: Thoughts for Today and Tomorrow. Washington D.C.: Regnery Gateway, 1979.

O'Connell, Richard, "Problemas Económicos de Cuba en el Período de Transición: Comments." Fundación Sociedad Económica de Amigos del País, London England, n.d.

Pazos, Felipe. "Problemas Económicos de Cuba en el Período de Transición." Invited address to the members of the Asociation for the Study of the Cuban Economy, Inter-American Development Bank, Washington, DC, December 28, 1990.

Polopolus, Leo C. and José Alvarez. Marketing Sugar and Other Sweeteners. Amsterdam, Netherlands: Elsevier Science Publishers, 1991 (In Press).

Rausser, G.C. and K. R. Farrell (Eds.). Alternative Agricultural and Food Policies and the 1985 Farm Bill. Berkeley, CA: University of California, 1984.

Schmitz, A., R. Allen and G. M. Leu. in G.C. Rausser and K.R. Farrell (Eds.). "The U.S. Sugar Program and Its Effects," Chapter 10.

Schmitz, A. and D. Christian. "U.S. Sugar," Paper presented at the U.S. State Department Conference on Sugar Markets in the 1990s, Washington, DC, May 23, 1990.

Schmitz, Andrew and James Vercammen. "Trade Liberalization in the World Market: Playing on a Level Field?," Working Paper No. 563, Department of Agricultural and Resource Economics, Giannini Foundation of Agricultural Economics, University of California, Berkeley, CA, November 1990.

Suchlicki, Jaime, Antonio Jorge and Damián Fernández (Eds.). Cuba: Continuity and Change. Miami, FL: University of Miami, 1985.

Torralbas-González, Diocles. "The Development and Prospects for Cuban Sugar Production," Sugar y Azúcar 78:2 (1983) 95-98.

Zimbalist, Andrew (Ed.) Cuba's Socialist Economy Toward the 1990s. Boulder, CO: Lynne Rienner Publishers, Inc., 1987.

Appendix 1

Gross Estimate of the Value of Assets in the Cuban Sugar Industry

Statistics on the value of assets of the Cuban sugar industry are not available, let alone on recapitalization needs. This note attempts to estimate gross figures by extrapolating Florida data to Cuba's current daily milling capacity.

The 1989 sugar cane enterprise budget of the USDA imputes $0.84 per net short ton as non-land capital in Florida, by multiplying the adjusted book value (ABV) of assets times the 10-year US Treasury bond rate (Clauson et al., 1991, p. 40).

Since total Florida sugar cane production in the 1989 season amounted to 13,435 net short tons, the ABV of assets can be calculated with the formula:

$$ABV \times 0.075 = \$0.84; \text{ or}$$

13,435,000

$$ABV = \frac{0.84 \times 13,435,000}{0.075} = 150,471,989 = \frac{\$21,495,998/mill}{7 \text{ mills}}$$

An average value of $21.5 million per mill in Florida, with an average daily capacity of 16,000 short tons, results in a value of $1,344 per short ton of daily milling capacity ($21.5 m/16,000 short tons).

In the 1980s, Cuba had an average daily milling capacity of 619,000 tones (682,138 short tons) in its 155 mills (Buzanell and Alonso, 1989, p. 23), although with a longer season. Thus:

$$682,138 \times 1,344 = \frac{\$916,793,472}{155 \text{ mills}} = \$5,914,797$$

Thus, a gross estimate of the value of assets in the Cuban sugar industry would be $917 million, or an average of $5.9 million per mill. Daily milling capacity, however, must be adjusted for the length of the season caused by the inefficiencies inherent in current production. In the 1950s, the season averaged 87 days, with a high of 120 days, while total cane production averaged 47,937,000 short tons. In the 1980s, (until the 1986-87 season), the average length of the season was 112 days, with a low of 99 days, while total cane production averaged 75,817,610 short tons (ibid.). Thus,

$$\frac{75,817,610}{87} = 871,467 \times 1,344 = \$1,171,252,000$$

Since adjusting the figures with data from the 1960s and 1970s also rendered similar results, the figure of about $1 billion is used in the assumptions.

Appendix 2

Modeling SUGPRICE and LIBOR

The holding period return (six months in this manuscript) is defined as:

$$Rt = (Pt - Pt\text{-}1)/Pt\text{-}1 \qquad (1)$$

with simple algebra, the continuously componded return can be shown to be:

$$\text{Ln}(1+Rt) = \text{Ln } Pt - \text{Ln } Pt\text{-}1 \qquad (2)$$

We can also write:

$$Pt = Pt\text{-}1 * ex \text{ , where } x = \text{Ln}(1+Rt), \qquad (3)$$

since this relationship is identical to (2):

The two financial prices of interest for this manuscript are the London Inter Bank Offered Rate (LIBOR) and the world sugar price (SUGPRICE). Both LIBOR and SUGPRICE were simulated using the following relationship:

$$Pt = Pt\text{-}1 * ex ,$$

where x is Distributed Normal (μ,σ) and the parameters are those estimated from monthly data.

To test for log-normality of the percentage rate of change from period to period we used the procedure HIST from Micro TSP Version 7.0. The data were monthly prices from 1979.09 to 1989.10. Data sources were Citibase for LIBOR and Commodity Systems Inc.(CSI) for SUGPRICE. For LIBOR, Ln (1+Rt) was distributed Normal with μ = -0.0243634, and σ = 0.2063901 (The Jarque-Bera normality test statistic was 1.206165, which means that we failed to reject the hypothesis that Ln (1+Rt) was normally distributed for LIBOR for six month holding periods from 1979.09 to 1989.10) For SUGPRICE, Ln $(1+Rt)$ was distributed Normal with μ = -0.0043599, and σ = 0.3907529 (The Jarque-Bera normality test statistic was 3.053901, which means that we failed to reject the hypothesis that Ln $(1+Rt)$ was normally distributed for SUGPRICE for six month holding periods from 1979.09 to 1989.10).

Notas Sobre una Estrategia Agropecuaria Para Cuba

Raúl Fernández

"Para verdades trabajamos, y no para sueños."
José Martí

La inevitable terminación de la tiranía castrista dará a los cubanos una singular oportunidad de replantear la estructura de la nación. De la forma en que el pueblo de Cuba aproveche tal coyuntura dependerá en gran medida el destino del país. Son por ello de la mayor importancia los esfuerzos que como los de la ASCE en la presente reunión, permiten adelantar el estudio necesario para aprovechar esa extraordinaria oportunidad. Quiero dejar constancia de mi reconocimiento a los amigos Roger R. Betancourt y Armando Lago por haberme brindado la oportunidad de compartir con ustedes este evento y presentar algunas ideas sobre el sector agropecuario en el período de transición.

Permítaseme señalar brevemente la naturaleza y límites de este trabajo, así como la definición de algunos conceptos. Una exposición completa de una estrategia agropecuaria para Cuba exigiría un tiempo y otros recursos que caen fuera de los parámetros ahora disponibles. Por ello limitamos el presente trabajo al período de unos tres años inmediatamente siguiente al esperado derrumbe del régimen castrocomunista. En ese período serán cruciales la estabilidad del gobierno provisional y el mantenimiento de la paz. Sin ambos, la reconstrucción de Cuba se haría imposible.

Un concepto básico que ha normado nuestro trabajo es el de la interdependencia de cuanto se relaciona con la sociedad. Por eso, cuando hablamos de "sector agropecuario" lo hacemos por una conveniencia metodológica, pero ese sector no existe como algo independiente o autónomo. En realidad ese sector es influído y a la vez influye una multitud de aspectos de las más diversas actividades humanas. Es por eso que en los párrafos que siguen nos veremos obligados a entrar brevemente en otros campos. Lo haremos, sin embargo, sólo en la medida indispensable para dar perspectiva y realismo a la estrategia del sector. Si no lo hiciéramos, caeríamos en el vicio conocido de trabajar en torres de marfil, de espaldas a la sociedad.

Usamos la palabra estrategia como el arte y la ciencia de emplear, en las oportunidades y lugares críticos, los recursos políticos, diplomáticos, económicos, psicológicos, militares, etc., con el objeto de dar el máximo apoyo a las políticas que se adopten. Tales políticas conviene clasificarlas según se pretenda lograr resultados a corto, mediano o largo plazo. Un plan estratégico se requiere para orientar a las autoridades en las complejas relaciones del sector, así como ayudar a tomar las acciones detalladas que constantemente deberán adoptarse. Tal vez, las dificultades que sufren algunos países en su transición hacia un régimen de libre mercado se deben, en parte, a la falta de un buen plan estratégico o a la incapacidad de ponerlo en práctica.

La forma en que termine la tiranía, tendrá un efecto marcado, y en algunos casos determinante, sobre las políticas y la estrategia que se sigan. Pero como es necesario fijar un marco de referencia, supongamos el siguiente escenario. Los hermanos Castro y sus más leales seguidores serían desalojados del poder y neutralizados totalmente por un movimiento en el que participarían las Fuerzas Armadas, elementos descontentos dentro del actual gobierno, grupos disidentes de la población y representantes de la comunidad cubana del exilio. Habría un mínimo de violencia, destrucción y derramamiento de sangre. El nuevo gobierno, de carácter provisional, denunciaría el marxismo, pero trataría de mantener relaciones constructivas con la URSS y China, al mismo tiempo que ejecutaría una campaña diplomática para restablecer o mejorar, en su caso, las relaciones con Estados Unidos, otros países de Occidente y América Latina, (especialmente Venezuela y México), así como con las organizaciones internacionales. Una de las primeras tareas del Gobierno será consolidar su posición dentro y fuera de Cuba. Para lo primero tendrá que contrarrestar las fuentes de descontento y desorden en el país.... Este escenario podría ser considerado como poco realista, pero téngase en cuenta que situaciones no muy diferentes se han desarrollado en Europa Oriental. Tomémoslo como marco de referencia.

En esa situación, el sector agropecuario puede jugar un papel muy significativo a corto, mediano y largo plazo. Trataremos sólo del corto plazo. La escasez de alimentos que ha caracterizado a la tiranía, debería aliviarse o eliminarse tan pronto como fuera posible, usando el potencial de la agricultura cubana. Ello, al satisfacer una necesidad humana tan básica, contribuiría a la estabilidad y a la paz, así como a proporcionar a las autoridades un número mayor de opciones, internas y externas. La mayoría de las cosechas de Cuba destinadas a la alimentación, se obtienen entre tres y cinco meses, a partir de la siembra, y los animales como pollos y cerdos se producen en pocas semanas o meses, por lo que los beneficios de un aumento de su producción podrían notarse enseguida. Por tanto, el énfasis inicial debe concentrarse en estimular la producción tanto de dichas cosechas como de los animales de cría, incluyendo las vacas de leche, así como la pesca.

Este curso de acción se siguió con éxito a la caída del régimen de Trujillo en la República Dominicana en 1962. Entonces, el agro dominicano, como el resto de la economía, se había deteriorado considerablemente, como consecuencia de las sanciones de la OEA que siguieron al intento de asesinato del Presidente Rómulo Betancourt de Venezuela. Después de un período de debilitamiento general de la economía dominicana, cayó finalmente el régimen y el Consejo de Estado tomó el poder como gobierno provisional. Ante las grandes convulsiones sociales, políticas y económicas que se experimentaban, el Consejo intentó y logró estabilizar la situación mediante programas de obras públicas y otros que pusieron dinero en los bolsillos de la gente de escasos recursos, lo que incrementó considerablemente la demanda de alimentos de una población famélica, justamente cuando el anémico sector agropecuario no podía satisfacer esa demanda adicional. En esas circunstancias se empezó a impulsar una pronunciada espiral inflacionaria. Las siguientes cifras ilustran esa situación.

-        El nivel de salarios se hizo aumentar en un 34% en apenas 12 meses

-        El índice del costo de la vida, que había registrado el punto mas bajo de 209 en septiembre de 1961, durante la recesión de los dias finales de la tiranía trujillista, subió un 20% para llegar a 252, ocho meses más tarde, luego de instaurarse en el poder el Consejo de Estado.

- Entre el primer semestre de 1961 y el primer semestre de 1962 se produjeron los siguientes incrementos en el consumo: harina de trigo, 37%; grasa comestible, 79%; y arroz, 93%. Nótese que con respecto al arroz, que constituye el alimento básico de los dominicanos y de los cubanos, el consumo practicamente se duplicó en apenas 12 meses.

Con el objeto de remediar esta peligrosa situación, el Banco Agrícola de la República Dominicana organizó, tan rapidamente como fue posible, una campaña masiva de crédito dirigido a los agricultores pequeños y medianos. El dinero prestado en dicha campaña, pronto se transformó en más arroz, más maíz, más pollos, más cerdos, más viandas, en fin, en más alimentos que equilibraron la oferta con la demanda, y que hicieron un aporte apreciable a la paz social. Contribuyeron además a aumentar la oferta de arroz, las importaciones de ese grano de los Estados Unidos, bajo los términos de la Ley 480. Dichas importaciones tuvieron el efecto adicional de engrosar los recursos que el Banco Agrícola destinaba a financiar a los agricultores, ya que el producto de la venta del arroz importado se canalizó al Banco. Con tales medidas, el incremento del índice del costo de la vida se detuvo, estabilizándose a un nivel inferior al mencionado 252.Se celebraron elecciones a finales de 1962 y se dió posesión al primer gobierno democraticamente electo en tres décadas.[1]

La experiencia de los países que tratan de abandonar el marxismo en Europa o Centroamérica, indica que no es fácil realizar los cambios. En el citado caso de la República Dominicana se trabajó con las estructuras económicas existentes y se proveyó crédito agrícola de producción. La combinación de demanda, buenos precios para lo producido, y crédito accesible, estimuló rapidamente el aparato productivo del país, lo que aumentó la disponibilidad de bienes y ayudó a contener una amenazadora inflación. Como corolario se redujeron las tensiones sociales. En los países con viejas estructuras marxistas, la situación es más difícil, pero muchos de los principios a aplicar son similares. Lo que se requiere es una programación y ejecución más cuidadosas. Con esta observación, creemos que lo relatado en relación con la República Dominicana debe ser tenido en cuenta respecto del caso de Cuba.

No es posible concebir una estrategia agropecuaria para Cuba en un vacío de ideas y circunstancias. Por ello permítaseme recurrir a las hipótesis de trabajo para definir el marco dentro del cual continuaremos formulando nuestras Notas. Esas hipótesis no son rígidas, ni mucho menos definitivas. No creemos que representen el deseo unánime de los cubanos, pero estamos persuadidos de que la mayoría concordará con muchos de los

---

[1] Informe ante la Primera Reunión de Instituciones Financieras de Fomento, publicado por el Banco Agrícola de la República Dominicana en febrero de 1964 y presentado en la citada reunión en Caracas.

postulados de las hipótesis, y en el peor de los casos ellas representan ideas respetables.

Hipótesis de trabajo:

Primera. El Gobierno Provisional tendrá funciones limitadas a:

a) Mantener la paz y el orden

b) Reactivar la economía

c) Acometer sólo los cambios estructurales que sean imprescindibles para el desempeño de las funciones antes señaladas, o para corregir obvias y graves injusticias o ineficiencias. Cualquier cambio estructural que pueda comprometer el futuro del país, y que no esté comprendido en los casos anteriores, deberá esperar por la celebración de una asamblea constituyente y la instalación de un gobierno electo por el pueblo. Proceder de otra manera sería una violación a los principios de la democracia.Se llevarán a cabo privatizaciones selectivas, pero durante la provisionalidad no se intentará un programa masivo de privatización por las razones que veremos después.

d) Administrar el patrimonio nacional con diligencia y honestidad, velando por los intereses permanentes de la nación cubana. A los programas que fueran de beneficio para el país, como los de desarrollo de las frutas cítricas y de los subproductos de la caña, continuaríase dándoles el apoyo apropiado, independientemente de dónde hubiera partido la iniciativa para impulsarlos.

Segunda. La duración del Gobierno Provisional no excederá de tres años. Su gestión deberá culminar con la celebración de elecciones para una asamblea constituyente, seguidas de elecciones generales para establecer el primer gobierno constitucional después de la tiranía.

Consideremos ahora la privatización. Empecemos por recordar que casi toda la propiedad en Cuba ha pasado a manos del Estado. Si se intentara una privatización rápida en gran escala, sin las debidas previsiones legales e institucionales, se podría desembocar en una situación caótica, o darse lugar a todo tipo de prácticas corruptas, o a una liquidación de la riqueza cubana a precios irrisorios. Los países de la Europa del Este están experimentando grandes dificultades en sus programas de privatización. Aún países como Estados Unidos, con su admirable desarrollo institucional y tecnológico, ha encontrado múltiples dificultades para vender las propiedades resultantes de los fracasos de las asociaciones de ahorro y préstamos, las conocidas "savings and loan associations". Se ha dicho en Estados Unidos,inclusive, que el ritmo de las ventas de esas propiedades debe atemperarse a las condiciones de la demanda en el mercado, para no deprimir los precios. Nosotros creemos que eso es lógico. En Cuba, además, deben tenerse en cuenta otros factores, tales como si un gobierno no electo por el pueblo tiene la autoridad para acometer una privatización en masa, lo que equivaldría practicamente a enajenar el país. Como una de las excepciones necesarias, nos referimos adelante a la privatización de dos subsectores, lo cual creemos viable y deseable, por su relativo pequeño monto y su gran valor estratégico en la dinámica de la producción. Podría haber otras limitadas excepciones, pero volvamos ahora al papel del sector agropecuario.

La producción de alimentos deberá contribuir significativamente al bienestar y a la paz. A esos fines, el Gobierno Provisional debe estimular a los pequeños agricultores que no fueron totalmente absorbidos por el régimen, restableciendo la libertad de empresa y dándoles acceso a los insumos y recursos necesarios a la producción, así como permitiéndoles la libre concurrencia al mercado y proporcionándoles asistencia técnica. Además, el Gobierno usará provisionalmente algunas estructuras existentes tales como las cooperativas y las fincas estatales, y ajustará otras. Veamos:

Consideremos al sector agropecuario dividido en tres subsectores que llamaremos "provisión de insumos", "producción en fincas" y "comercialización". "Provisión de insumos" comprende todas las actividades de adquisición de semillas, fertilizantes, pesticidas, piezas de repuesto, maquinarias, equipos, combustibles, etc., así como la venta y distribución de dichos bienes a los agricultores. Respecto a este subsector se procuraría su privatización a la brevedad posible, velando por que se salvaguarden los intereses nacionales. El dinamismo que despliegue este subsector servirá como una fuerza que empujará, por así decirlo, al subsector de producción en fincas, que es el que lleva a cabo la producción agrícola propiamente dicha.

Mientras se adquieren los insumos, habrá que organizar con rapidez y eficacia, mecanismos de crédito, o sea, de canalización de recursos financieros, a los productores elegibles tales como agricultores independientes, cooperativas y empresas estatales, o a cualesquiera otro productor legítimo no previsto en estas Notas. El crédito se daría para producción, pero no se otorgaría en esta etapa para la adquisición de fincas. El Ingeniero Casto Ferragut, fundador y dirigente distinguido del Banco de Fomento Agrícola e Industrial de Cuba (BANFAIC), ha preparado una excelente monografía sobre esa organización la que podría servir como documento de referencia al estructurarse las nuevas instituciones de crédito. El BANFAIC, bajo el liderazgo de ilustres cubanos como el Dr. Justo Carrillo Hernández, resistió con éxito presiones de unos y de otros, en una época lamentablemente corrupta. Con vista al futuro, cabe enfatizar solamente, que el mecanismo de crédito que se utilice durante los primeros dos o tres años después de la liberación, debe ser esencialmente sencillo y ágil. Si hubiera algún mecanismo actualmente que, mediante su reforma y supervisión, pudiera rendir la tarea requerida, deberá utilizarse. Nosotros pensamos que el mayor riesgo que correría la democracia en Cuba sería la incapacidad del nuevo gobierno de remediar a corto plazo, al menos las más obvias deficiencias de la tiranía. Entre éstas ninguna es más irritante que la falta de alimentos.

Tanto los agricultores independientes así como las cooperativas y fincas estatales tendrían acceso a los insumos y a los recursos financieros. La responsabilidad que pesaría sobre todos los productores sería la de incrementar la producción y pagar los préstamos.

Además, deberán hacer un uso racional de los recursos naturales. El desempeño de unos y de otros constituirá un factor importante para determinar el tratamiento a dárseles en las etapas posteriores. El elemento crítico a resolver sería la obtención, por parte de Cuba, de semillas, fertilizantes, material de envase, combustibles y otros insumos, así como equipos, piezas de repuesto, y otros bienes necesarios a la producción, almacenamiento, refrigeración, transporte, distribución y venta de las cosechas. Pensamos que sería factible conseguir crédito de proveedores para esos propósitos.

Deberá merecer atenta consideración desde el principio el adiestramiento de quienes tendrán a su cargo funciones de administración y dirección. El hecho de que Cuba y los cubanos han sido sometidos durante más de tres décadas, no sólo al adoctrinamiento marxista sino a la privación de otras fuentes de información sociales y económicas, origina una deficiencia educacional que podría dificultar la transformación de la economía. La falta o distorsión de conceptos básicos de contabilidad, administración de empresas, economía y agronomía, deberá superarse mediante programas de adiestramiento imaginativos y masivos.

La comercialización eficiente de las cosechas y la reducción al mínimo de las pérdidas y desperdicios, deberán constituirse en una de las tareas de más alta prioridad. Todos sabemos el penoso espectáculo de los países comunistas con poblaciones carentes de alimentos al lado de cosechas destruidas por la intemperie o las plagas. Por eso, el subsector de "comercialización" sería privatizado a la brevedad posible bajo principios similares a los que se señalaron antes para el subsector de insumos. La libertad de comercio, incluyendo la fijación de precios según las leyes de la oferta y la demanda, sería una finalidad deseable desde la etapa inicial, pero no entraría en vigencia en aquellos casos excepcionales en que su aplicación pudiera generar graves conflictos sociales. Creemos que el dinamismo de la comercialización en manos de empresarios privados contribuirá a estimular la producción en fincas.

Resumiendo, a corto plazo se privatizarían los subsectores de insumos y comercialización y se daría apoyo prioritario a los pequeños agricultores no incorporados al aparato estatal marxista. A corto plazo no se privatizaría el sector de fincas estatales. Las cooperativas estarían sujetas al examen de las condiciones particulares de cada una. De no haber serios conflictos por la posesión y la propiedad de la tierra, se adelantaría todo lo posible la privatización de las cooperativas. El tratamiento diferenciado descrito anteriormente, podría ser ampliamente objetado. Ciertamente todos quisiéramos ver un desmantelamiento total e inmediato de la burocracia estatal. Sin embargo, a corto plazo y dadas las limitaciones de recursos internos y externos, nosotros vemos como única alternativa para evitar el posterior deterioro de las condiciones de vida del cubano, la del aprovechamiento temporal de parte del aparato productivo existente. Este sería supervisado y ajustado por el Gobierno Provisional, al mismo tiempo que se fortalece lo que ha quedado del sector privado, a fin de prepararlo para un desempeño de mayor envergadura después. A mediano y largo plazo se actuaría de acuerdo con lo que disponga el nuevo gobierno democraticamente electo, atendiendo a lo que dictamine la nueva constitución.

Si en vez de realizar cambios graduados, las autoridades provisionales intentaran demoler todo el aparato estatal, la legitimidad de esa actuación podría ser cuestionada por quienes creen que sólo a un gobierno elegido democraticamente corresponde tal atribución. Además, no parece factible que se lleve a cabo una radical e inmediata transformación sin que se entronice el desorden, tal vez el caos. Semejante cosa comprometería aún más el bajo nivel de producción actual. Nosotros creemos que el cambio de las estructuras debe tener lugar progresivamente y, en la medida que lo permita el carácter excepcional de la situación en Cuba, apoyarse en principios de derecho dentro de un régimen democrático. Ello empezaría a ser viable a partir del segundo año, y con plena autoridad, una vez que sea electo el primer gobierno democrático, unos 30 meses después del colapso del castrismo.

Desde un punto de vista técnico creemos que, a mediano y largo plazo, la estrategia debe propiciar una producción diversificada tanto en la naturaleza de lo producido como en los mercados, la que debe apoyarse en la investigación. Además, debe propenderse al uso racional de los recursos naturales. Cuba, en ningún momento, debe obtener una bonanza transitoria a cambio de la erosión de sus suelos, o su salinización, o de la destrucción y contaminación del ambiente. Aquí creemos necesario subrayar algunas ideas sobre la erosión de los suelos.

La creciente presión demográfica sobre los suelos agrícolas aumenta los riesgos de erosión y deterioro de éstos. La construcción de obras que prevengan esos daños, es una solución. Ahora bien, cuando el costo de esas obras se compara con el valor presente de los beneficios futuros que generarían, usualmente se descartan las obras, ya que el valor presente de beneficios que se materializarán muchos años en el futuro, puede llegar a ser insignificante. Sin embargo, como los pueblos son permanentes, la pérdida del suelo por erosión puede llegar a significar la ruina total del país como se observa ya en Las Antillas, al lado mismo de Cuba. Todo esto indica que hay un peligroso divorcio de algunos enfoques ecológicos de los de tipo económico correspondientes, así como que algunos métodos deben revisarse. Afortunadamente, distiguidos académicos y profesionales están trabajando ya en una "Ecología Económica", ciencia transdisciplinaria destinada a tratar las relaciones entre ecosistemas y sistemas económicos en su más amplia acepción. En contraste con el menosprecio que los países marxistas han demostrado por el habitat del hombre, Cuba democrática debería enarbolar una política ecológica de respeto por el patrimonio natural y el derecho que al disfrute del mismo tienen las generaciones venideras.

Hace cien años, cubanos en ciudades del exilio se preparaban para un regreso a Cuba cargado de presagios. Hoy, exactamente un siglo después, asambleas de cubanos pensantes que se preocupan por el destino de la patria, replican como un eco misterioso, aquellas reuniones de Tampa, de Nueva York, de Cayo Hueso. Hoy como entonces, la lucha es desigual. De un lado, la razón de la fuerza ha acumulado arsenales de armas junto a arsenales de odio. Pero como entonces, la razón de la fuerza será vencida por la fuerza de la razón. Nuestro deber, como orgullosos herederos de los hombre y mujeres de 1895, es rendir el homenaje de los cubanos de hoy a los heróicos cubanos de ayer, mediante la construcción, a las puertas de América, de una patria justa y feliz, con todos y para todos.

Comments by Antonio Gayoso

Presenters dealt with agricultural conditions and problems which a new Cuban Government would face in the future. Some approaches were discussed to address these problems. Foremost issue will be the role of the sugar sector. Major conclusion was that it will remain critical to Cuban economic well being. Given market conditions, continuous access to Soviet market will be an absolute necessity. Regarding food production, a complex package of incentives needed to increase supplies was discussed. It included price incentives, input supplies, and open marketing. The crucial issue of land tenure rights was a part of it. Discussion led to conclusion that, without settling tenure rights, such incentives would not work. Only eighteen percent of Cuban productive land is in private hands, who might be only ones responding to such standard economic incentives.

A proposal to use a commodity-linked transaction approach to access capital needed for future reconstruction was also presented. While attractive in principle, financial experts in the audience believed it could lead to unhealthy future indebtedness, without assurance of the desired payoff for the country.

Finally, keeping in mind the protracted litigation to settle ownership of land and other assets, currently underway in Eastern Europe, a notion was suggested to permit quick settlement of land tenure issues. In brief, land ownership would be granted to those who now till the land. Former owners would seek compensation from a special court created for that purpose and a land market would be developed to facilitate land purchases. It was felt that needed investment in agriculture will not occur as long as tenure rights are unsettled. This issue was not discussed for lack of time.

International Tourism in Cuba: An Economic Development Strategy?

María Dolores Espino

Introduction

After registering impressive rates of growth during the first half of the 80s, the Cuban economy beginning in 1986 entered into a deep economic crisis, from which it has yet to emerge. The factors contributing to this crisis are many and complex in nature and can be attributed to both internal and external factors.

The present Cuban economic crisis has been the subject of numerous studies by economists both inside and outside Cuba.[1] It is not the purpose of this paper to add to that body of work. Rather we will focus on the Cuban tourist industry, one sector of the Cuban economy which has maintained its positive performance throughout the decade. The tourist industry has been targeted as a key sector and prioritized during the "período especial en tiempo de paz", the Cuban economic readjustment program.

Tourism in Cuba

Tourism in pre-1959 Cuba was a major industry and a primary source of hard currency and employment for the nation. In 1957, 347,508 foreigners visited Cuba.[2] Tourist expenditures amounted to 62.1 million pesos that same year. By 1957, hard currency earnings from tourism had surpassed those from the tobacco industry (see Table 1). Tourism had become the second largest earner of foreign currency in the Cuban economy.

In the early years of the revolution, international tourism all but disappeared from the island. Although the major reason for its demise can be attributed to the U.S. embargo, ideological concerns also contributed. Tourism was perceived as too closely associated with the capitalists evils of prostitution, drugs, gambling and organized crime. The revolutionary government discounted tourism as a vehicle for economic growth and development. During the 1960s and early 70s, no major investment in tourism was undertaken. The vast tourist infrastructure, remaining from the pre-revolutionary years, was left for the use of Cuban citizens, internationalist guest from socialist and other friendly countries, or simply abandoned. Some 16 hotels where closed down and hotel capacity was reduced by 50

---

[1] See for example; Roca, Sergio G. "Cuba y la Nueva Economía Internacional: Tiempos Duros, Decisiones Difíciles," paper presented at the Latin American Studies Association meetings, Washington, D.C., April 1991; Rodríguez, José Luis "The Cuban Economy: A current Assessment" in Transformation and Struggle: Cuba faces the 1990's, S. Halebsky and John M. Kirk ed. Praeger, New York 1990; and Ritter, A.R.M. "Cuba's Convertible Currency Debt Problem". Cepal Review N. 36 December 1988, U.N. Cepal, Santiago, Chile.

[2] Data on Foreign visitors and tourist to Cuba prior to 1959 and cited in a number of studies among these; Truslow, Adams Francis, Chief of Mission, Economic and Technical Mission to Cuba International Bank for Reconstruction and Development, 1950; Grupo Cubano de Investigación Económica, Un Estudio Sobre Cuba, University of Miami Press, 1963; and Martín Fernández, Ramón," El turismo y su desarrollo," Economía y Desarrollo No. 5, Año 1968.

Table 1

Table 1. Cuba's Hard Currency Receipts from Merchandise Trade and Tourism: 1953–1958
(In Million Pesos)

	1953	1954	1955	1956	1957	1958
Total All Merchandise	640.4	539	594.2	666.2	807.2	733.5
Sugar and Sugar Products	530.1	432.9	474.4	525.1	656.3	593.1
Tobacco	41.9	41.2	43.5	43.8	47.9	49.6
Tourist Receipts	19.6	24	27.8	38.1	62.1	56.9

Sources: Banco Nacional de Cuba, Memoria 1958–1959, La Habana Cuba; and Banco Nacional de Cuba, Programa de Desarrollo Economico, Informe N 4, Habana, Cuba, 1958

percent.[3]

By the mid 1970s visitors from capitalist nations started trickling back to Cuba. In 1974, 8.4 thousand visitors from the capitalist countries visited Cuba. By 1987, this figure had increased to 217.9 thousand.

In 1976, recognizing Cuba's comparative advantage as a vacation spot and realizing the potential economic benefits that would be derived from international tourism, the Cuban government created the Instituto Nacional de Turismo (INTUR). INTUR became the agency primarily responsible for developing policy for both national and international tourism, as well as for collecting data on tourist arrivals and tourist expenditures.

In recent years Cuba has started promoting tourism strongly in capitalist countries. In 1987 another tourist development agency, Cubanacan, S.A. was created in the island. Cubanacan shares responsibilities with INTUR for policy making in the international tourist industry. Cubanacan is also the major Cuban corporation which engages foreign capital for joint-venture investments in the Cuba tourist industry. A smaller corporation Gaviota, S.A. also operates in Cuba and engages in joint-ventures.

Indicators of International Tourist Activity

The best and most reliable statistics that can be use as indicators of international tourist activity is the number of foreign travelers arriving at a given country. The Cuban government collects two different and distinct series on international visitors.[4] One series includes only visitors which arrive at the country through travel agencies. This series is compiled by the Cuban tourist corporations (INTUR, Cubanacan, etc) and published in the Anuario Estadístico de Cuba. A second, much broader series is compiled by the Direción de Immigración y Extranjeria and includes all foreign visitors arriving at the border. This series is published by the World Tourism Organization, in the Yearbook of Tourism Statistics and by the Banco Nacional de Cuba in its Informe Económico.

All sources corroborate that during the 1980's, Cuba experienced rapid growth in international tourism. (See Tables 2-4). International visits more than doubled from 132.9 thousand in 1981 to 340.3 thousand in 1990.

The bulk of international visitors to Cuba is from capitalist nations. In 1990, Western Europe, North America and Latin America accounted for almost 90 percent of all international visitors to Cuba. The country generating the highest number of tourists to

---

[3] Cited by Hector Ayala Castro in "Notas Sobre el Turismo," series de Estudios Sobre la Economía Cubana, Universidad de la Habana, Cuba, June 1991, p. 15.

[4] For the exact definition used, see Anuario Estadístico de Cuba, Comité Estatal de Estadísticas, Habana Cuba, 1986, 1987, 1988.

Table 2

Table 2: Foreign Visitors to Cuba, by Area of Origin

	1980	1981	1982	1983	1984	1985	1986	1987	1988
Socialist Nations	29,696	34,634	28,963	20,007	23,909	28,322	34,083	31,446	31,393
% of Total	22.9	32.7	27.2	16.9	15.1	16.4	17.5	15.1	12.7
Capitalist Nations	98,678	69,543	75,662	95	126,796	139,856	152,005	166,606	205,326
% of Total	76.1	65.6	71,1	79.5	80.2	81.0	78.1	80.0	83.1
Other	1,217	1,859	1,814	4,208	7,330	4,398	8,443	10,189	10,361
	1.0	1.7	1.7	3.6	4.6	2.6	4.4	4.9	4.2
Total	129,591	106,036	106,399	118,308	158,035	172,578	194,531	208,241	247,080

% Growth	1981	1982	1983	1984	1985	1986	1987	1988
Socialist Nations	16.6	-16.4	-30.9	-19.5	18.5	20.3	-7.7	-0.2
Capitalist Nations	-29.5	8.7	24.4	34.8	10.3	8.7	9.6	23.2
Total	-18.2	0.3	11.3	33.6	9.2	12.7	7.0	18.7

Source: Comite Estatal de Estadisticas: Anuario Estadistico de Cuba, 1986, 1987, 1988.

a: Visitors through travel agencies

Table 3
International Visitors to Cuba
(In Thousands)

	Total Visitors	% Change	Visitor from Capitalist Nations	% Change
1982	150.7	13.39	101.5	
1983	174.1	15.53	124.9	23.05
1984	218.3	25.39	168.5	34.91
1985	243.0	11.31	193.2	14.54
1986	281.9	16.01	217.9	12.78
1987	298.3	4.06	237.3	8.90
1988	309.2	5.40		
1989	326.3	5.53		
1990	340.3	4.30		

Source: Direción de Immigración y Extranjeria estadistica de frontera, unpublished series; and Banco Nacional de Cuba, Informe Economico varies issues.

Table 4
International Visitors to Cuba by Selected
Area of Origins

	1981	1985	1990	% Change 1990/1981
North America	29,511	44,116	81,810	177.22
Latin America	24,667	46,267	81,985	232.37
Western Europe	22,675	77,578	138,757	511.94
Eastern Europe	30,388	31,332	30,031	-.01
Total	132,902	243,026	340,329	156.08
% Share of Total				
North America	22.21	18.15	24.04	
Latin American	18.56	19.04	24.09	
Western Europe	17.06	31.92	40.77	
Eastern Europe	22.86	12.89	8.82	
Other	19.31	18.0	2.28	
Total	100.00	100.00	100.00	

Source: Direción de Immigración y extranjeria, estadistica de frontera, unpublished series.

Table 5

Foreign Visitors to Cuba by Major Country of Origin
(in thousands)

	1981	1985	1990
Canada	23.6	40.7	74.4
Spain	9.0	18.2	33.9
Italy	2.5	15.7	16.9
Germany	3.2	21.9	59.5
Mexico	12.7	22.6	34.5
Venezuela	.8	.3	17.3
U.S.S.R.	17.6	12.9	18.7

Source: Direción de Immigración y Extranjeria, estadistica de frontera, unpublished series.

Cuba is Canada with 74.4 thousand visitors, followed by Germany with 59.5 thousand, Mexico with 34.5 thousand and Spain with 33.9 thousand. Other major suppliers of tourism to Cuba, are the Soviet Union, Venezuela and Italy.

During the 1980s most visitors to Cuba were tourist, that is their stay in the island lasted for longer than 24 hours. Very few excursionist visited Cuba during that period. In 1988 only 4, 746 excursionist were registered compared to 231,973 tourists. The tourist/excursionist breakdown of Cuba, in the 80s is quite different from that prevailing in pre-revolutionary Cuba, and from the current pattern in most of the Caribbean. During the 1950s a major portion of the tourist trade could be attributed to excursionist. In 1957, 75,200 and in 1958 90,000 excursionist visited the island. The low number of excursionists which presently visit Cuba can be attributed to the island's isolation from the sea-cruise circuit, which generates a significant number of visits for the rest of the Caribbean.

In terms of tourist arrivals, Cuba exhibited one of the strongest growth rate in the Caribbean (see table 7). From 1981 to 1987, tourist arrivals to Cuba more than doubled increasing at a rate of 133.1 percent. The rate of growth for the Caribbean as a whole, for the same period of time was of 42.0 percent. In spite of this strong growth, Cuba's share of total tourist arrivals to the region is still rather small and insignificant, especially when compared to the island's size. In 1987, Cuba accounted for only 2.9 percent of all tourist arrivals to the region. In comparison, the Dominican Republic's share for 1987 was of 9.5 percent.

In terms of tourist receipts, measured in U.S. dollars, Cuba's share of the region's tourist activity is even smaller, only 1.8 percent in 1987 (see Table 8).[5] Cuba's tourist receipts from 1981 to 1987 grew by 159.3 percent compared to a 61.5 percent growth rate for the Caribbean as a whole.

The performance of Cuba's tourist industry is not as favorable in terms of tourist receipt as it is in terms of tourist arrivals. Hard currency tourist receipts have not grown as fast as tourist arrivals from capitalist countries, the generators of hard currency. As can be seen in Table 9, average receipts per visitor from capitalist countries have been declining.[6] In 1982, average hard currency receipts per capitalist-nation visitor was $501. In 1987 this figure had fallen to $470.

Cuba's success in attracting visitors from capitalist countries might be due in part to the price advantage over other comparable sites that Cuba offers to visitors. In Table 10, average receipts per visitor night have been calculated for selected Caribbean nations.[7]

---

[5] Tourist receipts cited here exclude fare's for international travel.

[6] Due to the small percentage of visitors to Cuba which can be categories as excursionist, only 1.9 percent in 1988, what is true of the average visitor statistic also applies to average tourist.

[7] Country selection was base on availability of data. For Cuba, 1984 data on average length of stay is the latest figure avaiable.

Table 6

Table 6: International Travelers to Cuba by Category

Year	Visitors	Tourist	Excursionist
1980	129,521	99,671	28,703
1981	106,399	98,536	6,059
1982	106,399	98,526	6,206
1983	118,308	107,894	4,604
1984	158,035	146,101	4,604
1985	172,527	163,434	4,744
1986	194,531	179,911	6,177
1987	208,241	194,614	3,473
1988	247,080	231,973	4,746

Sources: Comite Estatal de Estadisticas, Anuario Estadistico de Cuba,
1986, 1987, 1988.

Table 7
Table 7: Arrival of Tourists from Abroad for Selected Caribbean Nations
(In Thousands)

	1981	1982	1983	1984	1985	1986	1987	% Change: 1987/81
Antigua & Barbuda	85	87	111	139	149	159	173	103.5
Aruba	221	220	195	210	206	181	232	4.9
Bahamas	1,031	1,101	1,200	1,278	1,368	1,375	1,480	43.5
Barbados	353	304	328	368	359	370	422	19.5
Bermuda	430	417	447	417	407	460	478	11.2
Virgin Islands	110	114	119	122	130	164	170	54.5
Cayman Islands	125	121	131	148	145	166	209	67.2
Cuba	121	139	164	207	240	298	282	133.1
Curacao	176	174	111	130	128	128	135	-23.3
Dominican Republic	451	460	502	562	660	747	902	100.4
Guadalupe	133	189	194	163	151	148	153	15.0
Haiti	158	158	150	145	144	112	122	-22.8
Jamaica	406	468	566	603	572	663	739	82.0
Martinique	157	178	176	184	191	183	234	49.0
Puerto Rico	1,573	1,564	1,530	1,496	1,532	1,573	1,872	19.0
St. Lucia	68	70	78	86	95	112	123	78.3
St. Marteen	190	213	263	318	398	439	496	161.1
Trinidad & Tobago	187	184	189	191	187	191	202	8.0
U.S. Virgin Islands	344	340	345	370	412	470	580	68.6
Total Caribbean	6,626	6,845	7,033	7,388	7,827	8,297	9,412	42.0
% Cuba/Caribbean	1.8	2	2.3	2.8	3.1	3.4	2.9	

Source: World Tourist Org., Yearbook of Tourist Statistics, Madrid, Spain, 1986, 1988.

Table 8

Table 8: Tourist Receipts for Selected Caribbean Countries
(In Million U.S.Dollars)

	1981	1982	1983	1984	1985	1986	1987	% Change: 1987/81
Antigua & Barbuda	46	44	59	89	101	114	131	184.8
Aruba	156	163	115	110	111	144	203	30.1
Bahamas	639	655	765	796	994	1,104	1,174	83.7
Barbados	264	251	252	284	309	337	379	43.6
Bermuda	306	314	326	339	357	422	475	55.2
Virgin Islands	54	66	82	86	97	120	140	159.3
Cayman Islands	53	56	62	71	86	94	120	126.4
Cuba	44	51	59	76	87	98	112	154.5
Curacao	158	155	78	69	71	89	94	-40.5
Dominican Republic	223	229	282	315	368	464	500	124.2
Haiti	85	80	85	83	95	84	93	9.4
Jamaica	284	338	399	407	407	516	595	109.5
Martinique	85	82	83	87	93	92	100	17.6
Puerto Rico	626	678	691	681	723	723	866	38.3
St. Lucia	29	32	40	42	56	73	78	169.0
St. Marteen	115	117	122	128	150	160	170	47.8
Trinidad & Tobago	152	179	206	198	197	83	92	-39.5
U.S. Virgin Islands	318	313	356	440	507	509	623	95.9
Total Caribbean	3,793	3,978	4,219	4,427	4,954	5,394	6,127	61.5
% Cuba/Caribbean	1.2	1.4	1.4	1.7	1.8	1.8	1.8	

Source: World Tourist Org., Yearbook of Tourist Statistics, Madrid, Spain, 1986, 1988.

Table 9

Table 9: Arrivals from Capitalist Nations and Hard Currency Receipts

	1982	1983	1984	1985	1986	1987
Number of Visitors from Capitalist Nations (In Thousands)	101.5	124.9	168.5	193.2	217.9	237.3
Visitors Receipts in Hard Currency (In Million Pesos)	50.9	59.4	75.7	87.3	97.7	111.7
Average Receipts per Visitors from Capitalist Nations (In Pesos)	501	476	449	452	448	470

Source: Banco Nacional de Cuba, Informe Economico: various issues.

Cuba has the lowest average receipts per visitor night, of all major Caribbean countries. This is true, whether calculations are made using all visitors or only capitalist countries visitor. Average receipts per visitor night in Cuba is $42.59 for all visitors and $50.54 when calculated for capitalist countries visitors only.[8] The highest figure in the area is the one estimated for Puerto Rico of $117.67 per visitor night, more than twice the Cuban figure.

It is impossible from the data available to calculate receipts per tourist and receipts per tourist night, which gives a better picture of the comparative cost of alternative Caribbean vacation day. However, due to the insignificant percentage of visitors to Cuba, which fall in the excursionist category, the figures for tourist would be very closed to those calculated for visitor. This is not true of the rest of the Caribbean, where a great percentage of visitors are excursionist, staying less than a day in the country.[9] By definition, excursionists do not spend money on lodging within the country, and, therefore, receipts per day for excursionists tend to be less than that of tourists. Excluding excursionists from our calculations would have significantly increased the average receipts per day for most countries in the Caribbean but not for Cuba, further emphasizing Cuba's price advantage in the region.

In spite of the price advantage Cuba offers over alternative Caribbean vacation spots, annual growth rates of visitors to Cuba started to slow down in the late 80's. The average annual growth rate for total visitors during 1982-1986 was of 16.3 percent while, for 1987-1990 the annual average rate fell to 4.8 percent. While sharp decline in growth rates can be attributed to the almost total disappearance of visitor from the former Socialist block (excluding the Soviet Union), growth in visits from capitalist area has also slowed down. The average annual growth rate for European visitors has fallen from 36.81 percent during 1982-1986 to 11.0 percent during 1987-1990, and the average annual growth rate for visits from North America has decline from 15.2 percent to 11.2 percent in 1987-1990. Latin America is the only area which exhibits increased average annual growth rates in visitors to Cuba in the late 80's.

It is unlikely that Cuba's share of the Caribbean tourist market will increase significantly as long as the trade embargo imposed by the U.S. remains in effect. There are a number of reasons for this, first, the embargo prohibits travel for pleasure to Cuba by U.S. citizens to Cuba. This blocks Cuba's access to the U.S. travel market, its "natural partner." Its affluence and proximity to the region makes the U.S. the major supplier of tourist to the Caribbean. Over 60 percent of all visitors to the region originate in the U.S., Cuba has tried to overcome the handicap of U.S. travel restrictions to the island by catering to the Canadian and European market. Canada, however, does not have the depth of the U.S.

---

[8] Visitor's receipt reported for Cuba are hard currency receipts, so the correct calculation of both, receipts per visitor and receipts per visitor night should only include visitors from capitalist country, the only generators of hard currency.

[9] For example excursionist make-up 24 percent of Puerto Rico's international visitors in 1987, 28 percent of Jamaica's and 16 percent of the Dominican Republic. In comparison in 1987 only 1.7 percent of all visitors to Cuba are excursionist.

Table 10

Table 10: Average Receipt per Visitor, and Average Receipt per Visitor Night for Selected Caribbean Nations, 1987

	Visitors Arrivals (In 000)	Average Receipts per Visitor (In U.S. $)	Average Length of Stay (days)	Average Receipts Visitor Night (In U.S. $)
Aruba	318	638	7.0	91.14
Bahamas	2,914	403	5.9	68.31
Barbados	651	582	10.0	58.2
Bermuda	631	753	6.5	115.85
Cuba (All Visitors)	298	396	9.3*	42.59
Cuba (Visitors from Capitalist Countries)	237	470	9.3*	50.54
Curacao	242	388	6.5	59.69
Dominican Republic	1,069	468	8.3	56.38
Jamaica	1,031	577	10.2	56.57
Puerto Rico	2,456	353	3.0	117.67

Source: Author's computations from Yearbook of Tourist Statistics, 1986, 1988 and Banco Nacional de Cuba, Informe Economico, Junio, 1988

*1984 Statistics for all visitors

Table 11

Growth Rates of Visitors to Cuba by Major Area of Origin

	Total Visitors	North America	Latin America	Western Europe	Eastern Europe
1982	13.39	19.95	2.5	6.1	22.14
1983	15.53	4.87	22.12	30.00	-1.51
1984	25.39	-20.59	42.16	113.27	-2.09
1985	11.31	49.66	5.34	16.25	-15.88
1986	16.01	22.65	9.4	18.41	-26.19
1987	4.06	6.81	39.92	4.60	0.82
1988	5.40	9.35	7.79	16.15	3.73
1989	5.53	26.01	13.99	11.78	-40.72
1990	4.30	2.73	2.11	11.3	-18.69
Average Annual % Change					
1982 – 1986	16.33	15.22	16.30	36.81	-4.71
1987 – 1990	4.8	11.2	15.9	11.0	-13.7

Source: Authors calculations from, Direción de Immigración y Extranjeria, estadistica de frontera, unpublish series.

market, and the distance between Europe and Cuba, significantly raises the cost of a Cuban vacation once international travel fares are included.

Secondly, as long as the embargo is in place, Cuba will continue to be left out of the lucrative sea-cruise industry. The industry is based in Miami and the embargo presently prohibits Cuba's ports to be included in the cruises.

Finally, the U.S. embargo prohibits U.S. citizens, corporations or U.S. affiliates overseas from investing in Cuba. This closes the door to important funding sources at a time when Cuba is seeking foreign investment to finance and build its tourist infrastructure. Failure to expand the existing infrastructure may place serious constraint on the growth of international visits to Cuba.

Investment in Cuba's Tourist Infrastructure

The Cuban government has targeted as a priority investment in the tourist infrastructure.

During the eighties tourist accommodations expanded across the island. New hotel and motels were built and others rehabilitated. In 1988, 321 hotels and motels were operating in the island.[10] Fifty four more than at the beginning of the decade. Available capacity in hotel and motels increased at an even faster pace, with 21,108 rooms available at the end of 1988 almost double the number available in 1980.[11]

Accommodations capacity in establishments other than hotels and motels (Villas, houses, apartments, cabanas, camps etc.) increased only minimally. In 1988, there were only 470 more beds available in these establishments than in 1980.[12]

In total, 30,697 rooms where available in the island at the end of 1988. Of this 43% were in Ciudad Habana and 9.3% in the traditional beach resort of Varadero.[13]

The Cuban tourist development plan calls for a step-up in the expansion of tourist accommodations and the development of new tourist centers throughout the island.

Of the rooms available in the island at the end of 1988, around 8,000 thousands were

---

[10] Anuario Estadístico de Cuba, 1986, 1987, 1988.

[11] Anuario Estadístico de Cuba, 1986, 1987, 1988.

[12] Anuario Estadístico de Cuba, 1986, 1987, 1988.

[13] Anuario Estadístico de Cuba, 1988, pg. 613.

available for international tourist.[14]   Of these, about 6,500 were manage by INTUR.[15] Through new construction an rehabilitation INTUR plans to increase its accommodation capacity by 60% by the end of 1991. The task of renovating and rehabilitating already build facilities in Havana and Varadero, falls mainly to INTUR.[16]

Since its creation in 1987, the bulk of new construction of tourist accommodations, has been undertaken by Cubanacan, S.A. Cubanacan's plans for 1988-1992 calls for an expansion of 16,800 more rooms throughout the island. Of these rooms 2,962 are planned for in Habana and 4,860 in Varadero.[17]

The development of new tourist resorts in the North-Eastern coast of Cuba and near Santiago and Sierra Maestra will primarily be under Cubanacan leadership. Cubanacan plans to expand room capacity in the Santa Lucia area by 2,614 rooms and in the Holguin area by 3,776 rooms. Plans for Santiago call for an additional 1,490 rooms, while 130 rooms are planned to be build in the Gramma province.[18]

In 1989 and 1990 capacity for international tourism stood as follows:[19]

	1989 Installations/Rooms		1990 Installations/Rooms	
INTUR	91	10,815	92	10,551
Cubanacan	71	2,069	22	3,600
Gaviota	3	126	7	465
Other	6	536	6	536
Total	117	13,541	127	15,151

Cuba's success in accomplishing this ambitious investment plan hinges on a large extend in its ability to attract foreign investment to finance hotel and motel construction. In fact, one of the main task assigned to Cubanacan upon its creation in 1987, was that of attracting foreign capital for joint ventures in tourism.

Foreign investment in the form of joint-ventures have been allowed in Cuba since

---

[14]   This figure is cited by Jane McManis in South, June 1990, pg. 56 and by, Casanova and Monreal in "Cuba and the United States the Potential of Their Economic Relations" in U.S. - Cuban Relations in the 1990's, pg. 248.

[15]   Author's calculations. Of the 8,000 rooms available for international tourism in 1988, Cubanacán managed 1,562. Gramma Weekly, May 7, 1989.

[16]   Cuban Foreign Trade, 1, 1989 pg. 11.

[17]   Gramma Weekly, May 7, 1989.

[18]   Ibid.

[19]   INTUR statistics, unpublished.

Law-decree No. 50, was enacted in 1982. Under Law-decree No. 50, mix corporations with up to 49 percent foreign ownership are allowed to operate in Cuba.[20]

It is clear that one of the objectives of the joint-venture law was to open the door of the tourist industry to foreign capital. The decree establishes especial provisions for foreign capital in tourism which are significantly more favorable than for other industries. In particular, joint-ventures in international tourism may be exempt from all taxes and licenses and subject to more favorable regulation. Additionally foreign managers of joint-ventures in international tourism are allowed to directly lease Cuban installations and to directly hire Cuban workers.[21] Finally it has been rumored for several years, and recently reported by Cuban tourist officials, that the 1982 joint-venture law is being amended to allow majority foreign ownership in approved international tourism ventures.[22]

Cuba has been somewhat successful in attracting joint-ventures in the tourist industry. In 1990, two hotels constructed and operated under joint-venture agreements opened their doors in Varadero. The Las Palmas hotel is a joint-venture between Cuba and Spanish interests and the Tuxpan hotel is the product of a Cuban and German joint-venture.[23]

There is presently no way to accurately estimate the total amount of foreign investment that Cuba has been able to attract. Nor is it possible to ascertain the exact terms under which existing joint venture agreements have been negotiated. The terms, however, are reported to be quite favorable to foreign investor and to include: 1) free lease on the land where the project is constructed 2) exemption from tariffs on imported inputs 3) tax-free repatriation of profits and 4) guaranteed ownership rights for 25 year, renegotiable to up to 50 years.[24]

To date tourism is the only sector of the Cuban economy that has managed to attract any significant amount of foreign investment funds. This might be due to some extend to the special provisions granted to industry under Law decree No. 50, but is more likely attributed to the nature of the tourist industry itself. Tourism in Cuba does not have to depend on the internally depressed Cuban market for its viability. It is an export industry. In fact, it is the only major Cuban export industry which caters to, and depends on, primarily the capitalist countries. Under the status-quo foreign investors are assured a steady growth market, guarantees of ownership and favorable business terms. The future might even bring

[20] Far an indepth analysis of Cuba's joint venture law see, Jorge Pérez-López, The 1982 Joint Venture Law Context, Assessment and Prospects.

[21] Ibid, pg. 45-46.

[22] Business Monday, the Miami Herald, Dec. 10, 1990 and the New York Times, Travel Section, Sunday March 31, 1991.

[23] Gramma Weekly Review. January 13, 1991.

[24] El Nuevo Herald, February 23, 1991.

a windfall, better U.S.A.-Cuba relations, the lifting of the trade embargo and the opening up of the lucrative U.S. market.

The Economic Impact of International Tourism in Cuba

The real importance of international tourism lies in its ability to generate benefits for the host country. Economic benefits derived from tourism include the following:

- improvements in the balance of payments
- generation of government revenues
- creation of income and employment and
- promotion of economic growth and development

Tourist Exports and Cuba's Balance of Payments

International tourist receipts represent the consumption of domestic goods and services by foreigners and are therefore considered an exports activity. Cuba's tourist exports are accounted for in the service and invisible category of Cuba's balance of payment accounts. In 1987, tourist exports (receipts) were estimated at 111.7 million pesos hard currency, over one-third of the inflows in the service category of the balance of payments account.[25] All hard currency tourist receipts are attributed to tourist from capitalist countries.

Tourist exports are fast becoming a major source of hard-currency receipts for Cuba. The increasing importance of tourism as a export industry is best exemplified by comparing tourist receipts with hard currency receipts generated by other industries. In 1981, tourist receipts were 43.6 million pesos in hard currency, 3.1 percent as much as hard currency receipts from total merchandise trade. By 1987 tourist receipts had reached 111.7 million pesos, 11.6 percent as much as hard currency receipts from total merchandise trade and 16.5 percent, if one elcude oil re-exports. (see Table 12)

By 1987, tourist receipts were the third largest earner of hard currency in Cuba, excluding oil re-exports.[26] Only sugar, and fish products exports generated more hard currency for the Cuban economy than did international tourism.

Tourist receipts are forecasted to reach the one billion dollar mark by the year 2000. Cuban government officials project that by the end of the century the international tourist industry will be the most significant generator of hard currency in the island's economy.[27]

---

[25] Banco Nacional de Cuba, Informe Económico, June 1988, pg. 10-11.

[26] Banco Nacional de Cuba, Informe Económico, June 1988, pg. 10.

[27] South, June 1990, pg. 55.

Table 12

Table 12: Hard Currency Merchandise Exports and Tourist Receipts
(In Million Pesos)

	1981	1982	1983	1984	1985	1986	1987
Total Merchandise	1,405.8	1,355.9	1,233.9	1,135.7	1,244.4	907.3	964.7
Sugar	866.3	648.3	263.2	250.0	171.2	209.9	222.5
Oil Re−exports	151.4	262.1	497.7	484.4	526.9	248.5	286.3
Other	388.1	445.5	473.0	401.3	546.3	448.9	455.9
Total Merchandise Excluding Oil Re−exports	1,254.4	1,093.8	736.2	651.3	717.5	658.8	678.4
Tourist Receipts	43.6	50.9	59.4	75.7	87.3	97.7	111.7
Percentage of Tourist Receipts/Total Merchandise	3.1	3.8	4.8	6.7	7.0	10.8	11.6
Percentage of Tourist Receipts/Merchandise Excluding Oil Re−exports	3.5	4.7	8.1	11.6	12.2	14.8	16.5

Source: Banco Nacional de Cuba, Informe Economico, Various Issues

Table 13
Estimated Value of Tourist Income Multipliers

Location	Tourist Income Multipliers
Dominica	1.20
Antigua	.88
Bermuda	1.03
Hong Kong	1.02
India Ocean Islands	.95 – 1.03
Hawaii	.90 – 1.30
Bahamas	.78
Figi	.65
Cayman Islands	.65
British Virgin Islands	.58
Jamaica	1.58

Source: Archer, B.H., "The Value of Multipliers and their Policy Implication,"
Tourism Management, 3(4) 1982 and CTRC. The Contribution of Tourism
to Economic Development in the Caribbean.

Even if tourist receipts fall short of the one billion dollars forecasted by Cuban tourist officials, the relative importance of tourism as an export industry is sure to increase in the future due to the poor prognostic for Cuba's other major hard currency earning activities.

Notwithstanding the large weight of tourist receipts on total hard currency receipts, it must be stressed that at present Cuba's tourist receipt are small and insignificant. Particularly, if compared to total tourist receipts in the Caribbean area, or to Cuba imports needs.

Furthermore, gross receipts do not accurately reflect the true contribution of international tourism to the balance of payments. A better measure would be net receipt, that is gross receipts minus associated hard currency cost or import component. The input component of tourist receipts is affected by a number of factors:

- The cost of imported goods and services used by tourist.

- The foreign exchange cost of capital investment.

- Payments abroad in the form of, profits, interest payments, royalties and management fees, payment due to foreign travel agents, etc.

- Promotion and publicity abroad.

- Overseas training of personnel.

Estimates of the import component of tourist receipts of Caribbean countries range between 25.2 percent to 44.8 percent.[28] Cuban sources, citing INTUR studies, report that the import component of Cuba's tourist receipts to be between 30 to 38 percent.[29] Though it falls within the range estimated for Caribbean countries, there is at present no way to corraborate this estimate.

International Tourism and Government Revenues

A major economic benefit associated with international tourism, is the sector's ability to generate government revenues. Government's direct and indirect tax revenues derived from tourism include:

- airport departure taxes

---

[28] Pearce, Douglas, Tourist Development, pg. 197.

[29] Ayala Castro, Hector in "Notas Sobre el Turismo", pg. 19.

- hotel occupancy tax
- aircraft landing fees
- sales tax on tourist purchases
- import duties on goods and services, used by tourists
- corporate taxes and profit repatriation taxes
- other licenses and fee's

Revenues generated by international tourism allows the host nation to export a portion of its tax burden. The portion of government revenue's exported via international tourism in countries in the Caribbean is estimated to be quite high ranging from 20 percent in St. Lucia to 62 percent in Bahamas.[30]

It is hard to ascertain the impact of international tourism on government revenues in Cuba. On the one hand Cuba does not have a comprehensive tax structure, but on the other hand the majority of Cuba's factor of production are government owned.

We will just point out here that present concessions to foreign capital on profits repatriations and import tariffs might seriously curtail Cuba's ability to maximize benefits from international tourism. As Cuba moves towards a mix economy, care should be taken to install a tax structure which enhances the exportability of government revenues via tourism.

International Tourism Impact on Income and Employment

Tourist expenditures represent a direct injection of outside money into the local economy. The direct impact of this expenditure is to create income and employment for those entities which sell their goods and services to tourist. The economic impact of tourist expenditures does not stop here, however. Recipients of tourist expenditures spend out of these funds. As expenditures circulate through the economy, a multiplier effect is created, generating more income and jobs.

The total impact of an original injection of tourist expenditures on the local economy is the combination of direct and induced effects. The total impact is captured by multiplying tourist expenditures by a tourist income and/or employment multiplier.

Tourist income multipliers have been estimated for a number of regions. Estimated values of the tourist income multiplier for small island economies range from .58 for the British Virgin Islands to 1.58 for Jamaica. (See table 13)

The value of the multiplier depends on the portion of income that leaks out of the local economy at each round of circulation. This leakages include: payments for export of

---

[30] CTRC, The Contribution of Tourism to Economic Growth and Development in the Caribbean, pg. 11.

raw material and factors of production, rent and profits paid to non-residents and savings by residents. Leakages are minimized the larger and more self-sustained the economy in question, leading to a larger multiplier value.

The value of the multiplier is also affected by supply constraints. The multiplier concept rest on the premises that demand creates its own supply. The present structure of the Cuban economy does not facilitates induced supply creation. The multiplier effect of tourist expenditures is further curtailed by government policy that is designed to keep the tourist sector separated from the rest of the economy. The total impact of tourist expenditures on the Cuban economy is probably not much larger than the direct income and employment that these expenditures create.

Some partial estimates of the direct income and employment attributable to international tourism in Cuba have been calculated by INTUR. INTUR reports that during 1988, entities under its control contributed 455.9 million pesos to the national economy and employed 42,000 workers. The contribution to production and services is broken down by sectors as follows:[31]

	Millions of Pesos
Alojamiento	319.0
Turismo y Descanso	37.6
Arte	8.0
Comercio Interior	5.2
Abastecimiento Técnico-material	52.5
Construcción y Maquinarias	5.3
Construcción y Montaje	9.5
Transporte Automotor	13.3
Otras Actividades	4.4
Total	455.9

In, 1988 INTUR operated around 80 percent of all the rooms available for international tourists in Cuba. Assuming that its total share is also of 80 percent, the total direct impact of international tourism in Cuba can be estimated at 547.08 million pesos and 50,400 jobs. This represents only 2.08 percent of total Cuba's Social Global Product (SGP) and 1.35 of total employment. For purposes of comparison, tourism contribution to Jamaica's Gross Domestic Product has been estimated at 28 percent, in Bahamas at 33 percent, and in Antigua at 40 percent.[32]

---

[31] Ayala Castro, Héctor, op. cit. pg. 23.

[32] CTRC, op. cit., pg. 10.

Tourist Export-Led Growth

In recent years many developing countries have turned towards international tourism to promote economic growth and development. Tourist exports offer several advantages over other Third World exports both traditional and non-traditional including:

- international tourism is a growth industry. World wide tourist arrivals increased at an annual average rate of 6.5 percent during the eighties.

- long-run prospects for international tourism growth are bright. Tourist demand is highly income elastic.

- tourist exports exhibit more stability than export earning from traditional primary commodities.

- unlike trade in manufactures, developed nations place very few restrictions and barriers to international travel.

Strong growth in an export sector, however, will not by itself promote economic growth and development in a nation. The ability of the sector to stimulate economic growth depends on the linkages between the sector and the rest of the economy.

A number of researchers have expressed serious doubts about the ability of the international tourist sector to establish inter- industry linkages.[33] Weak linkages are especially a problem when the international tourism sector is isolated in enclaves apart from the rest of the economy.

When an enclave mode is abandoned and mass tourism promoted the possibility for inter-industry linkages are enhanced. The experiences of the Mediterranean countries bodes well for mass tourism as a stimulus of economic growth and development.[34]

The ability to establish effective inter-industry linkages between the tourist sector and the rest of the economy depends also on other factors. Among these, the structure of the economy, capacity of the labor force, internal demand and capability for income substitution.

At present the tourist enclave mode adopted by the Cuban government and the structure of the Cuban economy curtail the formation of inter-industry linkages.

---

[33] See far example Bryden, J. Tourism and Development: a Case Study of the Commonwealth Caribbean, and Griffith, Wiston, "Tourism in the Commonwealth Caribbean: A Case Study" in The Troubled and Troubling Caribbean.

[34] See for example, William, Allen and Gareth Shaw, Tourism and Development: Western European Experiences.

Concluding Remarks

In spite of the slow down in the rate of tourist arrivals in Cuba in the later part of the 80's, tourism to Cuba will probably increased in the next few years at rates above either the World's or Caribbean's averages. Travelers to Cuba will continue to be attracted by low-price packages.

Average expenditures by tourist decline throughout most of the 80's. This trend will probably continue. One indication of this is the increasing weight of Latin America's share of Cuba's tourist arrivals.

At present the primary economic benefit derived from tourism in Cuba, is its ability to generate hard-currency. The quest for hard currency seems to be the main motivation behind Cuba tourist policy. It has led the Cuban government to prioritized this sector inspite of potential social and political costs. Trying to minimize these costs, however, the Cuban government is presuing an enclave mode, keeping the tourist sector separate from the rest of the economy. In doing so other potential economic benefits are being foregone.

The weight of the tourist sector an the Cuban economy is still very small, and its overall economic impact rather insignificant. It remains however, the one bright spot in an otherwise dismal economic performance.

References

Ayala Castro, Hector, Notas Sobre el Turimo", series de Estudios Sobre la Economía Cubana, Universidad de la Habana, June, 1991.

Banco Nacional de Cuba Informe Económico, La Habana Cuba, 1960.

Banco Nacional de Cuba, Memoria 1958-1959, La Habana Cuba 1960.

Banco Nacional de Cuba, Programa de Desarollo Económico, Informe N. 4, La Habana Cuba 1960.

Business Monday, "Trade Winds: Cuba", The Miami Herald, Dec. 10, 1990.

Bryden, J. Tourism and Development: a Case Study of the Commonwealth Caribbean, Cambridge University Press, New York, 1973.

Cabrera, Carlos, "A Challenging 12 Months" Granma Weekly, January 13, 1991.

Caribbean Tourism Research and Development Centre (CITRC), The Contribution of Tourism to Economic Growth and Development in the Caribbean 1987.

Casanova Montero, Alfonso and Pedro Monreal González, "Cuba and the United States: The Potential of Their Economic Relations" in U.S. Cuban Relations in the 1990's, Jorge

I. Domínguez and Rafael Hernández ed. Westview Press, Boulder, Col. 1989.

Castells García, Jesús, "Tourism in Revolution" Cuba Foreign Trade, 1189.

Comité Estatal de Estadísticas, Anuario Estadístico de Cuba, La Habana, Cuba, 1986, 1987, 1988.

French, Howard, W., "Cuba's New Hotels Dream of Dollars", The New York Times: Travel, March 31, 1991.

Griffth, Wiston, "Tourism in the commonwealth Caribbean: A Case Study " in Roy Glasgon and Wiston Langley, ed., The Troubled and Troubling Caribbean, The Edwin Mellen press, Lewiston, N.Y., 1989.

Grupo Cubano de Investigación Económica, Un Estudio Sobre Cuba, University of Miami Press, Miami, Fl. 1963.

Martín Fernández, Ramón, "El Turismo y Su Desarrollo," Economía y Desarollo No. 5, Año 1968, La habana, Cuba.

McManus, Jane, "Cashing in on the Caribbean" South Survey, June 1990.

Mena, Jesús, "Quality Service for International Tourism", Gramma Weekly, May 7, 1989.

Pearce, Douglas, Tourist Development, John Wiley and Sons, Inc., N.Y. 1989.

Pérez-López, Jorge, "Sugar and the Cuban Economy: Implications After Thirty Years." Paper presented to the Association for the Study of the Cuban Economy. Washington, D.C., Oct. 18, 1990.

Pérez-López, Jorge, "Cuban Hard-Currency Trade and Oil Reexports" in Socialist Cuba: Past Interpretations and Future Challenges, Sergio G. Roca ed. Westview Press, Boulder, Colorado 1988.

Pérez-López, Jorge, The 1982 Cuban Joint Venture Law, Context, Assessment and Prospects, Institute of Interamerican Studies, University of Miami, Monograph, July 1985.

Roca, Sergio G: "Cuba y la Nueva Economía Internacional: Tiempos Duros, Decisiones Difíciles," paper presented at the latin American Studies Association Meetings, Washington, D.C., April 1991.

Rodríguez, José Luis, "Una imperiosa necesidad de cambios" <u>Cuba Internacional</u>, La Habana, June 1990.

Rodríguez, José Luis, "The Cuban Economy: A Current Assessment" in <u>Transformation and Struggle: Cuba faces the 1990's</u> Sandor Halebsky and John M. Kirk ed. Praeger, New York, 1990.

Ritter, A.R.M., "Cuba's Convertible Currency Debt Problem," <u>Cepal Review</u> No. 36, December 1988. U.N. Cepal Santiago, Chile.

Truslow, Adams, Francis, Chief of Mission <u>Economic and Technical Mission to Cuba</u>, Inter Bank for Reconstruction and Development, Washington, D.C. 1950.

Williams, Allan M. and Gareth Shaw, ed., <u>Tourism and Economic Development: Western European Experiences</u>, Belhaven Press, London 1988.

Cuba's Transition to Market-Based Energy Prices

Jorge F. Pérez-López

The Cuban-Soviet trade protocol for 1991, concluded in December 1990, introduced a number of important changes to the trading relationship between the two countries. One of those changes was the shift, effective on 1 January 1991 (but apparently delayed until the second half of the year), to world market prices and convertible currency payments for all traded commodities.

Since 1960 the Soviet Union has been, for all practical purposes, Cuba's exclusive supplier of energy products. For certain time periods, Soviet sales of oil and oil products to Cuba were made at concessional (below world market) prices; prior to 1991, all Soviet energy products exported to Cuba were priced on the basis of transferable rubles, the medium of exchange used by members of the recently-dissolved Council for Mutual Economic Assistance (CMEA), and were essentially bartered for Cuban goods, especially sugar. Five-year trade agreements and annual protocols committed the Soviet Union to supply Cuba each year with specific levels of energy products, a practice that introduced a certain degree of certainty into Cuba's planning function.

The shift to market prices and convertible currencies in Cuban-Soviet trade in energy products has already brought--or is likely to bring--a number of adjustments to the Cuban economy. First, it has affected the balance of trade and will further affect it as bartering of overvalued Cuban sugar exports for energy imports ceases to be an alternative. Second, the shift to commercial terms in trade relations, combined with the apparent unwillingness of the Soviet Union to supply Cuba with more than 10 million tons of oil and oil products per annum, rather than the 12-13 million tons supplied in former years, will mean the scaling down, or even the end, of the island's ability to reexport Soviet oil and oil products and close off an important source of convertible currency earnings. Third, it is bound to lead to shifts in energy consumption patterns to achieve higher efficiency in the allocation of resources economywide. And fourth, it is likely to accelerate efforts to alter the structure of energy supply, to give a heavier weight to alternative energy sources, especially nuclear power.

This paper represents a preliminary attempt to assess the implications of the transition to market-based energy prices on the Cuban economy. Because the requisite data to carry out a substantive assessment are either not available or are not timely,[1] the results are quite tentative. The paper begins with a brief discussion of the Cuban energy balance and then addresses four areas which may be affected by the shift to market-based energy prices. It closes with some observations regarding long-term adjustments in the economy related to changes in energy prices.

---

[1] The most recent issue of the Cuban statistical yearbook generally available to researchers is for 1988. This publication contains comprehensive statistics through 1988 in most economic activities, except for energy trade. See Comité Estatal de Estadísticas, Anuario estadístico de Cuba 1988 (La Habana, 1990).

I.   Energy and the Cuban Economy

With the exception of bagasse -- produced by the sugar industry and consumed almost exclusively by that same industry -- Cuba's output of primary energy products is very modest. No significant coal deposits have been found in the island. Hydroelectric resources are limited: Cuban rivers have low heads, carry relatively small volumes of water, and are subject to uneven rates of flow throughout the year. Commercial oil production increased significantly in the 1980s, but domestic output is quite small relative to domestic needs.[2]

Table 1 presents estimates of Cuba's total energy requirements in 1988, the most recent year for which these data are available. It is based on statistics compiled by the United Nations; data on production or trade of individual energy products have been converted to a common measure -- tons of oil equivalent -- in order to permit aggregation.

Energy sources: The Cuban energy balance is heavily tilted toward liquid fuels: crude oil, light oil products, and heavy oil products. In 1988, Cuba met nearly 70 percent of its energy requirements with liquid fuels, about 29 percent with biomass, and the remaining one percent with several other energy sources (coal, coke, electricity).

Biomass products (mostly bagasse, but also some fuelwood and charcoal) provide the lion's share of domestic production of primary energy. In 1988, biomass accounted for 86 percent of Cuba's primary energy production, with crude oil production accounting for about 13 percent, and electricity (in the form of hydroelectricity) for 0.4 percent.

Energy imports: Imported energy products are critical to Cuban economic activity. In 1988, total energy imports amounted to about 2.6 times the magnitude of domestic primary energy production, while net imports (imports less exports) were about twice as large. The most significant imported energy products, by far, are oil and oil products; in 1988, they accounted for over 99 percent of the value of imported energy products, with imports of coal and coke accounting for less than 1 percent.

The heavy reliance on imported oil and oil products is evident from data in Table 2. Columns 1-3 present official Cuban data on crude oil production and on imports and exports of oil and oil products for 1958-88. Using these data, apparent energy consumption (production + imports-exports), and the share of such apparent consumption accounted for by domestic production, have been calculated.

In the 1960s and 1970s, Cuba's domestic oil production accounted for a very low percentage of apparent consumption of oil and oil products. In most years, it hovered around 1-2 percent, although it rose to above 3 percent in 1968-69. In the 1980s, domestic production rose significantly and the domestic share of apparent consumption climbed to

---

[2] See Jorge F. Pérez-López, "Energy Production, Imports and Consumption in Revolutionary Cuba," <u>Latin American Research Review</u> 16:3 (1981), pp. 111-137.

Table 1: Energy Balance, 1988
(thousand metric tons of oil equivalent)

	Production of Primary Energy	Imports	Exports	Marine/Aviation Bunkers	Change in Stocks	Total Energy Requirements
Hard Coal, Lignite & Peat		66.5			13.3	79.8
Coke Briquettes and Coke		41.6			0.6	42.2
Crude Oil	717.0	8500.4	-1150.1		-100.0	7967.3
Light Oil Products		559.8	-526.4	-88.8	-0.4	-55.8
Heavy Oil Products		4867.7	-1572.9	-121.4	72.8	3246.2
Other Oil Products					3.0	3.0
LPG & Oil Gases					2.2	2.2
Natural Gas	19.3					19.3
Electricity	6.3					6.3
Primary Biomass	4651.6				0.9	4652.5
Derived Biomass					1.4	1.4
Total	5394.2	14036.0	-3249.4	-210.2	-6.2	15964.4

Source: United Nations, Energy Balances and Electricity Profiles 1988 (New York: United Nations, 1990), pp. 80-81

Table 2: Apparent Consumption of Oil and Oil Products, 1959-88
(thousand metric tons)

Year	Domestic Production	Imports	Exports	Apparent Consumption	Domestic Production as Percentage of Consumption
1959	28	3010	767	2271	1.2
1960	25	5428	164	5289	0.5
1961	28	3869		3897	0.7
1962	43	4456		4499	1.0
1963	31	4078	7	4102	0.8
1964	37	4543	22	4558	0.8
1965	57	4526		4583	1.2
1966	69	5020		5089	1.4
1967	116	5060		5176	2.2
1968	198	5207		5405	3.7
1969	206	5604		5810	3.6
1970	159	6001		6160	2.6
1971	120	6805		6925	1.7
1972	112	6720		6832	1.6
1973	138	7186	90	7234	1.9
1974	168	7814	45	7937	2.1
1975	226	7789	36	7979	2.8
1976	235	8419	63	8591	2.7
1977	256	9375	917	8714	2.9
1978	288	9843	479	9652	3.0
1979	288	9826	249	9865	2.9
1980	274	10448	885	9837	2.8
1981	259	10999	906	10352	2.5
1982	541	11556	1978	10119	5.3
1983	742	12329	3119	9952	7.5
1984	770	12474	2797	10447	7.4
1985	868	13500	3511	10857	8.0
1986	938	13157	3698	10397	9.0
1987	895	13510	3177	11228	8.0
1988	717	13442	2385	11744	6.1

Sources: 1959-87: Comité Estatal de Estadísticas, Compendio estadístico de energía 1989.
1988: United Nations, 1989 Energy Statistics Yearbook.

Table 3: Energy and Sugar Trade, 1980-88

(in million pesos)

	Total Imports	Energy Imports	% Energy/ Total Imports	Total Exports	Sugar Exports	% Sugar/ Total Exports	Sugar/ Energy
1980	4627.0	911.5	19.7	3966.7	3279.2	82.7	3.6
1981	5114.0	1166.2	22.8	4223.8	3300.8	78.1	2.8
1982	5530.6	1497.9	27.1	4933.2	3771.5	76.5	2.5
1983	6222.1	1857.5	29.9	5534.1	4078.2	73.7	2.2
1984	7227.5	2219.1	30.7	5476.5	4090.1	74.7	1.8
1985	8035.0	2655.6	33.1	5991.5	4441.5	74.1	1.7
1986	7596.1	2533.5	33.4	5321.5	4069.1	76.5	1.6
1987	7583.6	2621.0	34.6	5402.1	3987.3	73.8	1.5
1988	7579.8	2588.9	34.2	5518.1	4086.5	74.1	1.6

Source: Based on data in Comité Estatal de Estadísticas, Anuario
estadístico de Cuba 1988 and earlier issues.

5.3 percent in 1982, 8.0 percent in 1985, and 9.0 percent in 1986. Domestic oil production peaked in 1986 (when it reached 938,000 metric tons) and declined in 1987 and 1988. Consequently, the domestic share of apparent consumption of oil and oil products fell to 8.0 percent and 6.1 percent in 1987 and 1988, respectively.

II.   Energy and the Trade Balance

Annual merchandise trade deficits, financed by "credits" from the Soviet Union and other socialist countries, have been the norm in revolutionary Cuba.[3] According to official Cuban data, the average annual merchandise trade deficit (in million pesos) over certain time periods was:

1961-65	-210.3
1966-70	-377.8
1971-75	-281.0
1976-80	-402.6
1981-85	-1193.9
1986-88	-2172.5

The increase in the merchandise trade deficit in the 1980s reflected, in part, the rise in the value of energy products imported from the Soviet Union. Between 1980 and 1988, the value of energy imports rose from 911.5 million pesos to nearly 2.6 million pesos; the share of energy within the total value of imports rose from 19.7 percent in 1980 to 34.2 in 1988 (see Table 3). The shift to market-based prices in all trade with the Soviet Union means that the possibility of bartering overvalued sugar exports to the Soviet Union for energy products will disappear, with a consequent deterioration in the trade balance.

Soviet sales of oil and oil products to Cuba: Cuba began to barter sugar for Soviet crude oil in the spring of 1960. One of the arguments used by the Cuban government to justify purchasing Soviet crude oil was that its price was lower than the market price by about 33 percent. Upon the nationalization of the oil refineries operated by the international oil companies (in June 1960), Soviet oil and oil products began to flow into the island in increasing volumes, with the Soviet Union becoming, for all practical purposes, Cuba's exclusive supplier of these products.[4]

In October 1973, an embargo on oil sales by Arab members of the Organization of Petroleum Exporting Countries (OPEC) led to a four-fold increase in world oil prices. Cuba, as well as other socialist countries who depended on the Soviet Union for oil supplies, was not affected immediately by the price increases, since the Soviet Union lived up to its

---

[3] Over the 30-year period 1959-88, Cuba's merchandise trade balance has been in the black only twice, in 1960 and 1974. See Anuario estadístico de Cuba 1988, p. 410.

[4] Some of the oil consumed by Cuba might actually be Venezuelan, pursuant to a swap arrangement between the Soviet Union and Venezuela. Since Venezuelan oil shipments to Cuba respond to terms and conditions set by Cuba and the Soviet Union, they can be considered as Soviet exports for analytical purposes.

commitments to maintain commodity prices fixed in trade with its CMEA allies. Thus, Cuba was spared from the sudden quadrupling of the price of oil imports and serious balance of payments problems that affected other oil-importing countries.

In 1975, the Soviet Union implemented a new pricing policy for oil exports to its CMEA allies aimed at closing the gap between oil world market prices and the intra-CMEA export price. It consisted of a formula whereby annual adjustments to oil prices would be made based on the moving average of world market prices during the previous five years. Throughout the 1970s and early 1980s, as oil world market prices rose, Cuba benefitted from this arrangement as the five-year moving average price was consistently below the world market price. However, as oil world market prices softened beginning in 1983, the arrangement worked to Cuba's disadvantage since the five-year moving average price continued to rise or fell at a slow pace. In particular, Cuba did not benefit fully from the sharp fall in oil world market prices that occurred in 1986.

For 1982-87 the average price (import unit value) of Cuban crude oil imports from the Soviet Union (in pesos/barrel) and the average oil world market price (in U.S. dollars/barrel) were:[5]

	Import Unit Value	World Market Price
1982	17.7	33.5
1983	20.1	29.3
1984	23.8	27.5
1985	26.5	26.7
1986	26.1	13.1
1987	26.2	16.9

These data suggest that by 1986, Cuba was no longer benefitting from concessional prices in oil and oil products imports from the Soviet Union.

Cuban sugar sales to the Soviet Union: Pursuant to agreements reached in 1975, the Soviet Union guaranteed Cuba a "minimum" price of 500 rubles per ton of raw sugar (about 30.40 centavos/pound), with the price to be adjusted upwardly in step with changes in the price of a basket of Cuban imports from the Soviet Union. Although the components of the basket of imports, their base period price levels, and their weights have not been made public, it has been reported that oil played a prominent role; some Cuban officials have gone so far as to describe the mechanism as merely compensating Cuba (via increases in the price of sugar exports) for increases in the price of oil imports from the Soviet Union.[6]

---

[5] Cuban oil import unit values calculated from data in Anuario estadístico de Cuba 1988. Oil world market prices from International Monetary Fund, International Financial Statistics.

[6] For a fuller discussion of pricing of Cuban sugar exports to the Soviet Union see Jorge F. Pérez-López, "Cuban-Soviet Sugar Trade: Price and Subsidy Issues," Bulletin of Latin American Research 7:1 (1988), especially pp. 123-134.

As the data below demonstrate, during 1982-88 the average export price (export unit value) of Cuban sugar to the Soviet Union (in centavos/pound) was several-fold higher than the world market price (in U.S. cents/pound):[7]

	Export Unit Value	World Market Price
1982	28.4	8.4
1983	39.6	8.5
1984	39.4	5.2
1985	44.8	4.1
1986	39.3	6.1
1987	38.7	6.8
1988	41.8	10.2

The effect of the heavily-subsidized prices for sugar exports to the Soviet Union within Cuba's export basket is shown in Table 3. Thus, in the 1980s, sugar exports accounted for over three-fourths of the value of Cuba's total exports. Despite the very high price subsidies for Cuban sugar exports, Cuba's trade deficit grew rapidly in the 1980s. Clearly, the deficits would have been much higher had the subsidies not been present.

Sugar-for-energy barter: Table 3 presents data on overall Cuban foreign trade and on energy and sugar trade in the 1980s. It should be noted that the columns labelled energy imports and sugar exports in the table refer to all transactions, i.e., not only to trade with the Soviet Union. In the case of oil, imports from the Soviet Union and overall imports are essentially synonymous, considering the overwhelming importance of this nation as a supplier of oil and oil products; in the case of sugar, exports to the Soviet Union ranged from 62 to 83 percent of total annual exports in 1980-88.

The last column of Table 3 presents the ratio of the value of sugar exports to that of energy imports. Over the 1980s this barter ratio fell dramatically, from 3.6 in 1980 to 1.5-1.7 in 1985-88. This means that while Cuba could finance 3.6 times its energy imports in 1980 through sugar exports, it could finance only roughly 1.5 times its energy imports by the mid- to late-1980s. Although more recent trade statistics are not available, it is likely that this barter exchange relationship worsened for Cuba in 1989-90.

There is reason to believe that the sugar-for-energy exchange will deteriorate even further in 1991 and beyond. Cuban officials have indicated that the Soviet Union would pay a price for Cuban sugar imports in 1991 in line with that paid by the European Economic Community for preferential imports from Pacific, Asian, and Caribbean beneficiaries under the Lome Convention; this price would be lower than prevailed in 1990 in Cuban-Soviet

---

[7] Cuban sugar export unit values calculated from data in Anuario estadístico de Cuba 1988. Sugar world market prices from International Monetary Fund, International Financial Statistics.

Cuban-Soviet trade relations made such reexporting economically feasible for Cuba: 1) imports of Soviet oil and oil products were priced below world market prices; 2) Soviet oil and oil imports were obtained through barter for Cuban sugar (i.e., they were priced in transferable rubles), while Cuba could sell them for convertible currency; and 3) the Soviet Union was willing to provide oil and oil products to Cuba in amounts exceeding domestic demand thereby making the arrangement feasible.

Because of shortfalls in sugar production, at least in 1984 and 1985 Cuba actually bought sugar in the world market (using convertible currency), bartered it to the Soviet Union for oil and oil products, and then resold these products to convertible currency buyers. These deals were quite profitable for Cuba. In 1985, for example,[13]

- Cuba bought sugar for 100 million pesos (in convertible currency) in the world market;

- the sugar obtained through this transaction was then "sold" to the Soviet Union. It generated the equivalent of 1012 million pesos (in soft currency), for a net gain of 912 million pesos;

- this gain permitted Cuba to finance the import of 4.214 million metric tons of Soviet oil and oil products (priced in soft currency);

- a portion of the oil and oil products (1.978 million metric tons) was reexported to convertible currency purchasers and the rest (2.236 million metric tons) used for domestic consumption.

Considering that the world spot market price for crude oil was around $27 per barrel ($203 per metric ton) in 1985, it can be estimated that Cuba earned around $400 million (in convertible currency) in this sale. That is, by virtue of its arrangements with the Soviet Union, Cuba turned a $100 million convertible currency sugar purchase into a $400 million return.

Reexports and convertible currency revenue: In the 1980s, at a time when sugar world market prices were depressed and Cuba had serious difficulties in generating convertible currencies to service its debt and to purchase goods and services not available from the socialist countries, oil reexports became a key source of convertible currency.

Table 4 presents data on Cuba's convertible currency exports during 1981-88. In 1981, sugar exports generated 62 percent of hard currency revenues and oil and oil products about 11 percent. In 1983-87, however, oil and oil products reexports actually overtook sugar as the island's most significant source of convertible currencies. Incredibly, in 1983-85

---

[13] Banco Nacional de Cuba, <u>Economic Report</u> (February 1985), p. 35.

Table 4: Convertible Currency Exports

(in million pesos)

	Total Exports	Sugar Value	%	Oil & Oil Products Value	%
1981	1405.8	866.3	62	151.4	11
1982	1355.9	648.3	48	262.1	19
1983	1233.9	263.2	21	497.7	40
1984	1135.7	250.0	22	484.4	43
1985	1244.4	171.2	14	526.9	42
1986	907.3	209.9	23	248.5	27
1987	964.7	222.5	23	286.3	30
1988	1113.3	393.4	35	184.9	17

Source: Banco Nacional de Cuba, Economic Report (May 1989) and earlier issues.

Table 5. Consumption of Oil and Oil Products in 1988
(in thousand metric tons)

	Industry	Construction	Agriculture	Transportation	Population	Other	Total
Crude Oil		7.3				0.1	7.4
Natural Gas	20.9	0.4				0.6	21.9
Fuel Oil	5356.4	31.8	12.0	233.4		258.6	5892.2
Diesel Fuel	831.5	308.8	358.0	512.6	3.0	482.9	2496.8
Motor Gasoline	166.8	138.5	87.8	236.9	149.0	362.5	1141.5
Kerosene	7.6	2.4	1.3	0.5	632.8	8.6	653.2
Naphtha	183.9						183.9
Aviation Gasoline			7.9	4.0			11.9
Jet Fuel				336.6			336.6
Liquifi. Natural Gas	14.9	0.3	0.3	0.3	98.0	17.7	131.5
Solvents	8.3	1.2	0.5	1.5	0.2	3.7	15.4
Asphalt	16.0	236.3				1.4	253.7
Total	6606.3	727.0	467.8	1325.8	883.0	1136.1	11146.0

Source: Comité Estatal de Estadísticas, Compendio estadístico de energía 1989.

oil and oil products reexports accounted for over 40 percent of Cuba's convertible currency revenue, twice the share of convertible currency revenue generated by sugar!

The sharp drop in oil world market prices in 1986 eroded Cuba's convertible currency earnings from oil and oil products reexports. Nevertheless, liquid fuel reexports made substantial contributions to convertible currency earnings in 1986-88, when they accounted for about one-fourth of such convertible currency earnings. In 1988, sugar exports again overtook oil and oil products reexports as the main source of convertible currency revenue, in part because of the recovery of sugar world market prices.

The future of oil reexports: The shift to market-based prices and terms of sale in Cuban-Soviet trade casts serious doubts on the feasibility of generating substantial volumes of hard currency earnings through oil reexports. In essence, oil reexports constituted a form of arbitrage, with Cuba exploiting the differences in trade relations between, on the one hand, the socialist countries, and on the other, the market economies. To the extent that those differences have disappeared--or will disappear as a result of economic reforms in the Soviet Union--so would the possibility of arbitrage and the economic rationale behind reexports.

Moreover, the purported 10 million ton per annum limit that the Soviet Union has placed on liquid fuel exports to Cuba (down from the 13 million plus metric tons per annum in the late 1980s) further constrains Cuba's ability to reexport liquid fuels. According to data in Table 2, Cuba's apparent consumption of oil and oil products in 1984-88 averaged about 11 million metric tons per annum. Considering that domestic oil production is probably in the range of 500,000-700,000 metric tons per annum, Cuba will barely be able to continue to meet domestic requirements from the combination of domestic production and imports, and it will not have the physical capacity to engage in substantial reexporting unless it reduces domestic consumption very sharply.

It is also not clear that Cuba can count on annual imports of 10 million tons of oil and oil products from the Soviet Union in the out years. The Soviet energy industry has been going through a very difficult period, described by analysts as "bordering on collapse," with output of oil and coal in the first two months of 1991 more than 8 percent below the levels extracted in a comparable period in 1990.[14] Moreover, differences between the central government and the republics regarding ownership of natural resources--including oil--threatens the ability of the Soviet central government to direct oil exports to specific customers. Finally, the weakened condition of the Soviet economy, and its severe requirements for hard currency revenues, places a premium on exportable products such as oil and oil and oil products that can generate hard currency in international markers.

---

[14] "Crisis Deepens for Soviet Energy Industry," Oil and Gas Journal (8 April 1991), p. 91. See also, Mikhail B. Korchemkin, "Soviet Energy: The Uncertain 1990s," Energy Policy 18:5 (June 1990), pp. 399-405; "Soviet Union: Exports under Threat," Petroleum Economist (February 1991), p. 18; and Isabel Gorst, "Oil Exports Tumble," Petroleum Economist (August 1990), pp. 23-24.

In what may be an analogous situation, Czechoslovakian officials have recently reported that, despite contacts at the Ministerial level, the Soviets have "absolutely refused" to discuss oil export levels for 1992 and to make any commitments on export levels for 1992 or for the out years. Czechoslovakia's oil purchases from the Soviet Union were cut back to about 12 million tons in 1990 from 16.4 million tons in 1989; for 1991, the Soviet Union promised to export to Czechoslovakia 7.5 million tons of oil for hard currency.[15] At the end of 1990, Cuba sought a five-year commitment from the Soviets on oil supplies, but that country would only enter into a one-year arrangement (1991), leaving future levels of supply to negotiation.[16]

IV. Shifting Energy Consumption Patterns

Central planning and cheap Soviet oil supplies contributed importantly to the relatively low efficiency of energy use in the socialist countries. In a study comparing energy consumption in Western and Eastern Europe, Moroney found that the European centrally planned economies (CPEs) consumed far more--approximately twice as much--energy relative to gross domestic product and capital than the European market economies.[17] According to Moroney, "this pattern of intensive energy use may well be a rational response by end users to historical energy subsidies and to central planning emphasizing energy-intensive industry."[18] In the development strategy of CPEs, "energy was conceived as a significant, abundant and cheap factor for achieving extensive growth."[19]

Data on apparent consumption of oil and oil products in revolutionary Cuba (Table 2) suggest that the pattern of high energy consumption observed in European socialist countries also applied to that country. Apparent consumption of oil and oil products rose from about 2.3 million MT in 1959 to 11.7 million MT in 1988, nearly a five-fold increase or a 5.6 percent average annual growth rate.

The availability of cheap Soviet oil has affected Cuba's development strategy, particularly in the industrial sector. Slavishly applying the heavy industrialization model pursued by the Soviet Union and Eastern Europe, Cuba invested in energy-intensive industries such as steel mills and machinery production. Nickel-refining, cement, and

---

[15] "Czechoslovakia Fears Problems With Supplies of Soviet Oil," The Journal of Commerce (29 July 1991), p. 7B.

[16] See interview with Carlos Rafael Rodríguez, as reported in "Cuba's Predicament," op. cit., p. 13.

[17] John R. Moroney, "Energy Consumption, Capital and Real Output: A Comparison of Market and Planned Economies," Journal of Comparative Economics 14:2 (June 1990), p. 201. According to Adam Gwiazda, "The decline of Comecon and its impact on the crude oil foreign trade of Eastern European countries," OPEC Review 15:1 (Spring 1991), p. 81, "the economies of Comecon countries use, on average, at least 2.5 times the amount of primary energy in the production of one unit of gross domestic product, compared with the highly industrialized Western countries."

[18] Moroney, "Energy Consumption, Capital and Real Output," op. cit., p. 212.

[19] Economic Commission for Europe, Energy Reforms in Central and Eastern Europe: The First Year, ECE Energy Series No. 7 (New York: United Nations, 1991), p. 5.

fertilizer plants that have been built may rely on technologies imported from the Soviet Union and Eastern Europe that have low energy efficiency. Mechanization of sugar harvesting appears to have been driven by political rather than by economic considerations.

Energy consumption and economic growth: Measuring the relationship between national income and energy consumption growth (the "energy elasticity") in revolutionary Cuba is very difficult because of the lack of adequate data on total energy consumption and on national income. Relying primarily on official statistics, a Cuban economist has estimated that over the period 1959-88, the nation's material product grew at an average annual rate of 4.3 percent.[20] Independent estimates of Cuban gross domestic product, developed using a different approach (that relies heavily on physical production data), suggest that real economic growth was much slower, roughly about one-half the growth rate obtained from official statistics.[21]

In either case, it is clear that the growth in consumption of oil and oil products (5.6 percent per annum) exceeded national income growth over the period 1959-88; the elasticity of oil and oil products consumption therefore was well above unity and may have approached two or higher. This high elasticity coefficient suggests that revolutionary Cuba, like other CPEs, also used oil and oil products extensively. Thus, Cuban economists have described the island's energy problem as follows:

> The essence of our energy problem is that the growth of consumption has been based fundamentally in increases in oil imports. Bagasse is used by the sugar industry in a closed cycle, and small amounts [of bagasse] are used as raw material. Meanwhile, the contribution of other energy sources and domestically-produced oil are not significant yet.[22]

Energy consumption by fuel type: Table 5 presents official Cuban data on consumption of oil and oil products in 1988 by broad consuming sectors: industry, construction, agriculture, transportation, population, and other. Table 6 presents the same data in terms of shares of consumption by consuming sector and type of oil product. Unfortunately, more detailed information on consumption within these broad sectors (e.g., by specific economic activity within the industrial sector) are not available.

According to data in Tables 5 and 6, over one-half (52.9 percent) of Cuba's consumption of oil and oil products in 1988 was of residual fuel oil. This is not surprising since residual fuel oil is typically used in boilers in industrial facilities and in thermoelectric

---

[20] José Luis Rodríguez, Estrategia del desarrollo económico en Cuba (La Habana: Editorial de Ciencias Sociales, 1990), p. 279-280.

[21] Jorge F. Pérez-López, Measuring Cuban Economic Performance (Austin: The University of Texas Press, 1987). The estimates cover the period 1965-82.

[22] Rigoberto González Rodríguez, Jorge A. San Emeterio Bordas, Armando J. Díaz Rodríguez, and Eduardo Villareal Sando, "Cuba: Energía y desarrollo en la perspectiva 2000," Economía y Desarrollo, no. 95 (November-December 1986), p. 77.

plants. In 1988, Cuba consumed nearly 6 million MT of residual fuel oil; 3.9 million MT were refined in Cuba from domestic and imported crude oil, and the rest imported.[23]

Diesel fuel, also used in industrial applications as well as in agriculture and transportation, accounted for 22.4 percent of consumption of oil and oil products, with gasoline accounting for 10.2 percent. About one-half (1.2 million tons) of the diesel fuel consumed in 1988 was produced in Cuban refineries, while the same was the case for 89 percent of gasoline consumption. Kerosene, used primarily by the population (as cooking fuel) accounted for 5.9 percent of consumption. Other fuels (crude oil, natural gas, naphtha, aviation gasoline, jet fuel, liquified natural gas, solvents, asphalt) were less significant in terms of consumption.

Consumption by sectors: Nearly 60 percent of Cuba's consumption of oil and oil products in 1988 was associated with the industrial sector. The other consuming sectors, and their shares of total consumption, are: transportation, 11.9 percent; "other" activities (which might include defense), 10.2 percent; population, 7.9 percent; construction, 6.5 percent; and agriculture, 4.2 percent. While more efficient use of energy resources across all consuming sectors would have a salutary effect, clearly the industrial sector offered the greatest potential for energy savings.

Since the mid-1980s, Cuba has made energy conservation a high national priority.[24] A National Program for the Conservation and Rational Use of Energy (Programa Nacional para el Ahorro y Uso Racional de Energía) was made part of the economic development plan for 1986-90. It consisted of a web of measures to increase efficiency of energy consumption in the industrial sector (especially thermoelectric plants), improvements in electricity distribution networks to reduce transmission losses, cogeneration in the sugar industry, changes in the technology of cement production to emphasize more energy-efficient processes, reduction in household electricity consumption, etc. Domestic and foreign specialists estimated that Cuba could reduce energy consumption by 30 percent without affecting the level of economic activity.[25]

An assessment of the success--or lack thereof--of the national energy conservation plan is not possible because of the lack of adequate data. One indicator that is available, consumption of oil products in the production of electricity in thermoelectric plants, suggests

---

[23] Refinery output data are from <u>Anuario estadístico de Cuba 1988</u>, p. 251. This source does not contain data on imports of oil and oil products in 1988.

[24] See, e.g., Serafín Hernández Cruz, "El ahorro de energía: Nueva fuente de recursos energéticos," <u>Revista Estadística</u> 9:20 (April 1987), pp. 5-42.

[25] Hernández Cruz, "El ahorro de energía," <u>op</u>. <u>cit</u>., p. 36.

Table 6. Structure of Consumption of Oil Products
(percent)

	Industry	Construction	Agriculture	Transportation	Population	Other	Total
Crude Oil		1.0					0.1
Natural Gas	0.3						0.2
Fuel Oil	81.1	4.4	2.6	17.6		22.8	52.9
Diesel Fuel	12.6	42.5	76.5	38.7	0.3	42.5	22.4
Motor Gasoline	2.5	19.1	18.8	17.9	16.9	31.9	10.2
Kerosene	0.1	0.3	0.3		71.7	0.8	5.9
Naphtha	2.8						1.6
Aviation Gasoline			1.7	0.3			0.1
Jet Fuel				25.4			3.0
Liquified Natural Gas	0.2				11.1	1.6	1.2
Solvents	0.1	0.2	0.1	0.1		0.3	0.1
Asphalt	0.3	32.5				0.1	2.3
Total	100.0	100.0	100.0	100.0	100.0	100.0	100.0

Source: Computed from data in Table 5.

Table 7: Electric Industry Statistics

	1983	1984	1985	1986	1987	1988
Installed generation capacity (a)	3000	3111	3229	3419	3532	3853
Hydroelectric	46	45	45	46	49	49
Thermoelectric	2954	3066	3184	3373	3483	3804
Gross electricity production (b)	11551	12292	12199	13176	13594	14453
Hydroelectric	63	70	54	59	44	73
Thermoelectric	11488	12222	12145	13117	13550	14470
Liquid fuel input (c)	2634	2805	2753	3032	3112	3337
Crude oil				127	152	73
Residual fuel oil	2634	2805	2753	2905	2990	3264

(a)   In thousand kilowatts
(b)   In million kilowatt-hours
(c)   In thousand metric tons

Source: United Nations, Energy Balances and Electricity Profiles 1988.

that no significant gains were made on this score.[26]

Faced with incipient disruptions in supplies of oil and oil products from the Soviet Union, in late May 1990 the Cuban Government announced a plan to save approximately 150,000 MT of oil products in the largest 45 industrial users in the nation.[27] The plan consisted of primarily of measures to use energy more efficiently and to improve maintenance of machinery and equipment. Implementation of this plan was overtaken by severe input shortages later that summer.

Response to energy shortages: In August 1990, the Cuban government announced the imposition of mandatory energy conservation measures to address a 2-million ton shortfall in Soviet deliveries of oil and oil products. Among the energy conservation measures were:

- reduction of daily gasoline and fuel oil deliveries to the state sector by 50 percent and of gasoline deliveries to the private sector by 30 percent;

- cutting back hours of operation in cement and construction material plants;

- shutting down of the Punta Gorda nickel production plant;

- halting start-up of an oil refinery built in Cienfuegos;

- cutting back household electricity consumption by 10 percent; and

- implementing a nationwide project to replace agricultural tractors and combines with draft animals.[28]

Subsequent events suggest that the energy crunch worsened in the second half of 1990:

- the Construction Materials Industry announced an effort to use of domestically-

---

[26] According to official Cuban data (Anuario estadístico de Cuba 1988, p. 260), consumption of liquid fuels in the production of electricity (in gallons/kilowatt hour generated) were:

1983	265.4
1984	264.8
1985	260.0
1986	265.1
1987	263.8
1988	262.3

[27] Mimi Whitefield, "Castro admite problemas con petróleo," El Nuevo Herald (20 June 1990), pp. 1A, 5A.

[28] "Cuba Restricts Fuel Use, Halts Refinery Start-Up," The Journal of Commerce (31 August 1990), p. 6B; "Cuba Cuts Fuel Consumption as Soviet Oil Deliveries Fall," The Washington Post (30 August 1990), p. A39.

produced crude oil at several cement factories that rely on the so-called wet-process;[29]

•   to ease bottlenecks in public transportation, the government announced the importation of large number of bicycles and expressed the intention to build plants to produce bicycles domestically; and

•   the Ministry of Light Industry was forced to cut back hours of operation of 321 plants nationwide within its purview from 40 to 24 hours per week.[30]

V.   Changing the Energy Mix

As discussed above, Cuba's efforts to conserve energy and to diversify its energy mix to reduce the reliance on imported liquid fuels are not new. As discussed above, on the energy demand side the Cuba has undertaken several initiatives to curb energy consumption in enterprises, reduce electricity consumption by households, etc. On the energy supply side, Cuba has turned to a number of alternative sources of energy, including solar heaters, wind power, and small hydroelectric plants. Each of these efforts, while making a contribution, has had very little impact on the overall energy balance. The one energy source that has the potential to substantially alter the energy mix, and the one behind which Cuba has been willing to put resources, is nuclear power.

The nuclear power program: Cuba's plans to build several nuclear power plants for commercial electricity generation stem from the early 1970s. In 1974, President Castro announced that construction of a nuclear power complex in Cuba's southern coast at Juraguá, near Cienfuegos, would begin in 1977-78 and the first reactor at that site would be operational by 1985. Subsequently, the intentions to build a second plant in the eastern region of the country, near Holguín, and a third plant in the western region have been announced.[31]

Ground was broken at Juraguá in the late 1970s, and construction of support facilities for the plant--which ultimately would have four nuclear reactors--have been completed or are near completion. The structure that houses the vessel of the first reactor is also approaching completion. Press reports circulating in early 1991 indicated that Cuba was about to receive some key pieces of nuclear hardware for the plant from the Soviet Union. The best estimate is that, assuming hardware and fissionable materials arrive from the

---

[29] "Fuel Conservation in Construction Outlined," Tele Rebelde Network, 3 October 1990, as reproduced in FBIS-LAT-90-193 (4 October 1990), p. 7. The wet process of cement production is almost 40 percent more energy-intensive than the dry process. See John E. Jankowski, "Energy Use and Conservation in Developing Country Industries," Natural Resources Forum 7:2 (1983), p. 151.

[30] "Paralización en industria ligera," El Nuevo Herald (18 October 1990), p. 3A.

[31] This section draws heavily from Jorge F. Pérez-López, "Nuclear Power in Cuba after Chernobyl," Journal of Interamerican Studies and World Affairs 29:2 (Summer 1987), pp. 79-117.

Soviet Union relatively close to schedule, construction of the first Juraguá reactor might be completed in 1993-94.

The reactors for the Juraguá plant, and presumably for other Cuban nuclear power plants as well, are Soviet-designed pressurized water reactors with 440 megawatt (MW) electricity generation capacity, commonly known as VVER-440. Like pressurized water reactors built in the West, VVER-440s are fueled with enriched uranium and use water as a moderator. VVER-440s have been in operation since the early 1970s in the Soviet Union. Ten VVER-440s are in operation in the Soviet Union and several others in Eastern Europe.

Electricity generation and nuclear power: In 1988, the Cuban electricity system had a generation capacity of 3.853 megawatts (MW); in that year, Cuba generated 14.453 gigawatt-hours (GWH) of electricity, with 99.5 percent of the electricity produced by thermoelectric plants (Table 7).

Thermoelectric plants, fueled with residual fuel oil and crude oil, used up over 3.3 million tons of liquid fuels in 1988. Electricity generation, then, accounted for over 28 percent of total apparent consumption of oil and oil products (Table 2) and about one-half of oil and oil products consumed by the industrial sector (Table 5).

According to Cuban officials, each 440 MW nuclear reactor will have the potential to displace thermoelectric generation capacity consuming 600,000 MT of oil products per annum. This explains, to a large degree, the high priority that Cuba has accorded to its nuclear power program. Despite the austerity program associated with rectification and the cut back in investments in social services, resources continue to flow into the construction of the Juraguá plant. Although more recent statistics are not available, during the period 1985-88, over 19 percent of national investment in the industrial sector was devoted to the electric industry, with a large share aimed at nuclear power; in comparison, the sugar sector, Cuba's most important generator of exportable commodities, was the recipient of slightly less than 17 percent of industrial sector investment over the same period.[32]

VI. Concluding Observations

The legacy of central planning and cheap Soviet oil supplies is a Cuban economy that is heavily dependent on imported oil and oil products. During the period 1961-1989, the Soviet Union met virtually all of Cuba's growing needs for imported oil and oil products and even permitted Cuba to reexport a portion of these fuels as a form of foreign aid.

Cuba's rapidly-growing demand for liquid fuels resulted, in part, from a deliberate Soviet trade policy consisting of commodity barter and energy priced at below-market prices. This policy did not create incentives for efficiency in the use of energy resources and

---

[32] Based on data in Anuario estadístico de Cuba 1988, p. 215.

contributed to questionable investment decisions in energy-intensive industries and to wasteful energy consumption practices.

Cuba is ill prepared to meet the challenges of a shift to market-based energy prices. Since 1986, the economy has been mired in a recession; trade deficits are large; the option of borrowing in international markets has been foreclosed; the exports are concentrated on sugar and a handful of other basic and semimanufactured commodities. Cuba's ability to generate hard currency through exports to be able to obtain energy supplies from the world market is extremely limited. The shift to market prices and hard currency for energy imports compounds the already-difficult economic situation. Some Cuban officials have warned that the situation might deteriorate, and the "option zero" (meaning "zero fuel, zero energy, zero supply") might have to be invoked.

Arguably, Cuba's economic plight associated with the shift to market-based energy prices is worse than that of Eastern European socialist nations. Those economies 1) rely less heavily on imports of oil and oil products than Cuba's;[33] and 2) are more diversified than Cuba's and are able to sell a broader variety of products--including high-quality manufactured products--in the world market. Moreover, because the Eastern European countries are already engaged in a process of economic reform and adoption of market mechanisms, they have been able to use market instruments (energy price increases, reduction of subsidies, creation of markets, abolition of foreign trade monopolies) to rationalize energy consumption.[34] These options are not available to Cuba, adamant about holding the line on reforms.

While nuclear power offers Cuba the possibility to reduce dependency on imported oil and oil products, it will not reduce the overall dependence on imported energy. Nuclear hardware for the application of the nuclear technologies is imported, and so are fissionable materials to fuel the reactors. Cuba will also have to depend on a foreign concern--whether in the Soviet Union or elsewhere--for storing and reprocessing irradiated fuels. The international controversy over the safety of the Juraguá reactors is sure to slow down their construction and commissioning and put further into the future the contribution of that technology to energy supplies.[35]

---

[33] The economies of Poland, Czechoslovakia, and the Eastern part of Germany (formally the German Democratic Republic) are heavily coal-based, with coal covering between 60 and 70 percent of their total primary energy needs. On average, all Eastern European countries satisfied only 21 percent of their energy needs with oil. Gwiazda, "The decline of Comecon," op. cit., p. 81.

[34] Economic Commission for Europe, Energy Reforms, op. cit., pp. 12-14. For example, since the beginning of reforms (around 1989), energy prices have risen typically of the order of 2-3 times in nominal terms in all Eastern European countries (p. 12).

[35] See, e.g., "Cuba to Invite Nuclear Reactor Inspectors," The Washington Post (26 July 1991), p. A16.

Comments

Juan J. Buttari

The papers by Espino and Pérez-López are informative useful works which provide a basis for start exploring the policy prospects for tourism and energy in a post-Castro Cuba. While I don't have fundamental disagreements on the thrust of both works, I would have liked the authors to go further and address policy implications for a future Cuba as they relate to the two sectors.

The main points that **Espino** makes is that in spite of Cuba's efforts to encourage tourism, the economic contribution of tourism remains insignificant and that, under existing conditions, prospects are not bright. While agreeing with this main point, I would raise the following issues :

1. The strong post-1981 growth in tourist arrivals is at least in part a reflection of the very low base -- one of the lowest in the Caribbean. Accordingly, the rise is less meaningful than it would seem.

2. Most likely, cost advantages are not the only reason why average receipts per visitor are very low -- perhaps there are very limited alternatives in which to spend.

3. While the paper attributes to tourism some success in attracting joint-ventures, it can only substantiate two hotels constructed under joint ventures. Not that impressive. (The paper adds that there is no way to estimate the foreign investment that Cuba has been able to attract.)

4. The paper indicates that the economic benefits from tourism include improvements in the balance of payments, generation of government revenues, income and employment creation, and promotion of growth and development. However, this can be said of any exports industry. Moreover, in many of the Caribbean islands the real significant impact is on employment.

5. The estimate of an import coefficient of 30 to 38 percent of imports seems quite low for an enclave economy.

6. The paper recommends a greater tax burden on tourism when a mixed economy is adopted. The problem here is that this seems to imply a differential tax treatment among industries, thus possibly biasing investment flows and discouraging investment in tourism. Such approach would be inconsistent with a "level playing field" objective which would be neutral with respect to industry taxing -- ie we should not continue to attempt to pick winners but let the competitive market do it. (In this connection, one is also concerned about references to administered and potentially subsidized credit made by other participants in the conference.)

7. While the paper underscores the isolation of the tourist sector and blames policy for such situation, it doesn't elaborate on the nature of such policies. To do so would be important for this seems a key aspect for the future. Is the author referring to the overall inefficiency and lack of incentives in the economy? What policies would the author recommend so as to strengthen the linkages between tourism and the rest of the economy? In a democratic Cuba, what policy approach vis-a-vis tourism is advisable?

Pérez-López' paper depicts how neglect of the price system has led to a grossly inefficient use of energy resources.

The major points the paper makes are:

1. The country is highly dependent on energy imports.

2. Even with highly subsidized prices for sugar exports, Cuba has experienced in recent years rapidly growing merchandise trade deficits.

3. Oil reexports have been a very important source of foreign exchange, but Cuba will not be able to continue reexporting oil at the same levels as in the past.

4. Existing industry is not energy efficient. Moreover, because past policy implicitly took oil as an abundant resource, the economy has had very high energy coefficients.

5. Given Cuba's very limited ability to earn convertible currencies through exports, the energy situation amounts to a major crisis.

In its present format the paper could be enhanced by illustrating the balance of payments implications of financing the energy imports required to sustain target rates of growth -- such exercise would be also useful for future negotiations with international financing institutions. Moreover, the paper could elaborate more on past and potential efforts to exploit nonconventional energy sources.

The points raised in the paper are relevant for economic policy in post-Castro Cuba. The implications are :

1. Most of Cuba's economic sectors require energy as a primary input. However, Cuba will have to continue importing most of its energy requirements.

2. In part, economic growth is going to be a function of whether the country is able to finance its energy needs.

3. The future government will have to deal with the issue of how to address the serious constraints to the country's capacity to finance energy imports.

4. Such situation adds urgency to the need to follow adequate foreign exchange and trade policies which do not discriminate against exports or other sources of foreign exchange.

5. In such light, the need for exchange rate policies which do not overvalue the domestic currency, for an open trade regime, and for a foreign investment regime which attracts the foreign investor are of key importance.

6. Likewise, the energy situation imposes the need to move rapidly toward the efficient use and conservation of energy resources. This means that allowing prices to reflect scarcity costs of energy resources will be urgent. In such context, the government will have to make painful decisions regarding targeted subsidization of energy resources --especially electricity and fuels -- and the mechanisms for such subsidies if some subsidization is adopted.

The above implications are consistent with three principles on which, in my opinion, energy policy would be based :

- encourage competition in the supply and distribution of energy

- regulate only to counter monopoly advantages and for environmental protection

- regulations and policies should encourage the use of energy conservation

In preparation for the implementation of policy based on such principles the following analytical work is advisable :

1. On price policy :

-- identify how to introduce marginal cost pricing (ie what it costs to deliver additional electricity to users)

-- as a subitem, one should determine how electricity and energy prices should be decontrolled and the extent to which they should be

2. On subsidization :

-- Is some subsidization warranted? To whom? How much?

-- What are the most efficient channels for subsidization of energy use?

3. On institutions in the energy sector :

-- What should the regime for foreign investors in the energy sector be?

-- In letting market forces by and large guide changes and the development of the energy sector, what are the roles of the private and public sectors?

-- Should there be a centralized institution responsible for energy policy?

-- What should be the legal regime covering technological transfers

-- What should tax policies affecting the energy sector be?

4. On energy and the environment

-- What has been the environmental impact of energy practices in Cuba. One can venture that if it is at all like what has taken place in Eastern Europe, much is to be done. What regulations should be adopted in this respect?

APPENDIX A

Cátedra Carlos F. Díaz Alejandro

Problemas Económicos de Cuba en el Período de Transición

Felipe Pazos

Introducción

Agradezco mucho a Roger Betancourt y a todos los miembros de esta Asociación, a la mayor parte de los cuales me unen viejos lazos de afecto, haberme pedido inaugurar la cátedra Carlos Díaz Alejandro, lo que para mi constituye un gran honor y una enorme satisfacción dada la gran amistad que tuve con Carlos, quien me hacía el altísimo honor de considerarse mi discípulo. No puedo vanagloriarme publicamente de un hecho del que no hay mas constancia que mi palabra, pero a ustedes si puedo decirles que uno de mis grandes orgullos intelectuales es haber sido considerado como maestro por un profesor de Minnesota, de Yale y de Columbia, que poco tiempo antes de morir había sido designado para ocupar una Cátedra Fundacional en Harvard.

Desgraciadamente, no está aquí Carlos para ayudarnos a pensar sobre los problemas de Cuba que vamos a discutir hoy, y que tendremos que seguir discutiendo hasta que se produzca el cambio; o, para hablar mas propiamente, que tendremos que seguir discutiendo antes del cambio, durante el cambio y después del cambio. Los economistas cubanos no hemos examinado con suficiente detenimiento los problemas de transición al nuevo régimen, ni las políticas necesarias para resolverlos, por considerar que estos problemas y estas políticas dependerán de las circunstancias en que se produzca la caída de Castro, por lo que son difíciles si no imposibles de preveer; pero ese razonamiento es solo parcialmente válido, porque los problemas y las políticas de transición serán muy similares cualesquiera que sean las circunstancias en que esta ocurra. Los problemas de la transición serán mas difíciles si el cambio de regimen requiere una lucha larga y cruenta, que dañe gravemente el aparato productivo; pero los problemas de como realizar la privatización de las empresas y retornar a una economía de mercado, de que orientación dar a nuestro comercio exterior y de como evitar la caída de la producción en los primeros meses, así como los de la probable insuficiencia de la ayuda externa y de la casi inevitable emergencia de deficits fiscales en los primeros tiempos, serían basicamente de igual naturaleza; por que pueden y deben ser estudiados.

Debemos tener en cuenta, desde luego, que las políticas del período de transición serán diferentes si son aplicadas por una junta militar formada por oficiales del actual ejército, que con toda probabilidad restablecerían mas gradualmente un régimen de libre empresa que un gobierno de ex-exiliados (la palabra es fea pero suena muy grata al oído); y que tendrían también una actitud de defensa de los actuales dirigentes civiles, no permitiendo que estos fuesen substituídos en forma masiva por recién llegados del exterior.

Hace ocho o diez meses hablé en Puerto Rico sobre estos problemas y sobre las medidas que podrían adoptarse para resolverlos o atenuar su gravedad. Al hacer este examen, expresé preferencia por algunas políticas; pero no fué mi intención entonces, como no lo es ahora, formular un programa económico para Cuba democrática, sino definir con la mayor claridad posible los problemas a que tendremos que hacer frente. Mi propósito es analizar con el máximo cuidado la situación en que se encontrará Cuba a la caída de Castro, que será una situación llena de complejos problemas que requerirá un programa especial de transición, en el que en algunos aspectos no sería posible o aconsejable aplicar las políticas de carácter permanente que deberán adoptarse una vez que esté normalizada la economía. Por ejemplo, para acelerar nuestro desarrollo deberemos estimular y facilitar la inversión extranjera, pero si los desequilibrios de la transición provocan una fuerte depreciación del peso, con la consiguiente caída en el valor de todos los activos cubanos en términos de moneda extranjera, la libre entrada de capital implicaría regalar la riqueza de Cuba a los nuevos inversionistas. Otro ejemplo, después de restablecida la normalidad deberemos adoptar un régimen arancelario de derechos muy bajos, pero el establecimiento de ese régimen antes de reequipar nuestra industria y restablecer la voluntad de trabajo de nuestra población, significaría inundarnos de importaciones y desequilibrar gravemente nuestra balanza de pagos. Un ejemplo más: Cuba tendrá que reincorporar a su economía a los empresarios, administradores, ingenieros y profesionales de todo tipo que están hoy en el exilio, pero esta reincorporación deberá ser hecha gradualmente porque, si se realizase en forma masiva, provocaría un choque económico, social y cultural con nuestros hermanos que permanecieron en Cuba, que podría crear graves obstáculos a la completa y absoluta reunificación patriótica de todos los cubanos. Además, los exilados no podemos abandonar subitamente nuestras actividades actuales. Estos ejemplos muestran, creo yo, que debemos diferenciar entre las políticas básicas que deberemos aplicar una vez que superemos los problemas de transición, y las medidas temporales que tendremos que adoptar inicialmente. Repitiendo lo dicho hace unos momentos, en este intercambio de ideas me concentraré en las medidas de transición, y no entraré a discutir las políticas posteriores.

Importancia de analizar los problemas de transición

Creo sumamente importante que comprendamos claramente los problemas de transición y que nos pongamos de acuerdo en las medidas que deberemos aplicar para resolverlos; y una vez que nos pongamos de acuerdo, será necesario convencer a las naciones industriales y a las instituciones internacionales de la necesidad de apoyar esas medidas a fin de facilitar la transición y, lo que es mas importante, acelerar su advenimiento. Cuando comencé a preparar las notas para esta charla, no pensaba que el análisis de los problemas de transición pudiera contribuir en forma alguna a acelerar el momento en que esta se produjera; pero ahora sí creo que podrá contribuir, y contribuir en forma decisiva. Me explicaré. Tengo la convicción de que la inmensa mayoría, si no la totalidad, de los miembros del ejército de Cuba está en total desacuerdo con la locura--más grave que la descrita en ningún texto de Psiquiatría--de hacer de Cuba el último bastión del comunismo internacional, y de condenar al hambre a nuestra población en una lucha irremisiblemente perdida de antemano: los militares cubanos son hombres inteligentes que no pueden estar de acuerdo con políticas absurdas, sin sentido ni lógica. Pero, además, yo tengo fe en que aman a su patria y que quisieran devolverle la paz, la tranquilidad y la prosperidad a Cuba, y la felicidad a todos los cubanos. Estoy convencido de que estos hombres tomarían el poder si no temiesen que las naciones industriales se abstendrían de reconocer la Junta Militar que ellos instaurasen, y que las instituciones financieras internacionales se negarían a conceder préstamo alguno a la Junta, lo que provocaría el rápido derrocamiento de ésta y, posiblemente, la condena a prisión de sus miembros por haber apoyado el régimen comunista. Tenemos que estar plenamente conscientes de esta situación y hacer todo lo que esté a nuestro alcance para disipar todo temor de esta naturaleza en los oficiales del ejército. Cuando lo logremos, habremos acelerado el advenimiento del período de transición.

Pero terminemos este largo prólogo y entremos de lleno en el tema de esta conferencia, que es examinar los problemas que confrontará Cuba a la caída del régimen actual que, debo adelantarles, no serán nada fáciles.

Enumeración de problemas

Al producirse el cambio, Cuba tendrá que hacer frente a graves y complejos problemas, los más importantes de los cuales serán los siguientes:

1. Reconversión de la economía estatal a una economía de mercado.

2. Orientación del comercio exterior.

3. Bajo nivel de ingresos, déficit fiscal y desequilibrio externo.

4. Realineación de precios para ajustarlos a los costos.

5. Inflación.

6. Restablecimiento del espíritu de trabajo.

7. Creación o reorganización de las instituciones requeridas para el funcionamiento eficiente de un sistema de libre empresa.

8. Atracción de capital privado extranjero; y

9. Reincorporación a la economía cubana de los empresarios, administradores, ingenieros y profesionales de toda clase actualmente en el exilio.

La reincorporación de los exilados no es un problema, sino una solución, pero una solución que tiene que ser aplicada con gran cuidado, porque de ese cuidado dependerá la pronta reunificación de todos los cubanos y la rápida reconstrucción de nuestra economía.

Reconversión de la economía estatal a una economía de mercado

El primero y más importante de los problemas a que tendremos que hacer frente será la reconversión de la economía estatal a un sistema de empresas privadas que compitan libremente en el mercado. Este objetivo puede lograrse mediante la aplicación conjunta o alternativa de las políticas siguientes:

a. devolución de las propiedades confiscadas;

b. venta a subasta de las unidades productivas a postores cubanos o extranjeros;

c. distribución de la totalidad o de una parte de la propiedad de las unidades productivas entre los trabajadores de cada unidad; y

d. distribución de la totalidad o de una parte de la propiedad de las unidades productivas entre toda la población del país.

La devolución de las propiedades confiscadas sería aparentemente la forma obvia de regresar a la empresa privada y a la economía de mercado; pero no sería un proceso fácil de realizar rápidamente porque requerirá la identificación y evaluación de las propiedades confiscadas, los títulos de sucesión de los herederos, etc., todo lo cual implicaría un proceso que tomaría tiempo. Esto plantearía también la cuestión de si deben, o no, ser devueltas sus propiedades a las empresas extranjeras, que han recuperado sus pérdidas, o una parte de ellas, deduciéndolas de sus impuestos. ¿Deben esas propiedades ser devueltas a las empresas o a los gobiernos que les dedujeron impuestos?

Estas dificultades parecen indicar que la indemnización a los propietarios confiscados debe ser hecha en bonos del Estado.

Una segunda vía sería poner en venta las unidades productivas en subastas que se realicen en el período más breve posible, a las que se invitarían postores cubanos y extranjeros. Este procedimiento tendría, sin embargo, el inconveniente del bajísimo precio que probablemente sería obtenido, lo que transferiría a los compradores la propiedad de la economía cubana por una pequeña compensación.

El tercer método se aplicaría distribuyendo entre los trabajadores de cada unidad de un 50 o un 70 por ciento de la propiedad de la unidad respectiva, reservandose el Estado el remanente a fin de intervenir en la administración de las empresas en caso de que los trabajadores no las manejasen bien.

El cuarto método, muy similar al tercero, tiene el propósito de convertir en propietarios no solamente a los trabajadores de las unidades privatizadas, sino también a los de los servicios de gobierno, hospitales, escuelas públicas, etc; pero su aplicación sería complicada y difícil.

Comercio exterior

En años recientes, Cuba ha exportado alrededor de 4 millones de toneladas de azúcar a la Unión Soviética y a los países de Europa Oriental, y alrededor de 2 millones de toneladas a la Comunidad Económica Europea. Al sobrevenir la liberación, los Estados Unidos no podrían comprar de inmediato, ni en el curso de varios años, todo el azúcar que está siendo ahora vendida al ára soviética, ni siquiera una parte significativa de esa cantidad, porque ello implicaría reducir su producción doméstica a los suministros que ahora reciben de Filipinas y de países de América Latina; pero como la Unión Soviética continuará necesitando todo ese azúcar, o una gran parte del mismo, podriamos continuar vendiendosela, bien en forma directa, o bien en forma indirecta a través de corredores, aunque desde luego a precios del mercado mundial.

Nuestro problema de comercio exterior no será, por consiguiente, la cantidad de azúcar que podremos exportar, sino el menor ingreso que recibiremos por esa exportación.

Bajo nivel de ingreso, déficit fiscal y desequilibrio externo

Cuando se produzca el cambio, Cuba estará en una situación crítica, con bajo nivel de ingresos, déficit fiscal y balanza de pagos desequilibrada, debido a los efectos acumulados de tres décadas de ineficiencia comunista, agravados por los problemas de la etapa final del régimen, que mientras mas se prolongue mas crítica hará la situación. A esto habrá que sumar la pérdida del subsidio soviético, que ha representado entre un 1.5 y un 2.0 por ciento del producto bruto, y los pagos de la deuda con la Unión Soviética y con los Bancos de Europa y de Japón, que pueden representar otro tanto; pero, lo que es mas grave, la economía cubana estará afectada también por la desorganización que provoca inevitablemente un cambio de régimen, que en nuestro caso sería especialmente intensa, por lo que deberemos hacer todos los esfuerzos que estén a nuestro alcance por reducirla al mínimo. Además el déficit de balance de pagos será tanto mayor cuanto mas rápidamente decidamos acelerar el reequipamiento y reconstrucción de nuestra economía.

No es posible predecir el nivel a que habrá caído el ingreso real cuando se produzca el cambio, ni el de los desequilibrios internos y externos que experimentará la economía en los primeros tiempos; pero podemos esperar que la caída en el nivel de ingreso será muy fuerte y que los déficit serán superiores a la cuantía de la ayuda externa. Si nos atenemos a los pronunciamientos recientes de Fidel Castro, el ingreso caerá a los niveles de una economía agraria primitiva, caída que será progresivamente mas profunda en la medida en que se prolongue la actual situación. A esto se añadirá, como digo antes, la pérdida del subsidio soviético, el servicio de la deuda y la inevitable desorganización del cambio de régimen. Según vimos antes, las dos primeras causas tendrán un efecto conjunto equivalente a un 3.0 o 4.0 por ciento del producto que será, sin embargo, insignificante comparado con la reducción de 20.0 o 30.0 por ciento del producto anterior a la crisis que provocará la disminución de suministros procedentes de Europa Oriental y de la Unión Soviética. Pero no podemos ignorar la última de las causas mencionadas de reducción del producto, porque la desorganización económica provocada por el cambio de un sistema comunista a uno de libre empresa puede ser muy grave.

Todas las unidades del producción de Cuba, con la sola excepción de las fincas pequeñas, están en la actualidad dirigidas por funcionarios del Gobierno, muchos de los cuales son miembros del Partido Comunista. Dada esta situación, el derrocamiento del régimen implicaría que en un gran número de empresas los trabajadores se rebelarían contra los directores y gerentes, con la consiguiente desorganización de la producción. Si a este proceso de rebeldía espontánea se sumase una política sistemática del nuevo Gobierno de destitución de los directores de empresa, el resultado sería una caída vertical de la producción.

Debe recordarse que aún en los países capitalistas, donde la producción está en manos de empresarios privados y de gerentes politicamente neutros, las revoluciones políticas provocan caídas en la producción y en el ingreso. La caída sería probablemente mucho más fuerte en Cuba, donde los gerentes de las unidades de producción son funcionarios públicos y presumiblemente corresponsables de los errores y abusos del régimen. Este es un problema del que debemos estar plenamente conscientes y al que tendremos que dedicar nuestra máxima atención.

Pero olvidemos momentáneamente el peligro de la desorganización económica provocada por el cambio de régimen y volvamos a las estimaciones. Cuando comience el período de transición, el producto nacional podrá estar 30.0 o 40.0 por ciento por debajo de su nivel de los últimos años "normales" del período comunista y el desequilibrio potencial de los pagos internacionales podrá ser también de 30.0 o 4.0 por ciento de las exportaciones "normales", es decir, podrá tener una cuantía de US$1.500 a US$2.000 millones.

Las cifras que acabo de mencionar son estimaciones gruesas que tienen el sólo propósito de cuantificar, siquiera sea burdamente, mi criterio de que los problemas serán sumamente graves, y de apoyar mi creencia de que el desequilibrio potencial de balanza de pagos durante los años iniciales del período de transición será casi seguramente muy superior a la ayuda que recibamos; y digo desequilibrio potencial, porque en la medida en que no haya financiamiento el déficit no se materializará aunque si creará todas las presiones, distorsiones y desequilibrios que provoca un déficit potencial no financiado.

Al volver al régimen democrático, Cuba debería recibir préstamos masivos de los Estados Unidos, de los países de Europa Occidental y del Japón, cuyo interés económico y político estaría en que triunfase plenamente nuestro país al volver al sistema de empresa privada. Cuba deberá luchar denodadamente por obtener la máxima ayuda posible de esas naciones, basando su solicitud en el enorme valor político para Occidente que tendría el rápido éxito económico de una nación al regresar al sistema capitalista. Dada la gran importancia política de ese éxito, es posible que Cuba reciba una cantidad relativamente alta de ayuda, pero dificilmente ésta alcanzará las enormes cifras que se requerirán. En todo caso, no sería realista planear sobre la base de que Cuba recibirá toda la ayuda necesaria.

Realineación de precios con costos

La reconversión de la economía estatal en un sistema de empresas independientes, que guíen la cantidad y composición de los bienes que produzcan por las señales que reciban del mercado, hará que los precios y costos sean realineados por las unidades de producción tan pronto éstas sean privatizadas o, aún antes de serlo, reciban autorización para decidir las cantidades que produzcan y precios que cobren, por lo que la realineación de precios y costos no será, en principio, un problema para el gobierno, pero si lo será la probable disminución de los salarios reales que resultará del aumento de los precios de los bienes y servicios de consumo popular en mayor medida que los precios de los bienes y servicios de más alta calidad. Yo no conozco la estructura de precios relativos en Cuba, pero supongo que, al igual que en los demás países comunistas, los bienes-salarios sean vendidos por un valor inferior a su costo, mientras ocurra lo contrario en el caso de los bienes no esenciales. Si este es el sistema prevaleciente en Cuba, la realineación reduciría los salarios reales, en adición a la reducción que estos probablemente experimentarán como consecuencia de las disminuciones en la producción ancional y en los suministros importados, que en una sección anterior hemos previsto. Debemos tener en cuenta el probable efecto depresivo de la realineación sobre los salarios, a fin de contrarrestarlo, en la medida de lo posible, mediante un sistema temporal de subsidios e impuestos de consumo. Hago esta advertencia no solamente porque debemos tratar de evitar que los salarios reales se deterioren en mayor medida que la inevitable, sino porque tenemos que hacer todo lo que esté a nuestro alcance para prevenir la inflación, que es un peligro que nos amenaza seriamente.

Inflación

En una sección anterior expresé la opinión de que al caer el régimen comunista la economía cubana se encontrará en una situación crítica, con un bajo nivel de producción, con déficit fiscal y con desequilibrio en la balanza de pagos; y estimé en forma muy tentativa que el producto nacional podría estar un 30.0 o 40.0 por ciento por debajo de su nivel de los últimos años "normales" del período comunista, y que el desequilibrio potencial de balanza de pagos sería probablemente superior a la ayuda externa que podríamos esperar. En esos cálculos tentativos no hice estimación alguna del posible monto del déficit fiscal debido a dos razones: una, la dificultad del cálculo y otra, más importante, que el déficit dependerá de la política que adopte el Gobierno: de la fuerza de voluntad que tenga para absorber solo una parte del desempleo y dejar desocupados durante uno o dos años a un número considerable de trabajadores, y en la pobreza a un número considerable de familias, a fin de evitar que se desate la inflación; que se desate una inflación que daría empleo momentáneo solo a un número pequeño de trabajadores adicionales; pero que en unos pocos meses se convertiría en hiperinflación y crearía un volumen de desocupación mucho mayor y dificultaría gravemente nuestra reconstrucción.

Desearía estar equivocado, pero creo que el peligro de inflación--de hiperinflación--es sumamente alto y que tendremos que hacer esfuerzos cuasi-heroicos para evitar esa gravísima amenaza. Evitar la inflación galopante obligará al Gobierno a señalarse un programa de reconstrucción más modesto, a reducir el volumen de obras públicas para dar empleo, y a disminuir a niveles muy bajos el subsidio a los desocupados, pero, a mi juicio, el peligro es evidente y tenemos que evitarlo.

Restablecimiento del espíritu de trabajo

La nueva Cuba tendrá que restablecer el espíritu de trabajo de la población y demostrar que la reconversión a una economía de mercado no se ha hecho para devolver sus propiedades a los exilados, sino para hacer libres, felices y prósperos a todos los cubanos, especialmente a los que no pudieron salir de Cuba, ya que los que salimos recobramos hace mucho tiempo nuestra libertad y, gracias a nuestro trabajo, hemos alcanzado un nivel de ingreso mas alto del que teniamos antes. A este respecto, debo manifestar a ustedes que favorezco decididamente el plan de distribuir un 70 por ciento de la propiedad de cada empresa entre sus trabajadores.

Organización o reorganización de las instituciones requeridas para el funcionamiento eficiente de un sistema de libre empresa

El funcionamiento de una economía de mercado requiere los servicios de instituciones auxiliares de distintos tipos--bancos, compañias de seguro, bolsas de valores, lonjas de comercio, casas de corretaje, etc.--que ayuden a las empresas a financiar su capital de trabajo, a asegurarse contra riesgos, a aumentar su capital accionario y a vender sus productos, por lo que será necesario crear o traer del extranjero instituciones de este tipo, pero esto no ofrecerá dificultad alguna, porque en el exilio hay personas preparadas en todas estas actividades, que podrían volver a Cuba como técnicos individuales, o llevar sucursales o agencias de las empresas que poseen; y, además porque Cuba podría abrir las puertas a empresas extranjeras que operan en estas actividades.

Dada la inexistencia en Cuba de entidades de servicios comerciales y financieros--excepto, desde luego, el Banco Nacional que presta estos servicios para las empresas del Estado--y dado el hecho de que estas empresas no irán a comprar activos a precios ínfimos, sino a movilizar ahorro nacional y traer recursos de afuera, será altamente aconsejable abrirles de par en par las puertas de nuestra economía.

Atracción de inversión directa extranjera

Repitiendo una afirmación hecha al principio de esta conferencia, Cuba deberá estimular y facilitar la entrada de capital extranjero a fin de acelerar su desarrollo económico, pero en las primeras fases del período de transición será necesario establecer algunas regulaciones a la entrada de capital si, como es probable, la economía experimenta desequilibrios que provoquen una caída en el valor de los activos cubanos en términos de la moneda de otros países. De ocurrir ésto, autorizar la libre entrada de capital sería vender activos cubanos a precios muy bajos a compradores de afuera: sería regalar nuestra riqueza al extranjero.

Si en las primeras fases del período de transición la baja en el valor de los activos fuese moderada, ésta estimularía la entrada de capital foráneo, lo que elevaría de nuevo ese valor, al propio tiempo que haría crecer la producción y el ingreso real, por lo que la pérdida que sufriría la economía del país al vender activos por algo menos de su valor estaría compensada por el mayor crecimiento económico; pero si la caída del valor de los activos nacionales fuese profunda, no podría permitirse su venta a un precio irrisorio. El problema es difícil, pero si se presenta habrá que afrontarlo con inteligencia y firmeza.

No puedo decir a ustedes, porque no he pensado con suficiente detenimiento en el problema, cuales deberían ser las reglas para canalizar las entradas de capital en los primeros tiempos, pero si puedo indicarles que, a mi juicio, estas deberían orientarse en la dirección de abrir las puertas al capital que venga a aumentar la producción de bienes y servicios, y cerrarlas al que pretenda entrar con el solo propósito de adquirir activos ya existentes. Este criterio no resuelve enteramente el problema, porque las inversiones dirigidas a aumentar la producción necesitan adquirir activos ya existentes--terrenos, edificios ya construídos--pero nos ayuda a decidir en sentido afirmativo o negativo, según la mayor importancia de uno u otro propósito.

El caso más difícil, y también el que habrá que afrontar con mas frecuencia, será el del inversionista extranjero que desea adquirir una industria nacional en operación, o una participación en su propiedad, para modernizarla y ampliarla, ya que no será fácil determinar que proporción del capital ampliado de la empresa deberán recibir los nuevos inversionistas y que proporción deberán mantener los antiguos propietarios (que en caso de Cuba en el futuro próximo serían el Estado o los trabajadores). Este es un problema que tenemos que resolver, de una manera u otra, porque su solución nos dará el criterio que deberemos aplicar a la inversión en Cuba del capital cubano en el exilio que, conjuntamente con el regreso de los técnicos exilados, serán los factores básicos de la reconstrucción de la economía cubana.

Reincorporación a la economía de los empresarios, administradores, ingenieros y profesionales de todas clases en el exilio

Al igual que en la sección anterior, debo comenzar ésta repitiendo conceptos ya enunciados: Cuba tendrá que reincorporar a su economía a los empresarios, administradores, ingeniéros y profesionales de todo tipo que están hoy en el exilio, pero esta reincorporación deberá ser hecha gradualmente porque, si se realizase en forma masiva, provocaría un choque económico, social y cultural con nuestros hermanos que permanecieron en Cuba, que podría crear graves obstáculos a la completa y absoluta reunificación patriótica de todos los cubanos.

El problema no será tal vez grave porque el grueso de los exilados está compuesto por funcionarios y empleados que no abandonarán sus puestos para ir a un país en crisis. El problema estará mas bien en los empresarios y capitalistas cubanos que quieran ir a adquirir unidades agrícolas, mineras o industriales, para modernizarlas y ampliarlas; para ponerlas a producir y a rendir dividendos. Como vimos en la sección anterior, tenemos que pensar en las normas que deberán regular estas inversiones.

Conclusiones

Siguiendo el mismo orden en que las he expuesto, podría resumir mis ideas y preocupaciones sobre el período de transición de la siguiente manera:

1. La forma mas aconsejable de reconvertir la economía estatal a un sistema de libre empresa sería distribuir una parte considerable de la propiedad de cada unidad productiva entre sus trabajadores. La indemnización a los propietarios consfiscados podría hacerse en bonos de valor garantizado contra la inflación.

2. El mercado principal para las exportaciones durante algunos años seguirá siendo la Unión Soviética, a la que se vendería el azúcar directamente o a través de terceros países.

3. Puede preverse un período de bajos niveles de producción e ingreso real, y fuertes desequilibrios fiscales y cambiarios, probablemente superiores a la ayuda externa que se reciba.

4. Dados los desequilibrios fiscales y cambiarios previsibles y el grave riesgo de inflación que ellos comportan, deberá procederse con gran cuidado en la aplicación de las políticas para realinear precios y costos.

5. Existe grave riesgo de inflación que será necesario evitar aplicando políticas económicas y financieras sumamente rigurosas, aún al costo de debilitar la lucha contra el desempleo y hacer mas lento el programa de reconstrucción.

6. Será necesario revivir el espiritu de trabajo, adormecido por el comunismo, y levantar la moral de los obreros y empleados, para lo cual sería aconsejable aplicar el plan de distribuir entre los trabajadores una alta proporción de la propiedad de las empresas.

7. Será necesario crear, reorganizar o traer del extranjero las instituciones financieras y comerciales necesarias para le buen funcionamiento de un régimen de libre empresa.

8. Deberá estimularse y facilitarse la inversión de capital extranjero, pero en las fases iniciales del período de transición la entrada deberá regularse a fin de evitar la venta a precios muy bajos de la riqueza del país; y

9. El regreso a Cuba de los empresarios, administradores y técnicos que están en el exilio deberá hacerse en forma gradual a fin de evitar choques con los actuales dirigentes de la economía cubana.

Las ideas desarrolladas a lo largo de esta conferencia, que acabo de resumir, son solo opiniones personales que espero puedan servir a ustedes como agenda para analizar y discutir los problemas que pueden presentarse en el período de transición, y las medidas alternativas que deban aplicarse para resolverlos o atenuarlos. Creo que la utilidad de esta exposición está en haber diferenciado las medidas de transición de las políticas que deberán adoptarse una vez que se normalice la economía, y, demás, en haber hecho un catálogo relativamente completo de los problemas que, a mi juicio, podrán presentarse.

Temo que mi análisis haya estado demasiado influído por la experiencia de los países de Europa Oriental, y que haya presentado los problemas de Cuba con una gravedad mayor de la que realmente tendrán; pero creo preferible que seamos precavidos a que los problemas nos agarren por sorpresa. No debemos ignorar que confrontaremos problemas, pero tenemos que estar seguros de que los superaremos. Tenemos que tener fe en que trabajando hombro con hombro los cubanos de adentro y los que estamos temporalmente afuera reconstruiremos una patria unida, libre, própera y feliz; una patria que volverá a ser orgullo de sus hijos, de América y del mundo.

Diciembre 12, 1990

APPENDIX B

Cuba: Una Opción por la Libertad, el Desarrollo y la Paz Social
(Propuesta de Lineamentos Estratégicos para la Completa Transformación de la Economía Socialista a una Economía Social de Mercado) 1/

Rolando H. Castañeda 2/

I. Introducción

A. Propósito

El propósito de este ensayo es presentar una propuesta concreta, pragmática y coherente de lineamentos estratégicos para hacer la completa transformación de la economía socialista a una economía social de mercado en Cuba, así como para enfrentar el país al reto del desarrollo y conducirlo adecuadamente hacia el siglo XXI. Para este fin se tienen en consideración el entorno internacional, la organización y la crítica situación de la economía nacional, las ventajas comparativas del país, así como los estudios y las experiencias recientes sobre la transformación de otros países socialistas.

La propuesta presupone un gobierno civil o militar con suficiente legitimidad política para emprender las reformas necesarias. El autor recomienda hacer los cambios institucionales y económicos orientados a la estabilización y la apertura económica en forma gradual y ordenada, pero progresiva, sistemática e integral. 3/ Además, encaminados a alentar el aumento de la oferta agregada de producción desde un principio; por lo tanto, la privatización de los medios de producción, la desregulación de la actividad económica y el desmantelamiento de los monopolios y oligopolios se deberán iniciar pronto y hacer rápidamente. Los cambios no buscan soluciones inmediatas para asegurar que el crecimiento sea sostenible social y políticamente.

Los cambios se efectuarían mediante políticas y medidas institucionales y macroeconómicas coherentes, interrelacionadas y que se apoyen mutuamente dentro de un marco general orientado al objetivo final de establecer una economía social de mercado muy competitiva y abierta, basada en la propiedad privada y en la libertad e iniciativa individuales, con un papel limitado y subsidiario del estado. La propuesta permitiría la modernización del país para mejorar las cada vez más deterioradas condiciones de vida de

---

1/ Versión revisada del ensayo presentado en la reunión de The Association for the Study of the Cuban Economy el 29 de enero de 1992.

2/ Economista del Departamento de Operaciones del Banco Interamericano de Desarrollo. Las opiniones sobre todos los temas tratados en este ensayo son estrictamente personales. El autor agradece los comentarios y sugerencias de Raúl Asón, Noel Belt, Ernesto Betancourt, Juan Buttari, Eduardo Caro, Alnunfo Carrandi, Don Arturo Cruz, Ramón Figueroa, José Antonio Herrero, Armando Lago, Jorge Lamas, Francisco León, Eloy Mestre, Lorenzo Pérez, Ricardo Puerta, Luis Rubio, Jairo Sánchez y Jorge Teller. Los temas tratados en este ensayo se ampliarán y se les dará un carácter multidisciplinario en un trabajo conjunto con Ricardo Puerta.

3/ El gradualismo que se propugna se refiere a no hacer todos los cambios y reformas estructurales en los sectores reales, financiero, fiscal y externo a la vez. Sin embargo, se recomienda un severo ajuste fiscal y de precios inicialmente, junto con significativas medidas en las otras áreas para lograr la indispensable estabilización. El objeto del gradualismo es evitar las experiencias negativas de otros países por conflictos entre las medidas de estabilización de corto plazo y las reformas estructurales de mediano y largo plazo, así como lograr efectos iniciales que compensen al menos en parte los grandes costos iniciales de las medidas estructurales.

los cubanos y crear bases sólidas para una sociedad libre y democrática, con participación ciudadana efectiva y paz social.

Con la propuesta se pretende responder, al menos parcialmente, al desafío que Felipe Pazos (1990) lanzara a los miembros de The Association for the Study of the Cuban Economy en su seminal ensayo sobre el tema (ver Capítulo IV, Sección D). La propuesta tiene sus raíces en la consigna de **libertad y vida** del movimiento de derechos humanos de Cuba en contraposición al cada vez más desacreditado lema de **socialismo o muerte** del gobierno socialista. También pretende alentar la presentación de otras propuestas alternativas sobre estos temas fundamentales para el futuro desarrollo de Cuba.

B. Organización

En el Capítulo II se presenta el entorno internacional. En el Capítulo III se resumen las principales características del socialismo barroco y la grave crisis de la economía cubana, que comenzó en 1986. En el Capítulo IV se consideran las condiciones políticas para efectuar los cambios y se desarrolla en detalle la propuesta tomando como base las ventajas comparativas de la economía cubana.

En los Anexos I a III se presentan algunas lecciones de los estudios sobre la materia y la experiencia reciente de otros países, que se tuvieron muy en cuenta para hacer la propuesta, ya que sería una verdadera necedad que los cubanos "redescubriéramos" lo que no se debe hacer.

Concretamente, en el Anexo I se exponen algunas consideraciones que surgen de la literatura reciente, en especial de la obra de Ronald McKinnon (1991), sobre cómo realizar en forma exitosa la estabilización, la liberalización y la privatización en la etapa de la transformación. En el Anexo II se destaca la experiencia de Chile en 1973-1991, el único país que ha pasado con éxito de una economía socialista a una economía de mercado muy abierta y que ha tenido un programa de privatizaciones sin precedentes. La experiencia chilena con algunos ajustes para corregir los errores de política económica cometidos y para darle mayor énfasis a las áreas sociales y al manejo y la conservación de los recursos naturales, debería ser el paradigma de la economía social de mercado a desarrollar en Cuba. En el Anexo III se resume el forzado y simultáneo plan polaco de estabilización y liberalización, pero que ha sido lento en la privatización. El plan polaco es considerado como el paradigma del cambio tipo gran explosión ("big bang"); no obstante, sus resultados iniciales no han sido positivos, a pesar de varias condiciones muy favorables.

II. El Entorno Internacional

El mundo, a través de tres bloques de países o megamercados, 4/ está envuelto

---

4/   Norteamérica, la Comunidad Económica Europea y Asia del Este.

en una rápida transformación hacia el comercio sin restricciones, la cual algunos autores han denominado la tercera revolución industrial. Especialmente en esos bloques prevalecen la interdependencia, la competencia y las continuas adaptaciones e innovaciones tecnológicas. La transformación se caracteriza por la significativa reducción o eliminación de las barreras y restricciones al libre movimiento de bienes y servicios, capitales, tecnologías e información, y se facilita por los sostenidos progresos en las computadoras, los transportes y las telecomunicaciones. En el área política hay una manifiesta tendencia hacia regímenes democráticos que facilitan la transformación integracionista.

Las empresas multinacionales tienen un destacado papel en el referido proceso, ya que trasladan sus sucursales y subsidiarias a los países donde pueden operar más eficientemente, sea para procesar sus insumos o bienes al menor costo, o para comercializar sus bienes o servicios finales para obtener mayores ingresos. Más aún, ahora las trasnacionales tienden a subcontratar muchos de los bienes y servicios que necesitan en el país de operación, en vez de que seguir creciendo para producirlos en forma directa, ya que un elemento muy importante de dichas empresas es la rapidez y flexibilidad con que puedan reaccionar a un entorno muy dinámico y cambiante. De ahí que un aspecto fundamental de los países en desarrollo debe ser el esfuerzo para la organización y progreso de los mercados internos a fin de que puedan tomar ventajas del entorno internacional.

Las pequeñas y medianas empresas industriales y de servicios de apoyo, que tienen una mayor intensidad en la utilización de mano de obra, han sido cruciales en el desarrollo industrial y la capacidad exportadora o de integración a los mercados internacionales de Japón, de los llamados cuatro dragones asiáticos (Corea del Sur, Hong Kong, Singapur y Taiwán) y de los países del ASEAN (Brunei, Filipinas, Indonesia, Malasia y Tailandia). En menos de 25 años, los dragones asiáticos pasaron de economías muy atrasadas con niveles de ingreso por habitante de pobreza a pujantes economías exportadoras con altos niveles de ingreso por habitante, mucho mayor que los países de América Latina.

Otra de las características del nuevo entorno internacional, es que el ahorro nacional de los países en desarrollo es más prescindible para lograr los niveles de inversión, tecnología y acceso a los mercados externos, ya que la existencia de condiciones adecuadas para la inversión privada extranjera pueden facilitarlos, tales como la organización y funcionamiento de mercados financieros. En este contexto, la educación, conocimientos, destrezas y ética de trabajo de los habitantes de un país; 5/ lo apropiado de su infraestructura básica, así como la solidez y lo apto de sus instituciones son elementos fundamentales en lograr la prosperidad en el futuro, atrayendo la inversión, la tecnología y el acceso a los mercados externos de las empresas multinacionales.

Guiada por nuevos líderes, muchos de ellos formados y con experiencias profesionales en las economías de mercado de los países desarrollados, América Latina está

5/   El acervo del capital humano (conocimientos, experiencias, habilidades, etc.) y la tecnología tienen cada vez una mayor importancia en los estudios recientes para explicar el crecimiento económico de los países.

envuelta en una serie de reformas para democratizar sus sociedades y para integrar sus economías entre sí, mediante acuerdos regionales, y a la economía mundial. La austeridad fiscal, la desreglamentación de la producción (eliminación de obstáculos burocráticos y legales), la promoción de la inversión extranjera, la apertura y reformas en los sectores financiero, externo y laboral, cada vez son más aceptadas como mecanismos eficientes y eficaces para lograr el crecimiento económico.

Lo mismo, sucede con la privatización de las empresas públicas, incluso de las que hasta hace poco se consideraban servicios que el estado debería brindar, debido a la frustración existente con la baja calidad de los servicios prestados, el déficit financiero en sus operaciones, al burocratismo y al clientelismo que las caracterizan. 6/ Ejemplos notables de la intensificación de los procesos de desreglamentación, apertura y privatización entre los países latinoamericanos son Argentina y México, los cuales tenían una larga tradición proteccionista, de intervención estatal y de empresas públicas y ahora están experimentando una notable mejoría económica con las reformas adoptadas.

Con el resurgir de las ideas democráticas y neoliberales, el fracaso de los intentos del socialismo de mercado 7/ y el desplome del socialismo en Europa Oriental y la antigua URSS, se ha generalizado el descrédito de la planificación y de la intervención del estado como gestor, administrador y empresario. Más aún se puede considerar que la economía de mercado basada en la libre empresa es el único modelo de desarrollo de América Latina y el Caribe en la actualidad. Tal vez esto explique la muy favorable acogida de la Iniciativa "Empresa para las Américas" del Presidente George Bush, que aspira a lograr el libre comercio en todo el Hemisferio Occidental, aumentar la inversión privada y reducir la deuda pública externa.

III. La Situación de Desbalances de la Economía Cubana.
Las Tres Décadas Perdidas o el Costo del Socialismo

En 1986, comenzó una recesión en Cuba, que se ha convertido en una severa crisis socioeconómica. Esta crisis se caracteriza por una marcada reducción en la producción; elevados niveles de desempleo abierto y disfrazado, de inflación reprimida, de déficit fiscal y de déficit en la cuenta corriente de la balanza de pagos; así como una deuda externa inmanejable, que hacen evidentes los desbalances estructurales internos y externos y la declinación de la economía. El problema de los desbalances es que no existen mecanismos de corrección que permitan resolverlos dentro del sistema vigente. Esta insostenible

---

6/   Recientemente, América Latina ha privatizado empresas aéreas, eléctricas y de teléfonos, bancos comerciales, explotaciones petroleras, plantas de tratamiento de agua, puertos, muelles, ferrocarriles y hasta zoológicos. En México hay una propuesta para privatizar los ejidos, una de las instituciones de la Revolución Mexicana, que supuestamente tenía sus orígenes en el sistema de tenencia de la tierra azteca. Guyana está vendiendo las tierras públicas.

7/   Hubo experiencias negativas en Polonia, Hungría, Yugoslavia, China y la antigua URSS. János Kornai, uno de sus propulsores iniciales, es uno de los convencidos de su total fracaso (Kornai, 1990, p 58-59). Parte del éxito húngaro en la década de los años 80 es atribuible a una economía paralela, ya que el gobierno socialista autorizó desarrollar actividades privadas en tiempo de ocio en restaurantes, servicios de reparación y taxis, pequeñas parcelas de tierra, etc., en adición al trabajo regular en las empresas estatales.

situación y el entorno internacional imponen un cambio sustantivo en el orden institucional y las políticas económicas del país a fin de sacarlo de la mediocridad y la declinación que lo está retrocediendo al siglo XIX en vez de encaminarlo al siglo XXI.

La crisis es resultado de un sistema de propiedad socialista de los medios de producción muy extenso e intenso y de un sistema de decisiones económicas muy centralizado, autoritario, burocrático y caracterizado por complejos monopólicos artificiales y una corrupción generalizada. 8/ Asimismo, del creciente aislamiento internacional, económico y político del gobierno socialista; 9/ de una economía muy dependiente de la producción y exportación del azúcar; así como del comercio exterior y de la ayuda externa que le proporcionaban los países de la Comisión de Ayuda Mutua Económica (CAME), es decir, la antigua Unión Soviética y otros seis países socialistas europeos (Alemania Oriental, Bulgaria, Checoslovaquia, Hungría, Polonia y Rumania). 10/

Los principales elementos de la crisis y otros desbalances estructurales internos y externos hacen intrincado el proceso de estabilización. La amplitud y profundidad de la propiedad socialista, la centralización y burocratización en las decisiones económicas y la estructura de precios muy distorsionada dificultan los procesos de privatización, desregulación y apertura, propios de una auténtica y radical solución.

A. La Amplitud y Profundidad del Sistema Socialista

Después de haber estatizado todas las grandes y medianas empresas y algunas pequeñas en el período 1960-1963, 11/ el gobierno socialista estatizó las restantes pequeñas empresas de servicios y el comercio al por menor en la "**Gran Ofensiva Revolucionaria**" de 1968; 58,012 negocios que comprendían desde talleres de reparación de autos, barberías, sastrerías, cafés, hasta vendedores ambulantes.

El 100% de la propiedad es estatal, y está establecida por la Constitución Política de 1976, en los sectores industrial, construcción, energía, transporte, comercio minorista y mayorista, comercio exterior y banca. En 1989, el 81% de la tierra agrícola era propiedad del estado, 10% de cooperativas de producción y 9% propiedad privada en forma de pequeñas parcelas familiares. Los agricultores privados están agrupados en la Asociación

---

8/ En Cuba, las corruptelas son conocidas eufemísticamente como "sociolismo" o beneficios obtenidos por conocimiento o amistad con el que presta el servicio, "bisneo" o actividades clandestinas de mercado negro, muchas de ellas resultado del robo a las empresas estatales y "trapicheo".

9/ El gobierno socialista apoyó la invasión rusa de Checoslovaquia en agosto de 1968, las actividades del General Jaruzelski contra Solidaridad en Polonia en 1981, al dictador Manuel Antonio Noriega en Panamá, la represión de la Plaza Tienanmen contra los estudiantes chinos y a Saddam Hussein de Irak vis a vis la coalición internacional en la Guerra del Golfo Pérsico en 1991.

10/ Esta dependencia es el resultado de la llamada división internacional de trabajo socialista y de la miopía de la dirigencia socialista cubana. Cuba exportaba azúcar, níquel, frutas cítricas y tabaco a cambio de maquinarias, equipos, alimentos, fertilizantes, repuestos y petróleo.

11/ La ley de reforma agraria en mayo de 1959, la estatización de las grandes y medianas empresas extranjeras en agosto de 1960, la estatización de las grandes y medianas empresas nacionales en octubre de 1960, la estatización del comercio minorista en diciembre de 1962 y la segunda ley de reforma agraria en agosto de 1963.

Nacional de Agricultores Pequeños, mediante la cual reciben las semillas, herramientas e insumos agrícolas, y se les fijan los precios y las metas de la producción a ser entregada a los centros de acopio estatales. No se permite la contratación privada de mano de obra, ni el arrendamiento de la tierra. Hay una gran presión del estado por integrar a los agricultores privados en cooperativas.

Las noticias referentes a que el IV Congreso del Partido Comunista Cubano, efectuado entre el 10 y el 14 de octubre de 1991, concedió de nuevo a los plomeros, carpinteros y otros obreros artesanos operar libremente, muestra los extremos absurdos del sistema socialista de Cuba.

B. Los Desbalances Internos

El punto de inflexión de la actual depresión comenzó con el estancamiento de 1986, coincidiendo y originado con el "**Proceso de Rectificación de Errores y Tendencias Negativas**", o sea la eliminación de las limitadas medidas de liberalización económica, que se habían adoptado dentro del Sistema de Dirección y Planificación Económica (SDPE), y con la suspensión de pagos de la deuda externa a las economías de mercado. El gobierno socialista lo atribuyó a las sequías de 1986 y 1987.

Las medidas de liberalización se iniciaron a finales de la década de los 70 y se intensificaron en la primera mitad de la década de los 80. Entre ellas se destacaron el mercado libre campesino, la venta libre de viviendas, las actividades artesanales y los servicios privados (peluquerías, sastrerías, talleres de reparación, vendedores ambulantes, transporte y servicios profesionales), que aún siendo tímidas y llenas de restricciones contribuyeron a aumentar la producción en 1981-1985 y que según los gobernantes socialistas estaban originando una nueva burguesía. 12/ De la misma manera, el Proceso de Rectificación, eliminó gran parte de los estímulos materiales laborales, la descentralización de las decisiones y la dependencia de los técnicos en las empresas que estaban acabando con el conformismo y el servilismo. Se impusieron severas restricciones a la construcción y venta privada de viviendas. Más aún se mantuvo la estructura de precios muy distorsionada y se abandonó el cálculo económico en las empresas. 13/

En diciembre de 1987 se impusieron severas sanciones a los delitos contra la economía nacional, enriquecimiento ilegal, uso personal de recursos estatales, la especulación y el acaparamiento, engaño a los consumidores, la falsificación de certificados médicos y el favoritismo.

El producto social global (PSG) a precios constantes se contrajo de 27,390 millones

---

12/   El III Congreso del Partido Comunista Cubano adoptó el Proceso de Rectificación en 1986, a pesar de que el período 1981-1985 fue el de mayor tasa de crecimiento en la época socialista (Rodríguez, 1990, tabla 10). Dicho proceso es el antiglasnot y antiperestroika cubano. La experiencia de la liberalización a principios de los años 80 hace prever una reacción muy favorable y fuerte del sector privado cuando se privatice y liberalice en Cuba.

13/   Carmelo Mesa-Lago (1991) presenta un excelente análisis del Proceso de Rectificación.

de pesos en 1986 a 27,233 millones de pesos en 1989, mientras la población continuó creciendo cerca del 1% anual. Estimados preliminares indican reducciones del PIB del 7% en 1990 y del 9% en 1991, resultado de la contracción del comercio exterior y la reducción de la masiva ayuda externa.

Esta declinación ha conllevado una creciente dificultad para brindar los bienes (y servicios) más básicos, en cantidad y calidad, a la población, como lo muestran la intensificación de los bienes sujetos a racionamiento y los bienes faltantes, con sus enormes costos humanos y económicos. 14/ Según la CEPAL (1990, p 349) en 1989 "la dieta alimenticia se resintió y la ingestión de calorías y proteínas por habitante fue la menor de la década". Las cuotas de racionamiento de carne, frijoles, arroz, café, azúcar y leche de 1989 fueron inferiores a las de 1962, año cuando se estableció el racionamiento (Clark, 1990, p 279); un claro indicador del retroceso en los niveles materiales de vida en las tres décadas de socialismo. Existe una situación de grave deterioro de viviendas. El número de viviendas construidas ha disminuido significativamente al punto que algunos estiman que las que se añaden son menos que las que se desahucian. Las bicicletas y la tracción animal están sustituyendo en forma creciente el transporte automotor y los tractores.

Otra de las causas del estancamiento del PSG es que la mayoría de los grandes proyectos de inversión, que el gobierno socialista inició a mediados de la década de los 80, permanecen inconclusos: la central termonuclear de Cienfuegos (con una tecnología obsoleta y peligrosa, tipo Chernobyl) y sus fábricas satélites, la planta de níquel de Moa debido a su ineficiente tecnología que consume mucho petróleo y la refinería de petróleo de Cienfuegos.

El empleo se expandió de 3,263 miles de trabajadores en 1986 a 3,527 miles de trabajadores en 1989, es decir en 8.1%, mientras la producción se redujo, lo que contribuyó a aumentar la baja en productividad y al desempleo disfrazado, 15/ y es resultado de la artificial "política de plena ocupación". A esto habría que añadir una expansión del desempleo abierto al 6% en 1988 y el retorno de unos 50,000 soldados de Angola.

El déficit fiscal aumentó al 4.4% del PSG en 1988 y al 5.2% en 1989, y fue financiado con emisión del banco central. En consecuencia, la expansión monetaria se incrementó, lo que aumentó el circulante disponible y acentuó las presiones inflacionarias reprimidas, ya que aún el denominado mercado paralelo, cada vez más limitado y eliminado finalmente en 1991, tenía los precios fijados. Además, el porcentaje de gastos militares se ha incrementado al 10% del PSG.

14/   Jorge Pérez-López y Carmelo Mesa-Lago (1990) señalan la marcada expansión de los bienes y servicios sujetos a racionamiento. David Lipton y Jeffrey Sachs (1990a, p 90-99) analizan la importante reducción del ingreso real, debido a los racionamientos y a los faltantes en las economías socialistas.

15/   Tradicionalmente ha habido un alto ausentismo y una pobre disciplina laboral en las empresas estatales, así como técnicos y profesionales prestando servicios en otros países. Además, el gobierno socialista tiene alrededor de 270,000 empleados en la seguridad interna y el ejército regular, así como unos 1,500,000 milicianos y 5,000,000 de personas en los Comités de Barrios.

C. Los Desbalances Externos

La contracción económica de 1986-1989 se ha venido agravando en forma sostenida a partir de 1990 con el colapso de la ayuda económica externa y del comercio exterior, lo que el gobierno socialista llamó primero "**un período especial en tiempos de paz**" en agosto de 1990 y después "**la opción cero**" en 1991, que significa ningún abastecimiento por la antigua Unión Soviética. Este colapso impide realizar las importaciones esenciales, tanto de bienes de consumo, como de combustibles, materias primas y piezas de repuestos. El sector externo ya presentaba brechas manifiestas, tales como: el abultado déficit comercial, las exportaciones fueron el 66% de las importaciones en 1989, y la dependencia de las reexportaciones petroleras y azucareras.

Desde mediados de la década de los 80, Cuba tuvo una asignación petrolera de 13 millones de toneladas métricas anuales de la antigua URSS y podía reexportar el sobrante que no utilizara, ya que su consumo neto era del orden de 10 millones de toneladas métricas. Los ingresos por este concepto alcanzaron unos 515 millones de pesos en 1983 (Jorge Pérez-López, 1989) y se estimaron en alrededor del 40% de los ingresos en monedas convertibles en 1983-1985. También Cuba podía comprar azúcar en el mercado mundial para revenderlo a la antigua URSS a los precios subsidiados.

El citado colapso del comercio exterior se debe a la drástica reducción, y posterior suspensión, de la masiva ayuda externa del CAME; a la terminación del comercio de muchos productos del CAME, que era dictado por razones políticas o que se hubiese hecho a precios internacionales y pagadero en divisas a partir de 1991; y a la eliminación de los créditos comerciales y de proveedores de los países de economías de mercado, por la moratoria del servicio de la deuda externa de 1986. Asimismo, el cambio de régimen en Panamá en diciembre de 1989 eliminó una importante válvula de escape al bloqueo comercial impuesto por los Estados Unidos de América (EUA).

La masiva ayuda económica externa tenía dos componentes principales y estaba enmarcada dentro de acuerdos comerciales quinquenales, el último fue el de 1986-1990. Además, hay que destacar la ayuda técnica y militar.

Un componente fue la ayuda "implícita" o transferencias recibidas al vender el azúcar a precios muy superiores al mercado mundial 16/ y al comprar el petróleo a precios por debajo del mercado mundial. Esto distorsionó la economía al desalentar la diversificación de la estructura productiva y mejoras en la eficiencia de la industria azucarera. De la misma manera, alentó el consumo exagerado de petróleo y sus derivados (fertilizantes, pesticidas e insecticidas), con sus consecuencias de deterioro ambiental,

---

16/ En 1989 Cuba vendió el azúcar a la URSS a 41.9 centavos de dólares en vez de a 12.81 centavos de dólares que prevalecieron en el mercado mundial, CEPAL (1990). Jorge Pérez-López (1991a) estimó la transferencia de recursos de la URSS a Cuba en US$4,201 millones en las exportaciones de azúcar en 1987 por concepto del diferencial de precios pagados sobre los imperantes en el mercado mundial.

actividades muy intensas en el uso de petróleo como el procesamiento de minerales y la utilización de las cosechadoras en el azúcar, y desmotivó el desarrollo de fuentes de energía alternas. El otro componente era la ayuda "explícita" para financiar el déficit de la balanza de pagos, 17/ consecuencia de la marcada sobrevalorización del peso y de los ineficientes regímenes de producción y comercialización existentes.

La ayuda económica externa recibida por Cuba de la antigua URSS alcanzó niveles inusitados. Ritter (1990, p 134) la estimó entre el 26% y el 37% del PIB en 1987. Las cifras comparables para los países de América Latina fueron en 1987: Haití 9.7%, El Salvador 9.0%, Bolivia 7.1% y Honduras 6.4%. 18/

En 1989, el 85% de las importaciones de bienes y el 80% de las exportaciones de bienes se efectuaron con los países del CAME. En 1986, el gobierno socialista suspendió el servicio de la deuda externa con las economías de mercado que ascendió a 6,165 millones de pesos en 1989, o sea unos US$600 por habitante o aproximadamente el 30% del PIB. 19/ Esta suspensión prácticamente paralizó la modernización y actualización tecnológica y cualitativa del país, desde entonces dependiente fundamentalmente de los equipos y tecnologías de los países socialistas europeos. Asimismo, Cuba tiene una deuda morosa de 16,100 millones de rublos, denominada en esa moneda, con la antigua URSS. Carmelo Mesa-Lago (1992a) estimó la deuda externa total por habitante de Cuba en US$2,970 en 1989, la mayor de América Latina.

Información preliminar de 1991 indica que la antigua URSS disminuyó los envíos petroleros de Cuba a 7 millones de toneladas métricas y estaba pagando el azúcar a unos 21 centavos de dólares por libra. Dadas las deterioradas condiciones económicas de la antigua URSS y la actitud de los nuevos dirigentes en 1992, es casi seguro que se reduzcan los envíos de petróleo y no se continué subsidiando el azúcar, por lo cual la depresión se agudizará notablemente por la eliminación de la ayuda externa económica y técnica y por la reducción del comercio exterior. Carmelo Mesa-Lago (1992c) ha estimado los efectos de la reducción de la ayuda externa económica soviética y de la reducción del comercio con los países de Europa Oriental en alrededor de US$7,100 millones; sin embargo, esta cifra habría que ajustarla para reflejar la baja calidad de los bienes recibidos por Cuba de los antiguos países socialistas.

En su desesperación por la captación de divisas, el gobierno socialista ha decidido

---

17/   Ya en noviembre de 1990, el mercado negro era de US$1 = 20 pesos comparado con el oficial de US$1 = 1 peso (Andrade, 1990, p 138).

18/   Carmelo Mesa-Lago y Fernando Gil (1989) ya habían destacado el nivel decisivo y extraordinario de dicha ayuda externa. La ayuda externa de la antigua URSS fue estimada en US$100 mil millones en 1961-1990 por Irina Zoriona de la Academia de Ciencias de la URSS (Andrade, p 128). Ritter (1990, p 126) estimó la ayuda en 31,2 mil millones de pesos en 1980-1987 sin contar el no servir la deuda. Sin dudas, esta ayuda masiva estuvo asociada a los "servicios" que Cuba prestó al expansionismo soviético en 1961-1990, primero en forma de guerrillas y subversión y después de ejército regular, principalmente en Etiopía y Angola, pero que se volvieron obsoletos al terminar la guerra fría. También la URSS utilizaba a Cuba como un modelo de la vía socialista del desarrollo para el Tercer Mundo.

19/   Con base en los cálculos de Ritter (1990, p 138).

desarrollar rápidamente el turismo, una de las claras ventajas comparativas del país, mediante empresas mixtas ("joint ventures") con inversionistas de Canadá, España, Jamaica y México, pero en un verdadero estilo de economía de enclave o, más aún, de "apartheid". Dicho desarrollo está limitando el turismo a uno de relajación y exacerbando las penurias y desbalances existentes, ya que impide a la población nacional el acceso a las playas, restaurantes y otros centros de los turistas pagaderos solamente en divisas, y ha suscitado el aumento de la delincuencia común, en especial entre la juventud. La situación se hará más difícil e insostenible, a medida que el turismo se expanda.

El desarrollo turístico pone de manifiesto la contradicción ideológica del gobierno socialista que ha decidido no utilizar y discrimina contra el sector privado nacional en la agricultura y en los otros sectores, mientras fomenta al sector privado extranjero en el turismo, dándole exenciones tributarias e incentivos. Más aún ha tenido que modificar la Constitución Política del país para permitir el abastecimiento de los hoteles por empresas privadas y la contratación de personal por los hoteles privados, ya que las empresas estatales cubanas son tan ineficientes que impiden que los "joint ventures" funcionen adecuadamente.

D. El Gobierno Socialista, 1960-1992

Además del desarrollo del turismo, el gobierno socialista trata de resolver la crisis con base en el aumento y diversificación de la producción agrícola destinada al consumo interno, mediante la movilización forzada del obrero urbano al campo e impulsando un aumento de la productividad por pequeñas obras de riego y por otras mejoras en la infraestructura. También impone un enfoque redistribucionista, con total indiferencia a la realidad de los niveles de producción, exportaciones y crecimiento de la economía y al entorno internacional, e ignorando los mercados y al sector privado que pudieran dinamizar la producción.

La oposición del gobierno socialista a hacer los ajustes requeridos está disminuyendo drásticamente los niveles de vida de la población y poniendo en peligro los logros alcanzados en más de tres décadas en el poder en los sectores educación y salud, como resultado de extender los servicios a los grupos de bajos ingresos urbanos y a la población rural.

Antes del gobierno socialista, Cuba tenía uno de los niveles de ingreso por habitante más altos en el continente y niveles elevados de educación, salud y nutrición (Thomas, Fauriol y Weiss, 1984). Después de tres décadas de socialismo, los niveles de ingreso por habitante han progresado modestamente, los intentos de diversificación agrícola e industrial han fracasado, la economía sigue basada en un producto de exportación, dispone de una maquinaria industrial obsoleta tecnológicamente e ineficiente económicamente, tiene una elevada deuda externa para sus niveles de producción y exportación y presenta serios desbalances externos e internos. El gobierno socialista tampoco ha respetado los derechos políticos y económicos básicos de la Declaración Universal de Derechos Humanos, de la cual Cuba es signataria. Algunos visitantes recientes comparan a Cuba con Albania y Vietnam, indicando que más que cubanizarse el socialismo, paradójicamente se socializó la cubanía (Timmerman, 1990).

El crecimiento de la economía en el período 1960-1991 ha sido limitado, aunque las estadísticas oficiales, señalan un crecimiento anual del 2.7% del PIB por habitante en los últimos 32 años, que sería el mayor de América Latina. Sin embargo, la calidad de la información estadística del gobierno socialista no es buena (Jorge Pérez-López, 1991a y Carmelo Mesa-Lago, 1992a) y los datos están sujetos a frecuentes cambios por razones metodológicas que no siempre se explican (Carmelo Mesa-Lago y Jorge Pérez-López, 1985) y con seguridad tienen un sesgo en el sentido de mostrar la situación mejor de lo que en realidad es. El gobierno socialista de Cuba es simplemente fiel a la larga tradición de fabulación estadística que ha caracterizado a todos los países socialistas. Un dato elocuente del estancamiento económico durante el régimen socialista es la reducción de los productos de consumo básico de la población, mencionada antes, ocurrida en el período 1962-1989. La situación a principios de 1992 es mucho peor.

Índices agregados de crecimiento de la producción de los sectores agropecuario, minero y de energía eléctrica **confirman** que el crecimiento de Cuba no ha sido mayor que los de otros países latinoamericanos, tales como: Costa Rica, Colombia y Chile, que supuestamente han crecido menos que Cuba. De hecho Cuba ocupa el tercer lugar de estos cuatro países en crecimiento de la producción agropecuaria y de energía eléctrica y el cuarto de la producción minera sobre un período de 15 años o más. No hay datos agregados comparables para el sector industrial. Otros datos corroboradores: la producción agrícola en 1969 fue entre 12% y 16% menor que en 1961 y el número de cabezas de ganado se redujo de 7.2 millones en 1967 a 5.0 millones en 1987 (Mesa-Lago, 1992a, p. 434).

Tasas Anuales de Crecimiento en Países Seleccionados, 1970-1990

Tasas Anuales de Crecimiento de Indices de Volumen Físico	Colombia	Costa Rica	Cuba	Chile
Producción Agropecuaria, 1975-1989	3.17	2.18	2.56	2.69
Producción Minera, 1970-1989	3.70	17.17	2.51	3.93
Producción de Energía Eléctrica, 1970-1988	8.62	6.50	6.24	4.58
Fuente: CEPAL (1991), p. 602-607, 668-669 y 696-697.				

En cuanto a las áreas socioeconómicas, en la primera mitad de la década de los años 60, Cuba tenía tasas de mortalidad y mortalidad infantil menores y una esperanza de vida al nacer mayor que Colombia, Costa Rica y Chile. En la segunda mitad de la década de los 80, Cuba tenía una tasa de mortalidad mayor que esos tres países, pero seguía con una esperanza de vida al nacer mayor y una tasa de mortalidad infantil menor. Sin embargo, los ritmos de progreso de los otros tres países fueron mayores en cuanto esperanza de vida al nacer y tasa de mortalidad, y Cuba seguía a Chile y Costa Rica en cuanto al ritmo de progreso en reducir la tasa de mortalidad infantil. En educación secundaria y terciaria, Cuba ocupaba la tercera posición de matriculados después de Costa

Índices Socioeconómicos en Países Seleccionados, 1960-1990

ÍNDICES	Colombia	Costa Rica	Cuba	Chile
Tasas de Mortalidad				
1960-1965	11.5	9.2	8.8	12.1
1985-1990	6.1	4.0	6.5	6.4
Progreso en 1985-1990/1960-1965	0.53	0.43	0.74	0.52
Años de Esperanza de Vida al Nacer				
1960-1965	57.9	63.0	65.4	58.0
1985-1990	68.2	74.7	75.2	71.5
Progreso en 1985-1990/1960-1965	1.18	1.19	1.15	1.23
Tasas de Mortalidad Infantil				
1960-1965	92.1	81.3	59.4	109.4
1985-1990	39.7	19.4	15.2	18.1
Progreso en 1985-1990/1960-1965	0.43	O.24	0.26	0.21
Tasas Brutas de Matrícula al Segundo Nivel				
1960	11.9	20.3	14.2	22.9
1987	56.0	40.4	84.6	70.0
Progreso en 1987/1960	4.71	1.99	5.96	3.06
Tasas Brutas de Matrícula al Tercer Nivel				
1960	1.8	4.8	3.1	4.2
1987	13.2	24.8	22.8	17.9
Progreso en 1987/1960	7.33	5.17	7.35	4.26
Fuente: CEPAL (1991), p. 14, 15, 49, 56 y 57.				

Rica y Chile en 1960. En 1987 Cuba ocupaba la primera posición en educación intermedia y la segunda en educación terciaria después de Costa Rica y experimentó un mayor ritmo de progreso en los niveles de matrícula bruta en los dos niveles que los otros tres países en esos 27 años.

En resumen, el crecimiento económico (y la creación de empleo productivo) ha sido modesto durante el gobierno socialista, lo cual contribuye a explicar, al menos parcialmente, varias medidas tales como: el fomento de la emigración, la ficticia política de pleno empleo, la reducción de las edades de jubilación, la expansión de los servicios de profesionales en el exterior, la extraordinaria militarización, etc. Considerando la disminución de la producción en 1990-1992, la disminución de la productividad o la expansión del desempleo disfrazado en 1986-1989 y el aumento del desempleo abierto a 6% en 1988, Cuba deberá tener el equivalente a un desempleo abierto del orden del 25% al 30% en 1992.

El autor considera que los logros sociales con esta base productiva endeble son artificiales y no son sostenibles, porque el país ha vivido por encima de su producción y se han financiado mediante las masivas transferencias soviéticas y el elevado endeudamiento externo. De hecho, Cuba permaneció aislada de los efectos depresivos del aumento de los precios de petróleo y de la crisis del servicio de la deuda externa en 1974-1985. Sin embargo, una vez eliminados las transferencias externas y el comercio artificial, los avances sociales son insostenibles mientras perdure el barroco sistema socialista de producción y la organización administrativa sumamente centralizada y burocrática que obstaculizan la capacidad creativa y la iniciativa productiva de los cubanos.

IV. Una Propuesta de Lineamentos Estratégicos para Reconstruir y Modernizar la Economía Cubana en la Etapa de la Transformación

Esta propuesta presenta las principales las orientaciones, medidas y políticas institucionales y macroeconómicas para plasmar una economía social de mercado muy competitiva y orientada al exterior en Cuba. Las mismas se recomiendan en consonancia con el entorno internacional; las ventajas comparativas del país; el ajuste gradualista, pero progresivo y completo de McKinnon (véase Anexo 1); y siguiendo el paradigma y la integralidad de las reformas chilenas (véase Anexo 2), pero ajustadas para dar más énfasis a los aspectos sociales y corregir algunos errores cometidos de política económica.

A. Condiciones Políticas para la Implantación de la Propuesta

La propuesta que se describe a continuación podría parecer ingenua; sin embargo, hay varios escenarios políticos en que podría implantarse, o al menos, ser útil. [20] Es posible que la dirigencia del gobierno socialista se retire voluntariamente del país ante la

---

[20] Ernesto Betancourt (1988) presenta un marco general y algunas alternativas de transición política para Cuba que deberían desembocar en una apertura económica y en el cambio del sistema socialista. Luis Aguilar (1991) presenta reflexiones históricas y políticas sobre la inminente caída del régimen socialista.

insostenible situación económica y política; o haga elecciones libres ante la creciente presión de los gobernantes latinoamericanos, bajo el decidido liderato del Presidente Carlos Menem de Argentina, 21/ y de los intelectuales latinoamericanos y cubanos 22/ para extender la democracia de casi todo el continente a Cuba. También Fidel Castro podría desaparecer por muerte natural, accidental o de otra forma. En los casos anteriores, la propuesta podría contribuir a la preparación de un plan de acción para un gobierno de transición y ser un elemento de la plataforma de los partidos democráticos de oposición al sistema existente.

Los militares podrían tomar el poder para restablecer el orden, después de algunas manifestaciones espontáneas que se repriman a la rumana, o sencillamente por lo insostenible de la situación, y decidan sentar las bases para la institucionalización del país apoyando un cambio estructural radical, como se hizo en Chile. 23/ Como señala Luis Aguilar (1991), el régimen socialista no tiene salida, pero los militares sí la tienen.

En cualquier caso es necesario que comience un debate nacional sobre el futuro del país. Que los cubanos de la isla y fuera de ella tengamos propuestas lo más completas y coherentes para sacar a Cuba de la mediocridad y la declinación que sufre, porque el gobierno socialista trata sin criterio de hacerla el último bastión socialista y de economía centralizada del mundo, aún desaparecida la ayuda del bloque soviético que lo sostuvo artificialmente. Posiblemente, esta posición extrema facilitará todo lo contrario, o sea el establecimiento de una economía social de mercado con el apoyo de la inmensa mayoría de la población, harta de no haber podido expresar su capacidad creativa y su iniciativa, salvo en forma clandestina y reprimida, por más de tres décadas.

B. Las Ventajas Comparativas de Cuba

Las principales ventajas de la economía cubana consisten en: (1) sus recursos naturales para la agricultura y el turismo; (2) su situación geográfica cercana a los EUA, el mayor mercado del mundo, ahora en proceso de integración con Canadá y México; y (3) lo excepcional de su clase empresarial, profesional, administradora y trabajadora, que parcialmente se radicó con éxito y ha ganado extraordinarias experiencias en los EUA, América Latina y Europa, aumentando así su capital humano.

Uno de los grandes errores del gobierno socialista ha sido propiciar oleadas de emigración, principalmente en 1960-1961, 1965-1971 (Camarioca y los vuelos de la libertad) y 1980 (Mariel). Asimismo, la salida de cubanos de la isla, por medios legales e ilegales, ha sido constante de los últimos 33 años. Con ello el gobierno socialista ha eliminado

---

21/ Declaración de los 13 Presidentes de los Países del Grupo de Río de Cartagena de Indias del 2 de diciembre de 1991.

22/ Bajo el liderato de la poetisa María Elena Cruz Varela del Grupo Criterio Alternativo, quién fuera sentenciada a dos años de prisión el 27 de noviembre de 1991.

23/ Cabe señalar que los cambios socioeconómicos de Chile tuvieron lugar en un período que no se entendieron bien debido al régimen autoritario que las implantó y a las ideas intervencionistas y socialistas que prevalecían en el continente. Además, se cometieron algunos errores socioeconómicos innecesarios.

oposición interna, confiscado riquezas y redujo el desempleo, pero produjo el drenaje de cerebros y del dinámico capital humano no conformista. No obstante, ha realizado un esfuerzo por invertir en capital humano; en consecuencia, el país dispone de una fuerza laboral educada y sana, pero que habría que adiestrar en técnicas modernas y particulares a una economía de mercado y ampliarle los horizontes que los profesionales pueden y deben cultivar. Esta población podría competir ventajosamente en la producción de bienes y servicios con otros países de la región, una vez fijada una tasa de cambio realista, realizados los ajustes requeridos en el aparato productivo.

Para aprovechar sus ventajas comparativas, Cuba debe crear condiciones para atraer el retorno de la población radicada en el exterior con sus conocimientos y experiencias empresariales, profesionales y administrativas; con sus recursos financieros y tecnológicos; y con sus contactos y conocimientos que facilitarían el acceso a los mercados externos. Asimismo, debe desarrollar la infraestructura básica y otras facilidades físicas (transporte, telecomunicaciones, energía eléctrica, agua potable y alcantarillado), humanas (salud y educación primaria, secundaria y técnica y vocacional) e institucionales, que permitan la producción eficiente de bienes y servicios principalmente para el mercado internacional, con énfasis en sus mercados geoeconómicos naturales.

En general, Cuba debería orientar su economía a actividades que utilicen intensivamente sus recursos de mano de obra, conocimientos tecnológicos, capacidad empresarial y recursos naturales. Cuba podría competir con rapidez en tres sectores orientando la producción a sus mercados geoeconómicos naturales (los EUA y el resto del Hemisferio Occidental): la agricultura y el procesamiento de su producción (la agroindustria), la pesca y el turismo. Es decir, con una reducida inversión inicial por lo excepcional de sus recursos naturales o por las inversiones realizadas por el gobierno socialista.

El sector agropecuario y las agroindustrias por la fertilidad de sus suelos, reforzada ahora por obras de irrigación, el mercado cubano-americano en los EUA y la complementariedad de climas con Canadá y los EUA. La pesca por las importantes inversiones realizadas en el sector. El turismo debido a que Cuba es una isla tropical con bellas y extensas playas y paisajes naturales, a la diversidad de sus aves, variedades marinas y su flora tropical, a las inversiones que se están realizando y a la posibilidad que la agricultura nacional genere la mayoría de los alimentos que requerirán los visitantes. Sólo los ingresos generados por los cubanos radicados en el exterior que decidan visitar la isla podrían ser muy significativos en el turismo. 24/ Igualmente se debería aprovechar el turismo ecológico.

24/   El turismo ha jugado un papel muy importante en el desarrollo de varios países del mediterráneo europeo: España, Italia y Grecia.

Dada la situación y las expectativas del mercado mundial del azúcar, 25/ deberá abandonarse la especialización artificial de Cuba para un mercado externo protegido, con las distorsiones que ello conllevaría en los sectores internos y externos del país.

C. La Propuesta

1. Conceptos generales

El autor considera que el objetivo final de la transformación de Cuba debería ser desarrollar una economía social de mercado muy competitiva y abierta con base en la propiedad privada y la libertad e iniciativa individuales, alentadoras del esfuerzo, el ingenio, la creatividad y la imaginación de los cubanos, dejando un papel limitado y subsidiario al estado. No obstante, la acción del estado tendrá que ser decidida y muy activa en la etapa de la transformación, precisamente para reducir su exagerado ámbito; sin embargo, no es estatizante por sus fines, ni en sus medios.

No es sólo desmantelar el régimen de propiedad socialista y la centralización autoritaria y burocrática, o sea las estructuras del atraso y la crisis, sino es crear las condiciones para una economía estable, moderna y dinámica en que todos seamos propietarios e inversionistas y que el estado tenga un compromiso con la población más pobre. También es descentralizar la acción del gobierno central a las provincias, los municipios y las comunidades y tener un sistema con una auténtica participación ciudadana.

A tal efecto el autor propone hacer la transformación de la economía socialista existente en Cuba a una de mercado dentro de un marco general y consistente de reformas graduales, pero progresivas, sistemáticas e integrales en lo referente a la estabilización y liberalización a fin de asegurar su efectividad y hacerlas sostenibles política y socialmente. Las medidas a adoptar en cada etapa serían flexibles, pero hay interrelaciones, interacciones y secuencias necesarias. Se seguiría el esquema completo de McKinnon, con algunas desviaciones y ampliaciones referentes a hacer más rápido e intenso el proceso de privatización y adoptar medidas institucionales de desregulación de la producción y de desmantelamiento de los monopolios y oligopolios artificiales que tengan resultados catalíticos sobre el aumento de la producción. La propuesta es congruente con el conjunto de reformas económicas básicas que Williamson (1990) definió como el consenso de las instituciones financieras de Washington.

25/ Actualmente prevalecen precios por debajo de los costos de producción debido al creciente desarrollo de sustitutos en la Comunidad Económica Europea y los EUA. Es de esperar que este tipo de desarrollo continué.

Metas, Objetivos e Instrumentos Económicos Generales de la Propuesta

Las Grandes Metas Globales de la Propuesta	Objetivos Más Inmediatos	Instrumentos y Reformas
Establecer y consolidar el ejercicio de las libertades y derechos individuales. Promover auténtica participación ciudadana y plena vigencia del estado de derechos.	Establecer y desarrollar una economía de mercado y una sociedad civil.	Dictar leyes de libertades y derechos económicos básicos. Privatizar medios de producción. Libre entrada a actividades económicas, profesiones y oficios. Eliminar controles de precios y salarios a las empresas privadas. Alentar entidades privadas sin fines de lucro.
	El estado tendrá un rol limitado y subsidiario y será descentralizado	Reformar integralmente el estado. Privatizar al menos parcialmente servicios públicos y sociales. Expandir papel de las provincias, los municipios y las comunidades.
Impulsar el crecimiento, desarrollo y modernización del país y encaminarlo adecuadamente al siglo XXI.	Desarrollar una economía competitiva.	Desregular actividades económicas. Desmantelar monopolios y oligopolios artificiales. El estado no otorgará concesiones económicas especiales.
	Desarrollar una economía muy abierta.	Otorgar baja protección efectiva. Alentar la inversión privada extranjera.
	Establecer y desarrollar una economía estable, moderna y dinámica.	Banco central autónomo. Regular y supervisar el crédito bancario. Reformas se harán gradual, pero progresiva e integralmente. Establecer balance en las finanzas públicas. Reformar integralmente el estado. Dictar ley de presupuesto balanceado. Privatizar por ventas o "leasing".
Promover la paz social.	Establecer una Red de Solidaridad e Inversión Social.	Otorgar asistencia temporal a los desempleados. Asegurar niveles mínimos de vida a la población de bajos ingresos. Fomentar el ahorro mediante subsidios.

Las Grandes Metas Globales de la Propuesta	Objetivos Más Inmediatos	Instrumentos y Reformas
Lograr la reconciliación nacional y la reunificación familiar.	Sustituir la confrontación por la cooperación y la solidaridad ciudadanas.	Eliminar los órganos de seguridad política, las milicias, los comités de barrios y las brigadas de respuesta rápida. Reducir el tamaño del ejército. Atraer y reintegrar a los cubanos radicados en el exterior.
Reinsertar a Cuba en la comunidad internacional.	Desarrollar una economía muy abierta.	Alentar la inversión privada extranjera. Entrar a organismos financieros internacionales.

Con base en el análisis de McKinnon y el similar de Fischer y Gelb (1990), así como en la experiencia gradual chilena, el autor recomienda cinco etapas de uno año y medio las dos primeras y de un año cada una de las restantes, o sea un total de 6 años, para asegurar que las reformas requeridas e insoslayables tengan resultados sostenibles y sinérgicos.

Las reformas suponen devolverle a los individuos funciones y actividades que les fueron despojados por el estado, incluyendo derechos básicos, tales como la libertad de asociación, la libertad de entrar y salir del país, la libertad de expresarse, la libertad de información, etc. Igualmente, el autor propone que las reformas incluyan privatizar muchos servicios públicos y sociales, siguiendo el exitoso ejemplo de Chile, que se consideraban dominio del estado en Cuba, aún antes del gobierno socialista. De esta manera la economía sería más eficiente y competitiva, lo cual es imprescindible no sólo por el entorno internacional, sino por el atraso y la situación de inferioridad de los cuales Cuba partirá.

La privatización debería ser por venta de las empresas, incluyendo la tierra y las empresas agrícolas, por las situaciones de la producción, las finanzas públicas, la deuda externa y el exceso de circulante, así como para que se pueda atender adecuadamente la red de solidaridad e inversión social. Sin embargo, se incluirían también privatizaciones por contratos de arrendamiento a largo plazo ("leasings") y contratos de administración.

La propuesta tiene en consideración los elevados costos sociales, expresados en el sufrimiento real y concreto de las personas afectadas, que estos procesos de reformas conllevan inevitablemente. Además, las medidas sociales son parte integral del plan de transformación económica. En consecuencia, considera indispensable la red de solidaridad e inversión social para hacer esta transición política y socialmente sustentables. La red financiaría programas para asegurar niveles de vida mínimos a la población pobre y par dar empleo **temporal** a los desempleados y adiestrarlos para aumentar su capital humano y para que puedan integrarse efectivamente a la economía de mercado. También les ayudaría a ahorrar dándoles subsidios para tener una solución habitacional.

Con base en la experiencia de los antiguos países socialistas europeos y en consideraciones prácticas, a los residentes en el país se les daría la opción de reclamar sus propiedades o continuar con la compensación establecida por el gobierno socialista. A los cubanos radicados en el exterior que sufrieron confiscaciones se les compensaría con bonos o títulos para compra de empresas, activos o de acciones de empresas estatales. Estos criterios se refieren a las tierras agropecuarias, bienes, bienes raíces incluyendo viviendas, empresas pequeñas, medianas y grandes.

La propuesta no supone un programa masivo de ayuda externa; en este sentido, es autosuficiente. No obstante, sí pretende crear las condiciones para estimular el retorno, la inversión, las visitas y la ayuda de los cubanos radicados en el exterior, así como abrir el país a la inversión privada extranjera, pero sin darle concesiones especiales. Sólo el mismo trato que al sector privado nacional, como se ha hecho en Chile. También pretende la entrada de Cuba a los organismos financieros internacionales para que colaboren técnica y financieramente en la transformación.

La ayuda externa que se recibiera debería ser preferentemente para dar apoyo directo a las pequeñas y medianas empresas privadas a que se capitalicen adecuadamente, para los programas de solidaridad e inversión social orientados a asegurar una calidad de vida mínima en la etapa de transición, para conseguir asistencia técnica temporal de los cubanos del exterior que decidan permanecer fuera del país y para renegociar y reducir la deuda externa.

Las reformas, medidas y políticas económicas durante toda la transformación y en cada una de sus etapas serían lo más simples y transparentes posibles, para que la población las entienda con claridad y se una nacionalmente, apoyando los objetivos y medidas propuestos. Los objetivos bien definidos y aceptados en un consenso nacional facilitarían el período de transformación y de reformas, al establecer la confianza y debido a la tradicional incapacidad del gobierno socialista de cumplir sus promesas de mejorar el nivel de vida de la población.

2. Detalles de las orientaciones, medidas y políticas

a. La etapa del ajuste fiscal y de precios

Se establecería que el objetivo principal inmediato del estado es que la sociedad y la economía funcionen en forma ordenada, pero cambiante al garantizar las libertades básicas establecidas en la Declaración Universal de Derechos Humanos, el cumplimiento de las leyes y la protección de la propiedad. Se aseguraría la integridad y autoridad de las instituciones de servicio público que definan y hagan cumplir las orientaciones, medidas y reglas del juego. Especialmente, es necesario un poder judicial respetable y respetuoso, en el cual todos los ciudadanos tengan la confianza y la expectativa de que su causa será debidamente atendida. Se indicaría que se cumplirían los compromisos internacionales y se someterían los diferendos a arbitraje, cuando no se llegue a acuerdos.

PRINCIPALES MEDIDAS Y POLÍTICAS PROPUESTAS PARA LA RECONSTRUCCIÓN DE CUBA

MEDIDAS REFORMAS Y POLÍTICAS	SANEAMIENTO O ESTABILIZACION (TRES AÑOS)		LIBERALIZACIÓN (TRES AÑOS)		
	ETAPA 1 (AJUSTE FISCAL Y DE PRECIOS)	ETAPA 2 (COMIENZO DE LA PRIVATIZACION Y AJUSTE MONETARIO-CREDITICIO)	ETAPA 3 (PROFUNDIZACIÓN DE LA PRIVATIZACION Y APERTURA FINANCIERA INTERNA)	ETAPA 4 (APERTURA COMERCIAL)	ETAPA 5 (APERTURA FINANCIERA EXTERNA)
INSTITUCIONALES Y JURÍDICAS	RESTABLECER, GARANTIZAR Y HACER CUMPLIR DERECHOS DE PROPIEDAD Y LIBRE CONTRATACION, LEYES DE COMERCIO Y DE QUIEBRAS, NORMAS DE CONTABILIDAD, LIBRE EJERCICIO DE PROFESIONES Y OFICIOS, LIBRE ENTRADA A NEGOCIOS Y SINDICALIZACION LIBRE Y DEMOCRÁTICA. DEFINIR TRAMITES SIMPLES Y EXPEDITOS PARA INSTALAR NEGOCIOS.	FORMULAR MODERNAS LEYES DE SOCIEDADES COMERCIALES Y DE CONTROL DE MONOPOLIOS Y OLIGOPOLIOS. ESTABLECER BOLSA DE VALORES.	FORMULAR MODERNA LEY LABORAL CON DERECHO A HUELGAS, A CONTRATACION COLECTIVA. EL MERCADO DETERMINA LOS SALARIOS.		INSTITUIR ESTADO DESCENTRALIZADO Y EFICIENTE CON PAPEL LIMITADO Y SUBSIDIARIO. AUMENTAR LA COMPETENCIA Y AUTONOMIA DE LAS AUTORIDADES PROVINCIALES, MUNICIPALES Y COMUNALES.
PRECIOS Y SALARIOS	LIBERAR TOTALMENTE LOS PRECIOS Y SALARIOS DE EMPRESAS PRIVADAS Y LOS PRECIOS DE LAS PEQUEÑAS Y MEDIANAS EMPRESAS ESTATALES. AJUSTAR PRECIOS DE EMPRESAS ESTATALES GRANDES PARA REFLEJAR COSTOS Y ESCASECES INTERNACIONALES. LOS SALARIOS DE EMPRESAS ESTATALES PERMANECERÁN CONGELADOS Y SE AJUSTARÍAN POR AUMENTOS DE PRODUCTIVIDAD.		ELIMINAR CONTROLES DE PRECIOS, EXCEPTO A EMPRESAS ESTATALES GRANDES. AJUSTES SALARIALES DE LAS EMPRESAS ESTATALES ESTARÁN SUJETOS A AUMENTOS PRODUCTIVIDAD.		
FINANCIERAS	EFECTUAR REFORMA MONETARIA, EMITIR NUEVO PESO. DOTAR EMPRESAS ESTATALES DE CAPITAL DE TRABAJO PARA OPERAR. MANTENER ESTRICTO CONTROL MONETARIO-CREDITICIO. ESTABLECER TASAS DE INTERÉS REALES Y POSITIVAS PARA DEPÓSITOS BANCARIOS PRIVADOS Y DE EMPRESAS LIBERALIZADAS.	ESTABLECER BANCO CENTRAL AUTÓNOMO Y SUPERINTENDENCIA BANCARIA CON ESTRICTAS REGULACION Y SUPERVISIÓN DEL CRÉDITO BANCARIO. INICIAR DEPÓSITOS Y DEUDAS A MEDIANO Y LARGO PLAZO.	PRIVATIZAR LA BANCA COMERCIAL ESTATAL. LIBERALIZAR TASAS DE INTERÉS. FORMULAR MODERNA LEY DE INSTITUCIONES FINANCIERAS, PERMITIR TODO TIPO DE INSTITUCIONES, PERO SUJETAS A ESTRICTAS REGULACIONES Y SUPERVISIÓN.		
FISCALES	LOGRAR BALANCE FISCAL. REDUCIR GASTOS DE DEFENSA Y SEGURIDAD Y ELIMINAR SUBSIDIOS. ESTABLECER IMPUESTOS IVA, SOBRE INGRESOS NETOS DE LAS EMPRESAS Y PERSONALES, AL CONSUMO DE BIENES SUNTUARIOS Y NO NECESARIOS, Y SOBRE BIENES RAÍCES. IMPULSAR REFORMA INTEGRAL DEL ESTADO. EMPLEAR TECNICAS DE COSTO/BENEFICIO PARA SELECCIONAR INVERSION PUBLICA Y LICITACION PUBLICA O CONCURSO DE PRECIOS PARA ADQUISICIONES.	ESTABLECER MATRICULAS PARA LA EDUCACIÓN SUPERIOR.	ELIMINAR TODOS LOS SUBSIDIOS. PRIVATIZAR LA PREVISIÓN SOCIAL.	DESCENTRALIZAR Y PRIVATIZAR PARCIALMENTE LA EDUCACIÓN PRIMARIA Y SECUNDARIA Y LA SALUD PUBLICA. EL ESTADO SEGUIRIA FINANCIANDO LOS SERVICIOS, PERO EL SECTOR PRIVADO LOS BRINDARIA.	ESTABLECER LEY DE PRESUPUESTO BALANCEADO.
PRIVATIZACION Y RESTRUCTURACION PRODUCTIVA	INCENTIVAR SEGUNDO EMPLEO PARA EMPLEADOS PUBLICOS Y PARCELAS AGRÍCOLAS INDIVIDUALES. CREAR COMISIÓN RECTORA DE LA PRIVATIZACION. DESCENTRALIZAR DECISIONES A EMPRESAS ESTATALES PEQUEÑAS Y MEDIANAS. IMPONER SEVERAS MULTAS A TRABAJADORES Y ADMINISTRADORES DEPREDADORES. FIJAR CRITERIOS PARA QUIEBRAS DE EMPRESAS ESTATALES Y PARA SEGMENTAR COMPLEJOS MONOPOLICOS.	PRIVATIZAR POR VENTA AL CONTADO O A CRÉDITO, O POR LEASING LAS EMPRESAS ESTATALES PEQUEÑAS Y MEDIANAS Y LAS VIVIENDAS ARRENDADAS. SEGMENTAR Y COMENZAR A VENDER LAS ACCIONES DE LAS EMPRESAS ESTATALES GRANDES.	PRIVATIZAR LAS EMPRESAS DE ELECTRICIDAD, TELECOMUNICACIONES, LA CONSTRUCCIÓN Y MANTENIMIENTO DE CARRETERAS Y LAS OPERACIONES DE AEROPUERTOS Y PUERTOS, SISTEMAS DE ACUEDUCTOS Y ALCANTARILLADOS.		

PRINCIPALES MEDIDAS Y POLÍTICAS PROPUESTAS PARA LA RECONSTRUCCIÓN DE CUBA
(CONTINUACIÓN)

MEDIDAS, REFORMAS Y POLÍTICAS	SANEAMIENTO O ESTABILIZACIÓN (TRES AÑOS)		LIBERALIZACIÓN (TRES AÑOS)		
	ETAPA 1 (AJUSTE FISCAL Y DE PRECIOS)	ETAPA 2 (COMIENZO DE LA PRIVATIZACIÓN Y AJUSTE MONETARIO-CREDITICIO)	ETAPA 3 (PROFUNDIZACIÓN DE LA PRIVATIZACIÓN Y APERTURA FINANCIERA INTERNA)	ETAPA 4 (APERTURA COMERCIAL)	ETAPA 5 (APERTURA FINANCIERA EXTERNA)
SECTOR EXTERNO	NEGOCIAR ACCESO AL MERCADO DE EUA. DEVALUAR EL PESO, UNIFICAR LA TASA CAMBIARIA, ELIMINAR CONTROLES CUANTITATIVOS Y FIJAR CONTROL DE CAMBIOS. FIJAR UNA TARIFA UNIFORME DE 100% PARA LOS BIENES DE CONSUMO FINAL Y DEL 20% PARA LOS BIENES DE CAPITAL E INTERMEDIOS.	REDUCIR AL 70% LA TARIFA UNIFORME PARA LOS BIENES DE CONSUMO FINAL. ESTABLECER LEY ANTIDUMPING.	REDUCIR AL 40% LA TARIFA UNIFORME PARA LOS BIENES DE CONSUMO FINAL.	FIJAR TARIFA UNIFORME DEL 10% PARA TODAS LAS IMPORTACIONES. LIBRE CONVERTIBILIDAD PARA LA CUENTA CORRIENTE DE LA BALANZA DE PAGOS.	LIBRE CONVERTIBILIDAD PARA TODAS LAS TRANSACCIONES FINANCIERAS DE LA BALANZA DE PAGOS, SUJETO A LEY DE INVERSIÓN EXTRANJERA.
SECTORES PRIORITARIOS	LA AGRICULTURA, LA AGROINDUSTRIA, LA PESCA Y EL TURISMO.		MANUFACTURA DE ENSAMBLAJE Y SERVICIOS CONEXOS PARA EXPORTACIÓN.		
INVERSIÓN EXTRANJERA	SEVERA RESTRICCIÓN PARA LA INVERSIÓN EN EMPRESAS ESTATALES.	FORMULAR MODERNA LEY PARA LA INVERSIÓN PRIVADA EXTRANJERA.			
RETORNO DE CIUDADANOS	PERMITIR ENTRADA DE MENAJES DOMÉSTICOS, RECIBO DE PENSIONES Y DE CAPITALES LIBRES DE IMPUESTOS. EL LIBRE EJERCICIO PROFESIONAL Y DE OFICIOS.			ENTRADA DE MENAJES DOMÉSTICOS SUJETOS A TARIFAS EXISTENTES.	
TRANSFERENCIAS UNILATERALES	LIBRE ENTRADA DE LAS TRANSFERENCIAS MONETARIAS A LA TASA DE CAMBIO OFICIAL. LAS ORGANIZACIONES PRIVADAS DE DESARROLLO Y HUMANITARIAS DE INTERÉS SOCIAL Y SIN FINES DE LUCRO PODRAN ABRIR OPERACIONES EN EL PAIS.				
COOPERACIÓN TÉCNICA Y FINANCIERA INTERNACIONAL	SOLICITAR MEMBRESIA COMO ASOCIADO A LAS INSTITUCIONES FINANCIERAS INTERNACIONALES PARA TENER ACCESO A COOPERACIÓN TÉCNICA Y COMENZAR A PREPARAR PROPUESTAS DE PRESTAMOS. SOLICITAR ASISTENCIA TECNICA AL GOBIERNO DE CHILE EN LA IMPLANTACION DE LAS REFORMAS ECONOMICAS PROPUESTAS.	LOGRAR COMPLETA MEMBRESIA Y ACCESO A LA COOPERACIÓN ECONOMICA Y TECNICA DE LAS INSTITUCIONES FINANCIERAS INTERNACIONALES.			
DEUDA EXTERNA	DISEÑAR UNA ESTRATEGIA PARA RENEGOCIAR Y REDUCIR LA DEUDA EXTERNA QUE INCLUYA OPERACIONES DE RECONVERSIÓN.	COMENZAR EL SERVICIO DE LA DEUDA EXTERNA Y LAS OPERACIONES DE RECONVERSIÓN.			

i. Medidas institucionales y jurídicas

Se restablecerían, garantizarían y harían cumplir las instituciones y normas jurídicas de una economía de mercado, tales como: los derechos de propiedad, incluyendo titulación, patentes, transferencias y venta de bienes; libre contratación de bienes y servicios, incluyendo procedimientos simples para la contratación, movilidad y despido de la fuerza laboral; 26/ el libre ejercicio de las profesiones y los oficios, especialmente los vinculados con la prensa; leyes comerciales y de control de prácticas desleales de comercio; normas y procedimientos de contabilidad y ley de quiebra de las empresas. Se prohibirían los trabajos y movilizaciones "voluntarios" para el estado. Se permitiría plena libertad y democracia sindical, incluyendo el derecho de los trabajadores a afiliarse o desafiliarse a los sindicatos, 27/ pero no se permitirían huelgas hasta la tercera etapa, debido a la crítica situación de la producción.

Se establecería la libre entrada de empresas privadas a las actividades económicas, servicios públicos y sociales, incluso a algunos que antes del gobierno socialista se consideraban ámbito exclusivo del sector público o monopolios estatales. Se definirían trámites simples y expeditos para instalar o cerrar negocios a fin de facilitar la creatividad y la iniciativa, frenadas por más de tres décadas de incompetencia y controles burocráticos, a fin de introducir nuevos productos, mercados y modernizar las técnicas de administración, producción y distribución.

Sería necesario un programa de reentrenamiento para jueces, abogados, contadores, auditores, administradores y economistas en las instituciones básicas de una economía de mercado.

Estas medidas sentarían las bases para el estado de derechos económicos y el proceso de privatización y de modernización del país.

ii. Ajuste de precios y salarios

Los precios y salarios del sector privado y los precios de los bienes y servicios de las pequeñas y medianas empresas estatales se liberalizarían completamente. Los precios de los bienes y servicios de las empresas estatales grandes, incluyendo las tarifas de los servicios públicos (teléfono, luz y combustibles), se ajustarían para reflejar sus costos y escaseces relativas en la economía mundial más que en la distorsionada economía nacional, con una corrección para los servicios no transables en el exterior, debido al amplio desempleo abierto y disfrazado existente. De esta forma, los precios de los monopolios de bienes no transables en el exterior se mantendrían controlados hasta el desmantelamiento del monopolio o hasta la tercera etapa.

26/   Se permitirían contratos estacionales y temporales de trabajo.
27/   Por votación directa, secreta y universal.

Se determinaría la autonomía de las empresas estatales para tomar decisiones de producción y empleo y se alentaría la competencia para mejorar los productos y reducir los costos.

Los salarios del sector público permanecerían congelados. El propósito sería reajustar los salarios o ingresos reales teóricos de los empleados de las empresas estatales para hacerlos similares a los ingresos reales efectivos debido a la deteriorada situación de la producción. 28/ Otra alternativa sería hacer parte de las remuneraciones en dinero y parte en certificados que sirvan para comprar las empresas estatales que se privatizarían o acciones de las mismas. Se sentaría el principio que una vez hecho este ajuste inicial, los salarios reales de las empresas estatales se ajustarían teniendo en consideración los aumentos de la productividad o se complementarían por participación en las ganancias de las empresas.

iii. Reforma monetaria y política monetario-crediticia

Se determinaría la legitimidad de la liquidez existente mediante una reforma monetaria con la emisión de un nuevo peso y se dotaría a las empresas estatales del circulante necesario para realizar las transacciones (capital de trabajo) y
para reponer los repuestos y otros bienes esenciales. Esta reforma precedería la descentralización de las decisiones a las pequeñas y medianas empresas estatales y pretende evitar beneficios indebidos a la nomenclatura, la mafia y los narcotraficantes, que han hecho acumulaciones ilegítimas de medios de pagos.

Se fijarían tasas de interés reales positivas y altas. El crédito de la banca estatal se limitaría a las grandes empresas estatales controladas. Las empresas privadas y las pequeñas y medianas empresas estatales liberalizadas, que recibirían intereses por sus depósitos en la banca estatal, podrían concederse créditos entre sí o obtenerlos de los ciudadanos, lo cual equivale a bancos comerciales con 100% de reserva.

iv. Política fiscal

Se haría un tratamiento tipo choque para balancear las finanzas del sector público con base en una rigurosa política fiscal a fin de reducir el exceso de demanda agregada y que el sector público tenga fuentes de financiamiento propias (presupuesto balanceado), con lo cual se eliminaría la causa principal de los desbalances internos y una de las causas más importantes de los desbalances externos. Así las funciones que el estado seguiría financiando o brindando facilitarían los procesos de expansión de las empresas privadas y la privatización de las empresas públicas.

Se reducirían marcadamente los gastos de defensa y de seguridad interna, 29/ y en

---

28/   Es decir, este ajuste tendría como propósito que la práctica muestre la realidad tal cual es.
29/   Eliminándose de inmediato las milicias, los comités de barrios y las brigadas de respuesta rápida.

general se eliminarían los subsidios. Los gastos de mantenimiento y reparación de vivienda serían responsabilidad de los propietarios. Las funciones principales que el estado seguiría brindando o financiando serían los servicios de educación, salud, previsión social, justicia, defensa, seguridad pública y una red de solidaridad e inversión social. Esta red ofrecería empleo **temporal** a los desempleados y garantizar niveles mínimos de ingresos, nutrición, solución habitacional y salud a los más pobres de la sociedad, especialmente a los niños menores de tres años, madres embarazadas y lactantes. Se preferirá a los organismos no-gubernamentales u organismos privados voluntarios para canalizar estos servicios y bienes a los beneficiarios en vez de que el gobierno los brinde directamente.

A los que queden desempleados por despido de las instituciones o empresas estatales se les podría dar la opción de un empleo temporal o un pago mayor por terminación de una sola vez que se podría utilizar para comprar acciones o empresas o para instalar nuevas empresas. Cualquier pago por desempleo temporal exigiría la contribución del beneficiario a un programa lotes con servicios (basado en el esfuerzo propio y la ayuda mutua), de servicios de apoyo al sector agropecuario o de obras públicas, así como el reentrenamiento técnico del beneficiario para incorporarlo efectivamente a una economía de mercado.

Se comenzaría una reforma integral del estado a fin de reducir las funciones e instituciones públicas innecesarias. Los servicios del estado deberán seguir procedimientos simples y ágiles. Se utilizarían las técnicas de costo beneficio para determinar la prioridad de las inversiones públicas. Las adquisiciones del estado estarían sujetas a concurso de precios o licitación pública.

Se establecería un sistema impositivo simple y de fácil administración que genere ingresos suficientes, mediante un impuesto uniforme al valor agregado (IVA) a todas las empresas no controladas, un impuesto uniforme a los ingresos netos de las empresas y a los personales deducibles en la fuente, 30/ con las excepciones correspondientes, impuestos al consumo de bienes no necesarios y suntuarios 31/ y un impuesto a los bienes raíces. Se eximirían del impuesto a la renta las ganancias reinvertidas hasta por un período máximo de 4 años, o sea hasta completar la tercera etapa.

El gobierno encautaría y pondría a venta pública las edificaciones, terrenos, viviendas, equipos, vehículos y otros activos, asignados al partido comunista, las milicias, los comités de barrios y las brigadas de respuesta rápida.

30/   El impuesto a la renta no debería ser progresivo. Su propósito sería alentar la igualdad de oportunidades, no buscar la igualdad de resultados.

31/   Vehículos de lujo, bebidas alcohólicas, joyas, cigarrillos, etc.

v. Restructuración productiva y definición de las bases del proceso de la privatización

Se autorizaría e incentivaría que los empleados públicos o de empresas estatales tomen un segundo trabajo privado. Aquellos que ulteriormente decidan quedarse en ese segundo trabajo a tiempo completo, se le daría un pago por terminación de empleo en certificados, que podrá utilizarse para la compra de empresas y propiedades estatales. También se alentaría que los agricultores se dividieran de común acuerdo y en partes iguales las tierras que cultivan colectivamente pertenecientes a las empresas agrícolas estatales y que comenzaran a trabajar en forma individual las parcelas divididas. La asignación de las parcelas individuales sería por sorteo. Se reinstalarían el mercado de viviendas y de tierras agrícolas.

Las pequeñas y medianas empresas estatales podrían determinar libremente cómo fijar sus precios, utilizar sus recursos y sus ganancias (qué, cuánto, cómo y para quién producir, cómo comercializar, en qué invertir, sus niveles de empleo, etc.). Sólo las empresas con ganancias podrían hacer inversiones. Además, los administradores y trabajadores tendrían una participación en las ganancias que hicieran o recibirían aumentos de salarios por incrementos en la productividad. Los administradores de empresas estatales no estarían autorizados para vender activos principales de las empresas o hacer contratos de largo plazo. Se establecerían severas multas y penalidades para los administradores y trabajadores que se apropien de una parte del capital social de las empresas, mediante decisiones empresariales depredadoras, evidentes conflictos de interés u obteniendo aumentos salariales o beneficios sociales especiales subsidiados por las empresas.

Se definiría que la privatización estaría orientada a que el sector privado adquiera la posesión de las empresas, los activos y la administración de la mayoría de las empresas estatales y que los nuevos propietarios podrían ejercer todas sus prerrogativas. A fin de hacer su operación más eficiente, aún las empresas estatales que se decidan mantener y las que no se puedan vender, tendrían contratos de administración con empresas privadas que estén dispuestas a comprar parte de las acciones.

Se establecería una comisión rectora temporal, que oriente, regule y controle el proceso de privatización y que sería integrada por técnicos y profesionales reconocidos y apolíticos. La comisión designaría a los nuevos administradores de las empresas estatales, que serían personal técnico capacitado. Aclararía que el objetivo no es desarrollar un sistema de propiedad y producción socialista de mercado, ni un sistema de diversidad de formas de propiedad. Definiría criterios para las condiciones en que las empresas estatales quebrarían automáticamente por su situación financiera de deudas con el sistema bancario o por la no entrega de impuestos o sobrantes al gobierno.

Se determinarían criterios para sanear, racionalizar, restructurar y segmentar en empresas más pequeñas, los complejos industriales que habían sido organizados en forma artificial vertical y horizontalmente, a fin de propiciar una economía muy competitiva, ágil, de mayor empleo y menos capital, de acuerdo con el entorno internacional descrito en el Capítulo II. Las empresas estatales grandes estarían sujetas a auditores externos independientes. Se prohibirían carteles o acuerdos orientados a reducir la competencia entre las empresas que producen los mismos bienes o servicios.

La privatización propuesta permitiría a los trabajadores participar en la propiedad y gestión de las empresas. Sería sana financieramente en el sentido que las empresas privadas pagarían el IVA e impuestos sobre las ganancias no retenidas para inversión y que se daría total preferencia a la venta, "leasing" o contratos de administración de empresas sobre su transferencia gratuita. La privatización sería rápida y generalizada (no caso por caso).

vi. Política sobre el sector externo

Después de una drástica devaluación para corregir la marcada sobrevalorización del peso, se unificaría la tasa de cambio para todas las transacciones externas y se eliminarían todas las barreras cuantitativas y el monopolio estatal a las actividades de exportación e importación, pero se mantendrían controles de cambio hasta la cuarta fase. Las divisas disponibles se licitarían entre los importadores y otros interesados, permitiendo así una flotación administrada del peso y una política monetario-crediticia más flexible.

Habría una protección temporal alta (tarifas arancelarias del 100%) para importaciones de bienes de consumo, a fin de facilitar los reajustes en las técnicas, tecnologías y equipos de producción y en la utilización de insumos y del empleo por las empresas. Las materias primas y los bienes de capital tendrían tarifas arancelarias bajas del 20%, excepto para las utilizadas por las exportaciones que estarían exentas y se reintegrarían en el momento de la exportación. También se eliminaría el IVA a los bienes utilizados en la producción de las exportaciones. Debería definirse que las tarifas se reducirían automáticamente y en fechas definidas hasta llegar a una tarifa uniforme del 10% en la cuarta etapa. La protección temporal alta tiene por objeto reducir los costos de producción y de empleo del proceso de ajuste, especialmente en la etapa inicial de estabilización.

El gobierno de Cuba debería entrar en negociaciones inmediatas para lograr un amplio acceso sin barreras al mercado de bienes y servicios de EUA, ya que en caso de que el país no progrese, habría una fortísima presión de la población para emigrar a los EUA, lo cual podría realizarse sin mayores dificultades utilizando los vínculos familiares de los cubano-americanos. Se ha estimado que un millón de cubanos desean emigrar a los EUA (Bergner, 1992). A corto plazo, esa emigración sería una solución para el gobierno de Cuba, pero un problema para el gobierno de EUA.

Se harían colocaciones de valores denominados en dólares entre los cubanos residentes en el exterior para captación con propósitos de desarrollo.

vii. Sectores prioritarios

Se establecerían la producción agropecuaria y agroindustrial, la pesca y el turismo como actividades prioritarias para el crédito a las empresas estatales grandes y los gastos y servicios públicos por las ventajas comparativas del país y por el acervo de capital existente en estos sectores.

El gobierno emplearía sus recursos en difundir información sobre métodos y procesos de producción agropecuaria, semillas, cultivos, procesamiento de productos, mantenimiento de plantas y equipos, envases, precios internacionales, normas de calidad, mejoramiento de suelos y protección de cuencas, directrices de protección ambiental, gerencia, contabilidad de empresas, etc.

viii. Retorno de ciudadanos

A todos los nacidos o antiguos residentes en el país que deseen radicarse permanentemente en el mismo, se les permitiría la entrada de menajes domésticos incluyendo un automóvil, el recibo de pagos de jubilación del exterior y la entrada de capitales libres de impuestos, así como el libre ejercicio profesional y de oficios.

ix. Transferencias unilaterales

Se permitiría la entrada de transferencias unilaterales o remesas personales del exterior en efectivo libre de impuestos. El envío de bienes estaría sujeto a las tarifas arancelarias vigentes. Las organizaciones privadas, humanitarias y de desarrollo, de interés social y sin fines de lucro, aunque sean extranjeras, podrán abrir operaciones no sujetas a impuestos en Cuba.

x. Inversión privada extranjera

Se permitiría la inversión privada extranjera mediante nuevos equipos y plantas en todos los sectores productivos, pero habría severa restricción para la adquisición de las empresas estatales existentes hasta la segunda etapa.

xi. Cooperación financiera y técnica internacional

Cuba debería solicitar ser miembro asociado en los organismos financieros internacionales de desarrollo (BID, BIRF y FMI) con objeto de recibir cooperación técnica para preparar planes detallados de las reformas y propuestas de préstamos para etapas posteriores, mientras se determina su cuota de entrada en los mismos. Cuba solicitaría al Gobierno de Chile asistencia técnica para la implantación de las reformas propuestas al sistema económico.

xii. Deuda externa

Se diseñaría una estrategia para negociar y reducir la deuda externa que incluya operaciones de reconversión, dando preferencia a proyectos ecológicos, asistenciales y de desarrollo local dirigidos a poblaciones de bajos ingresos.

b. Otras etapas

i. Segunda etapa: el comienzo de la privatización y el ajuste monetario-crediticio

Se formularían modernas leyes de sociedades comerciales y de control de monopolios y oligopolios. Se establecería una bolsa de valores.

Las pequeñas y medianas empresas estatales, incluyendo el comercio al detalle y al por mayor, las empresas y tierras estatales agrícolas, los servicios y la flota de transporte serían privatizados, mediante venta en oferta pública a los trabajadores y administradores o al mejor postor, o mediante devolución a los antiguos propietarios. También se venderían las viviendas a los arrendatarios. Las ventas a los trabajadores, administradores y a otros individuos o familias, podrían realizarse a crédito, pero sujeto a colateral, garantías o hipotecas de los propios bienes vendidos y serían realizados a través de los gobiernos provinciales y municipales. Igualmente habría la opción de alquileres a largo plazo ("leasings") o contratos de administración.

Una vez completado el esfuerzo de segmentar, racionalizar y sanear los complejos artificialmente grandes, se harían sociedades accionarias de las grandes empresas estatales y se venderían hasta el 50% de las acciones a empresas, individuos o suplidores, nacionales o extranjeros, quienes tomarían a su cargo la administración de las empresas. El resto de las acciones de las grandes empresas se distribuirían entre aquellas instituciones afectadas en forma directa por las mismas (fondos de pensión de las empresas, gobiernos provinciales y municipales) y se les vendería a los trabajadores hasta un 20% de las acciones a un descuento del 50%. Una forma legítima de privatización podría ser la de suplidores internacionales que estuvieran dispuestos a comprar a crédito y administrar una empresa, ofrezcan como garantía y aporte su propia inversión y pagaran ulteriormente con sus propias ganancias.

Se restablecería la autonomía del banco central con normas estrictas para el control monetario. Se establecería una fuerte superintendencia bancaria y de instituciones financieras con normas estrictas para la regulación y supervisión del crédito bancario, incluyendo normas sobre colaterales, garantías e hipotecas. En general, no se podría prestar a empresas que estén incurriendo en pérdidas; las empresas estatales en esta situación se liquidarían. Se liberalizarían los mercados financieros, se introducirían nuevos instrumentos de depósito y crédito a mediano y largo plazo para captar el exceso de liquidez existente.

Para modernizar y descentralizar la educación superior y continuar con la reforma fiscal, se establecerían matrículas para financiar los costos de la educación. El estado otorgaría préstamos a los estudiantes de familias de escasos recursos. Se alentaría que las universidades y otros centros de educación superior prestaran servicios de capacitación e investigación al sector privado.

Para proseguir con la apertura comercial, se reducirían sin excepciones las tarifas arancelarias a los bienes de consumo final al 70%. Se establecería una moderna ley "antidumping".

Se dictaría una ley de inversión privada extranjera mediante la cual se permita la inversión en todos los sectores de la economía, salvo aquellos que se considere que no convienen al interés o la seguridad del país, y se le daría a las empresas extranjeras el mismo trato que a las nacionales. Esto podría considerarse una extensión de la Doctrina Calvo que establece la igualdad ante la Ley de los nacionales y los extranjeros radicados en el país, siendo contrario a lo que ha hecho el gobierno socialista que les ha dado exención de impuestos. No se contemplarían incentivos, ni subsidios especiales, ni concesiones monopólicas, pero se permitirían operaciones de reconversión de deuda en capital de inversión, fijándose un monto mínimo por transacción. Se renegociarían los términos y condiciones de la deuda externa y se hará un esfuerzo para comenzar su servicio.

Cuba solicitaría ser miembro regular en los organismos financieros internacionales de desarrollo (BID, BIRF y FMI) con objeto de recibir cooperación financiera. Como Cuba no tiene ninguna deuda pendiente con los organismos internacionales, podría obtener significativos flujos positivos con propósitos de desarrollo.

ii. Tercera etapa: la profundización de la privatización y la apertura financiera interna

Se eliminarían todos los subsidios y casi todos los controles de precios (excepto los de las grandes empresas estatales no liberalizadas), mientras se autorizarían ajustes de salarios en las empresas estatales relacionados con los aumentos de productividad.

Se aprobaría una moderna legislación laboral que establezca el derecho a huelga, la negociación colectiva y que el mercado determina los salarios.

Se determinaría que la manufactura de ensamblaje para la exportación y sus servicios de apoyo son sectores prioritarios para el gasto y la inversión pública.

Se permitirían todo tipo de instituciones financieras sujetas a estrictas regulaciones y supervisión. Se liberalizarían las tasas de interés activas y pasivas. Se privatizarían, al menos parcialmente, mediante venta pública abierta, incluyendo a empresas extranjeras, 32/ la banca comercial, las empresas de electricidad, de teléfonos y otras telecomunicaciones, la contratación de la construcción y mantenimiento de carreteras mediante derechos de peaje, la operación de puertos y aeropuertos, los sistemas de acueductos y alcantarillados, así como el sistema de previsión social.

Para proseguir con la apertura comercial, se reducirían sin excepciones las tarifas arancelarias a los bienes de consumo final al 40%.

iii. Cuarta etapa: la apertura comercial

Se abriría el sector real al rigor y las oportunidades del mercado internacional, mediante la fijación de una baja tarifa arancelaria uniforme del 10% para todas las importaciones. Se establecería y mantendría la libre determinación y plena convertibilidad del peso para todas las transacciones de la cuenta corriente de la balanza de pagos a la tasa de cambio. Con ello se generaría competencia y mejoraría la asignación de recursos, aún para las empresas estatales que quedaran.

Se descentralizarían y privatizarían parcialmente la educación primaria y secundaria, así como la salud pública. El estado seguiría financiando estos servicios, pero el sector privado los brindaría.

Se permitiría la entrada de menajes domésticos, incluyendo un automóvil, sujetos a las tarifas arancelarias vigentes, a todos los nacidos o antiguos residentes en el país que deseen radicarse en el mismo.

iv. Quinta etapa: la apertura financiera externa

Se permitirían todas las transacciones externas, incluso las de la cuenta de capital de la balanza de pagos, mediante la libre convertibilidad de la moneda nacional conforme a lo dispuesto por la ley de inversión extranjera.

Se establecería una ley sobre presupuesto balanceado. Las funciones del estado deberían ser descentralizadas y eficientes, con un papel limitado y subsidiario, y con un compromiso cada vez mayor con las bases de la sociedad. Debería aumentarse la autonomía y competencia de las autoridades provinciales y municipales, así como de las comunidades rurales y urbanas.

D. Otras Propuestas Anteriores

En su cimental trabajo sobre el tema de este ensayo, Felipe Pazos (1990) aboga por un gradualismo para contener y dominar el exceso de demanda agregada (déficits fiscal y

---

32/   Dependiendo de la naturaleza de la empresa, podría ser por licitación o por negociación directa.

de balanza de pagos) y para propiciar la liberalización en línea con lo propugnado por McKinnon. Antonio Jorge (1990 y 1991) presenta una serie de argumentos muy sólidos por medidas graduales para que puedan ser asimiladas apropiadamente 33/ y en contra de las medidas simultáneas, la gran explosión o el "big bang". Antonio Jorge si bien menciona algunas posibles medidas, no entra a discutir un plan en detalle. Jorge Sanguinetty (1991) también apoya el gradualismo y pone mucho énfasis en desarrollar las instituciones y normas jurídicas que faciliten el establecimiento de una economía de mercado sin entrar en detalles específicos.

Pazos aboga por estimular la inversión extranjera; no obstante, debido a la magnitud de las presiones inflacionarias en la etapa de ajuste inicial, muestra una gran preocupación respecto a que la propiedad estatal se venda por debajo de su valor a extranjeros. En cambio recomienda que la propiedad de las unidades productivas estatales se distribuya en un 70% a los trabajadores de cada unidad, a fin de restablecer el espíritu y la moral de trabajo, compensando a los propietarios confiscados con bonos de valor garantizado contra la inflación. Pazos considera que Cuba tendría que continuar vendiendo azúcar al mercado mundial, principalmente a la antigua Unión Soviética, debido a los compromisos existentes en el mercado americano.

Ernesto Hernández-Catá (1991) presenta un caso para una política de tratamiento de choque, simultánea e inmediata para reducir el exceso de demanda agregada, justificándola en que muchos de estos aspectos deberán ser realizados de esa manera en un enfoque a largo plazo. Un argumento central de Hernández-Cata es evitar tasas inflacionarias altas que conllevan menor crecimiento económico, debido a la inestabilidad y las incertidumbres, que desalientan el turismo y la inversión y que estimulan la fuga de capitales financieros y humanos. Sin embargo, Hernández-Catá reconoce la conveniencia del enfoque escalonado o por etapas para establecer la paridad del peso con el dólar como régimen cambiario. Además, como señala Raúl Asón (1991), Hernández-Catá a veces ignora las complicaciones y los efectos negativos de los cursos de acción que propone, no siempre entra en los detalles que sus recomendaciones requieren y rechaza importantes cursos de acción que podrían impedir serios errores de política económica.

33/ Evitar la inestabilidad social, evitar detener el proceso de descolectivización, no todas las medidas se pueden realizar al mismo tiempo, etc.

ANEXO I

Consideraciones Sobre las Estrategias de Transición
de una Economía Socialista a una Economía de Mercado

A. Dos Enfoques sobre los Procesos de Estabilización y Liberalización

El desplome y fracaso del socialismo, no asegura la adecuada implantación de una economía de mercado. En su libro <u>The Order of Economic Liberalization</u>, Ronald McKinnon (1991) plantea que pasar en forma exitosa de una economía socialista o de una economía muy reprimida y distorsionada a una de mercado es tan difícil como atravesar un campo minado. Igualmente, que la estabilización y la liberalización se deberán hacer en forma gradual y siguiendo una secuencia y velocidad óptimas. La gradualidad puede evitar inconsistencias y errores de política económica, cuyos resultados son fracasos o retrocesos innecesarios, e impedir fuertes resistencias a los cambios requeridos, evitando quedarse en una economía con fuertes desequilibrios y un importante segmento de propiedad estatal. La población no debe asociar las reformas con recesión, desempleo y empobrecimiento. El propósito es ir incrementando la oferta agregada con las medidas tomadas.

Otros economistas recomiendan otras secuencias en los procesos de estabilización y liberalización o la acción simultánea (fuerte, completa e inmediata) en todas las áreas o la gran explosión, ver la experiencia polaca en el Anexo III y la posición de Hernández-Catá (ver Capítulo IV, Sección D). Jeffrey Sachs de la Universidad de Harvard, uno de los propulsores del enfoque gran explosión, considera que hay que romper de una sola vez los grandes intereses que se oponen a las reformas, asegurar consistencia y eliminar incertidumbres, aunque los grandes beneficios de la misma no se comenzarán a obtener hasta después de cinco años de reformas continuadas. También el tratamiento gran explosión y simultáneo conlleva mayor desempleo que se suele contrarrestar mediante transferencias a los desempleados y ayuda externa. Esto conlleva mayor carga social para las empresas que la financian a través de impuestos y mayores tasas de interés.

Es irónico que los que recomiendan la gran explosión en las medidas macroeconómicas, recomiendan proceder con la privatización más lentamente. Así, Kornai, defensor de la gran explosión en las medidas macroeconómicas, aconseja efectuar la privatización más lentamente. El Plan Polaco de 1990 hizo la estabilización y la apertura simultáneas, pero ha sido muy lento en cuanto a la privatización, ver Anexo III. Como señala Chris Allsop (1991) se debería tener la misma seriedad a nivel microeconómico e institucional que macroeconómico.

Cuando las presiones inflacionarias son elevadas, casi hay consenso en la literatura económica que se debe proceder primero con la estabilización y después con el proceso de liberalización. Además, casi hay consenso sobre que se debe realizar la apertura comercial antes que la apertura financiera externa, Edwards (1984, 1990). Como ha indicado el propio Sachs (1987), la adopción de profundas reformas de liberalización antes de tiempo pueden erosionar las acciones de política económica y disminuir la credibilidad de las autoridades, lo que es crucial en las etapas iniciales.

Calvo y Frenkel (1991) juzgan que el proceso de transformación es largo y complejo, y que las medidas a adoptar deben despertar la credibilidad en el gobierno y ser lo más simples y transparentes posibles, ya que con la apertura económica, los ordenamientos y las instituciones de los sistemas socialistas suelen tener un colapso abrupto y total, sin ser sustituidas por otros. Por lo tanto, las expectativas de los consumidores e inversionistas sobre las nuevas orientaciones, políticas y medidas, y en especial sobre las de precios, financiera, fiscal y del sector externo, pueden agudizar los desbalances existentes.

Al respecto, el proceso de reforma en los antiguos países socialistas europeos, presenta constantes conflictos entre grupos de presión que quieren, por un lado, deshacerse, a la brevedad posible, de las ineficiencias y la centralización de los sistemas de propiedad, producción y distribución socialistas y, por otro lado, que ven reducidos sus niveles de empleo e ingresos por los ajustes requeridos, así como por los errores y retrocesos en la implantación de la estabilización y liberalización. Estos últimos grupos de presión se ven reforzados o apoyados por los antiguos burócratas del partido comunista y de las estructuras no productivas, las organizaciones de masa, que destacan el enriquecimiento de la nueva burguesía y defienden la igualdad social sobre la eficiencia económica.

B. La Estrategia Gradual

McKinnon sugiere cinco fases para asegurar que las reformas necesarias tengan resultados sostenibles y satisfactorios, las cuales podrían requerir hasta una década, pero no indica cuanto duraría cada fase. También, Fischer y Gelb (1990) estiman que el proceso de transformación con las medidas requeridas, que no pueden adoptarse simultáneamente, tomaría cerca de una década.

Las fases de McKinnon se basan en su análisis de las experiencias relevantes en los últimos 20 años y considerando que antes de comenzar la liberalización hay que lograr la estabilización y que los sectores reales reaccionan más lentamente que los sectores financieros, tanto en los mercados internos como en los externos.

En el enfoque de McKinnon es imprescindible que cada fase se complete antes de comenzar la siguiente. Por ejemplo, es necesario balancear las finanzas públicas antes de emprender un esfuerzo de apertura financiera interna, de lo contrario dicho esfuerzo se vería distorsionado por las presiones inflacionarias creadas por el déficit del sector público y habría una demanda monetario-crediticia sobredimensionada que impediría el adecuado acceso del sector privado al crédito. La desreglamentación de la producción no respondería correctamente a las señales de precios en un ambiente de fuertes presiones inflacionarias que no concluiría hasta completar la racionalización financiera. La apertura comercial externa no deberá comenzar hasta que se hayan realizado ciertos ajustes fundamentales en la producción interna, ya que la producción nacional es de baja calidad y requiere más insumos; de lo contrario, se estaría sujeto a quiebras y desempleo innecesarios. Por último, la apertura financiera externa antes de tiempo podría atraer una entrada de capitales que paralice la apertura comercial, al perjudicar a los exportadores.

Lo anterior no significa que no se puedan iniciar reformas y adoptar varias medidas a la vez en las áreas fiscales, monetario-crediticias, productivas, comerciales y externo-financieras. No obstante, lograr en forma efectiva y simultánea la completa estabilización y la apertura en todas las áreas no es factible.

Un argumento que McKinnon no utiliza a fondo, es que las empresas estatales de tipo monopólico u ologopólico no reaccionan en la misma forma que las empresas privadas y que hay que ir privatizando las empresas y desmonopolizando para lograr los objetivos de la transición. De lo contrario los presupuestos suaves serían sustituidos por precios suaves. Es muy difícil tener una economía de mercado sin una verdadera competencia.

1. **La estabilización** (o la eliminación de las presiones inflacionarias)

Primera fase, asegurar un balance en las finanzas públicas con base en una rigurosa **política fiscal y de ajuste de precios**. El objetivo es reducir el déficit de las empresas estatales, el exceso de la demanda agregada y asegurar que el sector público tenga fuentes propias de financiamiento diferentes de los excedentes de las empresas estatales, las cuales estarán en proceso de privatización. Así el sector público podrá proveer en forma no inflacionaria los servicios esenciales 34/ que no impidan a través de emisiones monetarias y, por el contrario, faciliten los procesos de expansión de las empresas privadas y de privatización de las empresas estatales en los sectores productivos y en los servicios públicos.

Se requiere la reducción de los gastos de defensa y seguridad interna, la eliminación de los subsidios de los servicios básicos (agua, teléfono, luz y combustibles) y el establecimiento de un sistema impositivo de amplia base, pero de niveles bajos, que genere ingresos suficientes y no cree distorsiones económicas. Un impuesto al valor agregado (IVA) del orden de un 20% a todas las empresas no controladas, un impuesto a la renta o a los ingresos personales, hechas ciertas deducciones básicas, del orden del 25% al 35% e impuestos al consumo de bienes suntuarios y no necesarios, podrían generar los ingresos públicos requeridos.

Se deberán ajustar los precios de los bienes y factores para que estén más acordes con sus escaseces relativas y para reducir distorsiones, así como para descentralizar en forma eficaz las decisiones a las empresas estatales pequeñas y medianas. 35/ Sin embargo, aún no se liberan los precios de las grandes empresas estatales; se pueden ajustar, pero bajo

---

34/   Educación, salud, previsión social, justicia, defensa y seguridad.
35/   Kornai (1990) cuestiona este punto.

control. El ajuste de los precios disminuye el exceso de dinero real y no debe ir acompañado de una indexación de los salarios para evitar la creación de presiones inflacionarias, en especial si se está controlando la inflación.

McKinnon no discute que la liberalización de los controles de precios no hace mucho sentido en economías muy monopolizadas, como son las economías socialistas. Esta liberalización es contraria a la tradición en las economías de mercado de regular y controlar los monopolios. Dejar fijar sus precios libremente a los monopolios y oligopolios artificiales de las economías socialistas, significará, sin lugar a dudas, niveles menores de producción y mayores precios. No sólo por los ajustes que pudiera haber en los precios para reflejar costos de producción más realistas, sino por la conducta racional de un monopolista o un oligopolista de maximizar sus ganancias.

Medidas de Política Económica en las Fases de Estabilización
(Primera y Segunda Fases) Con Respecto a los Distintos Tipos de Empresas

Medidas respecto a:	Empresas Estatales Controladas a/	Empresas Estatales Liberalizadas b/	Empresas Privadas c/
Impuestos	Todas las ganancias al gobierno	IVA uniforme	IVA uniforme
Precios	Fijados por el gobierno, pero hay flexibilidad para hacer ajustes	Determinados por el mercado	Determinados por el mercado
Salarios	Techos fijados por el gobierno	Techos fijados por el gobierno	Determinados por el mercado
Ganancias residuales	Todas las ganancias al gobierno	Dividendos van al gobierno. Reinversión de ganancias retenidas	Dividendos a los propietarios. Ganancias retenidas para reinversión o para préstamos a otras empresas
Elegibilidad para créditos	Bancos comerciales	Extrabancario	Extrabancario
Depósitos bancarios	Sin intereses	Con intereses	Con intereses

a/   Empresas grandes monopólicas, servicios públicos y sectores de gran concentración industrial, cuyas decisiones básicas son determinadas por el gobierno.

b/   Empresas pequeñas y medianas que pueden fijar los niveles y composición de la producción, empleo (incluyendo contrataciones y despidos), insumos y selección de tecnología, precios, excepto salarios que tienen techos.

c/   Agricultores, artesanos y pequeñas tiendas.

Habrá un estricto control monetario y todavía habrá un grado de protección alto mediante tarifas arancelarias, ya que el valor agregado de muchas empresas suele ser negativo como consecuencia de la obsolescencia tecnológica y cualitativa, así como de la excesiva acumulación de inventarios en el sistema de producción socialista, que estimulaba su uso ineficiente. No obstante, se devalúa para establecer una tasa de cambio única realista para todas las transacciones externas que ahora las empresas podrán realizar en forma directa.

En esta fase se deberán establecer y hacer cumplir los derechos de propiedad e iniciativa privadas, libre contratación y se deberá fomentar la capacidad creativa y empresarial de la población, dejándola desarrollar libremente actividades frenadas por tantos años de controles y prohibiciones. Esto de por sí constituye una medida de gran trascendencia e importancia con base en la experiencia de los países de Europa Oriental. Según Kornai (1990, p 36), en Hungría, el florecimiento espontáneo de las actividades productivas fue increíble cuando se eliminaron los controles y restricciones.

Segunda fase, lograr la racionalización de los mercados financieros con la fijación de tasas de interés reales elevadas, en forma simultánea con estrictas disciplina monetaria y regulación y supervisión del crédito bancario (**política financiera**). Esto evitará las empresas estatales con restricciones presupuestarias suaves, posibilitará una más eficiente asignación y utilización de los recursos, y aumentará la proporción y la productividad de la inversión. La regulación del crédito bancario podría requerir que los bancos exigieran garantías o colaterales para sus préstamos en forma de inventarios, cuentas a cobrar, etc.

Existe un debate sobre si después del ajuste de precios, los individuos o familias tendrían todavía, o no, un exceso de liquidez suficiente para comprar acciones de las empresas estatales que facilite la privatización. Obviamente, debe haber una situación intermedia, en la que al menos parte de la población tenga un legítimo exceso de liquidez, y a la cual podría venderse parte de las acciones para esterilizar el exceso de liquidez existente.

McKinnon (1991, cap 11), uno de los pioneros de la literatura sobre la liberalización de los mercados financieros, considera que si las medidas de las dos primeras fases no se realizan en forma adecuada, es decir, las presiones inflacionarias no se detienen suficientemente, la liberalización podría conllevar mayores ineficiencias que antes y el proceso de privatización podría verse paralizado por razón del exceso de demanda. Las presiones así generadas impedirían a las empresas privadas y a las empresas estatales eficientes competir por los recursos escasos disponibles.

2. La liberalización

Tercera fase, la eliminación de todos los subsidios y de casi todos los controles de precios (excepto los de las empresas estatales no liberalizadas), mientras se mantiene la fijación de techos a los ajustes de salarios en el sector público (**política de**

desreglamentación de la producción). También se profundiza la liberalización financiera con la descentralización bancaria, con la autorización de bancos comerciales privados y con la introducción de instrumentos de ahorro y deuda a mediano y largo plazo. Sin embargo, no debería descentralizarse los préstamos a las empresas estatales controladas a la banca comercial privada.

Cuarta fase, la apertura del sector externo real mediante la eliminación de todas las barreras cuantitativas, el establecimiento de una baja tarifa uniforme, la libre determinación y plena convertibilidad de la moneda nacional para todas las transacciones de la cuenta corriente de la balanza de pagos a la tasa de cambio única **(política comercial).** Esta apertura generará competencia y mejorará la asignación de recursos, aún para las empresas estatales controladas. Se deberá continuar con el proceso de liberalización financiera para eliminar reservas legales muy altas para la banca comercial nacional.

Quinta fase, la apertura del sector externo para todas las transacciones, incluso la cuenta de capital de la balanza de pagos, mediante la libre convertibilidad de la moneda nacional **(política cambiaria).**

Según McKinnon, la ayuda externa en las primeras fases de las reformas aumenta el consumo de los bienes externos, distorsiona la inversión hacia los bienes para los cuales no hay competencia externa y podría demorar las reformas necesarias. En Polonia la ayuda de alimentos fue un elemento muy negativo para la producción agrícola nacional, ya que deprimió los precios y desalentó la producción.

La propuesta de McKinnon parece muy estricta en lo referente a los aspectos monetario-crediticios en la segunda fase, pues se hizo teniendo en consideración la antigua URSS, cuyos repúblicas tienen un marcado exceso de liquidez y la exitosa experiencia de China a partir de 1979. No obstante, parece insuficiente y lenta en lo relativo a la privatización de los medios de producción. McKinnon no trata en detalle el tema de la privatización, por eso a continuación se incluye una sección sobre el mismo.

C. El Proceso de Privatización

La privatización es el proceso de transferir la propiedad y la administración de los activos netos, o parte de ellos, de las empresas estatales al sector privado 36/ y que los nuevos propietarios puedan ejercer todas las prerrogativas del derecho de propiedad. Igualmente, la privatización en un concepto más amplio, incluye la desreglamentación para la libre entrada y salida del sector privado a actividades que eran ámbito exclusivo del sector público porque se consideraban necesarias o estratégicas, y las condiciones institucionales y jurídicas para el desarrollo de la actividad privada.

36/ Se entiende por sector privado a los individuos o sociedades de individuos, nacionales o extranjeros.

El objetivo de la privatización es poner la riqueza y el poder en los individuos y las empresas privadas y quitárselos al estado y a la burocracia. La privatización democratiza el poder económico al distribuir la riqueza concentrada en la nomenclatura; sin embargo, ese componente podría perderse si posteriormente el estado permite la concentración de la riqueza. La privatización permite crear las condiciones apropiadas para el fortalecimiento y desarrollo económico y político mediante la asignación y la producción eficiente de los bienes y servicios, utilizando el interés, la motivación, la administración, la organización y la iniciativa individuales. Otro objetivo importante de la misma es mejorar la situación financiera del estado, ya que éste generalmente incurre en pérdidas netas administrando empresas y tendrá una fuente de ingresos que le permita financiar el proceso de transformación.

Hay varios factores que dificultan la privatización en los antiguos países socialistas: la indefinición existente entre la posesión y la propiedad en el régimen socialista, las reclamaciones de los antiguos propietarios y de los actuales obreros sobre la propiedad existente, las distorsiones de precios existentes, la estructura monopólica u oligopólica de los medios de producción, la falta de una cultura empresarial, la carencia de mercados financieros y de bienes propiamente establecidos, la resistencia de la burocracia y el oportunismo de los administradores para continuar como clase dirigente. No obstante, es imprescindible iniciar el proceso, ya que la cultura empresarial se nutre de su propia experiencia y los mercados financieros y de bienes de numerosos accionistas y productores.

Para propósitos de privatización se distinguen tres tipos de empresas en un régimen socialista: las empresas privadas, incluyendo trabajadores por cuenta propia o empresas asociativas, como verdaderas cooperativas 37/ (agricultores, artesanos, comerciantes, pequeños productores industriales y de servicios); las pequeñas y las medianas empresas estatales; y las grandes empresas estatales (empresas grandes monopólicas, servicios públicos y sectores de gran concentración industrial).

Las empresas privadas necesitan decidir libremente de cómo utilizar sus recursos (qué producir, en qué invertir, cómo comercializar, etc.), cómo utilizar sus ganancias y cómo disponer de su futuro. Las pequeñas y medianas empresas estatales deben ser privatizadas a la brevedad posible, mediante venta a sus trabajadores, administradores o al mejor postor, nacional o extranjero, o devueltas a sus antiguos propietarios, ya que en la etapa de transición y ajuste existen conflictos de interés de gente trabajando en las empresas públicas y en el sector privado a la vez (Kornai, 1990, p 94-95). Asimismo, hay que expandir en forma rápida el ámbito de la actividad privada.

Las grandes empresas estatales presentan problemas especiales de cómo establecer un régimen de propiedad privada funcional, y cómo vender o distribuir la propiedad y

---

37/   Aquellas con libre entrada y salida de los socios, los miembros pueden elegir libremente sus ejecutivos y los socios que se retiran pueden retirar libremente su capital. El resto de las cooperativas se consideran pequeñas, medianas y grandes empresas estatales.

administrarla adecuadamente. Algunos autores señalan la necesidad de desagregar los complejos industriales de tipo monopólico u oligopólico creados artificialmente para hacer una economía más competitiva y que facilite la expansión de empresas más pequeñas, ágiles y dinámicas de acuerdo con una economía de mercado competitiva y con el entorno mundial.

Los esquemas propuestos usualmente para la privatización de las grandes empresas son: distribuir la propiedad de la empresa entre los trabajadores y administradores; distribuir "vouchers" o certificados a la población en general para la adquisición de las acciones de las empresas; distribuir las acciones de las empresas entre intermediarios financieros, cuyas acciones podrían ser compradas con los certificados de la población; distribuir las acciones de las empresas a los afectados en forma directa por las mismas (trabajadores, administradores, bancos comerciales, gobiernos locales, etc); los intermediarios financieros estarían a cargo de realizar directamente la privatización; y los intermediarios financieros recibirían las acciones directamente. Sin embargo, todos los esquemas presentan inconvenientes operativos para administrar las empresas y complicaciones financieras de que el estado deje de percibir ingresos por la disposición de la propiedad.

La privatización debe ser sana fiscalmente y equitativa en el sentido de vender las propiedades, al menos al crédito o con préstamos del propio estado, y beneficiar a todos los ciudadanos por igual, porque se está distribuyendo lo que pertenecía a todos los ciudadanos. Debe ser rápida y generalizada, no caso por caso a la húngara, pues de lo contrario hay un gran incentivo para que los administradores y trabajadores se apropien de una parte del capital social, mediante decisiones depredadoras, tal como vendiendo activos por debajo del precio, o obteniendo aumentos salariales o beneficios sociales especiales subsidiados por la empresa. Tiene que haber un marco jurídico que impida que las privatizaciones se puedan cuestionar legalmente.

Debe establecerse una agencia rectora temporal, cuya existencia se limitará al período de transformación, que oriente, regule y controle el proceso. Debe evitarse la transferencia y control de la propiedad a unos pocos intermediarios que actuen en la práctica como una especie de ministerios de producción.

En la medida que se privatice en un entorno de políticas fiscales y monetarias restrictivas, se favorece la inversión extranjera o de aquellas firmas nacionales que tienen acceso a ella.

En los países de Europa Oriental se le ha dado la opción a las personas que fueron confiscadas para que presenten sus reclamos en un plazo de tiempo razonable. Asimismo, se nota que hay una gran oposición a la inversión privada extranjera en esos países, ya que sufrieron la dominación extranjera desde comienzos de la Segunda Guerra Mundial de los alemanes y posteriormente de los rusos.

Los países de Europa Oriental han adoptado legislaciones que indican intenciones de privatización, más que planes y medidas concretos, como lo muestran entre otras las experiencias de la antigua URSS, Polonia, Hungría y Checoslovaquia. Además el concepto de privatización es mucho más limitado de lo que se ha hecho en Chile que es, como norma general, sacar al estado de la producción de bienes y servicios, incluyendo también los servicios públicos y los sociales.

ANEXO II

La Transformación Chilena 1973-1991

Durante la década de los ochenta, la mayoría de las experiencias de apertura económica fueron negativas o muy lentas, tanto en economías socialistas (por ejemplo, las de Europa Oriental, la URSS, China y Vietnam), como en economías con amplia intervención del estado, endémicamente reprimidas y muy distorsionadas (por ejemplo, las de varios países de América Latina y el Caribe). Así, la liberalización y la muy limitada privatización realizadas por la URSS en el período 1985-1991, conocidas como "perestroika", tuvieron resultados negativos y retrocesos frecuentes, lo cual explica la baja popularidad de Gorbachov en ese país, a pesar de haber sido el iniciador y promotor de las extraordinarias reformas logradas.

Chile: Indicadores Socioeconómicos, 1970-1990

	1970	1973	1981	1990
Índice de Remuneraciones Real (1982=100)	81.7	58.3	108.4	103.1
Tasa de Desempleo, incluyendo programas especiales de empleo (%)	3.5	4.8	16.0	6.0
Expectativa de Vida (%)	63.6	65.7	71.1	71.8
Tasa de Mortalidad Infantil (.1%)	82.2	65.8	27.0	18.9
Tasa de Nacimiento (%)	26.4	26.9	22.2	23.3
Tasa de Mortalidad (%)	8.7	8.1	6.6	5.8
Tasa de Alfabetismo (%)	89.0	89.6	91.0	94.3

En cambio, Chile logró una exitosa transformación de una economía con una tradicional y gran intervención del estado en la gestión económica (controles, prohibiciones y regulaciones), con una amplia socialización de los medios de producción en 1971-1973, hiperinflación, recesión y marcados desbalances internos y externos en 1973 a una economía de mercado orientada al exterior, muy sólida, dinámica y moderna. Además, con una abundante captación de inversión extranjera, importantes servicios públicos y sociales racionalizados, descentralizados y parcialmente privatizados, y con una participación limitada del estado. Las exportaciones como proporción del PIB han aumentado del 15% a principios de la década de 70 a más del 30% a principios de la década de 90.

En el período 1973-1990, Chile mostró mejorías en varios indicadores socioeconómicos, tales como: mortalidad infantil, mortalidad, alfabetismo y expectativa de vida. No obstante, todavía un porcentaje significativo de la población vive en la pobreza, los servicios sociales no se brindan adecuadamente a la población más pobre y hay serios problemas de contaminación del medio ambiente. Sin embargo, el futuro de Chile luce muy promisorio para un crecimiento económico sostenido con estabilidad y con equidad social.

A. La Estabilización y Liberalización

1. **1973-1980: la etapa de la estabilización, la privatización de las empresas confiscadas, la ley de inversión privada extranjera y las reformas laborales**

El gobierno militar (1973-1990) comenzó con dos objetivos básicos en 1973: desarrollar una economía de mercado y estabilizarla. Poco después se añadió la orientación de la economía al exterior. El déficit fiscal del 24.7% del PIB en 1973 se transformó en un superávit del 3.1% del PIB en 1980, a través de la disminución del gasto público del 44.9% del PIB en 1973 al 23.1% del PIB en 1980 y de una reforma tributaria con aumento de las recaudaciones. El gasto en los sectores sociales se redujo, pero se focalizó en los más pobres. Se racionalizó la inversión pública mediante la aplicación de las técnicas de costo/beneficio para priorizarlas y seleccionarlas.

Se independizó el banco central y se eliminaron los controles de crédito sectoriales. La tasa de inflación disminuyó del 508% en 1973 al 31.3% en 1980. Se eliminaron los controles de precios. Se establecieron elevadas tasas de interés real, tanto para depósitos como para préstamos, y posteriormente se eliminaron los techos para las tasas de interés; pero no hubo un adecuado control y supervisión del crédito bancario.

Se realizó un **Programa de Normalización de la Propiedad** mediante la devolución masiva de las empresas industriales expropiadas y del 28% de los predios agrícolas a sus antiguos propietarios, así como un importante programa de venta y titulación del 50% de las tierras expropiadas a los campesinos en forma de predios familiares. Asimismo se privatizaron algunos activos, empresas y bancos del estado por medio de licitación y ofreciéndole créditos a los compradores a 8-15 años de plazo y a una tasa de interés del 8 al 12% con garantía de los activos de la empresa.

Chile: Indicadores Económicos, 1970-1990

	1970	1973	1981	1990
PIB por habitante en US$ de 1988	1,932	1,893	2,325	2,451
Empleo (en miles)	2,720	2,784	3,191	4,384
Exportaciones de Bienes en millones de US$	1,113	1,316	3,836	8,310
Deuda externa en millones de US$	2,600	3,275	15,664	19,114

Chile realizó una proceso de apertura externa trascendental. Efectuó una significativa devaluación, unificó la tasa de cambio para todas las transacciones comerciales en 1973, convirtió todas las restricciones cuantitativas y prohibiciones en tarifas arancelarias con un nivel máximo del 200% en 1974 y redujo las tarifas paulatinamente hasta un nivel uniforme del 10% en 1979. El gobierno apoyó varios programas en el sector privado para incrementar la productividad de los sectores orientados a la exportación y hacer simplificaciones administrativas tendientes a agilizar el comercio exterior. Las exportaciones de bienes se expandieron de US$1,316 millones en 1973 a US$3,833 millones en 1979. Sin embargo, la tasa de cambio se sobrevaluó como consecuencia de que se congeló la tasa de cambio nominal en junio de 1979, a la vez que existía un mercado financiero con elevadas diferencias de las tasas de interés real entre el mercado interno y el externo, que atrajo la afluencia masiva de capitales del exterior.

El decreto-ley 600 de 1974 estableció condiciones muy favorables para la inversión extranjera. Se otorgó a los recursos del exterior (capital en efectivo, tecnología y bienes, incluso usados) igual tratamiento que a los inversionistas chilenos, libre acceso a casi todos los sectores de la economía y una normatividad de mínima interferencia gubernamental y ágil tramitación administrativa.

Después de un período de prohibición de huelgas y de imposición de severas restricciones al movimiento obrero organizado (1973-1978), se hizo la reforma laboral de 1979. Esta estableció la sindicalización libre y democrática, otorgó derechos a negociaciones colectivas de trabajo por empresa y a huelga con vínculo de trabajo de hasta 60 días, salvo en algunas actividades, tal como en los servicios públicos, donde habría arbitrajes obligatorios que se fallan aceptando en su integridad la posición de una de las partes. Los empleadores podían contratar personal de reemplazo durante el período de huelga. Según el Banco Mundial (World Bank, 1990), las reformas laborales han tenido un papel muy importante en la exitosa apertura comercial de Chile.

2. 1981-1991: la etapa de la crisis, la racionalización de la liberalización, la reforma de la previsión social y la profundización de la privatización

La transformación chilena no estuvo ajena de reveses y retrocesos importantes e innecesarios. Por ejemplo, la tasa de contracción del PIB fue del -13.6% en 1982, la mayor en medio siglo, y del -2.8% en 1983, o sea, una caída de más del 16% en dos años, y la tasa de desempleo se elevó al 30%. Incluso se llegaron a analizar las causas del fracaso del modelo chileno de desarrollo (Edwards y Cox-Edwards, 1986).

La aguda recesión de 1982-1983 se debió a varias causas. No hubo una adecuada regulación del crédito bancario, lo que llevó a una excesiva especulación financiera. La marcada y acumulada sobrevalorización del peso a partir de junio de 1979; la indexación de salarios incrementó el salario real al atarlo a la inflación del período anterior en una etapa de desaceleración inflacionaria. Esto coincidió con la severa crisis exógena del sector externo 38/ y la errada política macroeconómica para contrarrestar la recesión.

En dicho bienio, numerosas empresas productivas y en el sector financiero quebraron, el sistema bancario fue "intervenido" de nuevo en una operación de rehabilitación, los movimientos externos de capital fueron controlados y las tarifas arancelarias aumentadas al 35%. Esto después que la banca comercial y las empresas privadas, estatizadas o "intervenidas" en los tres años de la Unidad Popular (1971-1973), ya habían sido privatizadas, existía la libre convertibilidad del peso y las tarifas arancelarias habían sido reducidas al nivel generalizado del 10% en 1979.

El gobierno de Chile superó la crisis al adoptar estrictas medidas de regulación y supervisión del crédito bancario, al ofrecer precios de sustentación para productos agrícolas básicos, al eliminar la indexación de los salarios, al restablecer una tasa de cambio real competitiva 39/ y al hacer operaciones de reconversión de la deuda extranjera en capital de inversión. Igualmente profundizó el proceso de privatización de empresas que siempre habían sido estatales (teléfonos, electricidad, agua, salitre, seguros, carbón, etc.) mediante los llamados capitalismos institucional, laboral y popular, ver sección B de este Anexo. Asimismo, se vio favorecido con una mejoría en los precios internacionales del cobre y con el nuevo sistema de previsión social. Todo lo cual ha permitido un marcado y sostenido crecimiento de la producción y el empleo desde 1984.

En 1979 el decreto-ley 2,448 fijó la edad de jubilación mínima para los empleados en 60 años para las mujeres y 65 años para los hombres. En 1981 el decreto-ley 3,500 estableció el sistema de previsión social privado basado en la capitalización individual de los aportes de los empleados hasta un 20% de la remuneración, deducibles de la base impositiva, más los retornos de la inversión de estos fondos en los mercados financieros (a mayor aporte, a mayor beneficio), así como en la libertad para entrar o no al nuevo sistema

---

38/   Pérdida en los términos de intercambio, altas tasas internacionales de interés y recesión mundial.
39/   Además, se eliminó el IVA para los insumos utilizados en la producción de las exportaciones.

y para elegir las instituciones depositarias, denominadas Administradoras de Fondos de Pensiones (AFP). También hubo una drástica reorganización del sistema previsional de atención de salud, en el que se estableció una modalidad de seguros privados de salud.

Las AFP son sociedades anónimas, sujetas a requerimientos mínimos de capital y rentabilidad. Sus ingresos provienen de los aportes previsionales, invierten en instrumentos públicos y privados nacionales de alta rentabilidad y bajo riesgo definidos por la entidad supervisora. En enero de 1992, se autorizó una colocación limitada en títulos emitidos por organismos oficiales externos. Las AFP se financian mediante una comisión cobrada a los aportantes para cubrir los gastos de inversión y operación, que requiere el mantenimiento de cuentas individuales por empleado. El empleado puede elegir libremente distintas AFP y transferirse de una a otra en cualquier momento.

Las AFP compiten entre si sobre la base de las comisiones cobradas y las rentabilidades de sus fondos. Existe una separación entre el capital de las AFP y los fondos de pensión que administran, las AFP responden con su capital en caso de mala administración de los fondos de los afiliados, en tanto que el estado asegura una rentabilidad mínima en caso de quiebra de la AFP. Las AFP a través de los fondos de pensión que administran, han tenido un importante papel en la intensificación de la privatización, en que los trabajadores se sientan propietarios e inversionistas y otorgan pensiones superiores a las que se obtienen por el antiguo sistema.

El PIB real por habitante de Chile creció a una tasa anual del 1.0% en el período 1981-1990, la segunda más elevada de los países de América Latina y el Caribe, sólo superada por Colombia y supuestamente por Cuba, que habría tenido la mayor, (CEPAL, 1991, p 762). La expansión de las exportaciones y de la inversión fueron los principales motores del crecimiento económico, lo cual es atribuible a políticas de tasa de cambio realista, imposición baja sobre las ganancias, captación de inversión extranjera y al marco institucional del país.

El gobierno constitucional que asumió en marzo de 1990 decidió mantener las orientaciones económicas básicas del gobierno militar. Sin embargo, otorgó mayor prioridad a los sectores sociales (educación básica, vivienda y salud), a la atención a los pequeños productores y al entrenamiento de los grupos marginados para su incorporación efectiva al mercado laboral a fin de mejorar las condiciones de vida de los grupos de bajos ingresos. Además, dicha población estará más envuelta en la determinación y ejecución de los programas para mejorarla. Estos programas se están financiando mediante una reforma tributaria que aumentó el ingreso a la renta y el IVA. Igualmente el nuevo gobierno pretende profundizar el modelo exportador, fomentando la innovación tecnológica y el desarrollo financiero.

B. La Privatización

En 1973 había 533 empresas en poder del estado, que incluían la minería, el sector financiero, el comercio exterior, las grandes empresas mayoristas y las empresas industriales estratégicas, los transportes y las comunicaciones. En 1978, en cambio, había sólo 19 empresas estatales, aunque éstas tenían bastante importancia relativa en la minería y el gas. Los campesinos que habían recibido tierras se les otorgaron parcelas familiares, vendiéndoseles y dándoseles títulos de propiedad. El 28% de la tierra expropiada mediante la reforma agraria se consideró expropiada incorrectamente y fue devuelta a los propietarios originales y la Corporación de Reforma Agraria vendió el 20% de la tierra expropiada al sector privado. 40/ La privatización fue acelerada por el proceso de desregulación y simplificación administrativa, así como por la apertura financiera.

La experiencia chilena de privatización abarca importantes servicios sociales y servicios públicos, incluso algunos monopolios naturales, transcendiendo la transferencia al sector privado de las empresas en los sectores productivos, "intervenidas" o expropiadas en 1971-1973, así como la mayoría de las manejadas antes por la Corporación de Fomento de la Producción (CORFO). Las ventas de las empresas de CORFO se hizo principalmente en el período 1985-1989 al decidirse profundizar el proceso de privatización. Antes de iniciarse la privatización de las empresas públicas, se realizó un gran esfuerzo de racionalización de las mismas que se tradujo en la reducción de costos y en la fijación de tarifas a niveles económicamente aceptables.

La privatización de las empresas en los sectores productivos en la década de los setenta, fue realizada mediante venta a grupos empresariales. Ha sido criticada por haber vendido el capital social de las empresas por debajo de su valor en libros, a grupos de poca solidez financiera, creando sectores muy beneficiados del proceso y por haberse realizado prematuramente, contribuyendo a las quiebras del bienio 1982-1983. La privatización posterior fue a través de ventas a las AFP (capitalismo institucional), a los trabajadores de las empresas (capitalismo laboral), a los ciudadanos mediante incentivos tributarios para la compra de acciones de los bancos intervenidos y de las AFP en problemas (capitalismo popular), a la Bolsa de Comercio y por licitaciones a compradores previamente calificados.

La educación, los servicios de salud y nutrición, y la vivienda popular han sido descentralizados y parcialmente privatizados. Se licitan y contratan varias actividades con el sector privado comercial. Se subsidia la demanda en vez de la oferta. Los ministerios instituciones son rectoras, financiadoras, supervisoras y evaluadoras en vez de ejecutoras. Se han traspasado importantes decisiones a los usuarios finales o a instituciones cercanas a los usuarios finales (comunidades, municipios, organizaciones regionales, entidades sin fines de lucro). Con esto la prestación de los servicios se ha simplificado y desburocratizado mucho. También el manejo de las entidades de servicios públicos estatales fue descentralizado regionalmente.

En resumen, la exitosa experiencia chilena de estabilización, apertura y privatización

---

40/ Uno de los resultados de la reforma agraria, es que redujo la proporción de fincas con riego de mas de 80 has. del 55% al 3% del total.

fue gradual, a pesar de que las reformas fueron realizadas por un gobierno autocrático. Tal vez por ser pionera y tan abarcadora, se vio envuelta en algunos errores de política económica en el período 1979-1983, lo cual se agravó por dos fuertes recesiones mundiales en 1975 y en 1982-1983. La experiencia chilena, corregida y ajustada para evitar los errores que se cometieron y para dar el énfasis adecuado a los sectores sociales, debería ser el paradigma de la transformación para Cuba. Al evitarse los errores cometidos en la política económica, se podría atender eficazmente un mayor gasto social.

ANEXO III

El Plan Polaco 1990

Después de varios intentos parciales y fallidos de apertura económica y de tratar de implantar un socialismo descentralizado en la década de los 80, que condujeron al colapso total del sistema socialista en setiembre de 1989, el Gobierno de Polonia comenzó un plan completo y simultáneo de tratamiento macroeconómico del tipo "gran explosión" para la radical estabilización y liberalización en enero de 1990. Los planes de privatización sólo fueron esbozados. 41/ Este enfoque, que es más o menos el empleado por la antigua URSS desde enero de 1992, se podría considerar como el antiparadigma a lo planteado por McKinnon. También es sustancialmente diferente del empleado por Checoslovaquia y Hungría.

El plan de estabilización y liberalización simultáneos contempló fuertes medidas de austeridad fiscal, al reducir la inversión pública, eliminar casi todos los subsidios alimenticios y aumentar las tarifas de las empresas de servicios públicos. Además, se liberaron los precios, excepto de las empresas estatales grandes, y se fijaron de techos a los ajustes de salarios en las empresas públicas. Se aumentó la tasa de interés real y se impuso un control muy severo de la base monetaria y del crédito bancario. Se devaluó drásticamente y se anunció que se sostendría la nueva tasa de cambio. Se eliminaron las cuotas y se estableció la libre convertibilidad de la moneda nacional para las transacciones de la cuenta corriente de la balanza de pagos.

El programa resultó en la disminución de la producción industrial y el aumento del desempleo hasta el 10%. El PIB disminuyó en 12% en 1990 y en 9% en 1991. Ello ha creado fuertes presiones para la reactivación de la economía y para hacer más lento el proceso de ajuste. La reacción de las empresas estatales no ha sido igual que en las empresas privadas ante la estabilización y la liberalización, lo cual se ha visto acentuado por la lentitud del proceso de privatización.

41/   David Lipton y Jeffrey Sachs (1990, a y b) presentan excelentes resúmenes y análisis de los planes de Polonia sobre reformas macroeconómicas y privatización.

En junio de 1991 se definió un nuevo plan de privatización para las empresas grandes que contempla el establecimiento de sociedades por acciones (corporaciones) en tres años. Se distribuirían certificados a la población en general para adquirir un 33% de las acciones de las empresas que se otorgarían inicialmente a una compañía de inversión, que sería al principio el socio mayoritario y administraría las empresas. También se distribuirían acciones a los trabajadores (hasta 20%, a un descuento del 50%) y a otras compañías de inversión, tales como fondos de pensión (27%). El restante 20% de las acciones, las retendría el estado y las vendería después a grupos de inversión.

Ha existido una gran oposición a la adquisición de las empresas públicas por la inversión extranjera. Sólo el 29% de los polacos apoyan la propiedad y la inversión extranjera en empresas nacionales. Esta actitud se basa en la experiencia de Polonia durante la Segunda Guerra Mundial, a que todavía tiene territorios que eran alemanes hasta la Segunda Guerra Mundial y a que se desconfía mucho de la inversión alemana.

En junio de 1991 se modificó de nuevo la ley de inversión extranjera, por tercera vez desde 1988, y no se permite la mayoría de capital extranjero en los siguientes sectores: la operación de puertos y aeropuertos, servicios legales, transacciones de bienes raíces, estaciones de energía, la importación de bienes de consumo y las industrias de la defensa.

Hacer la liberalización externa de inmediato, no parece conveniente, ya que conlleva la pérdida de valor de los activos nacionales que no pueden ajustarse de inmediato a las nuevas condiciones y no es consistente con no permitir la adquisición de las empresas mayores por la inversión extranjera.

Los resultados del plan polaco no han sido tan satisfactorios como las autoridades esperaban, a pesar de que el país recibió una significativa ayuda externa en 1990-1991, había un gran respaldo del movimiento obrero organizado a los dirigentes políticos y la agricultura estaba en un 75% en poder del sector privado. En setiembre de 1991, el FMI decidió no otorgarle un nuevo "tranche" del acuerdo de ajuste estructural, el Banco Mundial considera que la privatización marcha en forma lenta y las negociaciones de la deuda externa con el Club de París se encuentran paralizadas.

El resultado de las elecciones de octubre de 1991 mostró un repunte de los partidos comunista y nacionalistas que quieren detener el proceso de restructuración de la economía. El sindicato "Solidaridad" se pronunció contra la forma de hacer los ajustes en enero de 1992 y efectuó un exitoso paro nacional de una hora el 13 de enero de 1992. El 28 de febrero de 1992, el Primer Ministro Jan Olszewski solicitó al FMI hacer el proceso de reformas de estabilización y liberalización más lentamente, aunque reconoció que había que acelerar las privatizaciones.

A principios de febrero de 1992, el Presidente Lech Walesa denunció ante el Parlamento Europeo que el Oeste no estaba apoyando adecuadamente a Polonia para que haga una rápida transición. Sin embargo, se debe analizar si el problema fundamental está en un plan de transformación con algunos problemas de diseño o en una insuficiente ayuda externa. Algunos planes de transformación se basan en adoptar muchas medidas y reformas de estabilización y liberalización en un corto período, que provocan que la población las rechace política y socialmente y que su éxito dependa de un volumen extraordinario de ayuda externa. Posiblemente, un plan más gradual sea más aceptable y no necesite ayuda externa de niveles extraordinarios. En este sentido, hay importantes lecciones para el plan que se propone para Cuba.

Bibliografía

Luis Aguilar León (1991), Cuba y su Futuro, Miami: Ediciones Universal.

Rafael Aldunate (1990), El Mundo en Chile, Santiago: Empresa Editora Zig-Zag, SA.

Chris Allsop (1991), The Polish "Shock Trearment". A Critical Assessemment, in La Sociedad Económica, London.

Ramiro Andrade (1991), Fidel Acorrolado y sin Salida, Bogotá

Elías R. Asón (1991), Comments to Ernesto Hernández-Catá's Long-Term Objectives and Transitional Policies--A Reflection on Pazos' Economic Problems of Cuba.

Ernesto Betancourt (1988), Cuban Leadership after Castro, Coral Gables, Florida: Research Institute for Cuban Studies.

Jeff Bergner (3 de enero de 1992), "Let's Stop Isolating Cuba", The Washington Post, Washington.

Eduardo Borensztein y Maumohan S. Kumar (1991), " Proposals for Privatization in Eastern Europe", IMF Staff Papers, Vol. 38, No. 2, pp 299-325.

Guillermo A. Calvo y Jacob A. Frenkel (1991), "From Centrally Planned to Market Economy", IMF Staff Papers, Vol. 38, No. 2, pp 268-298.

Tarsicio Castañeda (1990), Para Combatir la Pobreza, Santiago: Centro de Estudios Públicos.

Juan Clark (1990), Cuba, Mito y Realidad, Miami: Ediciones Saeta.

Comisión Económica para América Latina y el Caribe, Naciones Unidas (CEPAL, 1990), Estudio Económico de América Latina y el Caribe 1989, Santiago de Chile, diciembre.

Comisión Económica para América Latina y el Caribe, Naciones Unidas (CEPAL, 1991), Anuario Estadístico de América Latina y el Caribe 1990, Santiago de Chile, marzo.

Fabrizio Coricelli y Roberto de Rezende (1991), Stabilization Programs in Eastern Europe, Washington, D.C.: World Bank Working Papers, No. 732.

Farij Dhanji and Brako Milanovic, Privatization in Eastern and Central Europe, Washington, D.C.: World Bank Working Papers, No. 770.

Sebastián Edwards (1984), The Order of Liberalization of the Balance of Payments, Washington, D.C.: World Bank Staff Working Papers, No. 710.

Sebastián Edwards y Alejandra Cox-Edwards (1986), Monetarism and Liberalization, Cambridge, Massachusetts: Ballinger Publising Company.

Sebastián Edwards (1990), "Reformas Estructurales y Apertura en los Países en Desarrollo: El Problema de la Secuencia y Velocidad" en Apertura Económica y Sistema Financiero, Cali, Colombia: Asociación Bancaria Nacional,

Stanley Fischer y Alen Gelb (1990), Issues in Socialist Economic Reform, Washington, D.C.: World Bank Working Papers, No. 565.

Hans Genberg, On the Sequencing of Reforms in Eastern Europe, Washington, D.C.: International Monetary Fund Working Paper, No. 91/13.

Ernesto Hernández-Catá (1991), Long-Term Objectives and Transitional Policies--A Reflection on Pazos' "Economic Problems of Cuba".

Antonio Jorge (1990), "The Political Economy of the Cuban Revolution: Why the System Failed, Why Piecemeal Reform will not Succeed" en Cuba in Changing World, editado por Antonio Jorge, Jaime Suchlicki y Adolfo Leyva de Varona, pp 69-95, Miami: Research Institute for Cuban Studies.

Antonio Jorge (1991), A Reconstruction Strategy for Post-Castro Cuba. Miami, Florida: Research Institute for Cuban Studies, North-South Center, University of Miami.

János Kornai (1990), The Road to a Free Economy, New York: WN Norton & Company.

David Lipton y Jeffrey Sachs (1990a), "Creating a Market Economy in Eastern Europe: The Case of Poland", Brookings Papers on Economic Activity: 1 (Washington, DC: The Brookings Institution), pp 75-147.

David Lipton y Jeffrey Sachs (1990b), "Privatization in Eastern Europe: The Case of Poland", <u>Brookings Papers on Economic Activity</u>: 2 (Washington,DC: The Brookings Institution), pp 293-341.

Ronald McKinnon (1991), <u>The Order of Economic Liberalization</u>, Baltimore: The Johns Hopskins University Press.

Carmelo Mesa-Lago (1989), "Cuba's Economic Counter-Reform (Rectificación): Causes, Policies and Effects", <u>The Journal of Communist Studies</u>, 5/4; pp. 98-139.

Carmelo Mesa-Lago (1991), "El Proceso de Rectificación en Cuba: Causas, Política y Efectos Económicos, <u>Revista de Estudios Políticos</u>, No. 74, Octubre-Diciembre 1991, pp 497-530.

Carmelo Mesa-Lago (1992a), "Andrew Zimbalist and Claes Brundenius, The Cuban Economy: Measurement and Analysis of Socialist Performance" (book review), en <u>Economic Development and Cultural Change</u>, pp 432-438.

Carmelo Mesa-Lago (1992b), "Is There Life after the USSR?", <u>Hemisfile</u>, Vol 3, No. 1, pp 10-12.

Carmelo Mesa-Lago (1992c), "La Crisis del Socialismo Real en Cuba: Situación Económica Actual y Prespectivas", <u>Revista de Occidente</u>, a ser publicado próximamente.

Carmelo Mesa-Lago y Jorge Pérez-López (1985), <u>A Study of Cuba's Material Product System, Its Conversion to the System of National Accounts, and Estimation of Gross Domestic Product per Capita and Growth Rates</u>, Washington, D.C.: World Bank Staff Working Papers, No. 770.

Carmelo Mesa-Lago y Fernando Gil, "Soviet Economic Relations with Cuba" en <u>The USSR and Latin America</u>, Eusebio Mujal-León editor, Boston: Hyman, pp.183-232.

Felipe Pazos (1990), <u>Problemas Económicos de Cuba en el Período de Transición</u>.

Jorge Pérez-López (1989), "Cuba an Oil Exporter" en <u>The Cuban Economy: Dependency and Development</u>, Antonio Jorge y Jaime Suchlicki editores, Miami: Research Institute for Cuban Studies.

Jorge Pérez-López (1991a), "Bringing the Cuban Economy into Focus: Conceptual and Empirical Challenges", <u>Latin Economic Research Review</u>, Vol XXVI, pp.7-53.

Jorge Pérez-López (1991b), "Swimming Against the Tide: Implications for Cuba of Soviet and Eastern European Reforms in Economic Relations", <u>Journal of Interamerican Studies and World Affairs</u>, Vol. 33, No.2, pp.81-133.

Jorge Pérez-López y Carmelo Mesa Lago (1990), "Cuba: Counter Reform Accererates Crisis", <u>Transition</u>, Washington, DC: The World Bank

José Piñera (1990), <u>La Revolución Laboral en Chile</u>, Santiago: Empresa Editora Zig-Zag SA.

José Piñera (1991), <u>El Cascabel al Gato</u>, Santiago: Empresa Editora Zig-Zag, SA.

Susan Kaufman Purcell, "Collapsing Cuba", <u>Foreign Affairs</u>, Vol 71, No 1, pp 130-145.

Robert B. Reich (1991), <u>The Work of Nations</u>, New York: Alfred A. Knopf.

Archibald Ritter (1990), "The Cuban Economy in the 1990's", <u>Journal of Interamerican Studies and World Affairs</u>, Vol. 32, No. 3, pp. 117-149.

Archibald Ritter (1991), "Prospects for Economic and Political Change in Cuba in the 1990s" en Latin America to the Year 2000" Archibald Ritter editores, pp 235-252.

José Luis Rodríguez (1990), <u>Estrategia del Desarrollo Económico en Cuba</u>, La Habana: Editorial de Ciencias Sociales.

Jeffrey D. Sachs (1987), "Trade and Exchange Rate Policies in Growth-Oriented Adjustment Programs" en Vittorio Corbo, Morris Goldstein and Moshin Kahn editores, en <u>Growth-Oriented Adjustment Programs</u>, Washington: World Bank.

Jeffrey D. Sachs (1992), "Building a Market Economy in Poland", <u>Scientific American</u>, March 1992, pp 34-40.

Jorge Sanguinetty (1991), <u>El Desarrrollo de una Economía de Mercado: El Caso de Cuba</u>.

Hugh S. Thomas, George A. Fariol y Juan Carlos Weiss (1984), <u>The Cuban Revolution 25 Years Later</u>, Boulder: Westviwe Press.

Jacobo Timmerman (1990), <u>Cuba, a Journey</u>, New York: Alfred A. Knopf.

Eugenio Tironi (1990), <u>Autoritarismo, Modernización y Marginalidad</u>, Santiago: Ediciones Sur.

Delano Villanueva y Abbas Mirakhor (1990), <u>Interest Rate Policies, Stabilization and Bank Supervision in Developing Countries: Strategies for Financial Reform</u>, Washington, D.C.: International Monetary Fund Working Paper, No. 90/8.

John Williamson (1990), "What Washington Means by Policy Reform" en John Williamson editor, <u>Latin America How Much Has Happened?</u>, Washington: Institute of International Economics.

World Bank (1990), <u>Lessons in Trade Policy Reforms</u>, Policy and Research Series #10, Washington, DC: The World Bank.

English Abstracts

Development of a Market Economy: The Case of Cuba

Jorge Sanguinetty

The central topic of this paper is that the implementation of a free-market-oriented economic policy in Cuba should be preceded by finely tuned institutional and legal changes. A careless or dogmatic application of general economic policy principles could generate immediate imbalances that would complicate further implementation of a transition towards a free-market system.

The transition towards a market economy is expected to be very difficult since the Cuban government created an extreme case of state ownership, and has practically eliminated all free markets and the correlative institutional and legal infrastructure. Consistent with its Stalinist orthodoxy, the government also controls all output and factor prices, and keeps a high level of centralization of the flow of funds of its enterprises. Price and cost determination do not respond to any profit motive since state enterprises are managed to fulfill production quotas or targets. State enterprises will not be able to respond effectively to a new system of price flexibility, unless they are allowed to operate under a different set of rules.

Any transition government wanting to introduce a measure of liberalization will inherit a Stalinist system that cannot be changed overnight and, therefore, will have to be well managed to avoid further imbalances while it rapidly creates conditions for a successful transition. The first economic priority of a transition government will be to avoid any further deterioration of the already precarious agricultural production and distribution systems. Although highly inefficient, the current productive system could easily break down with the loosening of the discipline exercised by the Cuban Communist Party. Failure to manage this system before it can be changed could lead to a food emergency situation of unknown magnitude, political consequences and would inflict additional pain to the beleagured Cuban population.

All enterprises must have the opportunity to become financially self-sufficient as soon as possible, so they can respond to free maket signals, or else, declare bankruptcy. Privatization of such enterprises through rapid inflows of capital may not be feasible nor desirable until those enterprises reach a certain level of efficiency. Otherwise, the national stock of capital may be sold out for an unacceptably low amount. Therefore, state enterprises could be partially privatized by selling a proportion of its ownership (through newly issued shares) to their workers.

Simultaneously, legal measures must be enacted to enable enterprises to operate autonomously while they develop a new profit-maximizing managerial style in a competitive environment. Emergency credit facilities may have to be created by the transition government before private capitals can build a competitive financial system. Then, a gradual, but swift process of price liberalization could be implemented in output and factor markets. Especially, labor markets must be liberalized as soon as possible to allow enterprises reduce costs, increase productivity and improve competitiveness. Also, emergency measures may be necessary to compensate the displaced workers until more jobs are created by new investments.

Notes On An Agricultural Strategy For Cuba

Raúl Fernández

The unavoidable termination of Castro's tyranny will give the Cuban people a unique opportunity to redraw the structure of their nation. The future of Cuba will greatly depend on the way Cubans take advantage of that opportunity. For this reason, efforts like those of the Association for the Study of the Cuban Economy are necessary to advance the required research and discussion that will make possible, when the time comes, the emergence of a better country.

We assume that Castro's downfall will occur with a minimum of destruction and that a Provisional Government (P.G.) composed of non-communist leaders will take over. The P.G. will denounce Marxism but will maintain constructive relations with all nations, and will actively seek relations with the US and other Western countries and international organizations. Internally the P.G. will pursue the maintenance of peace and order and the reactivation of the economy. The provisional period (which I assume at 3 years), will end with elections for a constitutional assembly and general elections.

The agricultural sector must play a strategic role of support to the P.G. by increasing the production of food and thus addressing one of the most widely shared complaints of the population. Providing more food certainly will spare the P.G. and the people countless inconveniences and will free energies to tackle other problems.

The Dominican Republic faced a similar situation in 1962 when the remains of the Trujillo tyranny fell apart. The Agricultural Bank, through a massive rural credit program aimed at small and medium size farmers, achieved an important increase in the supply of food. The practical measure of that increase was given by the stabilization of previously run-away prices. Democratic elections followed, the first in three decades.

Cuba will face a somewhat different situation but an adjusted approach is suggested to compensate. First, lets consider that the agricultural sector is formed by three sub-sectors: provision of inputs; production in farms; and commercialization. Provision of inputs (fertilizers, pesticides, spare parts, etc.), as well as commercialization (marketing of crops and livestock) should be privatized as soon as possible, tapping the dynamism of private enterprise.

Production in farms includes crops and livestock produced by small farmers, big state and cooperative farms. Small farmers should receive technical assistance and, as all other producers should enjoy access to inputs, credit and a free and open market. State Farms should be supervised, and reorganized if necessary, pending what democratically elected bodies finally decide in due time. Cooperatives should be dealt with in accordance with the characteristics of each one. Respect for the environment should be of paramount importance. This plan requires the fast organization or adaptation of an agricultural credit system and an steady supply of inputs. This approach allows for the tapping of private initiatives, capital and know-how, while avoiding a massive restructuring of properties which not only may unsettle the country, but also should be reserved to democratically elected officials to decide.

The Carlos F. Díaz Alejandro Lecture

"The Economic Problems of the Period of Transition"

Felipe Pazos

The first Carlos F. Díaz Alejandro Lecture was delivered on December 28, 1990 at the "Salón de las Americas" of the Inter-American Development Bank by Dr. Felipe Pazos, Ex Officio President of ASCE. This presentation served to raise a number of important issues concerning the Cuban economy which have served as a framework for later discussions during the First Annual Meeting of the Association for the Study of the Cuban Economy. We decided, therefore, to reproduce the full text of the Spanish version of this lecture in this volume. An English summary of the main points covered follows:

Dr. Pazos' presentation centered on an outline of some of the main types of economic problems likely to be encountered by the Cuban economy during the period of transition. While recognizing that the problems to be faced will depend, in part, on the nature of the political process that leads into the period of transition, Dr. Pazos pointed out that some issues are likely to arise irrespective of how this process evolves, and that it is therefore important to give some thought as to how they might be addressed when they arise.

The main problems, as he sees them, are:

1) How to handle the reconversion of the economy from a centrally planned to a market determined system? In this context, one of the main issues will be how to bring about the privatization of the existing publicly owned enterprises?

2) How to manage the country's international trade policy during the period of transition?

3)   How to prevent economic activity from declining sharply in the initial stages of the transition and how to mobilize external economic and financial assistance?

4) How to implement a realignment of domestic prices, to bring them in line with costs of production, without depressing further the low levels of income of the population or giving rise to inflationary pressures?

5) How to keep the fiscal deficit under control and prevent the development of hyperinflation?

6) How to reestablish the work ethic to the population?

7) How to create the necessary institutions (financial and other) required for the proper functioning of a market economy?

8)   How to encourage external private capital inflows without selling off existing assets at bargain prices?

9)   How to reincorporate into the Cuban economy those entrepreneurs, administrators, technical personnel, and professionals now living in exile without creating undue friction and resentment in the population?

Dr. Pazos proceeded to explore in more detail the nature of these problems and to outline some possible strategies as to how to handle them. In doing so, he indicated, he did not wish to give a categorical solution to any of these problems but rather to highlight their complexity and to urge the members of the Association to begin to give some serious thoughts to possible approaches so as to be ready when the time comes.

In particular, he expressed a preference to see the reprivatization of the state enterprises to take place in a manner that resulted in a distribution of a portion of the ownership to the workers of the enterprises, while settling any indemnization claims of former owners through the issuance of government bonds. He felt that such an approach would encourage a rise in the productivity of the enterprises and contribute to the build-up of appropriate work ethics principles among the work force. He foresaw that the Soviet Union would have to continue to be a significant trade partner to Cuba -- at least during the transition period -- as it would not be easy or costless to bring about a prompt restructuring of international trade flows. Thus, we should be prepared to find a modus operandi that allows Cuba to continue exporting its sugar. He saw the risks of going through a period of large falls in output and real incomes, and the possible rise in fiscal disequilibrium, and called for a cautious approach to the process of realignment of domestic prices and for the implementation of rigorous economic and financial policies to avoid the development of hyperinflation. He supported the encouragement of external private investment, but saw the need for some regulations in the initial stages to prevent existing assets to be sold off at irrisory prices. Finally, he felt that the exile community could contribute a lot to the rebuilding of a new Cuba, but that their reintegration to the Cuban society had to be done gradually and in a manner that contributed to the revitalization of the economy, so as to minimize the frictions with the rest of the society.

(by Joaquín P. Pujol)

An Option for Freedom, Development and Social Harmony

Rolando H. Castañeda

The key topic of this paper is a concrete proposal for quick and deep reforms in the Cuban institutions and policies to completely transform the socialist economy into a free and very open market economy. The aims of the reforms are to establish and consolidate an economy with growth, stability and social justice.

In a world of increasing commercial and financial integration, the economic and political trends are both towards democracy and open market economies. However, Cuba confronts marked internal and external economic imbalances as a result of an extreme centralization and state ownership in all sectors. These imbalances are further accentuated due to the cessation of massive subsidies from the USSR. There has been a drastic decrease in the gross domestic product that started with a recession during the period 1986-1989 and became a profound depression in 1990 and 1991. There are also high disguised and open unemployment, enormous repressed inflationary pressures, extreme fiscal and balance of payment disequilibria, and an unmanageable external debt.

The implementation of sound and rigorous policies, based on a radical, but gradual approach, is recommended for the stabilization and liberalization of the economy. Simultaneously, with a swift process of enacting institutional and legal reforms for the deregulation of the economy, for the privatization of small and medium state enterprises, and for breaking down artificial monopolies and oligopolies to facilitate the transition. Failure to implement the proper transition could lead to a huge emigration to the United States based on the Cuban American family tie connections.

The gradual approach, as opposed to the "big bang" approach, is recommended to avoid any further deterioration of the already precarious situation of the Cuban economy while other conditions are established or developed to insure the proper response to the stabilization and liberalization measures. This gradual approach will assure internal consistency, certainty and it will limit political and social resistance. The proposal is based on Ronald McKinnon's recent book "The Proper Order of Liberalization"; the Chilean successful transformation from a situation of complete chaos in 1973 to a solid and growing economy; and, finally, the difficult transition associated with the "big-bang" approach in Poland.

At the outset of the transition, legal and institutional measures must be enacted to enable individuals to establish new enterprises. Fiscal and price adjustments will aim to reduce the level of excessive expenditures that is generating both inflationary pressures and balance of payment difficulties; to stop the expansion of the money supply; to establish the basis for a stable process of privatization in future years; and last, but not least, to initiate the implementation of a solidarity and investment social program for the low income people without sacrificing fiscal discipline. Subsidies should be eliminated. Defense and internal security expenditures must be reduced and a comprehensive, but simple, tax system should be put in place. A full price liberalization for private, small and medium size state enterprises will foster a competitive climate. Tight monetary policies and credit should be established to eliminate inflationary pressures. A drastic devaluation of the Cuban peso, the elimination of all quantitative barriers to trade, and the establishment of two uniform tariff levels will be needed to restore external equilibrium and competitiveness.

At the second stage of the transition, the encouragement of foreign investment and the privatization of state enterprises through cash or credit open sales are also necessary and desirable to expand the meager private sector and to improve the fiscal situation. For further details on the proposed measures, reforms and policies, see attached tables.

MAIN POLICIES AND MEASURES PROPOSED FOR THE RECONSTRUCTION OF THE CUBAN ECONOMY

MEASURES, REFORMS AND POLICIES	STABILIZATION (THREE YEARS)		LIBERALIZATION (THREE YEARS)		
	FIRST STAGE (FISCAL AND PRICE ADJUSTMENTS)	SECOND STAGE (BEGINNING OF THE PRIVATIZATION AND MONETARY AND CREDIT ADJUSTMENTS)	THIRD STAGE (PRIVATIZATION DEEPENING AND INTERNAL FINANCIAL LIBERALIZATION)	FOURTH STAGE (FOREIGN TRADE LIBERALIZATION)	FIFTH STAGE (EXTERNAL FINANCIAL LIBERALIZATION)
INSTITUTIONAL AND LEGAL	REESTABLISH, GUARANTEE AND ENFORCE PROPERTY RIGHTS AND PRIVATE CONTRACTS, TRADE AND BANKRUPTCY LAWS, ACCOUNTING STANDARDS, FREE ENTRY TO MARKETS, PROFESSIONS AND TRADES, FREE AND DEMOCRATIC UNIONS. ESTABLISH SIMPLE AND EXPEDITE PROCEDURES TO INITIATE BUSINESS ACTIVITIES.	DICTATE ANTI-MONOPOLY, ANTI-OLIGOPOLY AND MODERN BUSINESS LAWS. ESTABLISH A STOCK EXCHANGE.	DICTATE MODERN LABOR LAW WITH RIGHT TO STRIKES AND COLLECTIVE BARGAINING. ALLOW MARKETS TO DETERMINE WAGES.		ESTABLISH A DECENTRALIZE AND EFFICIENT STATE WITH A VERY LIMITED AND SUBSIDIARY ROLE. INCREASE THE AUTONOMY AND AUTHORITY OF PROVINCES, MUNICIPALITIES AND COMMUNITIES.
PRICES AND SALARIES	FULL LIBERALIZATION OF PRICES FOR PRIVATE, SMALL AND MEDIUM STATE ENTERPRISES. PRICE ADJUSTMENTS FOR LARGE STATE ENTERPRISES TO REFLECT INTERNATIONAL COSTS. STATE ENTERPRISES SALARIES SHOULD BE FROZEN AND MUST BE ADJUSTED BY PRODUCTIVITY INCREASES. LIBERALIZE PRIVATE ENTERPRISES SALARIES.		ELIMINATE ALL PRICE CONTROLS, EXCEPT FOR LARGE STATE ENTERPRISES. SALARY ADJUSTMENTS OF LARGE STATE ENTERPRISES SHOULD BE BASED ON PRODUCTIVITY INCREASES.		
FINANCIAL	EXECUTE A MONETARY REFORM ISSUING A NEW PESO. PROVIDE STATE ENTERPRISES WITH WORKING CAPITAL. ESTABLISH TIGHT MONETARY AND CREDIT POLICIES. ESTABLISH POSITIVE REAL INTEREST RATES FOR PRIVATE BANKING DEPOSITS AND FOR LIBERALIZED STATE ENTERPRISES.	ESTABLISH AN AUTONOMOUS CENTRAL BANK AND A BANKING INSTITUTION TO REGULATE COMMERCIAL BANKING CREDIT. DEVELOP FINANCIAL INSTRUMENTS FOR MEDIUM AND LONG TERM DEPOSITS AND DEBTS.	PRIVATIZE STATE COMMERCIAL BANKING. LIBERALIZE INTEREST RATES. DICTATE MODERN FINANCIAL INSTITUTIONS LAW. ALLOW ALL TYPES OF FINANCIAL INSTITUTIONS, BUT SUBJECT TO STRICT REGULATIONS AND SUPERVISION.		
FISCAL	MAINTAIN FISCAL BALANCE. REDUCE DEFENSE AND INTERNAL SECURITY EXPENSES. ELIMINATE SUBSIDIES. ESTABLISH VAT, INCOME TAX FOR ENTERPRISES AND INDIVIDUALS, LUXURY GOODS CONSUMPTION AND REAL ESTATE TAXES. DESIGN A COMPREHENSIVE REFORM OF THE STATE ROLE. USE COST AND BENEFIT ANALYSIS TO SELECT PUBLIC INVESTMENT AND ESTABLISH PUBLIC BIDDING FOR PUBLIC ACQUISITIONS.	CHARGE TUITION AND FEES FOR UNIVERSITY EDUCATION.	ELIMINATE ALL SUBSIDIES. PRIVATIZE PENSIONS PLANS.	PARTIAL DECENTRALIZATION AND PRIVATIZATION OF PRIMARY AND INTERMEDIATE EDUCATION AND PUBLIC HEALTH. THE STATE WOULD FINANCE THE SERVICES BUT THE PRIVATE SECTOR WILL PROVIDE THEM.	APPROVE BALANCE BUDGET LAW.
PRIVATIZATION AND PRODUCTIVE RESTRUCTURING	GIVE INCENTIVES TO PUBLIC EMPLOYEES FOR A SECOND JOB AND FOR THE PARTITION OF STATE FARMS INTO INDIVIDUAL LOTS. ESTABLISH A PRIVATIZATION COMMISSION. DECENTRALIZE DECISIONS TO SMALL AND MEDIUM STATE ENTERPRISES. ESTABLISH SEVERE PENALTIES TO MANAGERS AND WORKERS WHO STEAL FROM STATE PROPERTIES. ESTABLISH CRITERIA FOR THE BANKRUPTCY OF STATE ENTERPRISES AND TO DISMANTLE MONOPOLISTIC STATE ENTERPRISES.	PRIVATIZE PUBLIC HOUSING, SMALL AND MEDIUM STATE ENTERPRISES BY CASH/CREDIT SALES OR BY LEASING. DISMANTLE AND START SELLING STOCKS OF LARGE STATE ENTERPRISES.	PRIVATIZE ELECTRICITY AND TELECOMMUNICATIONS ENTERPRISES, HIGHWAY CONSTRUCTION AND MAINTENANCE, AIRPORTS AND PORT OPERATIONS, WATER AND SEWAGE SYSTEMS.		

MAIN POLICIES AND MEASURES PROPOSED FOR THE RECONSTRUCTION OF THE CUBAN ECONOMY
(CONTINUED)

MEASURES, REFORMS AND POLICIES	STABILIZATION (THREE YEARS)		LIBERALIZATION (THREE YEARS)		
	FIRST STAGE (FISCAL AND PRICE ADJUSTMENTS)	SECOND STAGE (BEGINNING OF THE PRIVATIZATION AND MONETARY AND CREDIT ADJUSTMENT)	THIRD STAGE (PRIVATIZATION DEEPENING AND INTERNAL FINANCIAL LIBERALIZATION)	FOURTH STAGE (FOREIGN TRADE LIBERALIZATION)	FIFTH STAGE (EXTERNAL FINANCIAL LIBERALIZATION)
EXTERNAL SECTOR	NEGOTIATE ACCESS TO THE USA MARKET. DEVALUATE AND UNIFY EXCHANGE RATE. ELIMINATE ALL QUANTITATIVE CONTROLS AND BARRIERS. ESTABLISH UNIFORM TARIFF OF 100% FOR CONSUMER GOODS, AND 20% FOR CAPITAL AND INTERMEDIATE GOODS. ESTABLISH TEMPORARY EXCHANGE CONTROLS.	REDUCE TO 70% UNIFORM TARIFF FOR FINAL CONSUMER GOODS. DICTATE ANTI-DUMPING LAW.	REDUCE TO 40% UNIFORM TARIFF FOR FINAL CONSUMER GOODS.	ESTABLISH 10% UNIFORM TARIFF FOR ALL GOODS. FREE CONVERTIBILITY FOR ALL TRANSACTIONS IN THE CURRENT ACCOUNT OF THE BALANCE OF PAYMENTS.	FREE CONVERTIBILITY FOR ALL TRANSACTIONS OF THE BALANCE OF PAYMENTS SUBJECT TO FOREIGN INVESTMENT LAW.
PRIORITY SECTORS	AGRICULTURE, AGROINDUSTRY, FISHERIES AND TOURISM.		EXPORT MANUFACTURING ASSEMBLY ACTIVITIES AND SUPPORTING SERVICES.		
CITIZENS AND FORMER RESIDENTS RETURN	ALLOW TAX FREE IMPORTATION OF HOUSEHOLD ITEMS, PENSION PAYMENTS, CAPITAL INVESTMENTS. FREEDOM OF PROFESSIONAL AND TRADE PRACTICES.			PERSONAL HOUSEHOLD ITEMS IMPORTATION SUBJECT TO EXISTING TARIFF.	
FOREIGN INVESTMENT	SEVERE RESTRICTION FOR INVESTMENT IN STATE ENTERPRISES.	FORMULATE MODERN FOREIGN INVESTMENT LAW.			
UNREQUITED TRANSFERS	FREE MONETARY TRANSFERS AT THE OFFICIAL EXCHANGE RATE. FOREIGN NON-PROFIT PRIVATE ORGANIZATIONS ARE ALLOWED TO OPEN ACTIVITIES.				
EXTERNAL FINANCIAL AND TECHNICAL COOPERATION	REQUEST ASSOCIATE MEMBERSHIP TO THE INTERNATIONAL FINANCIAL INSTITUTIONS FOR ACCESS TO TECHNICAL COOPERATION AND ORIENTATION AND ADVICE FOR FUTURE LOAN APPLICATIONS. SEEK TECHNICAL ASSISTANCE FROM THE CHILEAN GOVERNMENT FOR THE IMPLEMENTATION OF THE REFORMS.	REQUEST FULL MEMBERSHIP TO THE INTERNATIONAL FINANCIAL INSTITUTIONS FOR ACCESS TO ECONOMIC AND TECHNICAL COOPERATION.			
FOREIGN DEBT	OUTLINE STRATEGY TO RENEGOTIATE AND REDUCE EXTERNAL DEBT INCLUDING RECONVERSION SCHEMES.	RESTART FOREIGN DEBT SERVICE AND INITIATE RECONVERSION OPERATIONS.			

APPENDIX D

AUTHORS AND DISCUSSANTS

José F. Alonso is the Senior Economic Researcher of Radio Martí. He specialized in market studies and computer systems design, and over the past five years has been research economist for the U.S. Information Agency, where he has undertaken macroeconomic analyses of internal and external accounts and international trade studies. For 12 years he served as market economic analyst at the International Price Division, U.S. Bureau of Labor Statistics. He graduated in international economics and development from Catholic University of America.

Fernando Alvarez is a Ph.D. candidate at New York University. He is an Assistant Professor of Finance at Babson College, Massachusetts. His current research interests are in short-term financial management and in financing engineering.

José Alvarez is Professor of Food and Resource Economics at the University of Florida's Everglades Research and Education Center where his research and extension programs deal with farm management and production economics. He received his Ph.D. from the University of Florida. He is the senior author of <u>Microcomputers as Management Tools in the Sugar Cane Industry</u>, Amsterdam: Elsevier, 1985, and co-author of <u>Marketing Sugar and Other Sweeteners</u>, Amsterdam: Elsevier, 1991.

Elías R. Asón has a Ph.D. in economics from the University of California at Berkeley. He was Professor of Economics and Finance at the University of Puerto Rico and is also a former bank president. Currently he is working as a private economist and financial consultant.

Ernesto F. Betancourt is a consultant to the UNDP on institutional development and has done consulting work for the World Bank, IDB, AID and the OAS on that subject throughout Latin America. He also lectures on analysis of revolutionary propensity and is author of the recently-published Transaction book <u>Revolutionary Strategy: A Handbook for Practitioners</u>. He has an MPIA from the University of Pittsburgh, majoring in economic and social development. He has been Director of VOA's Radio Martí program directed at Cuba, Director of Organization Development and Director of Finance and Budget at the OAS, and Managing Director of the Cuban Bank of Foreign Trade. He was Castro's representative in Washington during the revolution against Batista.

Roger R. Betancourt is Professor of Economics at the University of Maryland-College Park. He received his Ph.D. from the University of Wisconsin-Madison. Many of his contributions to the analysis of capital utilization and shift-work systems are summarized in the entry on "Capital Utilization" in J. Eatwell, M. Milgate, and P. Newman (eds.), <u>The New Palgrave Dictionary of Economics</u>, The Stockton Press, 1987. In recent years he has been a Visiting Professor and Scholar at INSEAD (Fontainebleau, France) where he developed his current research interest in the analysis of distribution systems.

Juan J. Buttari is Senior Economist with the Agency for International Development (A.I.D.) and a member of the United States Foreign Service. Prior to joining A.I.D. he held positions with the International Labour Organization, United Nations Development Programme, and the Brookings Institution. He has taught, written and published on development issues. He holds a Ph.D. in economics from Georgetown University.

Rolando H. Castañeda is currently a Senior Operations Officer working with Chile and Peru at the Inter-American Development Bank (IDB), where he has held different positions since 1974. Before joining the IDB, he worked as an economist at the Organization of American States; the Rockefeller Foundation at the University of Cali, Colombia; the University of Puerto Rico at Río Piedras; and the Puerto Rican Planning Board. He has an M.A. and is a Ph.D. candidate at Yale University, majoring in monetary policy and econometrics.

Gonzalo de la Pezuela is currently an international economic consultant in Key Biscayne, Florida. He is a former official of the Inter-American Development Bank. Prior to that, he was the Economic Representative of the National Bank of Cuba in Washington, D.C., an economist with the Agricultural and Industrial Development Bank of Cuba (BANFAIC), Legal Consultant on tax matters at the Ministry of Finance in Cuba, an attorney at law in private practice, and Professor of the School of Economics at the University of Villanueva in Havana, Cuba.

José Ramón de la Torre is currently a Professor of International Business at the Anderson Graduate School of Management at the University of California at Los Angeles and Director of the Center for International Business Education and Research (CIBER) at UCLA. He received his Ph.D. from Harvard University. His main area of interest is the study of firms in an international setting. He was a Professor in the Department of Strategy and Environment at INSEAD from 1974 to 1985.

Jorge V. Domínguez is a Professor of Government and chairman of the Committee on Latin American and Iberian Studies at Harvard University. A former President of the Latin American Studies Association, he is currently President of the Institute of Cuban Studies and editor of the journal <u>Cuban Studies</u>. His most recent book is <u>To Make a World Safe for Revolution: Cuba's Foreign Policy</u>.

María Dolores Espino is currently an Assistant Professor of Economics at Florida International University. She received her Ph.D. from Florida State University. She has conducted research on the tourism industry in Florida and in Cuba. Her current research interests focus primarily on the Cuban economy.

Raúl Fernández is an agronomist who has worked extensively in agricultural projects in Cuba and in most of Latin America and the Caribbean. From 1962 to 1964 he coordinated an IDB mission to the Dominican Republic and was Professor of Agricultural Economics at the University of Santo Domingo. In Costa Rica and Brazil he directed major studies on the agricultural credit situation in those countries, which were published by the Pan American Union and the Central Bank of Brazil respectively. His book, <u>Metodología de la Investigación</u>, based on those studies, was published in Mexico in 1977 and reprinted in 1981 and 1983.

Antonio Gayoso is Agency Director of the Human Resources Directorate in the Bureau for Science and Technology at the Agency for International Development in Washington, D.C. He received an A.B.D. in agricultural economics, an M.A. in international trade and finance, and a B.S. in business Administration from the University of Florida, and a Lic. in economics from the University of Villanova. He has held various other positions at A.I.D. and the U.S. Department of State and was previously Professor at American University, Assistant Professor in the Department of Agricultural Economics of the University of Florida, and Junior Economist in the Ministry of Finance of the government of Cuba.

Alfredo Gutiérrez is currently a Vice President of Morgan Guaranty Trust Co. of New York. He received his Ph.D. in 1974 from the University of Michigan. His area of interest is Latin American economic development and trade policies. He acquired extensive experience in this area at the World Bank, for which he was Resident Representative in Colombia from 1979 to 1983.

Ernesto Hernández-Catá is Deputy Director of the Research Department, International Monetary Fund. He served previously as Chief of the Fund's North America Division and economist in the International Finance Division at the Board of Governors of the Federal Reserve System, and taught economics at The American University and the School of Advanced International Studies. He received his <u>Licence</u> in Political Science at the Graduate Institute of International Studies, Geneva, Switzerland, and his Ph.D. in economics from Yale University.

Armando M. Lago is President of Ecosometrics Inc., an economic consulting firm. He has a Ph.D. in economics from Harvard University. His specialties include demand analysis and pricing, models of urban growth and regional input-output analysis. He is the author of <u>The Politics of Psychiatry in Revolutionary Cuba</u>, Transaction Books, 1991.

Luis Locay received his Ph.D. in economics from the University of Chicago in 1983. He is currently Associate Professor in the Department of Economics at the University of Miami. He was previously Assistant Professor of Economics at the State University of New York at Stony Brook. His areas of specialization include development, economic demography, and applied microeconomics.

Luis R. Luis is currently a principal of Scudder, Stevens & Clark in Boston, where he directs investment research in emerging countries. Previously he was Director, Latin America Department, at the Institute of International Finance in Washington, D.C. Luis holds a Ph.D. in economics from the University of Notre Dame.

Kent Osband is an economist in the Research Department of the International Monetary Fund. He received his Ph.D. from the University of California at Berkeley, with a focus on Soviet-type economies. Before coming to the IMF, he worked at the Harvard Russian Research Center and the RAND Corporation, and also was a guest researcher at the Central Economics-Mathematics Institute in Moscow. He is currently working on a variety of issues related to the restructuring of Soviet interrepublican ties.

Felipe Pazos is a distinguished Cuban economist who has had a long, varied and eminently successful career. He has been an inspiring teacher, in the true sense of the term, for many ASCE members. His scholarly contributions on inflation are frequently cited. He has served with distinction in several international organizations, including the International Monetary Fund, the Committee of Nine of the Alliance for Progress, and the Inter-American Development Bank. One of the founders of the Cuban National Bank, he served twice as its president. Currently, he is a Senior Advisor to the Central Bank of Venezuela.

Lorenzo Pérez has a Ph.D. from the University of Pennsylvania, and his areas of professional interest are macroeconomics, international economics and economic development. He has been with the International Monetary Fund since 1978, after working at the U.S. Department of the Treasury and the Agency for International Development. He is currently Division Chief in the Western Hemisphere Department of the IMF.

Jorge F. Pérez-López is an international economist with the Bureau of International Labor Affairs, U.S. Department of Labor. His writings on international economic issues -- especially on the Cuban economy -- have appeared in professional journals and several edited volumes. He is the author of The Economics of Cuban Sugar, University of Pittsburgh Press, 1991. He received his Ph.D. from the State University of New York at Albany.

Marifeli Pérez-Stable is an Associate Professor of Sociology at the State University of New York at Old Westbury. She holds a 1991-1992 National Science Foundation Visiting Professorship for Women and is spending the year at the New School for Social Research doing research on the Cuban upper class between 1868 and 1960. She has also held American Council of Learned Societies (1988) and Social Science Research Council (1989) fellowships. Her book manuscript, Cuba: Nationalism and the Struggle for Social Justice, presents a political and structural analysis of the origins and outcomes of the revolution.

Francisco Proenza is currently an economist with the Food and Agriculture Organization in Rome. He received his Ph.D. from the University of Florida in 1981. His main interest is in agricultural economics, and has worked in this area at the U.S. Department of Agriculture and the Organization of American States. He has also served as a consultant to the World Bank.

Joaquín P. Pujol is currently Assistant Director in the Exchange and Trade Relations Department of the International Monetary Fund, with responsibility for the evaluation and review of all macroeconomic programs supported by the IMF. He served previously in various capacities in the Western Hemisphere Department of the IMF, including as Chief of the Mexico Latin Caribbean Division. He is a graduate of Wharton School and pursued post-graduate studies in economics and regional science at the University of Pennsylvania. Prior to joining the IMF he taught economics at the Wharton School and did research on economics and econometrics for the National Bureau of Economic Research, the Foreign Policy Research Institute, the Regional Science Institute and the Economic Unit of the University of Pennsylvania.

Nicolás Rivero is the Managing Director of Rivero International. Specialized in international trade and U.S. legislation, he led for 28 years commercial policy and export promotion programs at the Organization of American States. Since 1989 he has continued his specialization in international trade -- now in the private sector -- with particular emphasis on inter-American trade and U.S. legislative affairs. He is Director for Latin America on the Advisory Board of Information Resources, Inc., a research firm dealing with petrochemical and oxygenated fuel industries. He is an international economics graduate of Georgetown University.

Jorge Salazar-Carrillo is Director of the Center of Economic Research and Professor of Economics at Florida International University. He is also Non-Resident Staff Member of the Brookings Institution. His Ph.D. is from the University of California at Berkeley (1967), where he also obtained a Certificate in Development Programming. His two most recent books are The Latin American Debt, MacMillan-St. Martin's Press, forthcoming, and Comparisons of Prices and Real Products in Latin America, North Holland-Elsevier, 1990. He is a member of the executive board of directors of the Cuban American National Council, the National Association of Cuban-American Educators, and IESCARIBE, a Caribbean Basin research network composed of 45 institutions.

Jorge A. Sanguinetty is President of Development Technologies, Inc., a Washington, D.C.-based international and domestic economic consulting firm. He received his Ph.D. in economics from the City University of New York, and was Director of the Latin American Program in Applied Economics at The American University. He was head of National Investment Planning at the Central Planning Board in Cuba.

Carlos Seiglie is Assistant Professor at Rutgers University in Newark, New Jersey. A graduate of Rutgers, he received his Ph.D. in economics from the University of Chicago. He previously worked as a consultant for Arthur Andersen & Co. and taught economics at Northwestern Illinois University. He has published a number of articles and participated in numerous conferences on defense economics. He is a Phi Beta Kappa, a Rutgers Scholar and an Eli Lilly Fellow in Economics. He is a member of the Economics Division of the National Science Foundation and a Journal Referee for Conflict Management and Peace Science and for Defense Economics.